D1564422

FRANK O'HARA

The Poetics of Coterie

CONTEMPORARY

NORTH AMERICAN

POETRY SERIES

Series Editors

Alan Golding, Lynn Keller,

and Adalaide Morris

Frank O'Hara

THE POETICS OF COTERIE

by LYTLE SHAW

UNIVERSITY OF IOWA PRESS   IOWA CITY

University of Iowa Press, Iowa City 52242

http://www.uiowa.edu/uiowapress

Printed in the United States of America

Design by Richard Hendel

The University of Iowa Press is a member of Green Press Initiative and is committed to preserving natural resources.

Printed on acid-free paper

Library of Congress Cataloging-in-Publication Data

Shaw, Lytle.

Frank O'Hara: the poetics of coterie / by Lytle Shaw.

p. cm.—(Contemporary North American poetry series)

Includes bibliographical references and index.

ISBN 0-87745-984-3 (cloth)

1. O'Hara, Frank, 1926–1966. 2. O'Hara, Frank, 1926–1966—Homes and haunts—New York (State)—New York. 3. Art and literature—United States—History—20th century. 4. O'Hara, Frank, 1926–1966—Friends and associates. 5. New York (N.Y.)—Intellectual life—20th century. 6. Art museum curators—United States—Biography. 7. Poets, American—20th century—Biography. 8. Museum of Modern Art (New York, N.Y.). I. Title. II. Series.

PS3529.H28Z86 2006 2005054892

811'.54—dc22

[B]

06 07 08 09 10 C 5 4 3 2 1

FOR EMILIE

CONTENTS

ACKNOWLEDGMENTS

This book began as a doctoral dissertation in the English Department at the University of California, Berkeley, under the guidance of Charles Altieri, T. J. Clark, and Mitch Breitwieser. I am grateful to my committee (and to the late James E. B. Breslin) for their patience, support, and commentary as the project took shape.

The book has since benefited from many friends and colleagues in the Bay Area and New York: Kevin Attell, Faith Barrett, Bill Berkson, Kevin Davies, Lyn Hejinian, Anne Wagner, and Barrett Watten all read and responded to parts of the manuscript. Bob Perelman read the entire manuscript and made extremely helpful suggestions. Anselm Berrigan, Jimbo Blachly, Steve Clay, Kevin Cook, Alex Cory, Jeff Derksen, Florence Dore, Ben Friedlander, Robert Gamboa, Tim Griffin, Catherine Hollis, Levon Kazarian, Christina Kiaer, Pamela Lu, Lisa Robertson, Michael Scharf, Mauri Skinfill, and Brian Kim Stefans were all, at various points, crucial to my mental and emotional life as I wrote.

More recently, I owe thanks to Catherine de Zegher at the Drawing Center and to my colleagues at New York University, especially Phillip Brian Harper, Una Chaudhuri, John Guillory, and Patrick Deer.

For granting interviews or responding to questions I am indebted to John Ashbery, Irving Sandler, Waldo Rasmussen, David Shapiro, Alice Notley, and Ron Padgett.

For access to archival materials I want to thank the Museum of Modern Art Library, the Harry Ransom Center at the University of Texas, the Grey Art Gallery at NYU, the Mandeville Special Collections at the University of California, San Diego, the Getty Research Library, and Rutherford Whittus at the University of Connecticut, Storrs.

For text and photographic permissions I owe thanks to Maureen Granville-Smith, Grace Hartigan, Steve Dickison, Barney Rosset, and the Claes Oldenburg Studio.

Several preliminary versions of sections of this book were delivered as talks or published as articles. Parts of the introduction became a talk at the Tibor de Nagy Gallery in New York for the Poetry Society of America in

2000. Chapter 1 was first a talk at Small Press Traffic in San Francisco in 1998; my thanks to Kevin Killian and Dodie Bellamy for the invitation. This chapter was subsequently published as "On Coterie" in *Shark* 2 (1999) and, thanks to John Tranter, reprinted online in *Jacket* 10, October 1999. Chapter 2 was given as a talk at the 2000 conference "The Opening of the Field: North American Poetry in the 1960s" at the University of Maine, Orono. Chapter 5 was first published in *Qui Parle* 12:2 (2001). My thanks to guest editor Barrett Watten and to the *Qui Parle* editors. Portions of chapter 6 were given as a talk at the Berkeley Visual Studies Conference in 1996.

The project was completed in New York with generous support from a Getty Postdoctoral Grant in art history. The illustrations were made possible with a Stein Grant from the New York University English Department.

Selections from Frank O'Hara's *Collected Poems* are reprinted by permission of Alfred A. Knopf, a division of Random House, Inc. Selections from Frank O'Hara's *Lunch Poems* are reprinted by permission of City Lights.

I am also indebted to my copyeditor, Mary Russell Curran; to Holly Carver, Charlotte Wright, and Karen Copp at the University of Iowa Press; and to the Contemporary North American Poetry Series editors, Alan Golding, Lynn Keller, and Adalaide Morris.

I owe the deepest debt, finally, to my father, John Shaw.

ABBREVIATIONS

WORKS BY FRANK O'HARA

CP *The Collected Poems of Frank O'Hara*, ed. Donald Allen. New York: Knopf, 1972.

AC *Art Chronicles: 1954–1966*. New York: Braziller, 1975.

PR *Poems Retrieved*, ed. Donald Allen. Bolinas, CA: Grey Fox, 1977.

EW *Early Writing*, ed. Donald Allen. Bolinas, CA: Grey Fox, 1977.

SP *Selected Plays*. New York: Full Court Press, 1978.

SS *Standing Still and Walking in New York*, ed. Donald Allen. San Francisco: Grey Fox, 1983.

WW *What's with Modern Art: Selected Short Reviews and Other Writings*, ed. Bill Berkson. Austin: Mike and Dale's Press, 1999.

FREQUENTLY CITED CRITICAL WORKS

G Brad Gooch, *City Poet: The Life and Times of Frank O'Hara*. New York, Knopf, 1993.

P Marjorie Perloff, *Frank O'Hara: Poet among Painters*. Austin: University of Texas Press, 1977.

H Bill Berkson and Joe LeSueur, eds. *Homage to Frank O'Hara*. Bolinas: Big Sky, 1978.

Other abbreviations are noted in the chapter in which they first appear.

INTRODUCTION

he isn't the English composer
and I'm quite aware that everybody
doesn't have to know who everybody
else is
but why did he take Mrs Kennedy
to the Tibor de Nagy Gallery worthy
as it is of her attention
though I'm also
used to the fact that one day someone
called up Charles Egan from Grand Central
and asked if he had a small Rauschenberg
and Franz said "that's not a practical
joke"
yes many things can happen in
the "world" of art (look at Malraux!)
but who is William Walton?
— Frank O'Hara, "Who Is William Walton?"

Plotting an unknown proper name amid the known names of dealers, critics and artists, glamorous first ladies, New York landmarks, and someone named Franz, "Who Is William Walton?" is a meta–Frank O'Hara poem. Reading O'Hara frequently means taking up the position of this poem's speaker — a fact that has led many critics to think of O'Hara as a coterie poet. Marjorie Perloff's introduction to the 1997 reissue of her seminal 1977 *Frank O'Hara: Poet among Painters* begins with the suggestion that when her book was initially published, "O'Hara was a coterie figure — adored by his New York School friends and acolytes, especially by the painters whose work he exhibited and wrote about, but otherwise regarded (when regarded at all) as a charming minor poet" (P 1997 reprint xi). While the paragraph continues on to consider O'Hara's dramatic rise in reputation since 1977 (and the role Perloff's own book played in this rise), it is these first sentences that, to my mind, best focus the problem of O'Hara's reception. Perloff's claim that O'Hara was a coterie figure is, in a variety of different forms, a baseline to critical writing on O'Hara from the 1950s to the present. The idea of O'Hara as a coterie poet emerges both from his intimate links to a circle of famous artists and writers and from the intimate referential practices of his work, in particular his conspicuous use of proper names, especially those of his friends.

Born in Grafton, Massachusetts, in 1926, O'Hara saw action in the Pacific in World War II before attending Harvard, where he met John Ashbery and Kenneth Koch, graduating in 1950. After receiving an MA in English at the University of Michigan in 1951, O'Hara moved to New York City, where early on, in addition to an expanding circle of poets, his closest friends tended to be painters — Jane Freilicher, Larry Rivers, and Grace Hartigan in particular, each of whom was also an active and important reader of his poetry.[1] After working at the front desk of the Museum of Modern Art (MoMA) from late 1951 until early 1954, O'Hara joined the International Program there in 1955 — first as a special assistant and eventually, by 1965, moving up the ladder to curator. Over this period he both assisted with and directed numerous international exhibitions during the heyday of Abstract Expressionism, including ones by Franz Kline (probably the "Franz" in "Who Is William Walton?"), Robert Motherwell, and David Smith. In July 1966 O'Hara was struck by a jeep on Fire Island and died of complications from the injury. Before his death he was scheduled to curate both the Willem de Kooning and the Jackson Pollock retrospectives at MoMA.

Already by the late 1950s, O'Hara had an extremely wide range of friends, from the intimate circle of poets associated with the first generation of the New York School (John Ashbery, Barbara Guest, Kenneth Koch, and James Schuyler) to painters including Willem de Kooning, Joan Mitchell, and Jasper Johns; from poets outside the New York School designation (Allen Ginsberg, Amiri Baraka [then LeRoi Jones], and John Wieners) to musicians including Virgil Thomson and Morton Feldman. There were also museum officials, dancers, and filmmakers (he was an enormous fan of Hollywood movies and musicals). O'Hara's poems are a complex map of how he negotiated these transitions both between disciplines and between high and popular culture. Frequently printed outside of the poetry world (in art catalogs and magazines), his poems also *thematized* the idea of a close-knit audience through intimate, seemingly shared references, dedications, and the mention of proper names.

How to understand the relationship between O'Hara's life and the referential strategies he used in his writing has been an ongoing problem in his reception. Among the many negative responses, Pearl K. Bell's 1972 review of O'Hara's *Collected Poems* is typical: "Mainly, [O'Hara] drew upon his vast collection of celebrated friends, in an extended family album of Larry Rivers, John Cage, Edwin Denby, Virgil Thomson, Jackson Pollock, and a lesser cast of thousands. The names may glitter, but O'Hara's poems to and about them do not. For the reader, the cumulative effect of this colossally self-absorbed journal of happenings is numbness, not pleasure."[2] Similarly, in his 1966 review of *Lunch Poems*, Raymond Roseliep complains of a "wearisome cataloging of personalia" (qtd. in Elledge *To Be True to a City* 14). Even those who supported O'Hara often understood his poetry as bound to the intimate audience of those actually referred to in the poems. Gilbert Sorrentino, for instance, describes O'Hara's poems as "messages to a personal cosmopolitan elite, which apparently consists of O'Hara and his immediate friends" (qtd. in Elledge *To Be True to a City* 15). And though he admires O'Hara's "brisk and brilliant world" (ibid.), Sorrentino understands the poems primarily as elements within a discrete social formation: the poems are "communications from [O'Hara] to 'persons,' and are to be read as such" (ibid.). But even if one agreed with Sorrentino's characterization, which clearly places O'Hara as a coterie figure, it remains unclear how, precisely, one would read O'Hara's poems "as such."

Is a coterie writer merely one who chooses to thematize a small audience? Or is the problem with the *writing* and not with the writer, so that coterie writing would name instead a literary practice that reflects or can only be sustained within such a small audience? Do the many intimate references, dedications, and proper names among the writings of the Black Mountain, Beat, and San Francisco Renaissance poets, for instance, render theses groups coteries as well? Certainly their works are less frequently associated with the term: Libbie Rifkin, for example, refers both generally to "the coterie poetics of the New York School" and specifically to O'Hara himself as "the famous coterie poet" (29, 126). Thus, while Perloff suggests that the link between O'Hara and the idea of a coterie was a temporary and unfortunate one, something of this link nonetheless seems to persist in his much wider appreciation — even in readings that, paradoxically, depend little on actual knowledge of the intricacies of his life or his circle. In his book *Statutes of Liberty: The New York School of Poets*, Geoff Ward also considers O'Hara a coterie figure but goes on to say more about what this might mean:

> [T]he idea of a literary côterie, so important to O'Hara, might be read as a group symbol . . . that attempts to cheat temporality by ingesting and acknowledging certain of its powers. The artists' circle, be it in Second Empire Paris or New York in the 1960s is therefore, leaving aside its vanguardist claims, a microcosm of urban life which has itself replaced Nature by the City. ("New York / greater than the Rocky Mountains" CP 477) The lack of resemblance between the subject and Nature is conceded by the twentieth-century city-dweller who in places like New York has made a cult of living against the "natural" grain, *à rebours*. But the côterie is still a humanist refuge against temporality, seeking by the mutual support of its members to stave off the negative impact of time on each individual subject. This is of course to read the term "côterie" textually, but we have to a degree been invited by Romanticism to do just that, ever since Friedrich Schlegel and the Jena Circle published their debates about art in the form of staged conversations. (60–61)

Ward's simultaneously rich and troubling formulation is one important critical point of departure for what follows: a study of O'Hara's poetry and art criticism organized around the persistent problems of "reading" a coterie. But while Ward's admittedly brief passage on coterie plugs the term into a de Manian drama of symbolic versus allegorical understanding (which I will consider in more depth in chapter 1) my own goal will be to expand the term's senses both beyond the symbol-allegory opposition and beyond the range of more common-sense judgments with which the idea of coterie is usually bound up. Though I will be analyzing what one could call a rhetoric of coterie, this will not mean that coterie is ever a purely textual phenomenon. For it is central to the strangeness and compellingness of the term that it involves both a mode of address and an *actual* context for that address, both a range of rhetorical, formal strategies and a staging ground for these strategies in empirical life. Reading a coterie thus might be considered an exemplary problem in considering this seam between the textual and the empirical.

The claim that a writer writes for a coterie usually implies two kinds of seemingly opposite critical engagements: first, biographical fascination by those who care about the minute particulars of a literary or artistic circle. At the same time, the charge of coterie, leveled by those uninterested in biographical interpretation generally or in a particular biography, implies a secure pejorative judgment. A coterie writer is, in common usage, someone whose writing depends upon a small and implicitly antidemocratic model of audience, a model in which particularity has hijacked the universality "we" all know and want. This charge then implies the existence of a stable, knowable alternative: a model of audience in which common-sense notions of accessibility ensure a work's status as "public." Were critics forced to articulate the presuppositions implied by these ideas of audience, the charge of coterie would require a far more difficult account of an individual writer's relation to the concepts of universality and particularity, concepts that are themselves, arguably, historically constructed and thus shifting. Critics might ask what particularity and universality have meant, how they have operated, for instance, in Paris in 1855, or in Moscow in 1920, or in New York in 1958.

One corollary of such an approach might be to understand what gets called coterie writing, then, as a critique of literature's frequent rhetoric of universality. In the 1950s in America, this rhetoric was bound up with a range of now familiar New Critical and Eliotic strictures. Certainly O'Hara was critical of them, as both Marjorie Perloff and James Breslin have demonstrated.[3] O'Hara's response, though, was less to claim his own identity as particular (and thus authentically marginal to the rhetoric of universality) than, as chapter 1 argues, to destabilize and displace the markers of literary universality that would allow poetry to operate in an established, understood public sphere — a sphere characterized by norms of tone, canons of reference, and what O'Hara, referring specifically to the New Critics, calls "certain rather stupid ideas about . . . the comportment in diction that you adopt" (SS 22). After mentioning that he had been "reading heaps of Eluard, Char and Lorca" in a 1956 letter to Kenneth Koch, O'Hara writes, "they make me hum like a tuning-fork; who wants a 'voice' of his own? How did you like the measured pace of that poetry 'spread' in the *Times*? 'Wilbur is major and undoubtedly Pound has been useful' — R E A L L Y!!!"[4]

Not only does O'Hara object to the *Times* critic's understanding of a singular persona or "voice" as fundamental to poetry, but he also objects to the *form* of the critic's own judgments — the "measured pace" that is supposed to ensure the objectivity of terms like major and minor. It is precisely this authority-conferring tone that O'Hara puts into question. Characterizing O'Hara's idea of "Personism" — "founded by me after lunch with LeRoi Jones [Amiri Baraka] on August 27, 1959" — Baraka claims, "you could say exactly what was on your mind and you could say it in a kind of conversational tone rather than some haughty public tone for public consumption" (G 338). Baraka thus identifies "haughty public tone" as the marker of a false sense of the public sphere, ensuring not communication but consumption. By dramatizing both characters and cultural references operating, frequently, below "public" radar, O'Hara could enter into a paradoxically public social discourse from a position often misunderstood as private.

Familiarly presenting unfamiliar people, events, and attitudes, O'Hara's writing intentionally did not give the requisite context to render it public in any standard sense. This stance was bound up with O'Hara's concern with small collectivities, circles, or, in the pejorative sense, coteries. These marginal audience figures (and not merely empirical structures) certainly allowed O'Hara to challenge familiar midcentury rhetorics of universality. But perhaps more important, they also helped him to explore alternative models of kinship, both social and literary.

It is in this sense that his work might be understood to examine social and literary linkages — the bonds that both enforce and seem to explain relationships in terms of similarity and difference. Though for O'Hara these are primarily a matter of relationships among living persons (be they the organic links of familial structures, the contingent links of friendship, or the ideological links of national subjects), they also crucially involve the kinds of linkages that literature can establish with its own past.[5] These senses of linkage — synchronic/social and diachronic/intertextual — come together importantly in O'Hara's work, where the thematization of temporary queer families in the present (positioned in a parodic relationship to more normative familial structures) often gains momentum from a reading of literary history that attempts to unsettle both the idea of "Lineage" and the constellation of established literary fathers known as "The Tradition." In much the way that the present tense of O'Hara's poetry provocatively asserts the significance of an obscure referential field that often reads as a mock family of O'Hara's friends — Ashes, Bunny, Kenneth, Joe, Grace, and Jane — so its past tense builds a mock "tradition" for this present out of either an obscure cultural background treated heroically (Ivy Compton-Burnett, Ronald Firbank, John Wheelwright, and composers like Poulenc) or an inappropriately chummy or disrespectful relationship to canonical authors. Coterie, in these models of association, is as much an idea about the social possibilities of affinity as it is a concrete sociological fact; it is as much a shifting rhetoric or assertion as it is a retrievable archival tidbit. Understood in this way, coterie functions less as a pejorative charge or as an occasion for biographical detail than as a code of reading that emerges at and helps to articulate the seam between biographical, historical particulars and modes of rhetoric, between archival facts and theoretical models.[6]

One of the best treatments of writing that thematizes a problematic seam between biography and text is Svetlana Boym's *Death in Quotation Marks: Cultural Myths of the Modern Poet.* Updating and expanding the Russian Formalists' category of the literary fact through case studies of Mallarmé, Rimbaud, and Mayakovsky, Boym argues that it is now a "*literary fact* that prohibits clear boundaries between literature and life, revealing the uncanny 'literariness' of life and the transgressive vitality of texts" (13). In O'Hara, however, the interpretive problem is not merely the status of the shifting "I" but that of the other proper names with which the "I" is in dialog—the problem of intersubjectivity and "community."

Like the problem of coterie, interest in community often gives rise to an archival project that tends to valorize traditional concepts of biography. In a book on Andy Warhol's relation to New York School poets, for instance, Reva Wolf uses the production history of Warhol's photographs within *C Magazine* to claim that Warhol used "visual gossip" in his art "to make a personal connection" with various writers, among them O'Hara (19, 10). Wolf goes on to justify the importance of gossip in Warhol by claiming a parallel to O'Hara, for whom "gossip is 'deep' principally for the simple reason that he used it often and boldly in his poetry, and thereby acknowledged — even took for granted — that gossip *is* deep" (18). Because repetition of any device leads inevitably to depth, Warhol's work is no longer cool, detached, or affectless but instead "personal," "emotional" (1), and concerned with a community. Thus gossip and community saddle Warhol with precisely the kind of old-fashioned subjective interior his work so articulately displaces (often precisely through repetition). Like O'Hara's poetry, Warhol's art is clearly bound up with the particulars of his life. But it is in part *because* of Warhol's art that it is no longer possible to consider categories like the personal and the emotional as self-evident.[7] This gap between readings that stress the particulars of literary community and those that develop theoretical models for community is complicated by the fact that theorization of community (or of its problematic twin, coterie) can never operate independent of context.[8] One of the advantages the study of coterie can introduce into the often vague evocation of community, then, is that, because the charge of coterie tends to involve a claim about an aesthetic and social breach, it becomes a moment when historically inflected assumptions about community (and its relation to reading) get articulated. Through its sense of real or imagined social infraction, coterie introduces a self-reflexive component to the study of community.

Despite the limitations I mentioned, important theorization of community has taken place over the last twenty-five years — first, in philosophy and political theory. In *The Coming Community*, for instance, Gorgio Agamben writes of an "*inessential* commonality, a solidarity that in no way concerns an essence." He also stresses the temporal unfolding of this concept of community, calling it "not an event accomplished once and for all, but an infinite series of modal oscillations" (18–19). Agamben's writing helps to focus the idea of communities as temporary, tactical social compositions based on contingent rather than organic bonds, dissipating and reforming themselves frequently. Such a model is crucial to what follows, as is the idea that collectivity does not mean consensus. Agamben's thought finds an echo in recent political theory organized around the problem of radical democracy. Charting a new path between the traditions of Kantian liberalism and communitarianism, Chantal Mouffe, in her essay "Democratic Citizenship and the Political Community," argues, for instance, that

> We cannot say: here end my duties as a citizen and begins my freedom as an individual. Those two identities exist in a permanent tension that can never be reconciled. But this is precisely the tension between liberty and equality that characterizes modern democracy. It is the very life of such a regime and any attempt to bring about a perfect harmony, to realize a "true" democracy can only lead to its destruction. This is why a project of radical and plural democracy recognizes the impossibility of the complete realization of democracy and the final achievement of the political community. (238)

Similarly stressing democracy as an unfinished (and unfinishable) project, Mouffe argues that "the creation of political identities as radical democratic citizens depends . . . on a collective form of identification among the democratic demands found in a variety of movements: women, workers, black, gay, ecological, as well as several other 'new social movements'" (236). Rather than a unitary, prediscursive subject that brings itself autonomously to such identifications, Mouffe — like most post-structuralist democratic theorists — conceives of this agent "as the articulation of an ensemble of subject positions, constructed within specific discourses and always precariously and temporarily sutured at the intersection of those subject positions" (237).[9]

In the context of American poetry, the most articulate writing about community has been that of the Language writers — developed both in historical studies and in theorization of their own community.[10] In *The San*

Francisco Renaissance: Poetics and Community at Mid-Century, for instance, Michael Davidson examines this important precedent for his own generation not only in terms of "the sustaining fact of community" in its concrete manifestation within "the circles, salons, and bars" (16) but also in the ways such "facts" gave rise to competing myths of a community and its history. His book thus explores "the ways in which the San Francisco Renaissance was the creation of plural narratives of its origin and gestation, narratives in whose distortions and refractions we may see the postwar period more clearly" (6). As a whole, however, the Language writers have brought far less attention to the New York School than they have to Stein, Riding, the poets of the San Francisco Renaissance, and the Objectivists. And the exceptions are revealing: Barrett Watten's writing about O'Hara and Ted Berrigan at once stages a literary historical intergenerational conflict and brings up many of the central problems confronting any reader of the New York School.[11] In an article titled "The Conduit of Communication in Everyday Life," Watten quotes a passage from Henri Lefebvre about everyday life becoming "the locus of repression": "If tragedy still exists it is out of sight; the 'cool' prevails. Everything is ostensibly de-dramatized; instead of tragedy there are objects, certainties, 'values,' roles, satisfactions, jobs, situations, and functions. Yet there are powers, colossal and despicable, that swoop down on everyday life and pursue their prey in its evasions and departures, dreams and fantasies to crush it in their relentless grip."[12]

Charging the New York School's cultivation of the quotidian with these symptomatic "evasions and departures," Watten continues:

> Lefebvre writes at the same moment when everyday life in this sense is given a particular figure in American poetry, in the work of Frank O'Hara. There has long since ceased to seem anything like the natural in O'Hara's casual ironies of "objects, certainties, 'values,' roles, satisfactions, jobs, situations, and functions." In fact, looking back on the degree to which their fragile formulations were underscored by "colossal and despicable powers" — the Cuban missile crisis, the Kennedy assassination, the Vietnam war, which are either trivialized or ignored in his poetry — it's hard to imagine how O'Hara's "I do this, I do that," as Ted Berrigan put it, could be mistaken as natural, even if there is an entire literature built on the belief that it is. (ibid.)

For Watten, this "entire literature" would be the second and subsequent generations of the New York School — poets including Ron Padgett, Joe

Brainard, Bernadette Mayer, Alice Notley, Frank Lima, Joe Ceravolo, Anne Waldman, Tony Towle, and many others. While O'Hara's own poetry registers forces that mediate the would-be immediate, Watten takes O'Hara's interpreters, especially Berrigan, to misunderstand this process and to read O'Hara's poetry as a registration only of immediate dailiness, authentic everyday life unconditioned by institutional and social frames. O'Hara becomes a rallying point for a mystified relation to the quotidian in poetry, his death the occasion for generations of younger poets to take up his immediate life in poetry, blinding themselves repeatedly to the "colossal and despicable forces" that underwrite the quotidian, that give it its legibility: "It is a death that Berrigan, O'Hara's interpreter, later acted out in a repetition compulsion of 'I do this, I do that,' particularly in his physical incorporation of consumer culture in the form of Coke and Pepsi, to ensure the reception of historical romance as the proof of original intention" (ibid.).

Whether or not one agrees with this diagnosis of Berrigan and the younger New York School writers (a topic chapter 1 considers), Watten points to the fact that any successful reading of O'Hara will also need to be an articulation of the social and historical frames underlying, and possibly underwriting, the quotidian. Such an interpretive project is complicated by the fact that O'Hara is, as Watten suggests, an intense site of affect — an enormous point of cathexis for his friends and admirers, fueling numerous poetry careers and inspiring copious memoirs. This cathexis has decisively flavored O'Hara criticism. My approach to this problem is not to imagine a form of critical objectivity beyond identification but to construct an interpretive language that does not simply replicate the terms (primarily ones borrowed from O'Hara's writing, especially his essay "Personism") that currently constitute the field.[13]

For most O'Hara critics the line or short citation has been the primary unit of analysis — with multiple lines from different poems seeming to prove the same point and each chapter taking up a different thematic focus. The result has been to downplay the more social and analytical features of O'Hara's poetry and to construe it instead as a set of fragmentary, casual, speech-based "lines" — only occasionally brought together. In this reading "Personism" frequently becomes the core of O'Hara's theory. This decision is itself disputable because the poems, arguably, are more reflexive about his poetry than this one metapoetic statement. But even assuming that "Personism" is a central, and somehow ur-intention-bearing document, reading him exclusively in his own terms has a very traditional and limited effect, much like the one Jerome McGann criticizes readers of romanticism for adopting: using Wordsworth's and Coleridge's own terms, for instance, as a limiting framework for interpreting their work.[14] Such a stance has made this picture of O'Hara typical of the New York School, and this antitheoretical New York School, therefore, removed from, and innocent of, the larger social analyses of the Beats, Black Mountain, the San Francisco Renaissance, and later, the Language writers. Without collapsing O'Hara and his circle into kinds of analyses they didn't always take on consciously, this book challenges such a characterization.[15] And though I, too, will necessarily refer at times to isolated lines of O'Hara's poetry, my general approach has been to organize each chapter around a small cluster of O'Hara's poems — sometimes (as in chapters 3 and 6) even a single poem. My hope is that this heightened focus on the logic of individual poems can, in turn, open up a kind of thick description of O'Hara's dialog with the social, literary, and artistic worlds of the 1950s and 1960s.

All of which should suggest that I disagree with Watten's claim that both O'Hara and his followers lack terms through which to engage their historical moments. In introducing some of these terms, chapter 1 provides a social and philosophical context for O'Hara's attempt to denaturalize families — both literary and biological; the chapter then traces the transformation of O'Hara's afamilial legacy in its paradoxical heirs, especially Ted Berrigan. Chapter 2 then broadens the time frame by examining O'Hara's varying relationship to the social models encoded in a series of important modernist coteries — from Apollinaire, the Surrealists, and Auden to Ezra Pound. Chapter 3 expands the discussion of recoded families by looking at O'Hara's writing in relation to 1950s debates about how artistic communities, literal families, and discourses of nationalism all produce forms of sociality, of social linkage.

Clement Greenberg's and Michael Fried's dismissals of O'Hara's art writing are similarly predicated on a sense that O'Hara had a trivial relationship to the major historical "facts" of his moment — only the unavoidable contemporary facts that demand a response are now not the Cuban missile crisis or the Vietnam War, but, to shift the frame of reference a few years and into an aesthetic register, Jackson Pollock and the other New York School painters. In this art-historical context, O'Hara draws the charge of triviality, as chapter 5 argues, because he fails to pursue art history as the rigorous vocation Greenberg and Fried desired. "Things that would get expelled from other kinds of writing by laughter multiply and flourish in art writing," Greenberg fumes in his well-known 1962 article "How Art Writing Earns Its

Bad Name" (4:143). He then quotes three examples, the last of them from O'Hara's monograph on Jackson Pollock, in which O'Hara describes Pollock's *The Deep* as a "scornful, technical masterpiece, like the *Olympia* of Manet . . . one of the most provocative images of our time, an abyss of glamor encroached upon by a flood of innocence" (4:144). While my art historical chapters explore the functions that phrases like this perform in O'Hara's art writing (arguing, for instance, that O'Hara's association of abstract expressionism with Hollywood actually achieved a number of *demystifications*), I want to note here only the terms of Greenberg's angry response: "The widening gap between art and discourse solicits, as such widenings will, perversions and abortions of discourse: pseudo-description, pseudo-narrative; pseudo-exposition, pseudo-history, pseudo-philosophy, pseudo-psychology, and—worst of all—pseudo poetry" (ibid.).

Michael Fried shares this rage at the incursion of poetry into art criticism. Considering these charges against O'Hara, chapter 5 positions his poetry–based art writing not simply as a subversion of Greenberg's and Fried's dicta against interdisciplinarity but as a writing mode whose "inappropriate" closeness to its subjects, and failure to meet "professional" norms (both problems of coterie, I argue) allowed for modes of articulateness quite different from Greenberg's and Fried's. In particular, I examine how the readings of Pollock and de Kooning in O'Hara's poetry reimagine art writing as a collage of contingently joined critical discourses that, unfolding in the course of poetic lines, allows for a mobile and self-conscious consideration of how painterly gestures relate to interpretive contexts.

Disdain for O'Hara's art writing, however, is not limited to fans of the New York School painters. In perhaps the most famous attack on abstract expressionism, *How New York Stole the Idea of Modern Art*, Serge Guilbaut lumps O'Hara, as art historian, into the "tragedy of American modern art history" (9). Responsible in part for the "miles of pages filled by friends, promoters and admirers of the abstract artists," O'Hara's influence has contributed to the "cacophony of articles devoted to breathless discourses of stylistic influence" (ibid.). This uncritical praise has rendered those other critics "determined to see art in its original context and to reestablish the link between art and politics, particularly between abstract expressionism and the ideology of the Cold War . . . [isolated] voices . . . in the wilderness" (ibid.).[16] Chapters 4 and 5 seek to exonerate O'Hara from these charges by considering the critical functions O'Hara's art writing performs, including his attempts to produce a trans–Cold War dialog with

Mayakovsky and Pasternak — a dialog that considers the instrumental uses the concept of "freedom" was coming to have in the West (both in art and in literature) as an advertisement for capitalism over and against communism. O'Hara's dialog with these Russian writers is also, chapter 4 argues, an occasion for a heretical, queer account of "How New York Stole the Idea of Modern Art" from Paris.

Though my own thinking has undoubtedly benefited from the massive trend toward interdisciplinarity in the humanities over the past forty years, I am writing one study of O'Hara's contributions to two disciplines not through an a priori belief in the value of interdisciplinarity — a belief which, at this stage, risks becoming a piety. Interdisciplinary approaches now seem justified less by the would-be repression of interdisciplinarity generally than by specific potentialities such frameworks can bring to particular intellectual problems and contexts. In O'Hara's case, the questions that surround his art writing are an extension of those that complicate reading his poetry. Both involve the potentially pejorative senses of coterie: inappropriate closeness to his subjects, a troubling lack of formality, and a lack of professionalism within the disciplinary matrix as it was conceived at the historical moment in which he was writing. As chapter 5 argues, moreover, O'Hara's poetry is generally his most complex and rewarding art writing. Therefore, treating his poetry in the context of art history will require two types of contextualization. The first is the immediate job of bringing the poetry criticism into the same frame as the writing of Clement Greenberg, Harold Rosenberg, Michael Fried, and their most interesting subsequent interpreters, including Rosalind Krauss, Hal Foster, T. J. Clark, Benjamin Buchloch, Craig Owens, and Stephen Melville. But sketching this context must be followed by the more tricky job of establishing the terms by which O'Hara's painting poems might be understood as a kind of art criticism.

Articulating these terms can, I hope, help to combat the conspicuous lack of engagement that recent art criticism has had with post–WWII American poetry.[17] In the context of the influential journal *October*, for instance (in which all of the younger art historians I mention have published important essays), "twentieth-century literature" tends to mean surrealism and its exiles (Bataille and Artaud in particular) with an occasional reference to recent prose writers like Dennis Cooper on the one hand and Thomas Pynchon on the other. In *Formless: A User's Guide*, for instance, Yve-Alain Bois and Rosalind Krauss employ Georges Bataille's "operation" of the *informe* to organize a revisionary reading of modern art from the 1920s through the late 1970s.[18] Though the book suggestively uses Bataille to "brush modernism against the grain" (ibid.) — an extension of Krauss's previous arguments in *The Optical Unconscious*, which I will take up in chapters 5 and 6 — its relation to the category of the literary is deeply troubling. Unmistakably, Krauss and Bois frame the work of many post–WWII American artists in an interdisciplinary context: Richard Serra, Edward Ruscha, Robert Smithson, Cy Twombly, Robert Rauschenberg, Cindy Sherman, Jackson Pollock, Andy Warhol, Robert Morris, Claes Oldenburg, Bruce Nauman, Gordon Matta-Clark, and Mike Kelley all figure prominently. But the literary component of this context is exclusively the writing of early and midcentury France: Georges Bataille, André Breton, Louis Aragon, Michel Leiris, Raymond Queneau, Jacques Prévert, Francis Ponge, Benjamin Péret, Jean Paulhan, Henri Michaux, Jean Genet, Paul Eluard, Robert Desnos, and René Crevel. Were *Formless* an attempt to construct a countermodernism solely through Bataille, then the exclusion of all recent literature might follow. But when the book extends to this French literary context, and to it only, without an explanation of the omission of all other literatures, then one cannot help but begin to suspect that "the literary" exists for Bois and Krauss as a static set of examples from early and mid-twentieth-century France. Why not Allen Ginsberg or Charles Olson? Why not Borges or J. G. Ballard? And most particularly for those artists who operated in New York in the 1950s and 60s — like Pollock, Rauschenberg, Oldenburg, Warhol, and Twombly — why not John Ashbery or Frank O'Hara?

For many other art historians, poetry is less a pre–WWII French phenomenon than a self-evidently symptomatic category. We find the word *poetic*, for instance, serving a crucial function in the lexicon of Benjamin Buchloch: always uncoupled from any actual examples of poetry (modern or contemporary), the word indicates a straying from the path of critical self-reflexivity — as in the cases of Joseph Beuys and Anselm Kiefer.[19] More recently (and again with no reference at all to *actual poetry*), James Meyer has used the idea of "the poetic" to distinguish symptomatic from critical artistic engagements with the concept of travel.[20]

Poetry's poor reputation in art history seems matched only by the lack of specific attention directed to it. This may account to some extent for the refusal to consider O'Hara in the burst of recent work by art historians on the 1950s. Certainly O'Hara's reputation in art history has not been matched by his much stronger reputation in literary history. In art history his poetry tends to be ignored; O'Hara as art critic is cited alternatively as a bumbling nonprofessional (Greenberg), a MoMA stooge (Guilbaut), or, by those in his favor, as an enabler of ambience, a symbol of a rich, lost milieu. This book uses his painting poems to present terms for another reading of O'Hara. Testing out the relations between painterly gestures and interpretive contexts, these poems shift rapidly among language registers, melding colloquial idioms and pulp narration with dense continental philosophy, and tending all the while to look self-reflexively at the uses that an ideology of wildness and foreignness was coming to have for the U.S. state. Such a stance was far from symptomatic of a triumphant New York School ideologically proclaiming itself. At the same time I try to account for O'Hara's conflicted position as, simultaneously, a writer of this kind of poetry and also a curator of MoMA's International Program at the crucial moment of its ideological ambitions. As O'Hara's work shows, there is no easy synthesis between these two roles. But O'Hara's complex negotiation of these ambitions and institutional pressures provides, I want to argue, one of the richest views of midcentury American art available. Though I take up the question of O'Hara's relation to current art history written about New York art in the 1950s and 1960s throughout the second half of this study, it is chapter 6 — in the context of a reading of O'Hara's early advocacy of the art of Robert Rauschenberg — that positions O'Hara's art-historical writing within debates that have come in the wake of Michael Fried's 1967 "Art and Objecthood" — an essay which I am certainly not alone in taking as an almost exclusively negative focal point for much of the theoretical writing concerned with postmodernism in art history, including the formation of *October*. Chapter 6 uses O'Hara's writing on Rauschenberg to propose a version of postmodern allegory with a more workable politics. Articulating a way to read allegory between positivist iconography and pure difference, this revision is organized by the conceptual frameworks made available by my concept of coterie. In the second part of chapter 6, then, I expand the frame of reference to consider O'Hara's wider participation in the 1960s art world, a topic that none of his previous critics has examined in detail.

As a whole, this study uses the social and philosophical problems involved in reading a coterie to propose a new language for understanding O'Hara. My remapping is designed to make available the serious social implications of O'Hara's writing, relating the contours of his thought at once to several contemporary discourses of community from the 1950s and 60s (ranging from Paul Goodman to Ezra Pound, from the possibilities of fabricated families to the ways that nationalism and Cold War politics produce patterns of identification) and to more recent theoretical discourses organized around the problem of postmodernism in art and literature. In understanding the concept of coterie as a seam between the empirical and the rhetorical, this book tries to follow O'Hara's lead (though not always his terms) in conceptualizing the links between biography and textuality. But by reading the charges of coterie inside O'Hara's reception history, I have also sought to reflect more generally on the often-elided theoretical dimensions of community. As community's evil twin, coterie illuminates crucial assumptions about the ways that styles of referentiality are taken to encode models of audience. Because the charge of coterie marks a *breach* of an interpretive community's tacit standards, that is, it can also be understood to anatomize that community's operation as such.

1 NOMINAL FAMILIES
COTERIE, KINSHIP, AND LITERARY HISTORY

I don't think
Popeye is strictly Faulkner's property, do you? do
John Crowe and Allen T.? pass the noodles . . .
what were you fingering last 4th of July?
I remembering having sand on my balls
and a Bloody Mary
in my hand

— *Frank O'Hara, "Muy Bien"*

In an essay in *Homage to Frank O'Hara*, John Ashbery introduces his peer through an anecdote: at an opening for Edward Gorey's watercolors in 1949, while all three were still undergraduates at Harvard, Ashbery hears O'Hara "in a ridiculous voice that sounded to me like my own" suggest that Poulenc's *Les Sécheresses* was "greater than *Tristan*" (H 20). The "provocation," as Ashbery calls it, depends upon an educational regime at Harvard whose bias against contemporary composers makes mentioning Wagner and Poulenc in the same sentence impossible, let alone raising Poulenc above Wagner.

In his 1972 "Introduction" to O'Hara's *Collected Poems*, Ashbery had already seen a related provocation in a literary context. It was O'Hara's early cultivation of Rimbaud, Mallarmé, the Surrealists, Mayakovsky, and even lesser-known writers like Ronald Firbank, Jean Rhys, and Flann O'Brien — at a time when none of them had been digested by mainstream American poetry culture — that caused O'Hara's poetry to appear so "puzzling to readers." Their horizons of expectation had been produced by what Ashbery calls the "rules for modern American poetry that had been gradually drawn up from Pound and Eliot[1] down to the academic establishment of the 1940s" (*CP* vii).[2]

If O'Hara's work was puzzling, though, it was not only because it came out of a then-obscure tradition but also because, in deploying the proper

Joe LeSueur, photograph of Frank O'Hara (left) with John Ashbery at a taping for Daisy Aldan's poetry magazine, Folder 1, *November 1953.*

name as a prominent literary device, it provocatively advertised the representatives of this tradition and his then-unknown friends as explicit reference points within his work.[3] This provocation, moreover, was not merely the contents of O'Hara's eccentric canon,[4] the fact that certain names and not others appeared there, but what one might call the *syntax* of references within this canon more generally. Rather than using proper names as secure markers of property and identity, O'Hara tends to cast them as fluid and overdetermined cultural signs whose coding and overcoding provide a way to imagine experimental kinship structures, both social and literary.

In O'Hara's early writing, names are often those of a series of muse figures (Bunny Lang, Jane Freilicher, and Grace Hartigan) to whom the poems are addressed, e.g., "Oh Jane, is there no more frontier?" (*CP* 62) In the midperiod of his "I do this, I do that" poems, names tend to focus quotidian experience, including that of writing: "It is 12:10 in New York and I am wondering / if I will finish this in time to meet Norman for lunch" (*CP* 328). Though O'Hara also experiments with proper names in his wide range of prose poems, odes, occasional poems, and love poems, it is perhaps in his collage-based FYI poems of the early 1960s that names tend to function most actively and experimentally — here as markers of ambiguous cultural knowledge activated within wide fields of reference: "Busby Berkeley, kiss me / you have ended the war by simply singing in your Irene Dunne foreskin" (*CP* 437). At times, for instance, names explain one another in infinite regress: he presents Jackson Pollock in terms of Richard Burton and Fragonard, or James Dean in terms of Tiepolo and Turner. At other moments names wedge inextricably into each other: "better than Albert Schweitzer, Pablo Casals and Helen Keller / PUT TO GETHER" (*CP* 319). Throughout, this microdrama of the unstable semantic domains of proper names tends to analogize movements within O'Hara's poetics more generally: the rubbing of vernacular diction against opera and high art terminology; the cross-cutting of disciplines, from music to painting to dance to film; the collapsing of vocabulary registers ("Holy Cow, the cenotaph read" [*CP* 409]).

The primary response to O'Hara's conspicuous use of proper names and to his intimate referentiality more generally has been to understand him as a coterie poet.[5] But what precisely is a coterie poet? At what level is the figure of coterie meaningful? Is coterie an empirical context that determines meaning? Or is it a style of referentiality, a rhetoric even? Historically, when the term "coterie" has come up in literary criticism it has tended to designate, first off, a *size* of audience, one often identified, moreover, with a specific time. When Marjorie Perloff speaks of O'Hara's reputation until the mid-1970s as that of "a coterie figure — adored [primarily] by his New York School friends and acolytes" (P 1997 reprint xi) or Leroy Breunig claims that Apollinaire had only "a coterie of readers between the wars" (xviii), each critic is identifying an early phase of an avant-garde, before it had been disseminated.

When coterie is used as a pejorative, however, as it most often is, one takes issue with audience size itself as ineffectual, or antidemocratic, or both. On one end of the spectrum, then, is T. S. Eliot's complaint that the process of democratization has forced the poet to "talk to a coterie or to soliloquise" (*The Use of Poetry* 22).[6] The more common complaint, however, is the opposite: that the weakness of seeming to address a coterie is not ineffectuality but the refusal to engage a wider, would-be democratic public sphere.[7] In the case of O'Hara's reception history, as we will explore, critics tend to locate what they see as inappropriately specific references as markers of this fall into coterie.

An alternative, historicist approach has been to understand coterie as a determinate "context" that allows one to ground textual valences in specific empirical conditions. While this approach has the benefit of not stationing the critic as the upholder of supposedly universal standards of reference, it tends, as I will argue below, to hypostatize context. Neither of these models, I think, articulates what is most compelling about the problems of reading a coterie in general or in the specific instance of a poet like Frank O'Hara.

Though Marjorie Perloff established many of the central terms of O'Hara's poetry,[8] her strategy reduced both the social implications and the strangeness of O'Hara's relation to the problem of coterie by understanding his use of proper names as important only because "persons and places, books and films . . . are central to O'Hara's particular consciousness" (P 2, 130–31).[9] Even for Geoff Ward, who addresses coterie through a more theoretical framework, O'Hara's connection to a literary coterie takes on the consistent, singular meaning of "a humanist refuge against temporality" (Ward 61). That is, in the de Manian terms Ward uses, O'Hara's reliance on coterie as a figure — his thematization of a close-knit world of friends marked in the poems by proper names — represents an attempt to freeze time, to repress temporality and loss by filling these voids imaginatively with the would-be presence of a secure identity within a coterie. But symbolism in de Man's writing always marks not so much an actual refuge against time as a temporary delusion that must eventually give way to what de Man calls an "authentically temporal destiny" and links to allegory, which "prevents the self from an illusory identification with the non-self, which is now fully, though painfully, recognized as non-self."[10] Does this delusion that de Man links to the symbol apply, though, to O'Hara's model of coterie?[11] To answer this question negatively, as this chapter ultimately does, it will be necessary to give a more detailed account of how the problems of coterie connect to models of audience, kinship, and literary history and how these connections are mediated through the effects of the proper name.

Tension between inherently conservative and progressive roles is embedded in the etymology of the word *coterie*, which carries at once the force of cultural marginality and the authority of deeply established cultural interest. The literary and political uses of the term that became widespread in the eighteenth century were preceded by a very different sense, defined in Littré: "a certain number of peasants united together to hold land from a lord."[12] In this usage, the wretched condition of "cots" or "cottages" prompts their peasant owners to collectivize against their landlords.[13] But as the term gets used to designate privileged circles devoted to covert political or literary activity, the force of marginality associated with the medieval term gives way to the modern connotation of the clique. Its etymology, then, encodes competing senses of a marginal group engaged in a struggle to attain property rights and a private, privileged clique. The very movement from one meaning to the next is a well-established tension within the history of the avant-garde's attempts to avoid recuperation or co-option.[14]

The idea of coterie as a progressive strategy had entered O'Hara's reception by the late 1960s. Commenting on his reservations about calling the poets included a traditional "school," John Bernard Myers remarks, in the introduction to his 1969 anthology, *The Poets of the New York School*: "Perhaps, despite the pejorative flavor of the word, it might be more accurate to call them a 'coterie' — if we define as coterie a group of writers rejected by the literary establishment who found strength to continue with their work by what the anarchists used to call 'mutual aid' " (7–8). As director of the Tibor de Nagy Gallery, where many of the artists with whom O'Hara had the closest relationships exhibited their work, Myers was the first to publish O'Hara and Ashbery.[15] If by the mid-1950s the first generation of Abstract Expressionists had begun to establish a market for their painting — one from which O'Hara's second-generation painter friends, such as Mike Goldberg, Norman Bluhm, Alfred Leslie, and Grace Hartigan, would benefit — no equivalent institutional support existed for poets in O'Hara's circle. Accounts of limited audience are crucial to O'Hara's depiction of the origin of his work: "When we all arrived in New York or emerged as poets in the mid 50s or late 50s, painters were the only ones who were interested in any kind of experimental poetry and the general literary scene was not" (SS 3). Of course, such depictions of the marginal status of writing (as well as of painting) have a distinguished genealogy within modernism, since both have often looked to marginality as self-explanation.[16]

The historicist alternative to understanding coteries as either authentically or symptomatically marginal audience structures has been to read them as determinate "contexts," as frameworks that ground and explain textual ambiguities.[17] When Arthur Marotti published *John Donne, Coterie Poet* in 1986, for instance, it was a response to a series of decontextualizing readings, from the seventeenth century to the present, that had "falsified" the terms off Donne's "context-bound" writing (24, 3). Documenting Donne's coterie was a way to reestablish the "contextual particularity" (10) that the poems both referred to and depended upon, which Marotti describes as "the personal circumstances of the authors and . . . the social, economic, and political milieu they shared with their chosen audience" (ibid.). For Marotti, Donne's intention to keep his poems within a set of small communities should operate, even now, as a primary interpretive framework.

Such a stance therefore suggests a sympathy with Donne's own metaphoric complaint in "The Triple Fool" that, by setting his work to music and performing it in a context over which Donne had no control, other poets thereby free the very grief Donne had captured:

> Grief brought to numbers cannot be so fierce,
> For he tames it that fetters it in verse.
>
> But when I have done so,
> Some man, his art and voice to show,
> Doth set and sing my pain,
> And, by delighting many, frees again
> Grief, which verse did restrain. (Donne 7)

Identifying with what we might call Donne's contextual imperative,[18] Marotti claims that "the very act of anthologizing dislodged poems from their place in a system of transactions within polite or educated social circles and put them in the more fundamentally 'literary' environment of the handwritten or typographic-volume" (12–13). Understanding this literary environment as necessarily "formalist or ahistorical" (13), Marotti uses the idea of coterie as a way to "recover some of what has been lost through literary institutionalization of Donne's verse" (24).

A similar idea of recovery motivates historian Alan Charles Kors's *D'Holbach's Coterie: An Enlightenment in Paris.* Here the question, however, is not *whether* d'Holbach, Diderot, and Grimm, for instance, were involved in something we could call a coterie but rather what the functions and beliefs of this coterie in fact were.[19] Though Kors notes that the term itself comes from an attack on the group in Rousseau's *The Confessions,* he does not reflect more generally on how the word *coterie* works to transform a various and diverse social formation into a uniform site of doctrine, the fact of an association into a symptom. As in Marotti's book, coterie is understood as a binding context. The problem for Kors is to establish the actual frame of that context.

It is certainly true that the traditional refusal to understand literature as contextually bound (in any framework more specific than nation) has played a crucial ideological role in the development of the concept of "the literary." Clearly the range of pre–New Historicist imperatives to understand literary effects and values within a universal context served a number of now-familiar ideological agendas, including unifying English subjects across class lines in the wake of religion's ability to achieve this and defining a space of linguistic complexity and play outside what was characterized, alternatively, as scientific instrumentality and mass culture.[20]

But whatever the real problems (nationalism, classism, and fear of popular culture) that have, in different ways throughout history, attended this jump from writing to literature, resistance to the ideological ruses of the literary cannot effectively happen by tracing all literature back to its preliterary status in coteries — its position in constructed contexts of the sort Marotti sees as determinant for the meaning of Donne's poems. If we are always slightly uninformed readers of coteries, we need a way to articulate coterie's afterlife in literature that does not simply imply loss — as if the opposition were between proper historicism and the symptomatically literary. Writing's inherent relation to temporality enforces this literary condition.

Morton Feldman touches on this dynamic when he descibes the odd relation between O'Hara's colloquial tone and its seemingly opposite afterlife in literary history.

> In an extraordinary poem Frank O'Hara describes his love for the poet, Mayakovsky. After an outburst of feeling, he writes, "*but I'm turning to my verses / and my heart is closing / like a fist.*"
>
> What he is telling us is something unbelievably painful. Secreted in O'Hara's thought is the possibility that we create only as dead men. . . . Death seems the only metaphor distant enough to truly measure our existence. Frank understood this. That is why these poems, so colloquial, so conversational, nevertheless seem to be reaching us from some other, infinitely distant place. Bad artists throughout history have always tried to make art like life. Only the artist who is close to his own life gives us an art that is like death. (H 13–14)

O'Hara's quotidian yet paradoxically deathlike work thus gives Feldman an insight ("we create only as dead men") that seems to run directly counter to Donne's and Marotti's contextual imperative. As O'Hara's act of creation stretches temporally into literary history, it is "like death" (perhaps) in that the possibility of an immediate world of quotidian sense-experience evoked so forcefully by O'Hara's rhetoric becomes an oddly displaced, and possibly opposite, effect. As details and names accumulate, O'Hara's New York becomes, for later readers, an increasingly impossible imaginative act, one held in a fictive unity only by its absent experiential center. Should we read O'Hara as the immediate, intimate friend, the animated interlocutor laughing between sentences and facing us, for instance, in Fred McDarrah's 1959 photograph of the poet at his apartment on 441 East 9th Street? Or is it more accurate to understand him, despite the appearance of informality, despite the "colloquial, conversational" surface of his work, as Feldman suggests, as a more "distant" writer (as opposed to speaker) who has subtly shifted himself away from us precisely through his seemingly immediate writing, who is always "turning to my verses," aware that "we create only as dead men" — perhaps the poet who, as in Richard Moore's photograph, presents his back to us while addressing someone else in a phone conversation, working at his desk, maybe typing, and possibly contemplating the solidity and permanence of the brick wall in front of which he writes?

In his "Poem (Khrushchev is coming on the right day!)," O'Hara comments self-reflexively on these very problems.

> Ionesco is greater
> than Beckett, Vincent said, that's what I think, blueberry blintzes
> and Khrushchev was probably being carped at

Fred W. McDarrah, photograph of Frank O'Hara in his 441 East 9th Street apartment, September 26, 1959. © Fred W. McDarrah.

Richard Moore, photograph of Frank O'Hara at his desk, 1960s. © Richard Moore.

in Washington, no *politesse*
Vincent tells me about his mother's trip to Sweden
Hans tells us
about his father's life in Sweden, it sounds like Grace Hartigan's
painting Sweden
so I go home to bed and names drift through my head
Purgatorio Merchado, Gerhard Schwartz and Gaspar Gonzales, all
Unknown figures of the early morning as I go to work
(CP 340)

Embedded with the names of O'Hara's close friend (Grace), boyfriend (Vincent), as well as their remarks and judgments, this is a classic coterie poem. At one level, then, we can understand the poem in terms of the figure of a literal group whose shifting and nonprofessional valuations work to challenge the more distant and measured tonality poetry is supposed to adopt if it wants to be considered "public." In this sense, O'Hara's poem could be thought to produce what Michael Warner calls a counterpublic, a social formation that, while resisting the terms of dominant culture, is nonetheless characterized by "openness, accessibility, and unpredictablity" (97). So unpredictable is this space, in fact, that, as if anticipating the reader's inability to recontextualize O'Hara's copious use of proper names more generally, the poem's own speaker (as in "Who Is William Walton?") struggles unsuccessfully to link three such names to attributes, to identify them for use. As we have seen, these problems of decontextualization can be managed temporarily by asserting, even policing, the priority of an actual, literal coterie of readers. In O'Hara, as I have been suggesting, it is not that such an inner circle is an irrelevant figure but rather that he is aware of and interested in what happens when poetry seems to escape these contexts, intentionally or not.

I say "seems" because, as the name Khrushchev suggests, such escapes are always partial: the problem of context, that is, never simply disappears. Indeed this poem depends upon some knowledge of Khrushchev's position as leader of the Soviet Union. But if it asks us to associate *these* framing contextual attributes with *that* famous proper name, the poem's ultimate gesture is precisely to destabilize the broader set of attributes we are taught to associate with a world leader, so that what is at stake in the poem's self-consciously impossible personalization of politics is not the competition of ideologies but a subject's contingent experience of Manhattan — as though the right atmospheric conditions would somehow produce the right view of New York and, therefore, of the United States as a whole. In a sense, then, this rejection of a kind of normative context for the proper name Khrushchev is an example of O'Hara's common practice of appropriating and personalizing what we might think of as the operative associations that are supposed to govern our understanding of public figures.

This happens in a related way in O'Hara's well-known poem "Adieu to Norman, Bon Jour to Joan and Jean-Paul," which first considers the movements of a group of friends between Paris and New York: "Allen is back talking about god a lot / and Peter is back not talking very much / and Joe has a cold and is not coming to Kenneth's" (*CP* 328). This leads into speculation on how, despite this kind of fluidity, both cultural capitals and people maintain their identities: "the Seine continues / the Louvre stays open it continues it hardly closes at all / the Bar Américain continues to be French / de Gaulle continues to be Algerian as does Camus" (*CP* 329). The "continuing" (if also often paradoxically international) identities of French rivers, museums, bars, colonists, and postcolonial critics prepare the poem for its conclusion, which operates as a kind of playful performative act that would convert this catalog of fully embodied Frenchness into a guarantor of both secure identity and happiness for those in O'Hara's circle.

> and surely we shall not continue to be unhappy
> we shall be happy
> but we shall continue to be ourselves everything continues to be
>   possible
> René Char, Pierre Reverdy, Samuel Beckett it is possible isn't it
> I love Reverdy for saying yes, though I don't believe it

Paradoxically, then, it seems to be the inclusion of this string of French authors — Char, Reverdy, and Beckett — that allows the New York artists and writers at least the possibility of continuing to be themselves. But how, precisely, do the names do this? As bodies of exemplary writing, yes. But also, somehow, as better-known proper names — ones that already carry a charge of authority and are therefore in pointed contrast to the first names of O'Hara's still-obscure friends. Ultimately, though, it is this contrast that the last magical recitation of the French names might be thought to mitigate: as though by rubbing the two sets of names against each other O'Hara could effect a sort of temporary, improper canonization of his own friends — a project that will be taken up with different sets of names, from poem to poem.[21]

Each of these constellations of names operates, analogically, as a figure of kinship. Thus, if "Adieu," like "Poem (Khrushchev is coming on the right day!)," suggests how an idea of coterie could explore the performative power of canonization, it also suggests how a practice of coterie could be used to recode kinship structures. I mean kinship here in the sense that a coterie of friends produced through selection could come to supplant the naturalized bonds of the family. Acts of poetic canonization contain a buried moment of kinship: they come out of families; they form and reform families. When T. S. Eliot argues, for instance, that "the primary vehicle for the transmission of culture is the family," he, like many others both inside and outside of literature, seeks to preserve not only the biological family's "hereditary transmission of culture" (and the class distinctions that this transmission would confer) but a larger understanding of kinship more generally as naturalized or "organic" (*Notes* 48). The family then becomes the machine not merely for enforcing similarity and difference but for naturalizing this activity. It is in this sense that one might understand Eliot's thoughts on the family, by the late 1940s already backed by a formidable institutional apparatus and even a style and tone of public discourse, as a necessary extension of his claims about literary heredity and kinship.[22]

Anthropologists understand kinship in terms of two primary structures: alliance ("horizontal" association through marriage) and filiation ("vertical" association through birth). Heterosexual marriage and reproduction are, of course, the machines that drive the movements of this system, along with the incest taboo. O'Hara's version of coterie, we might say, recodes both of these movements. He recodes alliances by replacing the organic and fixed social model of the family with a contingent and shifting association of friends. He recodes filiation not merely by refusing to produce offspring but also by refusing to *be* one. O'Hara's attempt to exit the filiative model of the Great Tradition is coincident both with his cultivation of obscure, often campy, genealogical precedents and with his frequently heretical readings of canonical authors.[23]

Literary coterie's intimate relation to anthropological models of kinship also emerges in how critics claim to recognize coteries. In the frequent pejorative usage, noticing a coterie work is noticing a breach in the tacit referential norms literature is thought to establish with its audience. It is in this sense that one should understand Geoff Ward's taxonomy of referential modes in O'Hara, for instance. For Ward, O'Hara's references fall into three interpretive categories inasmuch as they elicit three types of response from readers: literal recognition, abstract identification, and coterie dismissal. In the first case one knows and enjoys the reference, or as O'Hara might say, "everything is too comprehensible / these are my delicate and caressing poems" (*CP* 356). In the second, one appreciates the situation as a common human one — without necessarily knowing the actual people mentioned. Of the poem "Adieu," mentioned earlier, Ward says that "any of us middle-class speaking subjects has a friend like Kenneth and a lunch appointment next week with our own Joan and Jean-Paul" (*W* 62). Ward contrasts the accessibility of the above poem with examples in which coterie can be dismissed as bad, claiming that "a line like 'It's another case of nature imitating Alfred Leslie!' . . . is simply an in-joke, conforming to the more incestuous associations of 'coterie' " (ibid.).

For Ward, coterie becomes a breach of literary decorum when he can no longer turn names and events into universally accessible experience. With the mention of Alfred Leslie, O'Hara's proper names have dropped below Ward's interpretive radar and somehow broken the pact he wants to establish with O'Hara. If O'Hara's lines depended upon our knowledge of all of his proper names, one might agree. But this example makes it clear that they do not. Holding in abeyance the identity of Alfred Leslie, one can notice that O'Hara's line literalizes Oscar Wilde's famous dictum that "life imitates art." For "art," O'Hara has plugged in a proper name. Whether or not one knows precisely who life is imitating, encountering a proper name in this revised pun encourages us to take the name as an example of an artist. O'Hara consciously chooses an obscure name with which to update Wilde so that life itself will seem subject to a wide number of potential artistic modes or styles. Mastering life now appears, in the logic of the pun, as a matter of learning an array of specific artistic styles. Not only could we have Rembrandt, Goya, or Picasso days; we could have Alfred Leslie days. Many people might be confused and frustrated on such days, much as they might be confused on a day in which, as O'Hara writes elsewhere, "the clouds are imitating Diana Adams" (*CP* 339).

In the example Ward has chosen, the referentiality of the name does not regulate entrance into an actual group, an empirical coterie, so much as it sets into motion a pun about the workings of names in general within the relation between art and life. Ward's frustration leaves him outside O'Hara's pun, not outside a reference that depends upon a reader's ability to associate specific attributes (beyond the contextually produced relation to art) with the name Alfred Leslie. Unrecognizable references, that is, can have a variety of functions other than providing raw material for abstract identification.

Some of these might be fleshed out by a brief turn to the study of proper names in linguistics and philosophy. Because proper names at once blur schemes of categorization and perform important and vast political work, situating the name within the social sciences has been a difficult and largely inconclusive project. Though theorists of the name have been unable to account for the ways in which names become differently weighted, seemingly tied to public systems of reference, the specific nature of their failures has relevance for our consideration of kinship and canonization. Ferdinand de Saussure, for instance, in his *Course in General Linguistics* brackets off the proper name from the processes that affect other linguistic elements. Of what he calls "analogy" in diachronic language development (a process whereby words from other languages replace existing ones through the laboratory of speech), Saussure writes: "The only forms over which analogy exercises no power are naturally isolated words, such as proper names, especially place names. . . . These admit of no analysis and consequently no interpretation of their elements. No rival creation emerges to challenge them" (171). Even if one accepts the terms *analysis* and *interpretation* strictly in Saussure's intended sense of etymology, exceptions to his rule come readily to mind: modifying family names and renaming streets, buildings, monuments, or even entire cities. What is each of these acts if not a "rival creation" that emerges to "challenge" a previous linguistic order? In his 1958 poem "With Barbara Guest in Paris," for instance, O'Hara asks the question: "Oh Barbara! do you think we'll ever / have anything named after us like / *rue Henri-Barbusse* or / *canard à l'Ouragan?*" (CP 310) For Saussure, however, these types of mutation fall outside his interest in linguistic evolution precisely because they are linked to conscious human agency, rendering them what he calls "external."

Analytic philosophers have encountered similar difficulties with the proper name. John Searle argues, for instance, that "the uniqueness and immense pragmatic convenience of proper names in our language lie precisely in the fact that they enable us to refer publicly to objects without being forced to raise issues and come to agreement on what descriptive characteristics exactly constitute the identity of the object" (172). Searle would seem to avoid raising these issues by understanding famous or overdetermined names through their ability to evoke a "family of descriptions"[24] or attributes — a given set of associations that would accompany famous names like Napoleon or Aristotle. Not surprisingly, Searle's proposition was quickly countered by questions from Saul Kripke and others about how such essential associations would be established. In his *Naming and Necessity*, Kripke concludes "our reference depends not just on what we think ourselves, but on other people in the community, the history of how the name reached one. . . . It is by following such a history that one gets to the reference" (95).[25] But precisely how one "follows such a history" is not a concern for Kripke, who states what may seem obvious: "More exact conditions are very complicated to give. They seem in a way somehow different in the case of a famous man and one who isn't so famous" (ibid.). In a schematic sense, then, Saussure shares the problem that analytic philosophers encounter with the name: names press the problem of a given background. If for Saussure this background is the inaccessible, because nonsystematic, world of external linguistics, for analytic philosophers the position of names is compromised because it at once depends upon, but cannot ensure, a public descriptive discourse. In each case, something like the index or marker encounters the disruptivenss of the unbounded sign. Kripke, Searle, and Saussure suggest what the (impossible) requirements would be for proper names to evoke a consistent, publicly known family of attributes.

In fact it seems in part *because* names cannot secure such attributes that O'Hara both saddles names with new connotations and uses them to imagine reformed, self-consciously constructed families. Overall, O'Hara's names might be grouped into three broad and sometimes overlapping categories — each of which disrupts the idea of an organic family of associations: first, names that are simply too obscure to register — ones that pointedly lack context, from "Miss Stillwagon" (*CP* 325) to "Walter Wanger" (*CP* 474) and "Helen Parker" (*PR* 129); second, those names, initially just as unknown, that pick up such a "family" only contextually, through a self-consciously minor form of canonization, in his work — O'Hara's friends, such as Alfred Leslie, Norman Bluhm, Bill Berkson, John Ashbery, Kenneth Koch, and Joe LeSueur, among many others; finally, better-known proper names that seem to loose more established (if contested) attributes and gain a surrogate, often queer, "family" of associations. Here one thinks of O'Hara's camp appropriations of Hollywood stars (James Dean, Richard Burton, Gretta Garbo, Myrna Loy, Marilyn Monroe, Ginger Rogers, and Lana Turner are among his favorites), prominent New York dancers and ballerinas (including Maria Tallchief, Mary Desti, and Diana Adams), abstract expressionist painters (Jackson Pollock, Willem de Kooning, and Franz Kline), and musicians (Rachmaninoff above all).

Each of these loose categories emerges, of course, only through multiple poems over the course of O'Hara's six-hundred-page *Collected Poems* — poems, often, in which names are not necessarily the most prominent feature. Still, their gradual accretion with different, contextual attributes produces a kind of phantom canon of reference inside O'Hara's constructed world, a canon that both overlaps with, and frequently undermines, those would-be public attributes associated with better-known proper names. Here, then, are some examples of these three types of provocative, coterie naming practices. For the first category — names whose effects depend upon their obscurity — the last lines of the Khrushchev poem will serve as a good point of departure: "so I go home to bed and names drift through my head / Purgatorio Merchado, Gerhard Schwartz and Gaspar Gonzales, all / Unknown figures of the early morning as I go to work" (CP 340).

To say that O'Hara is simply interested in the sounds of these or all proper names is not enough; here names are included at least in part because they fail to call to mind any would-be essential attributes. This experience of grasping unsuccessfully to link evocative proper names to "identities" crucially and self-reflexively puts O'Hara in the position of a reader of his own *Collected Poems*. In this instance, after names vanish below contextual radar they do not reemerge in the sky as archetypes. We can't be sure that, as Ward would have it, "any of us middle-class speaking subjects has a friend like" Gerhard Schwartz "and a lunch appointment next week with our own" (*W* 62) Purgatorio Merchado. And that's the point. The names are recalcitrant matter — designating identities from which we (and here this "we" includes O'Hara) are held at a careful distance. To universalize them is therefore not adequate; instead, they are strategic remainders that block our easy identification. The effect of these names depends upon a version of the contextual loss — at the double levels of speaker and reader — that Marotti and most readers of coteries seek earnestly to overcome. Though O'Hara is continually supplying context, he seems to be interested in what happens when it breaks down, when we encounter markers of identity that we cannot recuperate.

To turn to my second category, then, names that begin to accumulate attributes generally do so as they move through the context of the poems: repetition in different contexts teaches new glosses. Take the example of Kenneth, the poet Kenneth Koch, whose first name appears in fifteen of O'Hara's *Collected Poems*. In the simplest of these appearances, as when we are told that Kenneth is "large, locomotive" (CP 75) or "excitement-prone" (CP 328), characterizing details accumulate without a poem-to-poem plot structure that converts this accumulation into narrative actions. As we learn features of Kennethness — including the speaker's admiration for his writing — the result is similar to what Roland Barthes describes as "the novelestic without the novel" (Barthes *S/Z* 5). In other instances, though, O'Hara uses the name itself as a way to register some of the principles he seems to value inside it, as when, in the poem "Second Avenue," the name Kenneth morphs into an impossibly broad context of Surrealist-based association:

Now!
in cuneiform, of umbrella satrap square-carts with hotdogs
and onions of red syrup blended, of sand bejewelling the prepuce
in tank suits, of Majestic Camera Stores and Schuster's,
of Kenneth in an abandoned storeway on Sunday cutting ever more
insinuating lobotomies of a yet-to-be-more-yielding world
of ears, of a soprano rallying at night in a cadenza
(*CP* 146)

Thus, while O'Hara's *Collected Poems* does work toward a kind of improper canonization of Kenneth, it also complicates any sense of neat piths and gists that we would associate with the name. What counts as a nominal attribute often shifts rapidly and humorously and is rarely "as unpleasantly definitive as statuary" (*CP* 360).

To illustrate my third category, that of transforming the attributes of famous figures, I turn to several slightly less complicated examples of shifting the associative world of the proper name. As film and painting enter the poems, for instance, O'Hara tends to torque the language one might use for accomplishment, as in "Favorite Paintings in the Metropolitan": "Richard Burton / waves through de Kooning the / Wild West rides up out of the Pollock / and a Fragonard smiles no pinker / than your left ear, no bigger either" (*CP* 423).

Because the syntax of name placements allows for interdisciplinary, anachronistic montages, painters can become caricatures of Americana who feature Hollywood actors among their attributes. This happens in reverse in the first lines of "Thinking of James Dean": "Like a nickelodeon soaring over the island from sea to bay, / two pots of gold, and the flushed effulgence of a sky Tiepolo / and Turner had compiled in vistavision" (*CP* 230). Again, the point is a kind of energized connection that strips famous names of established connotations, while highlighting others. This process comes together perhaps most clearly and hilariously in BIOGRAPHIA LETTERARIA:

GERTRUDE STEIN
She hated herself because she wrote prose.

JAMES JOYCE
He was a very lovable person, though thorough.

RONALD FIRBANK
I will not go home with you, so perhaps I shall.

IVY COMPTON-BURNETT
My grandfather's lap was comfortable and becoming speaking is not becoming a cactus.

PHILIP ROTH
How do you do, Mr. Rahv; I hope you will print my friend.

CLEMENT GREENBERG
How Orphic?

CHARLES DICKENS
He hated pretense. He was the founder of Social Security.

LAWRENCE OF ARABIA
Cognac is not KY.
(CP 464–65)

Humorously elliptical glosses shift seamlessly from description of to statement from authors. Clement Greenberg, for instance, clearly has power to attach attributes to careers in art history, but his inability to read contemporary poetry here leaves him as a confused spectator. Similarly, Philip Roth's own writing vanishes, and he gets pictured only as a toady schmoozer. This heretical use of a proper name's would-be attributes is what allows O'Hara at once to playfully undercut powerful public figures and to situate his own alternative modernist influences, Firbank and Compton-Burnett, in a paradigmatic relation to Joyce and Stein. At once ruthless, oblique, and funny, this poem is an example of how O'Hara rethinks structures of literary kinship through the proper name. In "Cornkind," O'Hara takes up the question of kinship more explicitly, here in large part through a series of glosses and inversions of the name William Morris.

So the rain falls
it drops all over the place
and where it finds a little rock pool
it fills it up with dirt
and the corn grows
a green Bette Davis sits under it

reading a volume of William Morris
oh fertility! beloved of the Western world
you aren't so popular in China
though they fuck too

and do I really want a son
to carry my idiocy past the Horned Gates
poor kid   a staggering load

yet it can happen casually
and he lifts a little of the load each day
as I become more and more idiotic
and grows to be a strong strong man
and one day carries as I die
my final idiocy and the very gates
into a future of his choice

but what of William Morris
what of you Million Worries
(CP 387)

By asking about the fate of William Morris, the exterior voice identified as "Million Worries" initiates a series of reflexive questions that concludes the poem: "what of Hart Crane / what of phonograph records and gin // what of 'what of' // you are of me, that's what / and that's the meaning of fertility / hard and moist and moaning" (ibid.). As the poem turns back on what appears to have been Million Worries's naïve understanding, it suggests that how we think of the word *of* might determine how we understand fertility and the possible social linkages implied by it.[26] Casting aside William Morris's attempt to universalize heterosexuality in so-called "fertility motifs," the poem moves from fertility's "of" as heterosexual reproduction or filiation to "of" as something like inhabitation, coexistence, or alliance — concretized in the activity of gay sex, which would enact linkage in itself outside of representation and reproduction.[27] Giving up the desire to see one's idiocy carried forward by children parallels a renunciation of narrative, not caring, as Million Worries does, what happens to William Morris. And indeed, with this pun, O'Hara actually turns the name William Morris into a critique of heterosexual narrative by flipping the M and W upside down.

Throughout his work, O'Hara's pseudocanonizations of obscure friends and unknown influences, his revisions of famous names' "descriptive backing," as well as his heretical syntax of name juxtaposition can be read as a sustained, inventive engagement with the problem of how and in which contexts names take on meaning and who has the power to enforce this meaning.[28] All of this tends to shift the idea of coterie away from its more normative sense of a sociological entity toward that of a social rhetoric. Because we get to look at the edges of coterie — positions from which it does not cohere, from which names drop, add, and change their attributes — we begin to see coterie as a rhetoric capable of enacting experimental models of kinship, both social and literary. These models might provide one kind of answer to Judith Butler's question, in *Antigone's Claim*, about whether there is "a social life left for kinship . . . that might . . . accommodate change within kinship relations" (18).

Once coterie appears also as a fluid rhetoric, moreover, the historicist imperative to contextualize must be transformed: to reconstruct the codes by which gestures within coterie are meaningful is part of the work. But the second part consists in tracking such poems as they oscillate between this would-be immediate and singular context and a variety of new and more distant contexts, some of which we associate with the literary. By featuring the obscure as experience in itself, by canonizing the unknown, and by seeming to modify or disrupt the canonized, O'Hara anticipates this very oscillation. In view of this, O'Hara's model of coterie should be understood not as a symbolic stand against time but as a fluid and experimental way of conceptualizing literary and social linkage. It is because these linkages are based on appropriated, superimposed, chosen, and contingent principles — which operate outside the organic family — that coterie retains a demystifying force that is allegorical, not symbolic. Rather than the symptomatic delusion of an already-formed group, then, coterie in O'Hara might better be described as an invented form of kinship that uses the name, in particular, to reimagine the social logics that allow group formations in the first place.

• • •

> *This Sunday night (tonight) I went to the poetry reading by O'Hara and Koch at the New School. Koch was good but read old stuff. O'Hara was marvelous! He read from 2nd Avenue and his "odes" — which inspired me to rush home and write* Ode to Joe Brainard.
>
> — *Ted Berrigan, diary entry, June 9, 1963*

> *Ted said something the other day about finding a lot for today in great works of the recent past — that you can keep drawing on them the way he draws on O'Hara. It makes*

sense. It would be some kind of anchor. I'm tired of drifting aimlessly. I envy Ted his Frank O'Hara, his inspiration. ("It's all there, I don't need anything else.")
— Donna Dennis, "Excerpts from Journals"

Rewrite someone else's writing. Maybe someone formidable.
— Bernadette Mayer, "Experiments"

Whatever the suggestion in "Cornkind," O'Hara did, in fact, "see [his] idiocy carried forward" — even in his lifetime.[29] And had he lived beyond 1966, he would have seen it disseminated even more broadly. Not by biological children (obviously) and not by participation in a Great Literary Tradition, but primarily in the second and subsequent generations of New York School Poets.[30] If O'Hara's work resisted characterization as the kind of literary masterpiece that is understood to drive the engines of literary production in arenas like the *Norton Anthology of Poetry*, and yet O'Hara was consumed and somehow reproduced by a broad and significant range of poets, what, then, were the terms of this alternative transmission? Though the breadth of O'Hara's influence is far too wide to survey or inventory, focusing on a few paradoxes associated with this influence may help to expand the context and implications of the questions of coterie with which his work remains intimately tied.

Perhaps the major event that put O'Hara on the map for younger poets was the publication of Donald Allen's anthology *The New American Poetry* in 1960, in which O'Hara was given thirty-one pages (second behind Charles Olson's thirty-eight). Allen's anthology included not only shorter works like "The Day Lady Died" and "Why I Am Not a Painter" but also longer pieces like "In Memory of My Feelings" and "Ode to Michael Goldberg ('s Birth and Other Births)." There is ample testimony by younger writers — including Ted Berrigan, Ron Padgett, Anne Waldman, Lewis Warsh, David Shapiro, Tony Towle,[31] and many others — both about the importance of this anthology generally and about O'Hara's significant place in it in particular.[32] Berrigan mentions in a 1965 review of *Lunch Poems* that "[w]hile romping thru the assorted confessions, obsessions, concessions and blessings of the Allen book I was suddenly given an extremely close reading by O'Hara's poem WHY I AM NOT A PAINTER. For reasons I don't know this poem seemed to straighten all kinds of things out for me, as I immediately explained to Ron Padgett" (91). Later Berrigan will become *the* reader of O'Hara, the second-generation New York School poet who makes reading O'Hara into a kind of life practice; here, though, in this initial encounter, O'Hara's poem seems to read Berrigan. And Berrigan immediately "explains" this to his friend, the poet Ron Padgett. Padgett, in high school when the anthology came out, writes of "a certain high pitch in some of those poems that scared me, a certain kind of diction and intensity that I hadn't seen before" (G 354). Anne Waldman, also in high school at the time of the Allen anthology, mentions that the anthology led her "into whole books by authors" featured in it, including O'Hara (Waldman and Webb 295). O'Hara's biographer Brad Gooch concludes that "[b]ecause of the Allen anthology, teenage poets all around the country, who would eventually gravitate to New York and to O'Hara, were given their first tantalizing, if sometimes baffling exposure" (G 354).[33]

At the same time, O'Hara is typically characterized as a kind of antiteacher. In his book on John Ashbery, for instance, John Shoptaw writes: "Unlike the Black Mountain school, the New York School had no campus or lessons or poetics, other than the absence of a poetics, the very rules by which group discipline might be maintained. None of these founding members wrote anything like the manifestoes coming from Black Mountain" (48). While it's true that the group rejected manifestoes and that Ashbery in particular did not cultivate a circle of younger devotees, the stark opposition Shoptaw draws between the New York School and Black Mountain is not quite accurate. Koch and O'Hara both taught younger poets — in classrooms and outside them.[34] Koch's pedagogy (both at the New School and at Columbia, where he taught for over forty years) has been described by many former students. Bill Berkson, who took Koch's class at the New School in 1959, provides a detailed account of the older poet's teaching:

> Sitting very upright at one end of the long table, he invented as he went, uncertain in spots, but with surges of glee at the edges of his thought. Part of each lesson, the fun and suspense, was watching him steer the language toward describing graphically the pleasurable aspects of the poetry he liked — the poetry of Whitman, Rimbaud, Williams, Stevens, Auden, Lorca, Pasternak, Max Jacob and Apollinaire, as well as of his friends Frank O'Hara and John Ashbery. Then, too, he would make an analogy between some moment in a poem and the sensibilities of New York painting — the amplitude of a de Kooning, Larry Rivers' zippy, prodigiously distracted wit, or Jane Freilicher's way of imagining with her paint how the vase of jonquils felt to be on the window sill in that day's light. All of these things would dovetail into the writing assignments Kenneth gave us, which were designed to (and really did) help precipitate and sustain energy and surprise in our poems. (Kane 257–58)

We might note Koch's construction of an alternative genealogy (one that included his immediate circle of New York Poets), the interdisciplinary focus, and the attempt to bring all of these stimuli into productive contact with the students' own practice.[35] By all accounts, O'Hara's pedagogy was far less programmatic and, in fact, less organized. He taught formally just one semester, spring 1963, at the New School. His students included Tony Towle, Gerard Malanga, Joe Ceravolo, Jim Brodey, Frank Lima, and Diane Di Prima. Brad Gooch tells us that "[u]nlike Koch, whose brilliant teaching style included impromptu speeches given in iambic pentameter as well as clever assignments involving imitations of Williams or Stein or of elaborate verse forms such as sestinas, pantouns, or canzones" (G 400), O'Hara downplayed his role as professor: "One afternoon he would bring in the *Selected Poems* of Williams, read a few favorites, and ask students their opinion. Another afternoon he would read from W. H. Auden's *The Orators* or 'New York Letter.' He never gave assignments but wrote comments on any poems students chose to hand in" (ibid.).

If less dashing in the classroom than Koch, O'Hara extended his pedagogy into public in ways Koch's did not; he also covered topics beyond poetry—especially film and music.[36] This expanded domain caught Koch's attention: "He followed up his enthusiasms in a physical way. . . . I had all these wonderful students at the New School. But you didn't see them at my house. You didn't see me in bars with them. They became *friends* of Frank O'Hara" (G 401).[37] Tony Towle experienced the difference:

> [W]hen class was over, Kenneth quickly disappeared into the rest of his busy life; but with Frank it soon became known that any of us who wanted to could walk over to the Cedar with him and have a beer and shoot the breeze for another hour. I don't remember *how* this came to be known but I immediately and regularly availed myself of it, as did Jim Brodey and Allan Kaplan (there may have occasionally been another student or two along as well). . . . Nothing that was said stands out to me from these gatherings, except that poetry *per se* did not come up much. However, movies were always being mentioned, especially the 'old' movies of Frank's youth, in regard to which he often demonstrated his now legendary enthusiasm and expertise. (52–53)

To some extent, O'Hara's insistence on breaking down spatial and social hierarchies between student and teacher and his expansion of the sites of pedagogy from the classroom to the apartment, poetry reading, and bar anticipate some of the demands of the nascent student movement of the

1960s. Obviously O'Hara's power and authority did not simply evaporate in these newly configured relationships and sites. But their character did change. At his apartment, where most of this informal pedagogy took place, students like Tony Towle, Bill Berkson, Joe Ceravolo, Frank Lima, and Jim Brodey could watch O'Hara teach in his "natural habitat" — his own artwork and book collection replacing the supposedly neutral context of the seminar room. Towle says of his experience going to O'Hara's apartment, listening to Satie and Prokofiev: "Between pieces, and between movements during the pieces, O'Hara was coming out with a dazzling array of comments. He was communicating the same kind of excitement about art that Kenneth Koch projected in class" (56–57). Pedagogical distance was further broken down by collaborations and by sex.[38] But the lack of classroom structure did not mean that no formation, no transmission, was taking place.

Berkson, for instance, was careful to cite O'Hara in his long-winded bio for Padgett and Shapiro's *An Anthology of New York Poets*: "General 'cultural' education through friendship with Frank O'Hara . . . we read Wyatt together, recited Racine, skipped through galleries, collaborated on *The Hymns of St. Bridget* 1961–64" (547). But while O'Hara's "influence" on Berkson appears as a kind of cultural authority or pedigree bestowed directly by "Frank" — by proximity or touch, as it were — Ted Berrigan's O'Hara influence (ultimately perhaps stranger and more extreme) was developed through the more mediated practice of reading.[39] Berrigan did not know O'Hara nearly as well as Berkson did; they met, they exchanged some correspondence (begun when Berrigan sent O'Hara poems), but they were not especially close. Berrigan's legendary obsession with O'Hara played itself out most legibly at the level of literary devices, which Berrigan lifted from O'Hara in especially recognizable ways.[40] What is interesting here are the senses in which Berrigan did and did not transform O'Hara by a kind of friendly and self-admitted sampling.[41] Consider the first lines of Berrigan's second poem in *The Sonnets*.

> Dear Margie, hello. It is 5:15 a.m.
> dear Berrigan. He died
> Back to books. I read
> It's 8:30 p.m. in New York and I've been running around
>   all day
> old come-all-ye's streel into the streets. Yes, it is now,
> How Much Longer Shall I Be Able To Inhabit The Divine
> and the day is bright gray turning green
> feminine marvelous and tough

Isolated like this, such a poem may seem like an O'Hara rip-off in which the quotidian notations of a poem like "The Day Lady Died" ("It is 12:20 in New York a Friday" [CP 325]) get updated from a more explicitly bohemian subject position.[42] Marjorie Perloff, for instance, is quick to take up such a reading: "By 1964 or so, O'Hara's style, especially the style of the 'I do this, I do that' poems, was beginning to have a marked influence" (P 178). Of Berrigan's *Sonnets* and Ron Padgett's poem "16 November 1964," Perloff writes, "Such early imitations were, of course, merely derivative; in these poems, Berrigan and Padgett capture the O'Hara manner without the substance" (P 179). But the very fact that Berrigan chooses to repeat his opening line at the end of the poem — "Dear Margie, hello. It is 5:15 a.m. / fucked til 7 now she's late to work and I'm / 18 so why are my hands shaking I should know better" (8) — suggests that he already has an understanding of O'Hara's "manner" as a kind of substance. His repetition of his own first line, weaving the earlier time into the later section of the poem, undercuts the possibility that we hear the line as a simple expressive marker of the time at which the poem begins. Berrigan thus at once samples and recodes O'Hara's time referencing, treating it as a poetic device.

Moreover, sampling or appropriating such a device as exact time references will necessarily produce a different set of meanings when understood by readers as a kind of quotation or intertextuality.[43] In fact, Berrigan's act of borrowing and recontextualizing O'Hara's time references had the effect of making such a device all the more legible as the (now-borrowed) poetic property of Frank O'Hara — so that what would appear to be an abstract, impersonal device of trying to mark and capture an instant by using temporal shifters ("It is 12:20 in New York") became associated with the proper name Frank O'Hara. Berrigan, however, characterizes his transformation of O'Hara in a slightly different way:

> In 1960 and '61, I wrote a bunch of poems saying 'it's 5:15 a.m. in New York City & I'm doing this & that & now I think this & this & this, & next this happens, that happens, & in conclusion I can say blank blank & blank.' I thought I was blatantly imitating Frank O'Hara. But I was wonderfully dumb, and thank god! It turns out that when Frank was writing his poems and saying it is 4:16 a.m. in New York City, he meant that it wasn't 4:16 at all. It was a flashback. Whereas when I wrote my poems, whatever time I said it was, that's what time it was. So, I wrote an entirely different kind of poem than he did, and not only that, but in the language of the critical periodicals, I actually extended a formal

> idea of his into another area. . . . And my poems were pretty good too. And in fact they're not very much like Frank's at all, because I was too dumb to be like Frank. But I wasn't too dumb to be like somebody. (Berrigan, "Business" 67–68)

Berrigan here positions himself as stumbling onto a greater poetic immediacy by misunderstanding O'Hara. Though Berrigan's theory that all time references in O'Hara are flashbacks works to drive a convenient wedge between their practices, O'Hara's work presents important exceptions, such as the first lines of "Adieu to Norman, Bon Jour to Joan and Jean-Paul": "It is 12:10 in New York and I am wondering / if I will finish this in time to meet Norman for lunch." If the distinction between present tense and flashback does not quite separate Berrigan from O'Hara, one might still agree with Berrigan that he "extends a formal idea of his into another area" by considering the structure of *The Sonnets* as a whole. In the larger context of Berrigan's *Sonnets* the rhetoric of immediacy of each line actually gets undercut by the fact that most of the lines recirculate as collage elements that enter into new permutations: "I too am reading the technical journals" (16, 54, 62), "Rivers of annoyance undermine the arrangements" (19, 54), "And high upon the Brooklyn Bridge alone" (10, 13), "Keats was a baiter of bears" (18, 25, 61, 65), and "Harum-scarum haze on the Pollock streets" (24, 29, 42) are a few of the many phrases (and lines) that channel through the book, coupling and uncoupling with new contexts. The effect of this is especially important for the lines that seem to borrow from O'Hara, since these claim a rhetoric of access to the present. Sonnet 23, for instance, begins: "Dear Marge, hello. It is 5:15 a.m. / Outside my room atonal sounds of rain / In my head. Dreams of Larry Walker / Drum in the pre-dawn" (23). This immediate time reference then quickly becomes part of a series of different contexts:

> Now she guards her chalice in a temple of fear
> Each tree stands alone in stillness
> to gentle, pleasant strains
> Dear Marge, hello. It is 5:15 a.m.
> Andy Butt was drunk in the Parthenon
> Harum-scarum haze on the Pollock streets
> (Berrigan *Sonnets* 29)

Sonnet 62 ends thus: "Now night / Where Snow White sleeps amongst the silent dwarfs / Drifts of Johann Strauss / It is 5: 15 a.m. Dear Marge, hello" (38). Then, in sonnet 80, the name Chris substitutes for Marge: "Margie is dead / Patsy awakens in heat and ready to squabble / Dear Chris, hello. It is 5:15 a.m. / I rage in a blue shirt, at a brown desk" (66). The result is that Berrigan's book ultimately seems to have more of a connection to experimental poetry works that foreground procedure — like Jackson Mac Low's *Stanzas for Iris Lezak*, Ron Silliman's *Ketjak* and *Tjanting*, or Lyn Hejinian's *My Life* (all of which recirculate phrases or sentences) — than it does to O'Hara's *Lunch Poems*.

And yet Berrigan's connection to O'Hara is obviously real and substantial. "Only Frank's poems still send me right to the typewriter or the notebook," writes Berrigan in a letter to Joe Brainard (in Waldman *Nice to See You* 43). This connection operates, certainly and visibly, at the level of the proper names of his friends, with which Berrigan populates his poems — Ron Padgett, Dick Gallup, Joe Brainard, Patsy, Marge, and Grace. As in O'Hara, Berrigan *teaches* attributes: "Dear Ron: hello. Your name is now a household name, / As is mine. We, too, suffer black spells. This is called / 'Black Nausea' by seers, only to others, meaning poems" (*Sonnets* 69). In a tribute to Berrigan, David Shapiro noted that "it is easy to overlook the fact that Berrigan, with almost no resources except generosity and devotion, undertook to print what he considered to be the best poets of his time in . . . *C* [magazine], and that these poets may have seemed once a sort of squad, coterie, of friendly soldiers, but have become, after all, history: Ashbery, Schuyler, Burroughs, Koch, Denby, Ceravolo" ("On a Poet" 225). Shapiro goes on to link the selfless and yet coterie aspect of Berrigan's publishing enterprise back to O'Hara: "[F]riendship had become a topic and style in O'Hara's poetry, but in a way Ted was more obviously 'genial' than Frank ever was" ("On a Poet" 226). Here geniality is not merely a state of being or even a literary theme, but a style. For Shapiro, the trappings of Berrigan's geniality have to do with his willingness "to caricature and characterize himself as a creature among toilet papers and typewriters and pills" (ibid.).[44] One of the effects of this bohemian setting is to transform the smaller pantheon of names Berrigan is constantly referencing and publishing (especially O'Hara and Ashbery) into a kind of life-practice. Though such an "enactment" (or a kind of living out of intertextuality) is latent in O'Hara, it perhaps takes Berrigan to draw it out into something like a lifestyle. That Berrigan is "more obviously 'genial'" in this context may be one way of understanding how he attempts to transform the more defined edges of O'Hara's model of coterie — with its reliance on effects of distanciation and alienation — into a more explicit figure of community, one that relies on a rhetoric of accessibility. The two positions on the spectrum are, however, far from opposites.

Berrigan's eventual accumulation of institutional power, especially within the world of the St. Mark's Poetry Project, is a story that extends beyond our scope here. Some of its dynamics are hinted at, though, by Anne Waldman in her introduction to *Nice to See You: Homage to Ted Berrigan*: "If Ted's disciples were serious about making poems and interested in artistic 'community,' they invariably arrived on the Lower East Side where Ted held court, monitoring the cultural, aesthetic and social affairs of the day. Many former students and friends picked up the mannerisms of Ted's speech and poetry, and moved in their own ways from there. Ted's opinions, his 'takes,' rippled out into the community and carried a political influence within this extended family" (viii).

As I have been suggesting, this understanding of community is in large part a legacy of Berrigan's reading of Frank O'Hara — a reading that might be collapsed back oddly into the image in "Cornkind" of how filiation "can happen casually," the offspring lifting "a little of the load each day / as I become more and more idiotic / and grows to be a strong strong man / and one day carries as I die / my final idiocy and the very gates / into a future of his choice" (*CP* 387).[45] And if this different future could be imagined as Berrigan's idea of an "extended family," part of what makes it different is its ties to a literal, biological family. In this light we might consider the first section of the long poem "As You Like It," written by the poet Alice Notley, who married Berrigan in the late 1960s after meeting him when he was teaching at the University of Iowa.

I'm so with it I can't believe it.
Well yeah some were but I have this folder I keep.
Certainly.
Hi. You going out today?
You tell Mommy buy you ice cream.
You tell Mommy go fuck self.
Hi.
Okay.
Tell Bobby to call me up some time, there's a girl who's gonna
kill herself if Allen doesn't come to her farm.
Okay.
Listen when she's hypnotizing you let your mind do whatever
it wants & it'll all happen by itself.
Okay honey, have fun. Bye bye.
Shelley's getting hypnotized.

If you love a rainy night you'll love tonight.
Can we go outside? it's still light time.
Doll?
Hi, how are you?
He don't bother us no more.
This is CBS FM in a white tux & tails.
He's a good boy now?
We're not enemies no more.
These people that are nuts, they're mostly these
adolescents waiting for postcards. My sense of this one is
just to note it & let it go.
But I gave her a hug & a little squeeze.
We used to listen to La Boheme a lot.
It's very funny, they're unbelievable Bohemians, they
cough a lot.
Just like the days of old into the mystic.[46]

Certainly not all of Notley's writing is in significant dialog with O'Hara; an active and various poet and critic, she has written over twenty books. But "As You Like It" nonetheless points to another afterlife of a metafamilial, coterie poetics — one that both compliments and complicates Berrigan's. As the solicitous phone conversations in "As You Like It" suggest, Notley's writing, too, can be understood to extend the concept of family beyond the biological domain of offspring, siblings, and spouses. And yet it is the contact between these two models of family (nuclear and not) that is here illuminating. Notley, that is, treats the familial domain as the locus of what we might call a poetics of distraction that emerges, now, not as in O'Hara from the irruption into consciousness of midtown signage, "bargains in wristwatches" or laborers' "glistening torsos" (CP 257) but rather from children's requests — "Can we go outside? it's still light time" — during writing and phone conversations — from the oscillation, that is, between domestic and writerly labor.

In Berrigan's writing, O'Hara's seemingly spontaneous time references and proper names get reinscribed at once within a more insistently bohemian thematics (that of a nonnuclear, though heterosexual, family whose membership merges into a literary community) and within a formal structure that is, paradoxically, more procedural and defamiliarizing. The result is that while O'Hara's name and time references often seem grounded in empirical locations, in Berrigan such locations, though frequently included too, begin to uncouple themselves from singular speech acts and reemerge as iterable features of an even more self-conscious writing practice — a writing labor "Making vast apple strides toward 'The Poems'" (*Sonnets* 33). While both Berrigan and Notley recode the idea of family into an expanded model of coterie and link this recoding to textual and not merely biographical practices, Notley also invents a formal means of registering the unevenly distributed domestic labor that seems to underlie this social formation. In doing this, Notley does not merely extend a "formal idea" of O'Hara's "into another area" of poetry (as Berrigan had claimed of himself); she extends such an idea into another *discourse* — that of emergent feminism.[47]

2 COMPARATIVE COTERIES

MINING MODERNISMS

For today I think of a castle, half of which is necessarily in ruins; this castle belongs to me, I picture it in a rustic setting, not far from Paris. . . . A few of my friends are living here as permanent guests: there is Louis Aragon leaving; he only has time to say hello; Philippe Soupault gets up with the stars, and Paul Eluard, our great Eluard, has not yet come home. There are Robert Desnos and Roger Vitrac out on the grounds poring over an ancient edict on dueling.

—*André Breton,* Manifesto of Surrealism

[T]he invention of oneself as a writer in a community is only part of a larger question; it should be accompanied by the necessity for inventing that community, and thereby participating in the terms that, in turn, themselves play a crucial role in making invention possible.

—*Lyn Hejinian,* The Language of Inquiry

Considering the range of functions taken on in the American 1950s and 1960s by community's less-understood twin, coterie, chapter 1 dealt with the social and philosophical implications of coterie as a mode of writing rather than with the obviously quite different situations of writing within particular coteries. As a result, the chapter begged the question of whether there is such a thing as *bad* coterie, and whether, more generally, it is possible to make value judgments about coteries individually. In turning toward O'Hara's various and complex dialog with what could be characterized as modernist coteries, chapter 2 seeks both to answer these questions and to serve as a broader account of O'Hara's reading of key modernists.[1] If O'Hara refused to engage with, or even recognize, many of the 1950s' most influential poets (especially, as has already been suggested, T. S. Eliot and the New Critics), the objects of O'Hara's admiration, too, received atypical attention.[2] To influence O'Hara was often to provide a persona he could reoccupy and transform.[3] This process tended to take place, moreover, in the highly charged, shifting margin between literary techniques and more palpable social relations, between formal mechanisms or rhetorical modes and everyday experience. As life here becomes literature, as it gets motivated rhetorically and situated textually, it becomes what Roman Jakobson calls a "literary fact" (292).

As I mentioned in my introduction, Svetlana Boym argues that for Mayakovsky the literary fact takes on the special function of "revealing the uncanny 'literariness' of life and the transgressive vitality of texts" (13). For O'Hara (whose appropriations of Mayakovsky I consider in chapter 4), literary facts include not only the spectacular elements of his own biography but also an array of poetic personas he frequently borrows in order to produce a kind of hybrid writing that at once references the life of a poet like Apollinaire, for instance, and its stagy reoccupation in the world of Frank O'Hara. For O'Hara's world, too, by the late 1950s was gaining its own mythological status. This was occurring, in part, because so many of O'Hara's poems, including those based on appropriation of modernist personas, were positioned in a kind of intersocial matrix: as gifts for famous or not-so-famous painter friends included in letters; as funny, brash postcards sent to old roommates; as occasional poems read at friends' weddings; as thank-you notes; or as collaborative artworks.

Each of these acts brought a small, temporary collectivity into being; it helped to produce, highlight, or somehow change the terms of a social formation. And in doing this, O'Hara opened himself once again to the charge of being a coterie writer. But what did it mean to be a coterie writer who was often borrowing styles of subjectivity from a canon of modernist poets, using their personas as scaffoldings for new constructions? Looking briefly at O'Hara's use of Guillaume Apollinaire, the Surrealists, and W. H. Auden, the first part of this chapter sketches some terms for these appropriations.[4] Part of O'Hara's fascination with each of these poets or groups was, I think, the ways that their writing both operated in and thematized a closely knit social world — a world that often explored thresholds of membership, rhetorics of belonging, so-called *private* references, including proper names — in general, the range of formal and thematic indices of coterie writing, at least according to its negative critics. And O'Hara, too, could be such a critic. His negative reading of the social formations seeming to emanate from the work of Ezra Pound, which will organize the second part of this chapter, will be a case in point. Is it possible, then, to object to specific coteries while valuing others as demystifying structures? What are the social and textual coordinates by which such a case-by-case reading might proceed? Approaching these questions through the often-idiosyncratic terms of O'Hara's readings and appropriations of modernist poets (which themselves range from bubblingly enthusiastic to scathing, terse, and ungenerous), this chapter will also seek to expand the discussion of coterie beyond the strategic functions coterie's "problems" offered in the 1950s and early 1960s and beyond the primary focus on proper names. As O'Hara appropriates modernist writing strategies and personas, he tends in particular to displace the heterosexual family from its frequent position as the matrix of social similarity and difference, adopting instead a range of other structures of affinity, both social and textual.[5]

It is in part because of his displacements of both literary and social families that tracking O'Hara's influences becomes difficult. He opposes the idea of literary paternity not merely with the brashness characteristic of many avant-garde writers skeptical of the bland platitudes of value and authority underlying most constructions of the "Tradition" but with a more fundamental refusal to acknowledge paternity itself — and, in fact, with a positive, experimental model of affinity that would stand outside it. This value is central to O'Hara's cultivation of coterie writing, yet it forms the basis of his critique of several other coteries — so that even while O'Hara directly borrows the rhetorical strategies of an Apollinaire marriage poem, for instance, he also subtly displaces marriage from its center. These displacements, which run throughout O'Hara's often funny and subtle dialog with modernist poets, provide one vantage from which we can compare the social implications of coteries. For inasmuch as coteries are textual as well as sociological categories, rhetorical as well as biographical systems, their social implications emerge not from their mere existence but from the values they establish and promote. And while certainly O'Hara's reading of modernism was not constrained by some a priori sense that all relevant literature was produced in close collectivities or coteries, he was drawn to figures around whom social and literary codes collapsed into each other.

In "Memorial Day 1950," an early poem that announces itself as surveying debts to modernist figures — including Picasso, Stein, Ernst, Klee, "Fathers of Dada," Auden, Rimbaud, and Pasternak (all mentioned by name) — O'Hara writes, "I dress in oil cloth and read music / by Guillaume Apollinaire's clay candelabra" (*CP* 18). Compared to the poems of the mid-1950s and after, the use of proper names here is flatter, more an inventory than an inventive strategy; in this sense, the "debt" is more speculative and prospective than already enacted. Certainly O'Hara will transform the constellation of influences into more individualized contexts.

The way this happens with Apollinaire parallels what Apollinaire himself had written about his hero Alfred Jarry (and not so secretly about himself as well): "His smallest actions, his pranks, everything was literature" (Shattuck 271). O'Hara too certainly operated within an expanded concept of literature that linked writing practices to actions and personas, including the borrowed personas of writers like Apollinaire. Three and a half years after "Memorial Day 1950," for instance, O'Hara signed a 1953 postcard of the Chrysler Building sent to Robert Fizdale "Guillaume" (Archive December 26, 1953). Though a common enough gesture among writers, here the borrowed signature puts this architectural icon of midcentury New York modernism into dialog with the Parisian teens and casts O'Hara as the explicator or celebrant of this newer modernity. O'Hara's theatrical role at MoMA, which according to a friend he treated as "part salon of the *ancien regime*, part soundstage at Warner Brothers in the thirties" (*WW* 33), might similarly be seen in relation to Apollinaire's transformation of his life on the front of World War I into an opera production: "[It] seems that a soldier's life is the right life for me," Apollinaire writes in a 1915 letter, "I like that. My friend [Lou] keeps saying that I act all the time as if I were at the opera and it's true" (Shattuck 289). While the contrast between WWI trenches and the opera is obviously greater than that between MoMA events and either *ancien regime* salons or Warner Brothers soundstages, it is nonetheless important that such events for O'Hara similarly exceed their literal, professional functions and are instead appropriated and recoded as self-constructed theatrical productions. The contours of such productions might be grasped from a January 17, 1959, letter to Joe LeSueur from Paris describing an upcoming MoMA opening:

> Tonight Porter [McCray, O'Hara's boss in MoMA's International Program] and Julius Fleischmann . . . are giving an artists party at the *Closerie des Lilas* (where Apollinaire played chess with Lenin, will you ever!) and since John [Ashbery] and I had a hand in forming part of the invitation list you will not be surprised that Cocteau, Man Ray, René Lubowitz, Pierre Boulez, René Char, Gérard Philipe, Robert Bresson, Yves Montand, Simone Signoret, Alain Robbe-Grillet, Michel Butor, Nathalie Sarraute, Raymond Queneau, Henri Michaux *and* André Malraux are among those invited. (Archive)

With Ashbery's help, O'Hara turns the opening into a chance to rub shoulders with his French cultural heroes at a site whose oddly bohemian and revolutionary cachet has been established in part by Apollinaire himself. But this fawning appreciation of course masks a more complex dialog taking place with French culture generally and with Apollinaire specifically. Consider a January 1, 1957, letter to the Kochs describing O'Hara's move to University Place, which again links Apollinaire self-consciously to images of bohemian cultural production:

> Joe and I have moved to the free, glamorous Village. Would that you were here for midnight beers and liberated discussions of art, sex, friends, and above all, *techne*, which alone is said to free the poet from his limitations. I was reading some more of Apollinaire's letters to the girl he met on the train de Nice à Marseille, but I can't get out of my mind a quote which I think I quoted you in my previous letter "Discipline et personnalité, voilà les limites du style comme je l'entends . . ." Isn't that cute? I can't decide what it means. If only the personnalité came first I would understand. (Archive)

Rather than disagree outright, O'Hara pretends simply not to comprehend a style that seems to privilege discipline over personality. How such abstract terms take on more concrete values in O'Hara's dialog with Apollinaire, however, might be gleaned from O'Hara's transformation of Apollinaire's July 13, 1909, "Poèm lu au Mariage d'André Salmon,"[6] which begins: "When I saw the flags this morning I didn't say to myself / Behold the rich garments of the poor / Or democratic modesty desires to veil her sorrow for me / Or the liberty we honor is now causing people to imitate / The leaves O vegetable liberty the only earthly freedom" (*Alcools* 85). Apollinaire continues through a list of what the flags on the eve of Bastille Day do *not* mean before appropriating this citywide (and of course national) event for his friend: "I know that the only people to renew the world are those / grounded in poetry / They adorned Paris with flags because my friend André / Salmon is getting married there" (ibid.). The poem's middle stanza recounts the friends' meeting and their shared history before the last stanza returns to the first stanza's form, that of a list of mistaken readings (about why one should rejoice rather than why the flags are being waved) leading up to the supposedly real one: "Let us rejoice not because our friendship was the river that / enriched us" or for many other reasons, including that "flags flap at the windows of citizens content for a / century to have their lives and small things to defend / Or because grounded in poetry we have rights over those phrases / that shape and destroy the Universe" (ibid.). Instead, "Let us rejoice because the directory of fire and of poets / Love who fills as light does / All solid space between the stars and planets / Love determines that today my friend André Salmon gets / married" (ibid.). Whereas Apollinaire spends much of the poem drawing out the implications of this flag waving, pointing to the ideological logic by which Bastille Day produces national subjects who are "content for a century to have their lives and small things to defend" (87), he does not consider that marriage, too, might be producing usable forms of subjectivity, useful in part, also, to this same state. Though intentionally framed together, love's inevitable production of marriage provides the fundamental contrast with the waving of flags on Bastille Day's inevitable production of docile French subjects. Apollinaire has written explicitly in the poem that "grounded in poetry we have rights over those phrases / that shape and destroy the Universe" (88).

In his own similarly structured "Poem Read at Joan Mitchell's," which celebrates the marriage of his close friend the painter Jane Frelicher to Joe Hazan, O'Hara takes literally this phrase about having "rights over those phrases / that shape and destroy the Universe" and extends it precisely where Apollinaire won't — toward marriage and toward Apollinaire's own claim that the inevitable result of love is heterosexual marriage. This accounts for the conflicted tonality that runs conspicuously throughout O'Hara's poem.

> At last you are tired of being single
> the effort to be new does not upset you nor the effort to be other
> you are not tired of life together
>
> city noises are louder because you are together
> being together you are louder than calling separately across a tele-
> phone one to the other
> and there is no noise like the rare silence when you both sleep
> even country noises — a dog bays at the moon, but when it loves the
> moon it bows, and the hitherto frowning moon fawns and
> slips
>
> Only you in New York are not boring tonight
> it is most modern to affirm some one
> (we don't really love ideas, do we?)
> (CP 265)

O'Hara's poems rarely use such a string of negatives: "the effort to be new does not upset you"; "you are not tired of life together"; "Only you in New

York are not boring tonight" "(we don't really love ideas, do we?)." Beyond the grammatical level, the vocabulary (tired, upset, effort, louder, noise, boring) does not quite produce an ambience one would associate with the celebration of marriage. This hesitation over the value of marriage (especially that of a previously close friend) should recall the terms of my chapter 1 account of O'Hara's exploration of alternative kinship structures.[7] As the poem extends beyond the immediate framework of marriage it seems to value less equivocally the shared aspects of the interwoven lives both of absent friends (John Ashbery, Kenneth and Janice Koch) and of those present at Joan Mitchell's loft — especially the history of O'Hara's friendship with Jane Freilicher (previously one of O'Hara's central "muses," she is mentioned by name in twenty-five of O'Hara's poems), who is apostrophized consistently in the poem:

> Tonight you probably walked over here from Bethune Street
> down Greenwich Avenue with its sneaky little bars and the Women's
> Detention House,
> across 8th Street, by the acres of books and pillows and shoes and
> illuminating lampshades,
> past Cooper Union where we heard the piece by Mortie Feldman with
> "The Stars and Stripes Forever" in it
> and the Sagamore's terrific "coffee and, Andy," meaning "with a
> cheese Danish" —
> did you spit on your index fingers and rub the CEDAR's neon circle
> for luck?
> did you give a kind thought, hurrying, to Alger Hiss?
> (CP 265)

Flirting with sentimentality throughout, the poem poses this shared past against its possible obliteration at the hands of Freilicher's "peculiar desire to get married." Here and elsewhere, O'Hara values figurative over literal nuptial acts: "dear New York City Ballet company, you are / quite a bit like a wedding yourself!" (CP 266); and "John [Ashbery] and the nuptial quality / of his verses (he is always marrying the whole world)" (ibid.). Such "marriages" are temporary and contingent, emerging not from the core institution of traditional culture but from a metaphoric reading practice. That a literal marriage like Freilicher's runs the risk of transforming identity in a more problematic way is a question to which O'Hara will return in another poem that, incidentally, also compares Paris and New York. In "Adieu to Norman, Bon Jour to Joan and Jean-Paul," discussed in chapter 1, the middle section charts the international movements of O'Hara's friends in relation both to a desire for their continuous identities and to a catalog of more enduring cultural and architectural landmarks in Paris:

> and Jane Hazan continues to be Jane Freilicher (I think!)
> and Irving Sandler continues to be the balayeur des artistes
> and so do I (sometimes I think I'm "in love" with painting)
> and surely the Piscine Deligny continues to have water in it
> and the Flore continues to have tables and newspapers and people
>   under them
> (CP 329)

• • •

Describing O'Hara's first period at MoMA, in December 1951, Brad Gooch notes that "When [James] Schuyler dropped by the first time he came across O'Hara selling admission tickets to visitors while writing on a yellow lined pad a poem, since lost, titled 'It's the blue!' Resting beside him was a translation of André Breton's *Young Cherry Trees Secured against Hares*" (G 208). As in his reading of Apollinaire, O'Hara sought to integrate surrealism into his life, recoding and transforming it. The general outlines of this influence are well enough established: Marjorie Perloff, for instance, quotes O'Hara's reading lists of early-twentieth-century French poetry at Harvard and convincingly interprets his early work in relation to Desnos, Breton, Péret, Ernst, Aragon, and Tzara. Here I want to focus on another kind of dialog with surrealism — its fascination, for O'Hara, as *the* modernist experiment in artistic collectivity,[8] one in which this very collectivity, however, took on shifting and hotly contested meanings over time. What sort of group were members joined in? Was it a literary or a social group? Who was in control? How did desire express itself within the group? What were the limits of acceptable desires?

To contemporary critics, it is primarily the dissident Surrealists' experimental collectivities — like the College of Sociology — that provide the richest responses to these questions. In a 1939 talk for the College titled "Brotherhoods, Orders, Secret Societies, Churches," Roger Caillois argued (through Georges Bataille, who read the talk because Caillois was ill) that "since the end of the Dada period the project of a secret society charged with providing a sort of active reality to aspirations defined in part under the name of surrealism has always been a preoccupation" (Caillois 153). "Would not the 'secret society' or 'elective community' represent," Caillois/Bataille asked, "in every stage of historical development the means, and the sole means, for societies that have arrived at a real void, a static non-sense, that allows a sort of sloughing off that is explosive?" (ibid.)

While the College, like most avant-garde groups, suffered dissent, the structural allowance for this possibility — by Bataille in particular[9] — is one among many features that contrasts this group with the main line of avant-garde collectives, from the Dadaists through the Surrealists to the Situationists of the following generation.[10] When one looked at the most dominant form of surrealist collectivity, it seemed hierarchically organized around Breton as center, and this presented problems. Still, within this model, both collaborations and the various Surrealists' projects of recoding literary history into a kind of vertical structure of kinship seem to have been important for O'Hara.

In September 1919, at the beginning of André Breton's involvement with Dada, Tristan Tzara wrote to Breton: "I believe, my dear Breton, that you too are trying to find *men* . . . I am not a professional writer. I would have become a successful adventurer, making subtle gestures, if I had had the physical force and nervous stamina to achieve this one exploit: not be bored. One writes, too, because there aren't enough new men, out of habit, one publishes to try to find men, and to have an occupation" (Polizzotti 115). Tzara's analysis points both to the social dynamics of Breton's later career and to Breton's differences, as a professional writer, from Tzara, with whom he would violently fall out in 1924. As the string of these "excommunications" added up, readers of surrealism were forced to confront Breton's own central status. Summarizing numerous related accounts, Breton's biographer, Mark Polizzotti, writes that "the solemnity of Breton's manner; the frequently mystical turn of his thought; and the occult aura of the café meetings — not to mention the group's later practice of 'excommunicating' members deemed unworthy — gave Surrealism an intensely religious coloration in many observers' eyes, and Breton the distinct air of a pontiff. This air, regardless of Breton's feelings about the label, helped turn 'the Pope of Surrealism' from a rival's quip into an indelible stamp" (216).

It's unclear how much O'Hara knew specifically about the day-to-day politics of surrealism in the later 1920s under Breton.[11] But a nod toward the larger question of what constituted a surrealist collectivity and how it related to individual ambitions can be heard in O'Hara's January 1955 review: "Salvador Dali, the Marshal Rommel of Surrealism, prefaces his new show with an account of his recent 'campaign' in Europe, where he finds the forces of figuration everywhere rallying against abstraction" (*WW* 21). And if this model of the surrealist group as advancing army also had a humorous side, the fact that the military aspects of the Surrealists also included among many an ingrained homophobia was more of a lingering problem for the New York School writers. Americans were treated to this side of Breton, in particular, when, displaced to New York during World War II, he needed the support of the American poets Charles Henri Ford and Parker Tyler and their magazine *View*, which he nonetheless referred to privately as "pederasty international" (Polizzotti 508). The conflict, however, was not all behind the scenes: beginning in the mid 1930s, Ford and Breton had several open confrontations about homosexuality — Breton conceding, or pretending to concede, in part to keep a foot in American publishing.[12] The often-discussed influence of surrealism on Ashbery and O'Hara was certainly encouraged by *View*, which brought John Bernard Myers — the first publisher of both poets — his first job in New York.[13]

The conflict of surrealist sexual politics also included other, more sinister, examples. John Ashbery in particular linked André Breton's homophobia to the suicide of René Crevel, who was "excommunicated" by Breton during surrealism's act of closing ranks to present a unified, masculine image to the Communist Party: "As the Surrealist movement pursued its stormy course, exclusions, anathemas and even suicide followed in the wake of Breton's ruling and pronouncements. Sexual liberty, he proclaimed, meant every conceivable kind of sexual act except homosexuality — a notion that would have seemed odd to the Marquis de Sade, the Surrealists' unimpeachable authority on matters sexual."[14] Whether or not O'Hara knew of these dynamics, it was obviously still possible for him to identify with surrealist collectivity. And so it makes sense to understand his relation to surrealism not merely as a matter of syntactical structures or experiments with the unconscious but through the kinds of blurring and overlapping of subjectivities that can happen in collective enterprises such as collaboration and through the kinds of group formations that can occur by playfully appropriating literary history to the service of a contemporary literary formation — as the Surrealists did.

O'Hara collaborated throughout his career both on artworks and on theater productions[15] with an enormous number of artists, including Grace Hartigan, Mike Goldberg, Larry Rivers,[16] Norman Bluhm, Jane Freilicher, Nell Blaine, Elaine de Kooning, Jasper Johns,[17] Mario Schiffano, and Joe Brainard (their collaborative cartoons and collages will be discussed in chapter 6). He also collaborated with Bill Berkson on poems, with the composer Ned Rorem, and with the artist Alfred Leslie on a film.[18] And while most of these collaborations have been discussed in previous criticism, what is worth noting here is that many of these projects involved forms of collective improvisation, worked against the more hierarchical logic of illustration, and were frequently received in the art-critical context as coterie works — works whose primary, or at least initial, audience was those involved.[19]

Surrealist projects of recoding literary history (like those of the Dadaists) were also directed, in part, at a series of group members whose act of reorganizing the cultural field at once revised its values in accordance with those the group shared and also inscribed that group itself into the newly shuffled field of cultural monuments. In a Paris Dada article called "Liquidation," for instance, a group of historical and contemporary cultural figures (Anatole France, the unknown soldier, Beethoven, Jesus, Apollinaire, Charlie Chaplin, and the Dadaists themselves) were graded as in French schools (from −25 to +20) by members of Paris Dada. Taking up a tone very different from that of the magazine itself (which claimed "not to grade, but to degrade" [Polizzotti 151]), Breton explained the issue to his wealthy patron, Doucet: "I realize how shocking such a procedure must seem, but the resulting chart will say more, I believe, about the spirit of *Littérature* than a whole string of critical articles by its various contributors. It will have the advantage of situating us very clearly, and even of showing how we proceed, and we relate to, both what binds us together and what separates us" (Polizzotti 152).

Later, within surrealism, Breton's *First Manifesto* takes this revaluation a step further by not merely judging but also by recoding and appropriating literary history. Sade becomes "Surrealist in sadism"; Poe, "in adventure"; Swift, "in malice"; Baudelaire, "in morality"; Rimbaud, "in the way he lived, and elsewhere"; Reverdy, "at home"; etc. (Breton 27). "One of the book's main objectives," Polizzotti writes "was to define a distinct group of individuals, as indicated by the enormous number of proper names it contains. Foremost are those of Breton's close collaborators, the 'permanent guests' at a mythical castle 'not far from Paris': Aragon, Péret, Fraenkel; Desnos . . . Soupault . . . Éluard" (207).

While O'Hara doesn't comment directly in discursive prose on this genealogy- and circle-building aspect of surrealism, many of the "provocations" of the poems and letters we have thus far examined might be read in a similar light. At least initially, however, O'Hara tended to operate within smaller and less formalized circles (in the late 1940s and early 1950s they seem to be based on the poet and his "muse" figures; over the course of the 1950s they expand and shift). O'Hara also insisted that poetry itself, and not manifestoes or discursive prose, should be the primary space of the cultural discourse. Finally, and perhaps most important, O'Hara sought to conceive a collectivity's logic of affiliation, both toward itself and toward literary and cultural history, outside the model of the heterosexual family. And so when John Ashbery suggests that O'Hara expands "Breton's call for '*liberté totale*'" toward the "sacrosanct" (*CP* viii) structures of language, we might add that O'Hara's structural expansion also involves desire — be it of individual subjects or of groups.[20]

• • •

I think you (and John [Ashbery], too, for that matter) must watch what is always the great danger with any "surrealistic" style . . . namely of confusing authentic non-logical relations which arouse wonder with accidental ones which arouse mere surprise and in the end fatigue.

— W. H. Auden, June 3, 1955, letter to Frank O'Hara

As W. H. Auden once wrote, "Do thoughts grow like feathers, the dead end of life?" or something close to it.

— Frank O'Hara, February 10, 1956, letter to Grace Hartigan

Interest in the early works of W. H. Auden should not be seen simply as leading O'Hara out of surrealism. In fact, his rejection of Auden's criticism says a lot about both his sense of humor and his relation to authority: "I don't care what Wystan says, I'd rather be dead than not have France around me like a rhinestone dog-collar" (ibid.). But there are some important ways in which Auden's writing — and his life — suggested other significant strategies. Auden's collaborations, his cultivation of camp, his interest in popular culture and light verse, and his thematization of homosexual bonds all appealed to O'Hara.[21] It was Auden, in fact, who in 1947 was instrumental in convincing New Directions to republish O'Hara's cherished influence Ronald Firbank, whose works had been largely out of print since his death in 1926.[22] Auden had also given a 1937 broadcast talk titled "In Defense of Gossip," which claimed for gossip a fundamental social and artistic value.[23] O'Hara's favorite work by Auden, *The Orators* (1933), was explicitly concerned with cells and collectives. Perhaps more important, *The Orators* might be considered, as Edward Mendelson suggests, "a study of language; a transcript of the rhetorics that make a group coalesce and decay" (*Early Auden* 93).[24] These rhetorics include not only languages of collectivity — private vocabularies, proper names, and shared jokes — but also languages that construct enemies.

In his book *Early Auden*, Mendelson tracks what he calls Auden's "slow transformation into a public poet" (84). The main sign of this is an avoidance of so-called private names. But in the New York School's reading of Auden, and in O'Hara's especially, Auden's early work was his best, and not simply because it remained "private." The New York School poets saw the later work, which embraced Christianity and moved away from Auden's radical political positions of the 1930s, not as a move toward an objective, public quality but as a shift toward a more familiar, and ultimately more conservative, poetic mode — one that ensured Auden greater authority.[25] So much so that O'Hara could joke, in a November 28, 1964 letter to Mike Goldberg: "I was also greatly relieved to hear about your sexual STATE, as Bill [Berkson] and I have wasted several lunches in idle conjecture, feeling it was too delicate a subject to bring up in a written letter for all to see and collect in Auden's definitive edition of your letters."[26] Auden had by then, of course, edited a broad range of "definitive editions." But this Auden was not quite the same writer who had produced *The Orators* or his collaboration with Louise MacNeice, *Letters from Iceland*, which mixed ironic letters describing the country to friends back in England, collages of often-dark historical accounts of the country, an eclogue, and a campy poem written collectively by the two authors ("Auden and MacNeice: Their Last Will and Testament"), as well as a "Letter to Lord Byron," which characteristically figured England's decline in world prestige through a mix of high and popular culture:

> Byron, thou should'st be living at this hour!
> What would you do, I wonder, if you were?
> Britannia's lost prestige and cash and power,
> Her middle classes show some wear and tear,
> We've learned to bomb each other from the air,
> I can't imagine what the Duke of Wellington
> Would say about the music of Duke Ellington
> (*Letters from Iceland* 55)

But it was *The Orators* that a younger poet like Bill Berkson, who came under O'Hara's influence in 1959, would be urged to read.[27] The book became a canonical work for O'Hara and for the first-generation New York School poets. Mendelson describes the genesis of *The Orators* as follows:

> [Auden] wanted a wider unity-in-diversity, and during the next two years (1930–1931) he would hope to find it in what he called the group. . . . Freud had recently identified the primal horde, the band of brothers, as the earliest form of human society; and the group had emerged as the unit of the newest political movements, in the form of Communist or Fascist cells and in the Oxford Groups of the 1920s. Auden had already made glancing allusions to the companions of a tall unwounded leader. Now he returned to them for a closer look.
>
> A group requires a language common and also special to those within it, a language that gathers the group within its own borders and excludes those outside. Auden had earlier tried to find the abstract language that would be appropriate to the private acts of the mind. He now sought the different language that might constitute a group. (*Early Auden* 93)

Mendelson, however, follows the later Auden's judgment of this work and finds it mostly transitional, even in some senses a failure,[28] noting that "until the spring of 1930 all the names in his work honored private faces." The transition comes in certain sections: "[W]hen Auden wrote Ode IV . . . all the names he used enjoyed public currency — names of politicians, aristocrats, writers, censors — but with [some] outlandish exceptions" (*Early Auden* 120). These exceptions were derived from a private language Christopher Isherwood "and his friend Edward Upward invented in their university days and peopled with various grotesques" (ibid.) to lampoon Robert and Laura Graves, T. S. Eliot, and Wyndham Lewis. Later, the real names make their way in. "But the coterie air this revelation gave to Auden's lines was misleading," concludes Mendelson: "The Mortmere names served as apt disguises for the real targets of Auden's satire, who could not be identified in print" (ibid.).

Still, Mendelson's claim that the work's final reference system is strictly public undercuts much of the work's interest — its exploration of the threshold between public and private languages: "Speak the name only with meaning for us, meaning Him, a call to our clearing," Auden writes in the ode's first section (*English Auden* 64). Part of its related appeal for O'Hara seems to have been its construction of alternative kinship structures: "The true ancestral line is not necessarily a straight or continuous one" (*English Auden* 75–76). Another perhaps more direct point of interest for O'Hara was the Whitmanesque catalog of men in the poem

"III Statement," on whose "attitudes of play or labour" Auden lavishes great attention:

> One charms by thickness of wrist; one by variety of positions; one has a beautiful skin, one a fascinating smell. One has prominent eyes, is bold at accosting. One has water sense; he can dive like a swallow without using his hands. One is obeyed by dogs, one can bring down snipe on the wing. One can do cart wheels before theatre queues; one can skip through a narrow ring. One with a violin can conjure up images of running water; one is skilful at improvising a fugue; the bowel tremors at the pedal-entry. One amuses by pursing his lips; or can imitate the neigh of a randy stallion. One casts metal in black sand; one wipes the eccentrics of a great engine with cotton waste. One jumps out of windows for profit. One makes leather instruments of torture for titled masochists; one makes ink for his son out of oak galls and rusty nails. (*English Auden* 69)

Such a catalog might be read as a kind of inverse of the famous climax of O'Hara's "In Memory of My Feelings" (which we will consider in chapter 3), where a panorama of attitudes gets understood, instead, in terms of a self's proliferating feelings or states. But first we must turn to the question of coterie in one last modernist poet, Ezra Pound, to characterize O'Hara's dialog, now at slightly greater length.

• • •

Render unto Ez
the things that are Ezra's. and unto God
the things that are not ours. When the pupil
of the day came templar and cried "I must be
about my pater's business" you did not quiz him
if he be democratical or not.
—Frank O'Hara, "Poem (The rich cubicle's enclosure)"[29]

I've been thinking of how lovely you looked, like a mirage, the other day
and what an unexpected joy it was to see you, as in Ez's famous haiku:
The apparition of that face in such a motley crew
a petal in a brassy brasserie . . .
—Frank O'Hara, October 19, 1959, letter to Barbara Guest

These two quotations index one of the many complicated literary-historical relationships that poke out of the surfaces of O'Hara's poems and letters. In the parodic Poundian epiphany of O'Hara's letter to Guest, camp activates a reading of literary history that it would be unfair to call simply silly or brassy, though it is those as well. In the rest of chapter 2 I consider the significance of O'Hara's reading of Ezra Pound by unpacking and relating its two most significant moments: a little-known 1952 poem written in response to *The Pisan Cantos* and "Biotherm," composed in 1961–62, frequently associated with Pound, and now often considered one of the major long poems of the American 1960s. That a critique of the regressive social implications enacted in Pound's writing emerges in O'Hara and that this critique bears some important similarities to the now quite vast literature on the nature of Pound's fascism will be the first part of my argument. But my goal is not merely to add O'Hara's name to the chorus of Pound's detractors. Instead, it is to account more particularly for how his response to Pound informed O'Hara's own poetic practice and how O'Hara's relation to the concept of coterie might be clarified by comparison to the problems of space and discretion that underlie Pound's model of audience.

In August 1952 Pound was in his seventh year of captivity at St. Elizabeths Hospital in Washington, D.C. His *Pisan Cantos* had been published in 1948 and awarded the Bollingen prize in 1949. Though by 1952 he had reconstructed an active and influential literary life, certainly Pound's relationships at St. Elizabeths were less reciprocal than they had been in London, Paris, and Rapallo. Insofar as Pound was a member of a sociological coterie in St. Elizabeths, its logic was primarily unidirectional: students and followers learning from the master, publishing his work, explicating it to the public. Clearly Pound's position grew less easy to assimilate: from the comparatively open stance of the early cantos and the *ABC of Reading* to the crankier, more anti-Semitic, more overbearing *Pisan Cantos* and the *Guide to Kulchur*. Still, the example of the early cantos remained enormously important to a wide range of poets, even as Pound himself became increasingly a problem.[30] There is Zukofsky's massive influence at Pound's hands.[31] There is Olson's early and frequent appearance at St. Elizabeths and Ginsberg's public championing of Pound.[32] Then there are O'Hara's comments in an informal lecture — "The Image in Poetry and Painting" — at The Club in New York (a forum for painters and critics) in 1952.[33] In his notes O'Hara calls Pound "the father of modern poets in English" and goes on to suggest that Pound's "pervasive" influence "is almost invariably healthy in that it seldom detracts from the individuality of the poet who admires him; rather, it points up, clarifies it" (P 16). Marjorie Perloff takes these comments as the basis for her claims that Pound was one of O'Hara's "models" (ibid.), and that "O'Hara is squarely in the Pound . . . tradition" (P 130).

Though one tends not to think of O'Hara's *Collected Poems* as an epic or encyclopedic work, its field of reference does extend from Homer, Plato, Aristotle, and Cicero to Harpo Marx, Fred Astaire, and Marlene Dietrich, including along the way Warren Harding, Khrushchev, Michelangelo, and Florine Stettheimer. Clearly this world is far more quotidian than most other famous attempts by modern poets to synthesize or monumentalize cultural knowledge within poetic discourse. Even to speak of such an attempt on O'Hara's part is imprecise, since *The Collected Poems* was produced by his friends after his death; it is incomplete, quickly supplemented by *Early Writing* and *Poems Retrieved*. Unlike Olson and Williams, O'Hara did not write an epic in the shadow of *The Cantos*. And yet, part of what remains compelling about O'Hara's work is its broad inclusiveness, characterized well by Kenneth Koch's remarks about *The Collected Poems*: "In a book of twenty or thirty poems, certain of Frank O'Hara's subjects (lunch, movies) could seem trivial and willful because chosen at the expense of others; in this book of five hundred poems what strikes one is the breadth, sincerity, and exuberance of his concern for life. At first overwhelming, it is also liberating: by caring so much for so many things, he gives us back feelings of our own and permits us to respect them" (H 205).

Like Koch, Bill Berkson also notices what one might call a lowercase epic quality of O'Hara's work, which Berkson ties to O'Hara's reading of William Carlos Williams: "I remember him saying that perhaps Williams' work was all one long epic poem — not that the individual forays were insubstantial as such, but that they made supreme logic *together*, each suggesting the possibility (and necessity) of the next, all of them amounting to a total expression of a man's existence. O'Hara's work has this kind of complete articulation" (H 165).

This stress on articulating networks of quotidian fragments that operate collectively and yet resist the more recognizable trapping of epic makes it less surprising that O'Hara's statements about Pound as an important precursor (in O'Hara's talk at The Club) were significantly complicated within O'Hara's poems. Though O'Hara was unquestionably affected by reading *The Pisan Cantos*, for instance, his response is anything but admiring. Interested himself in the ways that a tight-knit interdisciplinary group could foster social and artistic possibilities, O'Hara saw the at once hierarchical and claustrophobic space of Pound's "cubicle" at St. Elizabeths as a kind of bad coterie — one in which lines of influence were unidirectional away from a fixed point of authority in Pound. And while Pound had certainly, and famously, been part of previous social/literary formations that included Wyndham Lewis, James Joyce, Ford Madox Ford, and T. S. Eliot, it was this later, far less glamorous literary formation that captured O'Hara's critical interest. In August 1952, in O'Hara's "Poem (The rich cubicle's enclosure)," not published in his lifetime, he considered Pound's imprisonment in Pisa, his situation at St. Elizabeths, his *Pisan Cantos*, and the larger question of the politics of sound and form. This poem is worth looking at closely not merely because it complicates O'Hara's would-be admiration for the late Pound but, far more specifically and interestingly, because the terms of O'Hara's disagreement provide a way to think about his *Collected Poems* as a kind of nontotalitarian *Cantos*—a work that jettisons the model of a citizen or third-person readership fundamental to epic in order to pursue a second-person model of audience. By reading "Poem (The rich cubicle's enclosure)" first in the context of Pound's *The Pisan Cantos* and later in relation to O'Hara's "Biotherm," one of what he called his FYI poems, I want to demonstrate how O'Hara recodes the educational program characteristic of Pound's late work, turning Pound's desire for discrete, bounded terms, proper names with carefully controlled piths and gists, and an epic third-person audience model into a referential field characterized by fluidity, appropriation, and "indiscrete" nods toward second-person audience figures inside the poems. These referential practices, which depend upon a blurring of boundaries between the writing subject and its reception framework, become analogs for less centralized and hierarchical models of social and intellectual interaction.

The best sympathetic readings of Pound tend to place his own drive toward totalitarianism as but one vector within a larger social and literary field, as a radical interestedness at the level of the individual subject that democracy anticipates, even thrives upon. Pound's obsessive and often offensive judgments, for Jerome McGann, initiate a chain of judgments to which they themselves then become subject as *The Cantos* begin to circulate as a literary text: "In Pound, only the work has 'Total Form,' there is no primal vision or ultimate knowledge. . . . Coming in judgement, the work thereby sets in motion a series of second comings by which it finds itself made subject to continuous judgement" (*Literature of Knowledge* 127). Pound's emphasis on a certainty of significance to be built out of references to historical figures and events places him, for Charles Altieri, not as an overbearing presence directing one's access to the poems but as one subject projecting an imaginary self through history within a social/literary field in which this activity remains an open possibility for others: "Depth equals intensiveness, the capacity to superimpose translations, so that although 'there is nothing . . . that's quite your own' . . . you manifest yourself by the quality of the relations you generate in, and as, your certitude" (*Painterly Abstraction* 305). Though it appears from his response to Pound that O'Hara could imagine the importance of such larger frameworks in any judgment of Pound, O'Hara would not have been satisfied with the justifications offered (much later) by McGann and Altieri. His objection is not simply that Pound's late poetry could be read as a weave of offensive statements but that the discrete structure of *The Pisan Cantos*, what I am calling its grammar of reference, is, like Pound's coterie at St. Elizabeths, itself totalitarian. That is, if, as Altieri recommends, we imagine *The Pisan Cantos* as the projection of a self through translation and intertextuality (a self whose certitude gets tested in a public forum), we might in turn imagine O'Hara's poem as such a test — one which could, however, not be carried out in public in 1952.[34] Rather than projecting a competing certitude, O'Hara works to demonstrate the social basis of the ever-so-certain self that was emerging from Pound's writing in the early 1950s. In particular, O'Hara suggests that the emphatic assertions of the self in *The Pisan Cantos* are symptomatic of Pound's social anxieties about controlling both the reception of his own writing and a larger view of culture. This negative moment in O'Hara's reading of Pound can then be read against the positive counterpractice of O'Hara's later FYI poems, in which he thoroughly and explicitly recodes the social implications and referential practices of *The Cantos*.

O'Hara begins to place *The Pisan Cantos* in the referential field of his "Poem (The rich cubicle's enclosure)" by borrowing Pound's "*Le Paradis n'est pas artificiel*" (a revision of Baudelaire's book *Les Paradis Artificiels*), which appears originally in the first Pisan Canto and then reappears throughout them as one of many repetitive motifs. Paradise is possible, not artificial: it is one of the goals of the Poundian epic to point out the steps toward its concrete realization. This epic model requires, as many critics have noted, the concept of a quasi-universal citizenship of readers, citizens with the same needs that can be remedied by learning the same facts from history and literature. To explain the terms of O'Hara's response, it will be necessary to return periodically to *The Pisan Cantos* themselves, unpacking several stanzas in some detail. In the context of Canto 74, for instance, one is encouraged to read the actuality of paradise as what *was* the grand potential in the now-thwarted dreams of Italian fascism, the “enormous tragedy of the dream in the peasant’s bent / shoulders” (*Cantos* 439) associated with the martyred Mussolini.

> Manes! Manes was tanned and stuffed,
> Thus Ben and la Clara *a Milano*
> by the heels at Milano
> That maggots shd / eat the dead bullock
> DIGONOS, Δίγονος, but the twice crucified
> where in history will you find it?
>
> (ibid.)

Mussolini is “twice crucified” by being shot and then hanged. For Pound there is also, of course, the ironic contradiction between his position in the cage in Pisa — to which *The Pisan Cantos* keeps circling back — and the potential of a paradise.[35]

> Pisa, in the 23rd year of the effort in sight of the tower
> and Till was hung yesterday
> for murder and rape with trimmings plus Cholkis
> plus mythology, thought he was Zeus ram or another one
> Hey Snag, wots in the bibl’?
> wot are the books ov the bible?
> Name ’em, don’t bullshit ME.
>
> (*Cantos* 444)

In Pisa, in the twenty-third year of Italian fascism, “the sun has gone down” (ibid.) on Pound’s efforts to bring about earthly paradise: dusk in his open-air cell. As the American GIs display their ignorance about the basics of Western culture, the caged Pound seems especially irked by his powerlessness to follow his self-appointed life project of combating ignorance by producing efficient guides to culture. This specific missed opportunity becomes, in *The Pisan Cantos*, a small part of the larger irony of fascist defeat, of the missed paradise.

It is the security of this irony for Pound, the sense that educated readers should share his grim smirk, that might be understood as O’Hara’s point of departure. O’Hara’s “Poem (The rich cubicle’s enclosure)” can be read as a sketch of the politics — at the levels of “cubicle,” stanza, and canto — of Pound’s not-so-ideal paradise. O’Hara’s poem begins thus:

> The rich cubicle’s enclosure
> with its verdant pasturage and fences

to keep the pussyfoots out
and its leagues of seaboard tentacles
of azure dripping down stalactites
or perhaps the simple sea of memory's dove
staying forever in the walled air which coos
sadly and (as it were) rancidly
(PR 82)

In the first stanza's complex sequences of images, O'Hara, like Pound himself in *The Pisan Cantos*, begins by punning on the seeming distance between actualized paradise and the spaces in which Pound is contained — the "cellicule" in Pisa, the "cubicle," possibly at St. Elizabeths. But unlike Pound's, these spaces of containment become for O'Hara a figure for the idealized goals — the "verdant pasturage," the paradise — Pound is in fact after.[36] Imagined as a space of writing, then, what gives the "cubicles" of Pound's *Cantos* their legibility is a strict system of "enclosure," one of "fences" and "walled air" — designed to keep out "pussyfoots." Hugh Kenner writes, "For the moral virtue Blake the engraver attributed to outlines Pound the poet associated with bounded sounds, and preferably bounded terms. Enunciation had its morality" (*Pound Era* 91). What feeds these discrete cells, in O'Hara's reading, is a set of "seaboard tentacles" — a kind of octopuslike intertextuality that allows Pound both to seize international (and transhistorical) counterpoints for the tragedy of the lost dream of Italian fascism and at a more literal level to act through his followers outside St. Elizabeths. To follow O'Hara's metaphor, what is disturbing about Pound's intertextuality is not merely its violent, sea-monster alterity but its desire to stuff the cubicles of *The Cantos* with what should be perishable goods.

In Canto 76 Pound repeatedly uses the line "dove sta memora" (where memory lives) to thematize a space of memory. Elsewhere in the stanza this image gets linked to "the timeless air over the sea-cliffs" (*Cantos* 469). O'Hara responds to this desire for timelessness by making the cooing of "memory's dove" grammatically indistinguishable from the discrete, even claustrophobic, space of "walled air" out of which the piths and gists of Pound's project implicitly become possible. Just as O'Hara hints that Pound, in his cubicle, is already in his paradise, so now he suggests that Pound's *Cantos* do, as Pound wishes, arrest sound and thought in a memorializing atmosphere — only too much so: "staying forever" in "walled air," lyric cooing becomes "rancid." This strategy of literalization works throughout O'Hara's poem and parallels contemporary negative readings of Pound. Jed Rasula, for instance, relates Pound's desire to fix history permanently to the doctrine of the New Critics: "When Pound professed to be writing a poem that 'included' history, his agrarian sympathizers would have understood this as, in effect, a containment policy: poetry subsuming the chaotic contingencies of history to a more durable transtemporal order, of which poetic structure was the exemplary paradigm" (118).

Rasula is right to point to a New Critical appropriation of Pound. But the fit between the two is perhaps not quite as clean as he suggests; nor was it so for O'Hara, who was more quick to dismiss the New Critics than he was Pound.[37] In an interview with Edward Lucie-Smith, O'Hara links the effects of New Criticism on American poetry to "stupid ideas . . . about . . . the comportment in diction that you adopt" (SS 12). Still, O'Hara will describe the slow reception of Zukofsky as a result of Pound's "being such a great genius that [Zukofsky] was associated more as a follower . . . than as an originator" (SS 22). Though O'Hara's poem presents a consistently negative image of the Pound of *The Pisan Cantos*, the book clearly exerted an important influence on him. And while it would be inaccurate to figure O'Hara in the Bloomian version of a dramatic struggle with a single poetic precedent (influence for O'Hara is too broad and interdisciplinary), there is an important way in which, for O'Hara, the possibilities of a poetry of cultural montage that Pound deployed needed to be disentangled from the disturbing political ends which they had come, increasingly, to serve.

Which is not to say that O'Hara wants to, or can, avoid attaching values to the many proper names in his writing; rather, as chapter 1 argued, his deployment of the name demonstrates an interest in what happens when these values and attributes undergo ambiguous shifts and transformations as functions of contexts beyond his control. Thus, if names do operate as sites of identification and affective intensity in O'Hara, these effects frequently shift from instance to instance. This is the case in part because, unlike Pound, O'Hara's art and literary criticism do not operate as a metadiscourse that would provide a global directory explaining the relative importance and essential attributes of each name once and for all.

O'Hara's playful attack on Poundian discretion in "Poem (The rich cubicle's enclosure)" operates both at a larger, thematic level and at a more minute formal level. Having suggested in stanza 1 that Pound, in St. Elizabeths, is already in his discrete, regulated paradise and that Pound's desire to fix the cultural significance of objects permanently in a kind of monumental poetry has, paradoxically, resulted in a crippling stasis,

O'Hara pursues these contradictions. "Because all of that had failed to find him" begins stanza 2. Rhetorically, "all of that" is the string of ironic contradictions that O'Hara has pointed out. But grammatically, "all of that" is a tangle of antecedents that intentionally, I think, flaunts Poundian precision and discretion: "the rich cubicle's enclosure," "verdant pasturage," "the pussyfoots," "seaboard tentacles," "stalactites," and "memory's dove" all drift within the nebulous "that."[38] In fact, if we expand the context of the passage quoted earlier about rendering "unto Ez / the things that are Ezra's" to the poem's conclusion, we see that O'Hara frames his entire poem, and thus his response to Pound, in terms of the social values O'Hara sees underlying Poundian notions of the precise or discrete.

> When the pupil
> of the day came templar and cried "I must be
> about my pater's business" you did not quiz him
> if he be democratical or not.
> those professors are not more nor less precise
> than us cowboys us bung-hole blowers of
> Venice-on-Hudson Atlantic New York.
> (PR 82)

Recalling O'Hara's poem "Commercial Variations" — written in April 1952, in which O'Hara refers to New York as "Sodom-on-Hudson" (*CP* 85) — the last two lines propose a decadent, queer New York as a challenge to Pound's rhetoric of discrete and so-called "precise" relations, a social rhetoric that, in O'Hara's reading, is also the logic of antidemocratic doctrine absorbed and then disseminated by the coterie of "pupils" and professors who visit Pound and bring his word from St. Elizabeths into the world, following the Poundian dicta to plunge "to the gist of the discourse / to sort out the animals" (*Cantos* 514).

Identifying the poem's "we" as part of a group of "bung-hole blowers" thus presents an exemplary indiscretion, one directed against both the spatial politics of the *Cantos* and against Pound's paternal attention to the lineage of ideas: the "bung-hole blower" does not reproduce, does not pass on traits "till our time." He is therefore outside Pound's heterosexual model of the citizen, the child producer and would-be researcher to whom Pound is speaking when he chides, "Infantilism increasing till our time, / attention to outlet, no attention to source, / That is: the problem of issue" (*Cantos* 583). In a sense, O'Hara simply brings out the queer implications of Pound's statement that "filial, fraternal affection is the root of humaneness / the root of the process" (*Cantos* 451). O'Hara presents a provocative and indiscrete attention to the fraternal "outlet" — the bunghole — one which, beyond the specific challenge to Pound's heterosexism, suggests that Poundian "precision" is less a form of intellectual rigor than a form of social anxiety about knowledge, an anxiety that holds in place the interrelated literary and social moments of Poundian thought. And it is in the name of this anxiety that the Poundian circle, the coterie of students, comes "templar."

Coming templar meant receiving Pound's wisdom on literature and politics. This religious, hierarchical image seems to point to O'Hara's dissatisfaction with Pound's model of social interaction, Pound's coterie at St. Elizabeths, where the patriarchal, conservative content of Pound's views was mirrored in the very structure of his coterie: "information" and influence, as all who were there reiterated, flowed in one direction — out from the center, especially toward those who were useful and could therefore be assigned tasks. "Conversation," writes David Heyman, "was Pound's chief mode of recreation at St. Elizabeths. Whether seated in the window alcove off his corridor or perched in an aluminum chair on the hospital lawn beneath elms, his first love was the monologue" (223). One of the goals of these monologs was the acquisition of converts — a process described by many of Pound's biographers: "No sooner did a disciple or group of followers fall away, or a magazine or journal he was trying to capture, prove unwilling, than he was busy gathering new followers, forming new groups, helping to establish or capture other publications" (Stock 569). Pound himself found a heroic precedent for this kind of government: "[Jefferson] governed with a limited suffrage, and by means of conversation with his more intelligent friends. Or rather he guided a limited electorate by what he wrote and said more or less privately" (M. Bernstein 71). Though Pound's model of audience is famously based on epic's demand for "citizen" readers, readers who are active members of the polis, the concrete model of social interactions both shown in *The Pisan Cantos* and enacted at St. Elizabeths points to the hollowness of the term *citizen*, lacking as it is, in agency and say.[39]

This, at least, is O'Hara's reading: ungenerous, partial, disputable, but compelling, I think. Not because its terms are unfamiliar now but *because they were then*, in 1952, when it was uncommon to conceptualize *The Cantos* as a kind of social space, one connected to the concrete social and intellectual practices that Pound was presiding over from St. Elizabeths, and moreover because these terms provide us with a new way to think about a large component of O'Hara's later writing (as I will argue below). But before turning to that writing it might be worth pointing out the basis on which another prominent critic, Clement Greenberg, objected to the public dissemination of Pound in the early 1950s, resenting not so much the structure of Pound's circle at St. Elizabeths, or even his views, but the official recognition these views received when he was awarded the Bollingen Prize for *The Pisan Cantos*: "Life includes and is more important than art, and it judges things by their consequences. I am not against the publication of *The Pisan Cantos*, even though they offend me; my perhaps irrational sensitivity as a Jew ceded to my fear of censorship in general, and to the anticipation of the pleasures to be gotten from reading poetry, and I have to swallow that consequence. But I wish the Fellows had been, or shown themselves, more aware of the additional consequences when they awarded their Bollingen Prize" (Heyman 219).

• • •

If a negative external perspective of a literary or artistic group is always possible, perhaps even inevitable (and the possibility of this perspective itself gives rise to the pejorative term *coterie*), contrasting group formations by the social and intellectual mechanisms under which they operate can nonetheless help to dispel the notion that the very fact of writing's having been produced in a small circle stamps that writing with a single, fixed social coding. In arguing that the problem of coterie in O'Hara oscillates between an empirical, actual group and a set of rhetorical strategies and audience structures that cannot be reduced simply to this group, thus far I have stressed the latter senses in which coterie exceeds the literal. Such an emphasis seems necessary to uncouple the concept of coterie from its usual positivist associations. But unlike other tropes and intertextual reference structures, the idea of coterie *depends* upon both conspicuous reference to and close involvement in a literal social formation. And while I have already pointed to a range of social and historical facts bound up with O'Hara's own social formation, I have not yet attempted any broader articulation of its structure, logic, or implications on this more material, sociological level. What, then, can one accurately say about O'Hara's coterie from such a perspective?

Because I will consider the artists and museums involved in this network in later chapters, let me begin here with O'Hara's circle of writers. Even here, though, one encounters problems of scale. Is O'Hara's coterie only that of first-generation New York School writers? How, even here, are the limits of membership drawn? Or does it include the second-generation students and friends? Could it even include those, like Ted Berrigan, whose primary encounter with O'Hara was textual but who nonetheless operated in the same milieu? Does one include the Beat writers with whom O'Hara was closest — like Ginsberg and Corso and Wieners? What about writers like Amiri Baraka, who, though less affiliated in the early 1960s with any school, were nonetheless close to O'Hara? The pragmatic answer is that — like other fluid social/literary networks from the Surrealists to Pound's circle at St. Elizabeths — O'Hara's coterie included different social configurations at different times. The clearest map of its shifting membership is perhaps provided by the proper names in O'Hara's poems — though of course not every name mentioned should be imagined as occupying the kind of interior audience position one associates with the idea of coterie.

Though obviously somewhat arbitrary, reducing this problem to its simplest perspective — in which O'Hara's "literary coterie" becomes primarily the members of the first-generation New York School — may allow a few useful, if incomplete, formulations. First, one might point to the comparatively horizontal social structure of this group: though there were tensions and jealousies, there was never — to the extent of Pound at St. Elizabeths — a clear center of authority.[40] As O'Hara's poems in particular demonstrate, the social field of the literary circle is a site of flux, of relatively temporary judgments and inventions spurred on by both literal collaboration and by a sense that the poems are emerging in, though not finally intended solely for, a sympathetic community of readers.

At the same time, the New York School poets tended to downplay or ignore the fact that their group status (in anthologies and at readings, for instance) created de facto power for them. Thus, they could be seen as an antimovement by refusing to write manifestoes and theory while in fact retaining much of the authority that those documents produce. If manifestoes and theory ran the risk of seeming like superfluous advertisements — and they seem to have appeared so to the New York poets — they nonetheless had the potential to provide a discourse through which the aesthetic and intellectual concerns of the group, and thus their power, could be openly debated. Their relatively few reviews, mock manifestoes, and some poems about these matters are the only traces by which one can reconstruct their ideas as a community of readers.[41] While this reconstruction is possible, it must occur behind the scenes of group poetic practice that sometimes appears to rely on a rhetoric of immanence. By the standard of creating discourse both about poetics and about group activity, then, the New York poets were certainly less active as an intellectual and artistic community than their contemporaries from the Spicer Circle to the Black Mountain poets — and also less active as a community than more recent groups, like the Language writers.[42] For the New York School, terms were comparatively implicit.

From the outside, to identify a group as a group — especially in the formulation of a "school" — is often to constitute it as a consistent site of method or doctrine.[43] Well before O'Hara's circle of poet friends was represented in any anthologies and before most of his painter friends had international reputations, they could appear to an outsider as a consistent, dead school. Here is Robert Rauschenberg, who would later become much closer to O'Hara, describing the very early days of O'Hara's New York scene:

> [Rauschenberg's Ninth Street Show with Kline and other Abstract Expressionists in 1951] was during the time that the Johnny Myers and the Tibor de Nagy gallery group were enemies of my art. The only good thing about them was that they didn't think I was serious enough to worry about. So they really didn't get in my way. Frank O'Hara was their spokesman. They were all busy doing washy paintings of each other. Helen Frankenthaler, Grace Hartigan and Alfred Leslie. I don't know what he has changed to now. Jane Freilicher and Joan Mitchell. It was a very powerful group of very strong people. Clem Greenberg got behind it later after he met Helen Frankenthaler. (Rose 41)

Though he does not use the term, Rauschenberg characterizes O'Hara's circle (artistic rather than literary) in the familiar negative terms associated with coterie. By describing their work as "washy paintings of each other," Rauschenberg suggests that the group's real function is social and not aesthetic, that its uniform, self-congratulatory mode precludes the sorts of challenges he was (implicitly) subjecting his own work to in the early 1950s.[44] Whether or not one agrees with Rauschenberg about the value of these paintings, he points (in a move characteristic of how one seems to spot a coterie) to the subterranean institutional machinery of this group in the Tibor de Nagy Gallery and in O'Hara's and Clement Greenberg's critical practices.[45] That Rauschenberg's statement is inaccurate in many respects is ultimately less important to my discussion than the characteristic features of his description, which identify him as someone *outside* a coterie.[46] O'Hara's scene is simultaneously what Rauschenberg would not want to be part of and what he could not be part of had he wanted to. Still, Rauschenberg's brief negative remarks do not quite put us in touch with valued terms that would be at the center of O'Hara's circle; they do not give us a sense, for instance, of what it would mean, or how it would be possible to "come templar"[47] within the world of the New York poets.[48]

• • •

well, that Past we have always with us, eh?
I am talking about the color of money
the dime so red and the 100 dollar bill so orchid
the sickly fuchsia of a 1 the optimistic
orange of a 5 the useless penny like a seed
the magnificent yellow zinnia of a 10
especially a roll of them the airy blue of a
50 how pretty a house is when it's filled with them
that's not a villa that's a bank
where's the ocean
now this is not a tract against usury it's just putting two and two together
and getting five (thank you, Mae).[49]

— Frank O'Hara, "Biotherm"

It makes sense that if most of the events in "Biotherm" center on the "meeting" of personal pronouns, the connections between them should be continually reinvented instead of grammatically enforced. Fragments converse across indents and silences.
— Bill Berkson, "Companion to Biotherm"

In the early 1960s, O'Hara's FYI poems, written mostly in June and July of 1961, return him to Pound and *The Cantos*. Like *The Cantos*, these poems develop a long, loose organization, establishing wide referential fields within which collagelike shifts of focus continually occur. If O'Hara's FYI poems similarly present broad cross-sections of cultural reference activated through montage, Pound's framing conceit of a solemn educational program gets recoded and deflated in O'Hara as the heading of an interoffice note or the preface to hushed gossip.[50] As the mention of "Mae" [West] in the middle of a reference to Pound's poetry of economics suggests, high and low culture (or levels of canonicity) meet in a way that also threatened Poundian discretion.[51] "I am having quite a bit of fun reading both *The Making of Americans* AND the Mae West story (which are not really too unlike each other, especially in their attitude towards parents and forebears in general)," O'Hara writes in a January 18, 1961, letter to Vincent Warren just before writing "Biotherm" (Archive).

These FYI poems challenge Poundian discretion both by pointedly abandoning his grammar of reference and by tying the relay of cultural information to a known second person — For *Your* Information — rather than to an assumed third person: as such, an audience figure disrupts their discrete status. Bill Berkson, the "you" of O'Hara's most famous FYI poem, "Biotherm," suggests that the poem "portrays the relationship of two very close friends in their ways of speaking together," something O'Hara calls "the appropriate sense of space — the fluctuating space that two people feel and invent between themselves."[52] Consider the poem's first lines:

> The best thing in the world   but I better be quick about it
> better be gone tomorrow
>   better be gone last night and
>   next Thursday better be gone
> better be
>   always   or what's the use the sky
> the endless clouds trailing we leading them by the bandanna, red
> ("Biotherm" *CP* 436)

As the opening to a poem that incorporates and thereby potentially memorializes a vast number of cultural artifacts (Pasteum Lucania, Kit Carson, Mozart's nephew, and Googie Withers, along with lines from Mallarmé, and Marilyn Monroe), this stanza paradoxically values transience — so much so that the very statement of this principle must itself get interrupted in order to remain "true" to itself. Rather than conceiving poetry as a place to fix the significance of cultural objects permanently — Pound's "dove sta memora" — O'Hara imagines the poem as a space in which made-up or misused references compete with actual ones.

>   extended vibrations
> ziggurats ZIG I to IV   stars of the Tigris-Euphrates basin
>   leading ultimates such as kickapoo joyjuice halvah Canton cheese
> in thimbles
>   paraded for gain, but yet a parade kiss me,
>   Busby Berkeley, kiss me

you have ended the war by simply singing in your Irene Dunne
    foreskin
"Practically Yours"
            with June Vincent, Lionello Venturi and Casper Citron
    a Universal-International release produced by G. Mennen Williams
                    directed by Florine Stettheimer
                    continuity by the Third Reich
                    ("Biotherm" *CP* 437)

Aztec ziggurats and the Tigris-Euphrates basin operate less as monuments of culture offered to a needy public than as self-conscious framing devices whose timeless monumentality tends to get undercut by what happens within and around them.[53] As the stanza continues, the "real" ultimates become contemporary food, like "kickapoo joyjuice" and "halvah Canton cheese" — a reference that, in the context of this panoply of international and world-historical references, one might read as mocking Pound's frequent evocation of Chinese history. For O'Hara, such a spectacle can be seen only in Hollywood terms, a "Universal-International release." As the stanza begins to play with the idea of the film credit, it misattributes intentionally: none of the people mentioned was in the movie *Practically Yours*, and only one is even an actor.

As monumentality implodes into appropriation, the flux of the referential field becomes an analogy for an open social field. One might say that the abstract morality of a third-person citizen learning timeless facts and principles has been replaced with the concrete ethics of the second person constructing meaning out of a referential space that brings an appropriated world history into humorous contact with the particularities of a microlinguistic community established, temporarily, between two people.[54] In "Biotherm," O'Hara's techniques can be understood in terms of spatial analogs: collapsing or shifting spaces take on social meaning at scales ranging from the minutely interpersonal to the broadly cultural. This happens because O'Hara interweaves an exploration of interpersonal lexicons with a larger-scale inquiry into how epic poetry creates effects of monumentality. The thematic raw material for this formal spatial construction is a set of interpersonal reference points that range from shared literary quotations (Wyatt and Wordsworth) to Hollywood movies (*Practically Yours*) and actors (June Vincent, Margaret Dumont, W. C. Fields, and Richard Widmark), to ballet dancers (Allegra Kent and Patricia Wilde) and artists (Florine Stettheimer), including along the way names that O'Hara and Berkson invented for each other (Angelicus and Fidelio Fobb) and phrases that took on meaning in their relationship, such as "*continuez, méme stupid garcon*" and "*do you love it?*"

The quotidian language of friendship also becomes a mechanism for linking sections, here not through shared vocabulary but through apostrophes:

> then you
> were making me happy otherwise I
> was staring into *Saturday Night* and flag
>
> . . . .
>
> One day   you are posing in your checkerboard bathing trunks
>
> . . . .
>
> I am rather irritated at your being born
> ("Biotherm" *CP* 440–43)

Despite the poem's emphasis on the second person, it would be inaccurate to understand Bill Berkson as a simple destination for all references. As O'Hara argues in "Personism," the second person is less a fixed and final reception context (what one associates with the negative implication of coterie) than a way of anchoring the poems in social relations, or, as O'Hara puts it, "sustaining love's life-giving vulgarity" (*CP* 499). The actual, empirical "you" to whom many of his poems are addressed (including numerous examples previous to the FYI poems) functions, according to "Personism," as an impetus for what he calls *abstraction*, a process whereby the concrete specificity of the second person operates not as a final container or destination for the significance of the poem but as an occasion projecting the poem out into the world.

Establishing how to read poetry that makes conspicuous use of the second person — be it an O'Hara joke to Berkson or a John Donne dedication — has remained a theoretical problem for critics, many of whom see the inscription of a second person, an internalized audience, as a threat to poetry's autonomy. Walter Benjamin, for instance, is categorical in his judgment, opening his famous essay "The Task of the Translator" with the claim that "in the appreciation of a work of art or an art form, consideration of the receiver never proves fruitful" (253). In O'Hara's case, use of the second person tends to be seen through interpretive lenses that either establish value *beyond* what is taken as the weakness or inappropriateness of writing to another or that valorize biography as the final goal. Thus, on the one hand, Marjorie Perloff cites Berkson's position as the addressee, and as the ideal recipient of O'Hara's movie references and personal jokes, as a liability that the poem must struggle to overcome: "Its endless puns, in-jokes, phonetic games, allusions, cataloguing, journalistic parodies, and irrelevant anecdotes may seem, on a first or even a later reading, merely tiresome" (P 174).[55] The poem does overcome this, unlike the rest of the FYI poems (which are for Perloff "curiously detached" and characterized by "self-conscious gamesmanship" and "sheer randomness" [P 173]), because "Biotherm" has greater unity: obscure references get repeated in modulated form, which are to Perloff proof of a masterful consciousness guiding the process.[56] On the other hand, however, Brad Gooch values the poem precisely because it is entirely about O'Hara's courtship of Berkson.[57] Poetry transcends biography, or it collapses into and is contained by it.[58]

But it seems more accurate to say that in the publication of "Biotherm" two frames of reception (Berkson as audience and everyone or anyone else as audience) come into awkward and revealing contact. The friction between these reception frameworks, friction that is typical of coterie writing at its most interesting, should be understood in the context of literary history, where the strange and compelling qualities of O'Hara's project can register more fully. As we read a poem like "Biotherm" now (and always) from a third-person position that overhears this conversation, the thematized, second-person inner-address qualifies the status of historical reference. But this qualification should not be seen simply as subsuming history within a personal code or as quarantining it by intending it for some other reader. As the poem circulates, the second person becomes less and less of a secure reception context. We do not explain "Biotherm" by imagining how Bill Berkson would have read it. Instead, this hypothetical reading becomes an internal frame of reference that necessarily comes into contact with a third-person reception framework. This contact produces a breakdown of discretion.

It should be emphasized that O'Hara's dialog with Pound is obviously less central and anxiety producing than the kinds of dialogs with Pound one sees in Williams, Zukofsky, or Olson and that O'Hara, more generally, did not seem to feel particularly oppressed by any of the living Modernists in the 1950s. Still, one must also understand "Poem (The rich cubicle's enclosure)" and "Biotherm" in the context of the failures of Pound's late work and in particular of the failures of *The Pisan Cantos.* These failures would be of little interest if the promise of the earlier sections of *The Cantos* were not a fixture of the imagination for so many poets, including O'Hara.

"Poem (The rich cubicle's enclosure)" suggests the cultural significance of this promise by providing a critical reading of *The Pisan Cantos* that implicitly guides the politics of space in O'Hara's longer, collage-based work, such as "Biotherm." The social logic of Pound's stanzaic "cubicle" is the pun on which this reading turns: in this tight room, the rhetoric of forms is also a rhetoric of community, the dialogism of the citizen masking the monologism of the autocrat. If "Biotherm" might be considered, among other things, an attempt to air this concept of the cubicle, this operation will depend upon conceptualizing audience not as discrete "citizens" in need of the same cultural remedies but as a theatrical relation to the second person. Placing literary and social history between two people, "Lucky Pierre style" (*CP* 499), allows references to emerge not as would-be explanatory piths and gists but as a tactical appropriation of a past for a group. Because such appropriations are fundamental to literary communities and to literary history more broadly, staging their contingency might have a demystifying force.

3 IN MEMORY OF MY FEELINGS
THE LIMITS OF KINSHIP

The essential [task of the] present-day advance-guard is the physical reestablishment of community. This is to solve the crisis of alienation in the simple way: the persons are estranged from themselves, from one another, and from their artist; he takes the initiative precisely by putting his arms around them and drawing them together. In literary terms this means: to write for them about them personally.

—Paul Goodman, "*Advance-Guard Writing, 1900–1950*"

In surveying O'Hara's reactions to Pound and Eliot and his transformations of Apollinaire, the Surrealists, and Auden, my first two chapters have focused primarily on what could be thought of as O'Hara's vertical or diachronic mining of modernism — especially his attempts to form alternative models of social and literary affinity. But O'Hara's involvement with literary community (and with social linkage more broadly) also took place within the horizon of his own historical moment and can thus be understood in relation to close-knit scenes like the San Francisco Renaissance and the Black Mountain poets. O'Hara's interest in the writings of Paul Goodman, for instance, was shared by several of the most important American poets of the 1950s, from Jack Spicer, who read Goodman both into textual strategies like dedications and occasional poems and into the more daily workings of his intimate community in San Francisco, to Charles Olson and Robert Creeley, who theorized Goodman into their own correspondence. Nor was reading Goodman the only way that 1950s poets and artists began to experiment with nonorganic families and even with coteries: many of O'Hara's painter friends, from Larry Rivers to Grace Hartigan, made work that, as O'Hara's commentaries suggest, rethought structures of social linkage.

This chapter examines O'Hara's well-known longer poem "In Memory of My Feelings" as a way to situate him more deeply within 1950s discussions about experimental models of community. One preliminary aim will be to demonstrate that the poem's concerns are not merely "the fragmentation and reintegration of the inner-self" (P 141), as Marjorie Perloff argues, but rather the larger social concern of how subjects imagine themselves as parts of collectivities within a given moment and historically. In order to reframe O'Hara's poem as such, I will need to stress, on the one hand, his modes of conceptualizing history (personally, nationally, and often through a campy vocabulary of the panorama or spectacle) and, on the other, the various ways the poem's concerns extend into social and material relations outside itself: from the various interpretations of Paul Goodman's writings about communities among 1950s poets to the (in some cases consequent) logic of Black Mountain, San Francisco Renaissance, and Beat coteries, to the critique of the family offered by the paintings of Grace Hartigan (the "Grace" at the center of the poem), and to the readings of "In Memory of My Feelings" developed at the time by O'Hara's peers in the poetry world, Amiri Baraka and Robert Duncan. These readings are crucial because in them, in different ways, Baraka and Duncan see "In Memory of My Feelings" as providing the terms central to O'Hara's understanding of and participation in community.

After a survey of influential early-twentieth-century avant-garde writers, Paul Goodman's 1950 essay "Advance-Guard Writing, 1900–1950"[1] divides contemporary literature's attempts to overcome alienation (a problem Goodman, who was openly gay, treats primarily within a masculine existentialist framework[2]) into three primary tacks — Genet's cult of criminality, Cocteau's attempts to please his audience, and the path he prefers, "occasional poetry": "As soon as the intimate community does exist . . . and the artist writes for it about its members, the advance-guard at once becomes a genre of the highest integrated art, namely Occasional Poetry — the poetry celebrating weddings, festivals, and so forth. 'Occasional Poetry,' said Goethe, 'is the highest kind' — for it gives the most real and detailed subject-matter, it is closest in its effect on the audience" (376).

"[T]he physical reestablishment of community" among a group of alienated writers who are "estranged from themselves, from one another, and from their artist" happens by a writer "putting his arms around" his audience and "drawing them together" by writing *"for them about them personally"* (375). For Goodman, such a writing practice works because readers recognize themselves in this literature: they are characters or names in other writers' works. Goodman is thus not worried about the pejorative sense of coterie. Nor is he concerned with precisely what is written, so long as it develops the intimate referential features he describes. Here, intimate reference brings a community of writers into collective self-consciousness:

> It makes no difference what the genre is, whether praise or satire or description, or whether the style is subtle or obscure, for any one will pay concentrated attention to a work in which he in his own name is a principal character. But such personal writing about the audience itself can occur only in a small community of acquaintances, where everybody knows everybody and understands what is at stake; in our estranged society, it is objected, just such intimate community is lacking. Of course it is lacking! The point is that the advance-guard action helps create such community, starting with the artist's primary friends. (Goodman 375–76)

Goodman found one immediately sympathetic reader in Charles Olson, who took up "Goethe, by way of Paul Goodman's article" in an August 9, 1951, letter to Robert Creeley: "all this damn funny recent verse — *all* of it, if you will notice, directed to *actual* persons, composted, actually, *by* and *for* OCCASION."[3] But beyond actual occasional poems, Olson also quickly theorized his correspondence with Creeley (which by then had grown to its seventh volume, as edited later by George Butterick) as producing two necessary changes that should be understood in terms of community: "(1), that you and I *restore society in the act of communicating to each other* . . . & (2), that what i mark about this correspondence is something i don't for a moment think is peculiar to thee et me — that the function of critique is more than the mere one of clarities (as, say, Flaubert, &, Mme Sand), it is even showing itself in the very form of our address to each other, and what work goes along with it" (Butterick *Complete Correspondence* 7:79). Olson added this: "I put it as of us, but, we do say to the Great Society, go fuck yrself (which Ez was not quite able to do!), and quietly create a society of our wives and friends — and without even trying to make it what DHL [D. H. Lawrence] wanted Trigaron or some such 'community' to be in Florida!" (ibid.).

Olson thus saw the signs of his and Creeley's invented male, heterosexual community[4] not merely in the volume of letters or in the practical help they provided but in the "very form" their "address to each other" took on — an invented language of intimacy that could substitute for the one offered by the Great Society.[5] "Without a ready-made reception," Libbie Rifkin writes, "they had to invent themselves as readers as well as writers; their poetic self-fashioning was the enactment — and ultimately the production — of an audience" (36).[6] As in O'Hara's reception history, Olson's too has involved charges of writing for a coterie. Donald Davie complains, for instance, about Olson's "A Bibliography on America for Ed Dorn":

> The slangy in-group flavor of that title, incidentally, as of much of the excited telegraphic prose which it introduces, is something that you may well find tiresome; but it is inevitable, given a movement which defines itself as all that organized society is not. Such a movement is an open conspiracy, which is only another word for a coterie, though an unusually ambitious and serious one. The same set of social circumstances produces the equally tiresome and not dissimilar telegraphese idiom of Ezra Pound's letters. (222)[7]

Like O'Hara and Olson, Jack Spicer too was interested in the "open conspiracy" of coterie writing and an eager reader of Paul Goodman's essay. Of the conspicuous dedications to friends in Spicer's book *After Lorca*, Lewis Ellingham and Kevin Killian write that "Spicer's comic way of justifying the dedications was 'at least you assure yourself of one reader,' but the multiple dedications serve — as they do in Frank O'Hara's work — to bring a world of others into the text, to create a community" (103). "This is no coincidence," Ellingham and Killian suggest in a note to this section, "since both O'Hara and Spicer were strongly influenced by the poet Paul Goodman's thinking on the subject. . . . Spicer and Goodman had argued over these issues in Berkeley during Goodman's 1949–50 tenure there. Spicer resisting, but now he came back to the fold" (390).[8] If Spicer's own relations to O'Hara were tenuous,[9] there were obviously important similarities between their projects — ones that did not escape their friends.[10] Still, Spicer never connected with New York writers. The painter John Button put it this way: "Jack was clearly over his head in New York. . . . He couldn't compete for coterie with Allen Ginsberg, Jack Kerouac, William Burroughs, James Agee, Paul Goodman, Wystan Auden, James Schuyler, John Ashbery or Frank O'Hara. . . . very soon he waxed nostalgic about the Bay Area" (in Ellingham and Killian 65–66). While we will return to Spicer's *After Lorca* in chapter 4, let me note here merely the extent of Goodman's influence within some of the most important microcommunities of American poetry in the 1950s.

O'Hara's interest in Goodman seems to have been strongest before he moved to New York and became part of an active artist and writer community. From Ann Arbor in 1951, for instance, O'Hara enthused about Goodman to Jan Freilicher: "The only pleasant thing that's happened to me since you left gal is that I read Paul Goodman's current manifesto in *Kenyon Review* and if you haven't devoured its delicious message, rush to your nearest newsstand. . . . It is really lucid about what's bothering us both besides sex, and it is so heartening to know that someone understands these things. . . .

[H]e is really the only one we have to look to now that Gide is dead, and just knowing that he is in the same city may give me the power to [hurl] myself into poetry" (G 187).[11] Clearly Goodman helped O'Hara focus interests: each was searching for social structures and genealogies that could support both avant-garde communities generally and gay writers operating outside of heterosexual narratives of community in particular. Still, Goodman's formulations would serve as a poor description of O'Hara's writing, in part because Goodman's occasional mode evokes a naïve realism: his claim that a poetry of proper names presents "the most real and detailed subject-matter" runs against O'Hara's more subtle take on rhetorics of realism, such as the claim, in O'Hara's essay "Nature and New Painting," that artists who turn away from abstraction are not more "real" or "detailed" than those who pursue it.[12] Value terms emerge in this essay not from the timeless pursuit of an empirical reality but from shifting, historically inflected senses that "nature" itself comes to take on.[13]

Still, Goodman's account of offending audiences (transposed, let's say, from the general categories of "advance-guard" poet and society to queer poet and heterosexual readers) might provide one way to focus the special flavor of O'Hara's early reception: "*Within* the advance-guard artist the norms of the audience, of 'society,' exist as an introjected, unassimilated mass; it is their irk that is his special inner problem; and his spontaneous attempt to vomit up or destroy and assimilate this irksome material that results in products that, as if willfully, offend, insult, or seek to disintegrate these same social norms" (359). Even the reception of O'Hara's 1951 master's manuscript, *A Byzantine Place*, which won the University of Michigan's Hopwood Prize, suggested an uncomfortableness with the lurking social implications of O'Hara's aesthetic.[14] Karl Shapiro, for instance, who thought the manuscript "far and away the best," felt it necessary to account for O'Hara's tone: "In spite of his parodistic leanings, he seems to be on his own; his affectations and frequently youthful lapses into games are perhaps too dangerous for him, but he seems to have courage and a full awareness of what he is doing" (G 183). What troubles Shapiro is not simply a general existentialist struggle against conventions (as Goodman might have it) but formal features identified as parodic, superficial, flirtatious, and finally dangerous. This is not Genet's representation of gay sex but a formal queerness of whose implications Shapiro believes O'Hara to be aware. In a letter to Freilicher which begins by bemoaning that his manuscript would not be published, O'Hara concludes, "Anyway you could fit the people I write for into your john, all at the same time without raising an eyebrow" (G 184). Stereotypical sentiments of a young poet romanticizing his marginality — true enough. But O'Hara's reception in the poetry world, then and to come, *was* importantly marked by the idea of a small, core audience, a group that might actually be in the john with him at the same time. In an odd inversion of a moral superego, the disapproving eyebrow is not raised against there being more than one person in the bathroom, only against a cramped gathering.

In fact, objections like Shapiro's continue in O'Hara's reception, even well after O'Hara was established in New York. Raising his eyebrow in a review of O'Hara's 1958 *Meditations in an Emergency*, for instance, Galway Kinnell complains that "O'Hara's flair is for mockery; though his poems are joyless, they never lack in wit. He mocks by modulating his voice, speaking either too seriously ('I cannot bring myself to prefer / Johnny Weissmuller to Lex Barker, I cannot!') or too casually ('And he was / there in the hall, flat on a sheet of blood that / ran down the stairs. I did appreciate it.')" (178). Wit, mockery, and tonal modulation irresponsibly elide the serious and the casual. Straying into diction that fails to match the situation's objective demands, the speaker perversely reneges on his contract with the reader. Whether or not one appreciates the self-consciously overstated aesthetic responses of the O'Hara lines Kinnell quotes, they are now clearly recognizable as a kind of queer camp. Like Shapiro, Kinnell finds these devices threatening and goes on to account for O'Hara's use of "childish diction" and "surrealism's paratactic devices" as a subset of O'Hara's problem with mockery.[15] For Kinnell it is as if, from an ethical point of view, details demanded a gradual unpacking (which would play itself out as symbolic development and unification) rather than metonymic accumulation. Kinnell's chastisement assumes the universality of his assumptions about poetic techniques and conventions. Mocking is therefore the activity of a child who eventually must, but as yet has not, recognized the authority of the father: in this case, the objective demands of poetry. And yet the familial and universal underpinnings of Kinnell's critique must now be seen in relation to camp's questioning of precisely these values: the universality of the family and the possibility of fixed, appropriate responses to given situations.

* * *

By the time O'Hara wrote "In Memory of My Feelings" in the summer of 1956, he was an active force within, and often the only common element among, a number of interdisciplinary communities, which included not only the New York poets but also several Beat poets, experimental musicians, dance critics, Abstract Expressionists, and neofigurative or gestural realist painters. The poem was finished during a transitional period in O'Hara's career. He had just returned from a somewhat bleak spring in Cambridge, Massachusetts (on a six-month fellowship at the Poets Theatre) and taken up his more serious, full-time position at MoMA. O'Hara wrote comparatively few poems in Cambridge, but he expanded and broadened his ties in the poetry world, especially to the Beat poets, who though not affected by Goodman as directly as were the San Francisco Renaissance and Black Mountain poets, were nonetheless in the process of working out their own important version of writing as a kind of social formation. In Cambridge, O'Hara met both Gregory Corso and John Wieners,[16] who had initially been a student at Black Mountain College under Olson but was quickly being championed by the Beats, especially Ginsberg. That O'Hara connected with these two poets in turn had the effect of strengthening his ties with Ginsberg. As Ginsberg says, "Frank admired Gregory's poetry and Wieners's and I think that's what locked me into him. . . . I was amazed he was so open and wasn't just caught in a narrow New York Manhattan Museum of Modern Art artworld cocktail ballet scene" (G 280). O'Hara's ties to the Beats were provisional and tentative and not without mutual suspicion and outright conflicts (including a shouting match with Kerouac, which will come into play in chapter 4), but they were nonetheless important.

From the Beats' perspective, it was decisively O'Hara — and not Ashbery or Koch or Schuyler or Guest — who both connected them to the midtown world and championed their work more generally.[17] As Ginsberg writes, "He taught me to really see New York for the first time, by making of the giant style of Midtown his intimate cocktail environment. It's like having Catullus change your view of the Forum in Rome" (G 288). Just as important, O'Hara defended the Beats[18] to his friends and to mainstream writers.[19] In a December 7, 1961, letter to John Ashbery, for instance, after remarking on Ashbery's positive,[20] Schuyler's undecided, and Koch's negative responses to John Wieners, O'Hara takes Koch to task: "Kenneth's opinion of it is spottier than I think it deserves. Come to think of it just the other day Kenneth remarked that he only liked 2 of the *Hotel Wentley Poems*, but of course they were all written in three days, a remark I intend to tax him with considering his own 'methods of composition'" (Archive). O'Hara was even more vocal in his support of Corso, whom he mentions in "To Hell with It" (about Ashbery's play *The Compromise*, performed the spring O'Hara was in Cambridge, with Corso acting a small part) and "The 'Unfinished'" (dedicated to the memory of Bunny Lang, who introduced Corso and O'Hara). O'Hara's strongest support of Corso, however, comes in an unpublished review of Corso's 1955 book, *The Vestal Lady on Brattle*, in which O'Hara seeks to uncouple the Beats from the fears they engendered in popular culture:

> The critical approach usually leveled against the "Beat" is one of very little use to any reader, all confused as it generally is with reactions to James Dean, jazz, juvenile delinquency, dope, miscegenation, and so on. If this line of reasoning were followed, could a Republican millionaire buy a Courbet . . . or an anti-Semite read Zola? The extraordinary beauties of Corso's poems, as of Ginsberg's, are not going to be revealed to petty-mined littérateurs who want their verse Georgian and their scandals Hollywoodian. (SS 82)

We will return in chapter 4 to O'Hara's pattern of linking Ginsberg to critiques of Hollywood. Here I want to reflect more generally on how the Beats' increasingly influential countercultural models of collectivity related to O'Hara's. For the Beats, the rethinking of social bonds tended to happen on male spiritual forays *out* of the city, conducted either alone (as part of an ethnographic/visionary journey recorded in epistolary form, as in Ginsberg and Burroughs' *Yage Letters*) or in small groups, as in many of Kerouac's novels. Part of O'Hara's dialog with the Beats involved his playfully contrary advice to remain in New York City and to stop turning toward religion (Eastern or Western). These are themes that run throughout O'Hara's remarks on Allen Ginsberg in particular, from "Allen and Peter why haven't you come back" (CP 324) in the July 15, 1959, poem "All That Gas" to the mention of their return three weeks later in "Adieu" — "Allen is back talking about god a lot" (CP 328) — to the direct question in the 1961 poem "Vincent and I Inaugurate a Movie Theatre": "Allen and Peter, why are you going away / our country's black and white past spread out / before us is no time to spread over India" (CP 399).

Despite disagreement on these points, O'Hara shared with the Beats the goal of cultivating both an alternative genealogy and an intimate, coterie audience for one's work, an immediate circle that anchored address, before it was, necessarily, overheard by a broader audience. In his many interviews and statements about the Beats, Ginsberg tends to locate the importance of Kerouac and Burroughs (as both writers and readers of his work)[21] on par with his reading of Blake, Shelley, and Williams and with his mystical experiences. In his "Notes for Howl and Other Poems" for Don Allen's *The New American Poetry*, for instance, Ginsberg claims that he had written the poem "for my own soul's ear and a few other golden ears" and that it involved "long saxophone-like chorus lines I knew Kerouac would hear the *sound* of" (415). As Ginsberg expands his account of the Beats into the present, he frequently mentions Corso and Wieners both as having made more recent formal contributions to this tradition and as sharing in the relevant models of sociality.[22] Far more than O'Hara, Ginsberg was willing to argue the genealogy of his own work (and of the Beats' work more generally) with academics — to insist on one constellation of influences and not another.[23] If O'Hara's relation to his own provenance and to that of the New York School poets was less polemical (and also less a matter of popular public debate), he would nonetheless aid Ginsberg in both this project and in the project of gaining converts — both of which Ginsberg clearly appreciated. Corso, Wieners, and Ginsberg were, however, not just an importantly allied social and literary group among O'Hara's expanding affiliations in 1956 but also a group whose subtle dissimilarities allowed O'Hara to articulate his own version of counterculture.

O'Hara's enthusiasm for them and their work seems to have coincided with a new post-Cambridge enthusiasm for his own and his friends' daily life in New York, which had been percolating formally at least since the previous summer, when O'Hara wrote what was arguably his first "I do this, I do that" poem, "At the Old Place."[24] "In Memory of My Feelings" is a more sustained meditation on the selves that emerge in these occasional poems. It is a poem that considers the social and philosophical conditions of possibility behind O'Hara's most famous poems of quotidian experience and friendship, from "A Step Away from Them" (written in August) and "Why I am Not a Painter" (also written in 1956, month uncertain) to "Poem Read at Joan Mitchell's" and "John Button Birthday" — both written in spring 1957.[25]

Unlike O'Hara's other poems, "In Memory of My Feelings" — which has been at the center of his reputation since it appeared in *Poetry* magazine in 1958 — does not feature a wide variety of contemporary proper names.[26] Instead, the poem is metacommunal in the sense that it explores the extent to which the self of an experience is also the self of one or several collectivities that frame that experience, conditioning its meaning. These collectivities are not simply present groups but pasts out of which one emerges: "The dead hunting / and the alive, ahunted" (CP 253). It is in this sense that one might understand the poem's first lines, where a "quietness" gets read or interpellated: "My quietness has a man in it, he is transparent / and carries me quietly, like a gondola, through the streets. / He has several likenesses, like stars and years, like numerals" (CP 252). As readers trace this quietness, its movement happens inside a space of multiple analogies, of likenesses.[27] Incidents, references, and "selves" proliferate so quickly that repeated motifs seem less to contain and unify the poem than to provide momentary rest stops and occasional internal loops amid an excess of detail.[28] As James Breslin notes, "the absence of a literal level derives from O'Hara's inability, made clear at the end of the poem, to reach any originating cause or source for his feelings, 'his selves'" (243). Still, *how* the poem proposes to search—from the destabilization of reference at the level of the line to the organization of five discrete sections—nonetheless becomes semantically charged.

The poem consistently links two kinds of necessary but impossible representations: that of experiences, always pluralized by the range of feelings from which they emerge and which they in turn generate; and that of identities, or selves, which at once depend upon and transcend the contexts and histories that would make them legible.[29] "Feelings" are linked to disparate selves: "One of me rushes / to window #13 and one of me raises his whip" (CP 253). This proliferation of experiential singularities, however, is at odds with the quasinarrative progression of the poem. In order for the poem to proceed, the multiple subjective selves and worlds of experience they make possible must be collapsed into at least temporary figures that (like the medusa at the end of section 1, the frieze of section 4, or the as-yet-to-be-murdered serpent of the final section) might contain these experiences by arresting them, transforming them into art, or (thereby) killing them.[30] In the same way that these images highlight the strained inadequacy of summary at the end of each section, so the poem explores a parallel gap between the various selves that keep emerging and the social and historical frameworks that would, but cannot quite, explain or contextualize them.

Section 2 of "In Memory of My Feelings" indicates the family as the first such social framework:

> The dead hunting
> and the alive, ahunted.
>   My father, my uncle,
> my grand-uncle and the several aunts. My
> grand-aunt dying for me, like a talisman, in the war,
> before I had even gone to Borneo

her blood vessel rushed to the surface
and bursts like rockets over the wrinkled
invasion of the Australians, her eyes aslant
like the invaded, but blue like mine.
(CP 253–54)

Though O'Hara superimposes "real" family details (an aunt's death) onto war images, the family drama appears as only one source of feelings among others, one force that unconsciously "hunts" the subject, here seemingly from beyond the grave. But as the section develops, death comes to be associated less with an actual aunt than with the family more generally as a constitutive category within identity — a concern that returns us to the arguments of chapter 1. The psychological space of the family proves to be provisional in much the way that marines jump from a "rusted barge" — "A hit? *ergo* swim" (CP 254), a line that is followed close after by a more definitive statement of this death and a subsequent affirmation of a theatrical play of subjective states in place of fixed familial identity:[31]

My
12 years since they all died, philosophically speaking.
And now the coolness of a mind
like a shuttered suite in the Grand Hotel
where mail arrives for my incognito,
whose façade
has been slipping into the Grand Canal for centuries;
rockets splay over a *sposalizio*,
fleeing into night
from their Chinese memories, and it is a celebration,
the trying desperately to count them as they die.
But who will stay to be these numbers
when all the lights are dead?
(CP 254)[32]

After "philosophically" killing off the family, the mind becomes a "shuttered suite" in the capital of theatricality, Venice, while the family's mail, its hunting — its desire for filiative inheritance — arrives only for an "incognito," made by the ambiguous grammar also the bearer of what should be the Grand Hotel's façade.[33] The last two lines of this passage distill the brewing conflict between empirical being and the functional categories (be they mathematical or social) that both structure being and work to make memory possible. If a number here can mark the *erasure* of

George Montgomery, photograph of Frank O'Hara posing as Ronald Firbank at Harvard, late 1940s. © George Montgomery.

family influence as easily as it can the actual influence, if identity can be understood as functional in such a way that it escapes the empirical determination of the family as the real origin of the self, what sort of identity is left ("who will stay to be these numbers") in the more theatrical world of postfamilial identification?

Section 3 proposes a range of historical moments as possible sources for identification, as temporary solutions for "the hand lifting towards a fig tree from hunger" (CP 254). By 1956 O'Hara had largely moved away from the high camp of his early poems, especially those involving Jane Freilicher.[34] Still, the excessive panoply of world history in what follows can be understood in a similar way.[35] Throughout the section, to identify with the host of historical figures and locales is in a sense to consume them as well — both through the literal act of eating that frames the section and through the stylized, easily digestible accounts: how, for instance, "the mountainous-minded Greeks could speak / of time as a river and step across it into Persia, leaving the pain / at home to be converted into statuary" (CP 254). The poem continues, "I adore the Roman copies." Camp appreciation of the copy is thus also an avoidance of art that would convert pain into stone monumentality. The mention of "ball gowns of the Directoire" (*CP* 255) similarly intertwines a revolutionary moment — " 'Destiny, Paris, destiny!' " (ibid.) — with campy attention to sartorial flair, the revolution itself becoming a fashion event. The section's concluding lines, then, give us a Hollywood history of the Middle East: "and lying in an oasis one day, / playing catch with coconuts, they suddenly smell oil" (ibid.). "A culture of surface" Andrew Ross claims in an article on O'Hara "is not simply a culture that declares its immunity to historical anxiety; it is also a culture that has become suspicious of History with a capital H, moving with awesome solemnity and depth through our lives, a culture which recognizes that history, for the most part, is also made out of the particulars by people whose everyday acts do not always add up to the grand aggregates of canonical martyrdom that make for *real* politics" ("The Death of Lady Day" 382).

Certainly O'Hara's version of camp — in this poem and elsewhere — works to deflate a notion of "History with a capital H." And yet for Ross, the politics of 1950s camp is a mode of what he calls survivalism:

> In the prepolitical climate of O'Hara's day, this survivalism found expression in the highly ironized flamboyance of the camp ethic — "laughing to keep from crying" — which structured a whole subculture around the act of imagining a *different* relation to the existing world of too strictly authorized and legitimized sexual positions. In this respect, camp has to be seen as an imaginative conquest of everyday conditions of oppression, where more articulate expressions of resistance or empowerment were impossible. ("The Death of Lady Day" 387–88)

Though this is the best critical statement about the powers camp held for O'Hara, its limitation is to see camp as merely a negative category, a mode of reaction.[36] Camp laughter would be useful only when one feels the desire to cry.[37] O'Hara's poetry does register some of the more disturbing facts of post–WWII American history; still, camp does not operate merely as a coping mechanism.[38] This is not to say that camp is devoid of social function. In fact it seems less accurate to treat camp's excessive aestheticism as a simple turn away from the social, as Susan Sontag does in her 1964 essay "Notes on Camp." Instead, camp in O'Hara might best be conceptualized in Jonathan Dollimore's terms, as a reception mode that operates as "a parodic critique of the essence of sensibility as conventionally understood."[39] Here we might position the "sensibility" opposed to camp as a desire to finalize and fix appropriate affective responses, mature responses. Certainly O'Hara's reading of Ezra Pound could serve as an example of this parody. Unwittingly, Galway Kinnell's response to O'Hara serves just as easily. By over- and underplaying affective responses to a wide variety of cultural objects and by changing the terms frequently, O'Hara turns the contingency of historical judgment into a value in itself, one around which imaginary, temporary collectivities frequently spring up. The fluidity of imagined collectivities is mirrored in the fluidity of judgment. Insofar as we understand camp in this sense, it remains intimately tied to O'Hara's use of obscure proper names with shifting and rapidly rebuilt "families of attributes."

Camp also underlies what O'Hara depicts as a nonpsychological "intimacy." Camp, that is, allows for communal identifications without basing community on the idea of consensus or on structures of familial, national, or world history:

> Rising,
> he wraps himself in the burnoose of memories against the heat of life
> and over the sands goes to take an algebraic position *in re*
> a sun of fear shining not too bravely. He will ask himself to
> vote on fear before he feels a tremor,
> as runners arrive from the mountains
> bearing snow, proof that the mind's obsolescence is still capable
> of intimacy.
> (CP 255)

Clothing oneself in spectacular histories remains a continual temptation throughout the poem, a defense mechanism employed by a "s[o]n of fear" against "the heat of life." Abandonment of these constitutive categories of nation and individual psyche is, however, as simple as a "vote on fear." One does not simply will them away. And yet O'Hara's resistance to psychology here can be further illuminated by remarks he makes in an article titled "Apollinaire's Pornographic Novels":

> Far from being an element of literature where the writer finds himself intimately engaged with his primal forces, pornography is the most difficult, limited, boring and laborious *genre* a writer could take on. And therefore it's an extremely interesting one. Personally, I wish the postal authorities would ban the detective novel, the autobiographical novel and the *roman à clef*, which, like the sonnet, are simple forms requiring only application, and let pornography run rampant. It, being some-

thing which requires great improvisatory skill, would undoubtedly yield some very interesting and out results, but in the direction of literary invention, rather than psychological revelation. (SS 157)

"In Memory of My Feelings" resists psychological revelation by refusing to depict events as clear causes for current feelings. The poem presents, instead, an excess of events that generate feelings and sites of historical fascination, which the authorial mind cannot simply synthesize. This refusal of what might be thought of as historical or experiential synthesis parallels the earlier refusal of familial synthesis: in the same way that the speaker is not a clear product of these historical tableaux, neither is he a simple product of a familial drama. The unsettling proliferation of sites of identification — "How many selves are there in a war hero asleep in names?" (CP 255) — operates in much the way Michel Foucault describes radical historiography, what he calls "counter-memory": "The search for descent is not the erecting of foundations: on the contrary, it disturbs what was previously considered immobile; it fragments what was thought unified; it shows the heterogeneity of what was imagined consistent with itself" (82). For O'Hara, a parade of historical inevitability (of the immobile foundations of the West, involving the Greeks, the Romans, the Arabs, and the Revolutionary French) marches past but does not connect with the present moment.[40] Its overstated progression provides only costumes, campy masks, incognitos. Foucault contrasts the status of soul and self in teleological history with Nietzsche's concept of genealogical history: "Where the soul pretends unification or the self fabricates a coherent identity, the genealogist sets out to study the beginning — numberless beginnings whose faint traces and hints of color are readily seen by an historical eye. The analysis of descent permits the dissociation of the self, its recognition and displacement as an empty synthesis, in liberating a profusion of lost events" (81). Rather than the structuralist idea of a failed or empty synthesis, however, O'Hara suggests a campy or mock synthesis whose critique registers through its excess. Dreams of identification turn in on themselves. "Beneath these lives / the ardent lover of history hides," begins section 4, "tongue out / leaving a globe of spit on a taut spear of grass / and leaves off rattling his tail a moment / to admire the flag" (CP 255).[41]

Identification with this version of world history makes possible a narrative — one O'Hara links to a pleasurable, temporary self-deception — in which individual nations rise and fall from the world historical stage; this is why the speaker ends the first part of section 4 by admiring the flag. The image of fellatio encoded in the tongue applied to the "taut spear of grass" thus might be taken as an intertextual wink at Walt Whitman.[42] "It is called *Leaves of Grass*, but don't let that fool you: it's really about sex," O'Hara writes elsewhere (*EW* 116). Whitman's epic of American, democratic grass famously uses moments of gay sex as allegories for actually receiving or coming in contact with the glad tidings of his picture of America as the cusp of a teleological history.

With Whitman suggesting a transition from world to national and sexual history, the poem moves to constructed afamilal friendships — those with Jane Freilicher and Grace Hartigan — as a possible explanatory context for feelings.[43] Details of a trip to Chicago with Freilicher and two paintings by Hartigan (superimposed again with war images) fuel what poses rhetorically as the poem's climax, or identificatory bonanza — the example of having the "Grace / to be born and live as variously as possible" (*CP* 256).[44] We will return to the various senses of "grace" in the line above. Here I want to emphasize only that O'Hara also includes "to be born" as the predicate of living "as variously as possible." Thus far the poem has explored being born into familial, world-historical, and national explanations of the self. In one sense, the poem seems to propose the afamilial bonds of friendship to Grace and Jane, the intimate linkages of coterie, as an alternative to the explanatory frameworks already considered.[45] Certainly it is in this section that the fantasy of living "as variously as possible" reaches its conclusion. But the fantasy of identification also seems to obliterate the logical progression of the poem thus far.

I am a Hittite in love with a horse. I don't know what blood's
in me I feel like an African prince I am a girl walking downstairs
in a red pleated dress with heels I am a champion taking a fall
I am a jockey with a sprained ass-hole I am the light mist
                                                                        in which a face appears
and it is another face of blonde I am a baboon eating a banana
I am a dictator looking at his wife I am a doctor eating a child
and the child's mother smiling I am a Chinaman climbing a mountain
I am a child smelling his father's underwear I am an Indian
sleeping on a scalp
                              and my pony is stamping in the birches,
and I've just caught sight of the *Niña*, the *Pinta* and the *Santa Maria*.
                              What land is this, so free?

(*CP* 256)

At one level, this catalog could be taken to echo Rimbaud's "bad blood" section of *A Season in Hell*, in which, as Kristin Ross claims, Rimbaud identifies himself with "barbarians" and Africans in part to appropriate the anti-Communard rhetoric of associating the workers with both. Such a linkage, according to Ross, also allowed Rimbaud to draw out "the political connection that indeed existed between workers in European capitals and the colonial oppressed at the historical moment when the most exotic lands were being opened to European mercantile interests" (757).[46] And yet if O'Hara's poem, too, makes links between metropolis and periphery, Rimbaud's concerns do not map neatly onto U.S. and world political conditions of 1956: the new scene is not one of opening up but rather of *transferring* colonial properties; and this operation is taking place not under the (differently hypocritical) French humanist rhetoric in which liberté is checked by égalité and fraternité but rather within the particular American rhetoric of singular and infinite "freedom." Living "as variously as possible" thus becomes — in the world of "a Hittite in love with a horse," "a sprained ass-hole," and "a doctor eating a child" — a kind of monstrosity (variously funny and not) in which the freedoms of "our democracy" (*CP* 256) get turned inside out through an "existence of emphasis" (*CP* 254) that produces anything but "humanism" (ibid.).[47] Though the catalog celebrates a kind of freedom, this freedom, as several critics have remarked, is both violent and imperial.[48] O'Hara's original version of the poem is revealing:

I don't know what blood's in me
I feel like an African prince
I am a girl walking downstairs
in a red pleated dress with heels
    what land is this, so free?

I am a champion taking a fall
I am a jockey with a sprained ass-hole
I am the light mist in which a face appears
and it is another face of blonde
    what land is this, so free?

I am a baboon eating a banana
I am a dictator looking at his wife
I am a doctor eating a child
and the child's mother smiling
    what land is this, so free?

I am a Chinaman climbing a mountain
I am a child smelling his father's underwear
I am an Indian sleeping on a scalp
and my pony is stamping in the birches
what land is this, so free?
(CP 538)

Here, the famous catalog exists as five-line stanzas ending with the ironic qualification "what land is this, so free?" used as a refrain. The easy irony of this last line probably began to seem pat to O'Hara. But the original indicates how firmly this poem was anchored, from the start, in a national context. One way to understand the expansion of the poem, then, is as the construction of larger frameworks that would demonstrate the possibilities and limitations of freedom in a more developed way. To an extent this involved putting these metademocratic images into more complex settings: the jockey, the father, and an African prince become part of familial, world-historical, national and afamilial dramas, part of the drama of the struggle to find a grace to live "as variously as possible."

• • •

The nature of this "grace" was a concern for many of O'Hara's readers, including several poets of O'Hara's generation. In his poem, "Look for You Yesterday, Here You Come Today," Amiri Baraka takes on the question directly:

Frank walked off the stage, singing
"My silence is as important as Jack's incessant yatter."

I am a mean hungry sorehead.
Do I have the capacity for grace??

To arise one smoking spring
& find one's youth has taken off
for greener parts.

A sudden blankness in the day
as if there were no afternoon.
& all my piddling joys retreated
to their own dopey mythic worlds.[49]

Looking at the event of a public reading (and alluding to O'Hara's line "My quietness has a man in it" [*CP* 252]), Baraka contrasts O'Hara's stance—

Fred W. McDarrah, photograph of Frank O'Hara reading at a benefit for Yugen Press at the Living Theater, New York, November 2, 1959. Left to right: O'Hara, Ray Bremser, LeRoi Jones (Amiri Baraka), and Allen Ginsberg. © Fred W. McDarrah.

understatement, "silence," and emphasis on "grace" — with Jack Kerouac's more macho "yatter."[50] Rather than simply writing off O'Hara's speculation as a "dopey mythic world," Baraka nonetheless questions the possibility, and perhaps the value, of grace for himself. In the larger context of Baraka's work over the next forty years, the playful self-deprecation involved in calling himself a "mean hungry sorehead" who may not have the "capacity for grace" operates also as a subtle critique of the theological implications of a term like *grace*,[51] (implications we will see more directly when we consider Michael Fried's attempt to link "presentness" and grace in chapter 6).[52] Simultaneously appreciating and creating a kind of separation, Baraka's reading of O'Hara seems poised between the earlier bohemian phase of his work, and the later activist phase.[53] But whatever his ambivalence, Baraka reads O'Hara's "grace" primarily as a value that should operate in the social world.

While Baraka would soon pursue an identity-based model of collectivity—the Black Arts movement[54]—in the context of Harlem and Newark, New Jersey, and would sever his ties to the downtown bohemian scene, his relationship to O'Hara[55] did not fall within the terms by which he tended to characterize this earlier scene: "For many of us who lived in the 'village' in New York, the political dimensions of the times were muted by the petty bourgeois anarchy[56] of the largely white soi disant arts community we lived in. But as the whole society heated up with struggle and rebellion and revolution, I suppose the most politically sensitive of us began to pull away from the bourgeois rubric that art and politics were separate and exclusive entities" (*Baraka Reader* 495).

O'Hara's practices as a writer challenged this separation in a number of ways. In 1961, for instance, O'Hara gave a benefit reading for the *Floating Bear* (a magazine that Baraka edited with Diane di Prima).[57] Four months later, as Brad Gooch notes, issues of the magazine were "seized on the grounds of obscenity for printing excerpts from William Burroughs's *Naked Lunch* and Jones's *The System of Dante's Hell*" (G 425). O'Hara's response was to write an open letter in support of the magazine. After noting that he had "the greatest respect and admiration for the *Floating Bear* as a publication more discerning and more adventurous than most, and for its editors Diane di Prima and LeRoi Jones, both as editors and as extraordinarily accomplished writers," O'Hara went further: "Mr. Jones' play [*The Dutchman*] I found powerful and moving. Part of a longer and not-yet published work, it is a strong indictment of moral turpitude. This work as a whole, *The System of Dante's Hell*, is to my mind a major contribution to recent literature, certainly the finest piece of American prose since Kerouac's first publications. I was therefore grateful for the publication of even this excerpt" (Archive October 21, 1961).

As the public reading became, throughout the early 1960s, an increasingly important forum for articulating social concerns, O'Hara participated by giving a series of benefit readings (sometimes with Baraka) both for small magazines and for people in need of money or support, including Baraka.[58] These commitments were interwoven with a larger imaginative investment in the Civil Rights movement. In an August 26, 1963, letter to Don Allen, for instance, O'Hara writes: "When are you coming to visit us all. Your fan club in New York is not so distracted by the Civil Rights movement or the treaty with Russia as not to miss you sorely" (Archive). Two days later, writing to Joan Mitchell, he laments not being able to go to "Washington for the Civil Rights march" but feels in some way compensated from hearing "Charlton Heston and Burt Lancaster being interviewed on the radio, and Jimmy Baldwin too, and it all sounded very grand" (Archive August 28, 1963). Considering O'Hara's race politics more fully would of course require moving beyond his participation in the emerging countercultural form of the benefit readings and his (at time self-consciously theatrical) expressions of support for the Civil Rights movement in his letters. For it is in the imagined communities and shuffled cultural monuments of O'Hara's poems that one can grasp the best picture of his race politics — an important project that is beyond my current scope. Suffice it to say here that, as a close reader of these poems, Baraka felt justified in contrasting O'Hara with other members of the New York School: "Frank at least had a political sense" (G 425). And if this sense seemed occasionally to drift toward a quasitheological concept of grace, Baraka could therefore indulge him to an extent.

Unlike Baraka's, Robert Duncan's response to "In Memory of My Feelings" does not register a reservation or a question but instead welcomes O'Hara into a would-be community. Duncan deals with the social world not as it emerges from "In Memory of My Feelings" directly but insofar as he sees the poem as proof of O'Hara's ability to exist in the poetic community that Duncan already occupies — a situation that can ultimately be read back into the poem. Consider Duncan's letter to O'Hara just after the poem was reprinted in *Evergreen Review*: "Your poem in the current (#6) *Evergreen Review* which I came at warily enuf has won me over — to re-search and see the section in MEASURE anew. . . . I write to tell you that you have another concerned reader: as I in turn have instances of joy." The letter is signed "With that love that we have for the secret writer of the poem who has reached into and touched a center that waited, Robert Duncan" (G 320). Duncan positions himself as a figure whose prejudices matter, one who has the power to welcome O'Hara into a secret society of poetic achievement from which, implicitly, O'Hara has previously been excluded. One can imagine O'Hara objecting both to Duncan's understanding of poetic groups and to his model of poetry. For Duncan, those writers who have already touched this waiting, fixed center appear to form a "we," the ones who can dispense "the love we have for the secret writer of the poem." Duncan's letter thus offers another version of interpellation by a fixed social group — the very problem that O'Hara has been dealing with throughout "In Memory of My Feelings." That O'Hara took Duncan this way was confirmed in a later exchange between Duncan and Allen Ginsberg. "[M]y relationship with the New York school has been very difficult," writes Duncan. "O'Hara was absolutely intolerant of my existence. My correspondence with O'Hara was only one long letter to him when I read a marvelous love poem of his and said, 'What a pouring-out of soul this is!' But for O'Hara it was wrong to have read his poem as a pouring out of soul, I guess, really" (H 63).

Ginsberg's response to Duncan nails the issue:

> [A]ll [O'Hara's] poetry was gossip, local gossip, social gossip, with sudden "ozone stalagmites," inspired images of New York, mixed with blueberry blintzes, also inspired. So that he felt any gesture he made was poetry, and poetry in that sense was totally democratic. So that there were no kings and queens of poetry. So when you wrote him, he saw you as the Queen of Poetry, giving him the scepter, and he said, "Well, I don't want a scepter from that old queen!" He wanted to be independent, or, in the New York context, he felt it was like a San Francisco plot, so he got paranoid, a little. (ibid.)

Ginsberg's suggestion that the proliferation of gossip, of seemingly inappropriate, intimate reference, becomes a kind of democratic writing gets at the very dynamic I see as fundamental to O'Hara's version of coterie writing. And it also suggests why O'Hara refused to take "a scepter from that old queen." Not one to have "reached into and touched a center that waited," O'Hara apparently felt himself being welcomed into a structure of community from which he felt alienated, both socially and poetically. Duncan's model suggests stasis, hierarchy, and even synthesis — all of which receive explicit critique in "In Memory of My Feelings." O'Hara ultimately did not respond to Duncan's letter, treating it like the familial communication in section 2 that, after the family has been killed off, "philosophically speaking," speaks from beyond the grave but reaches only "a shuttered suite in the Grand Hotel / where mail arrives for my incognito" (CP 254). Baraka's attempt to highlight the politics of grace and O'Hara's coldness to Duncan's idea of community both begin to indicate how "In Memory of My Feelings" might be understood as operating at a scale larger than the secret or private level of, in Perloff's words, "the fragmentation and reintegration of the inner-self."

• • •

> *and I have lost what is always and everywhere*
> *present, the scene of my selves, the occasion of these ruses*
> *— Frank O'Hara, "In Memory of My Feelings"*

Walter Silver, four photographs of Frank O'Hara and Grace Hartigan, 1952–1954. © *Estate of Walter Silver.*

By stressing scenes and occasions in O'Hara's famous lines, I have attempted thus far to demonstrate the ways "In Memory of My Feelings" explores the social and ideological contexts that selves necessarily rely on to explain their affinities to other subjects. To complete this picture, I must now track the crucial word and name *Grace* along the other side of the equation — toward the selves and ruses that were an active part of O'Hara's relationship with the painter Grace Hartigan (though this will also mean contextualizing the scenes and occasions that gave their friendship meaning). Over the course of this itinerary, we will encounter

O'Hara's art writing, which will gradually become the main focus of the second half of this study.

The lines "Grace / to be born and live as variously as possible" have been taken as characteristic of O'Hara's desire for variability: they are in fact etched on his tombstone. While variability is a crucial effect in O'Hara's writing, I would argue that the lines are characteristic also because they present a coincidence of proper name and value: that is, the lines crystallize a process that can be traced throughout O'Hara's writing in which proper names operate not simply as indexes for actual friends, nor conversely as universal symbols of friendship, but as uneasy hinges between the immediacies of a social situation and the transtemporal effects of poetic language.[59]

> One of me is standing in the waves, an ocean bather,
> or I am naked with a plate of devils at my hip.
>   Grace
> to be born and live as variously as possible. The conception
> of the masque barely suggests the sordid identifications.
> (CP 255–56)

The passage, as Marjorie Perloff notes, makes reference both to Hartigan's *Ocean Bathers* (1953) and to her *Frank O'Hara and the Demons* (1952), both of which, according to Hartigan, attempt to capture "Frank's body stance, his posture" (P 210). These are occasional paintings; they are also the "washy paintings of each other" that Rauschenberg snidely dismissed.[60] Hartigan, who began showing at the Tibor de Nagy Gallery in 1951, met O'Hara in early 1952. The significant period of their intense and mutually influential relationship lasted until 1960, when Hartigan married and moved to Baltimore. In 1956, when O'Hara was beginning to think of a cover for his *Meditations in an Emergency*, he wrote the following to Barney Rosset at Grove Press:

> While I admire [Bob Goodnough's] work very much and think he would undoubtedly do some lovely things, wouldn't it be more to the point to have some artist with whom I am more closely connected do this? The selection does seem important to the poems (if I'm not being too impressed by the French), and there are a few painters whose work has influenced the poems strongly, so shouldn't they at least be considered? I hope you will think of Grace Hartigan, anyway, and let me know what you think. . . . Perhaps it seems far fetched, but I do feel that Grace

and I have had a strong mutual influence on each other in our work and that this would make a certain effect in a book. (Archive April 9, 1956)

Early in their relationship, O'Hara was fascinated by Hartigan's use of the name George. John Bernard Myers claims that Hartigan took on the name as a practical response to sexism. Certainly this is part of the story. But Hartigan's own account suggests another level: "When I first met John Myers I was taken with the idea that homosexuals had camp names. I wanted another name too. So we decided on George since other famous women had chosen it and it began with G like Grace" (G 212). If camp identities, like pseudonyms for women painters in the American 1950s, suggest different (imaginative and practical) ways of coming to grips with real social pressures, O'Hara's writing on Hartigan's pseudonym, her incognito, hardly seems to fit Andrew Ross's model of camp as a strategy to "keep from crying." In 1952 O'Hara wrote *Grace and George: An Eclogue.* George remarks in the surrealist syntax of the eclogue, "[Y]ou may summon all the devils who amuse you across the anguished faces which crouch and beseech. You could conceive the emptiness as clarity, but who listens? who sees? It is as well to stroll on the edge of an abyss like the great Atlantic; uncharted it gave comfort to the last gargantuan sea-monsters, and in the clear light of the oceanographer did not fail to sink the Titanic" (SP 90).

Complete with stage directions that make it unactable, the eclogue pictures the gap between Grace and George's identities as a mock-romantic abyss, a camp rendition of "Manfred," (who of course attempts unsuccessfully to call the speaker in the first section of "In Memory of My Feelings.")[61] That O'Hara calls the play an eclogue suggests — given its subject of the slippage of identities between Grace and George — a sort of campy appropriation of the notion, common to pastoral poetry, of the urban poet nostalgically recalling the simplicities of rural life.[62]

But the eclogue — like O'Hara's other plays — consistently collapses the authenticity of speech into highly artificial, constructed writing[63] just as it turns practical stage directions into fantastic hallucinations.[64] O'Hara thus deals with the problem of dual identities by suggesting that there is no problem: enunciations need not be tied back to an explanatory source, a biographical being that then takes up a clear, consistent position within the matrix of gender divisions. By making theatrical speech uncontainable within a single character (or even a character conflict), *Grace and George: An Eclogue* celebrates the split between the two identities as productive rather than crippling.[65] This playfulness is perhaps what causes Mar-

Walter Silver, photograph of Frank O'Hara and Grace Hartigan on a picnic, 1954.

jorie Perloff to dismiss the play as "merely silly" (P 169); but the play's playfulness is in fact importantly tied, through the occasion of Hartigan's fabricated incognito, to O'Hara's ultimately serious consideration of the relations among speech, identity, character, and gender.

Grace and George: An Eclogue thus presents a concrete instance of how O'Hara's concepts of audience and psychology do not operate in the mimetic way Paul Goodman suggests. Like this one, O'Hara's other plays seem to have produced radical uncertainty about what sort of response was appropriate. "One event," writes Daniel Ellsberg in his 1951 review for the *Harvard Crimson* of O'Hara's play *Try! Try* "marred the evening for some. Thornton Wilder, after an appeal for funds, lectured the audience vehemently on its 'bad performance' during the O'Hara play, at which it had laughed loudly (and which got an extra curtain call). I think Mr. Wilder misjudged both the play and the audience's response; if so, his action was regrettable" (*SP* 223). It seems probable that the fluidity of identity and the lack of traditional interiority in O'Hara's play struck Thornton Wilder, for instance, as tragic, rather than practical. Certainly humor should have nothing to do with this crisis.

Although formally Grace Hartigan's paintings do not seem to have shocked anyone in the mid-1950s (quite the opposite in Rauschenberg's reading), many of their values were certainly coincident with O'Hara's. O'Hara writes, for instance, in his review of her 1954 show at Tibor de Nagy that "her paintings seem to be a means of dealing with experience on her own terms and insisting on her own meanings" (*WW* 11). Hartigan's 1954 painting *Masquerade* (see plate 1) is based on a photograph of the writers and artists associated with the literary magazine *Folder*. The photo, taken by Walter Silver for Hartigan, shows O'Hara, John Ashbery, James Schuyler, Jane Freilicher, and Hartigan herself along with several others, all in costumes.[66] Today, such a painting might be seen as a traditional coterie moment par excellence. In her journal, Hartigan writes of the work: "In the market Thursday I came upon piles of old clothes and costumes and bought some that excite me — a long black hooded cape, a red hunter's coat and beaded twenties dress. Since then I can think of nothing but making a large painting called 'Masquerade' for which I shall use all the Folder people" (Mattison 36).

The circumstances that surround *Masquerade* — the account of buying clothes, the title, the photographs, the known identities of the figures — all seem to charge the painting with a set of meanings that circulate around the play of identities. Such a reading is also borne out by the handling: brush strokes extend beyond figures, bleeding from one to another. Rubbed-out zones suggest vanished sections, or perhaps vanished attributes of figures. Each figure is composed of radically heterogeneous marks — dabs (especially in the two figures in the upper left corner), splotches, and surface modeling of whitish zones in both of the dresses that seem to detach themselves from the figures. Thick colored strokes frame heads and at times, evoking clothes, detach themselves from bodies.[67] Like Venetian theatricality, masquerade — enacted formally by the

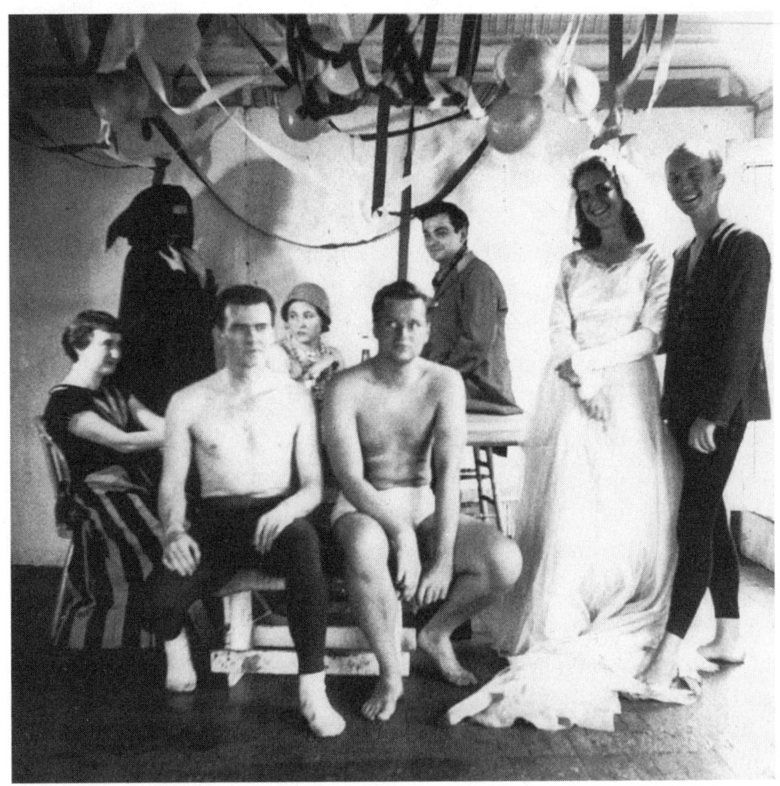

Walter Silver, photograph for Masquerade, 1954. *© Estate of Walter Silver.*

intersubjective dispersion of figures — would be a liberatory spectacle, an occasion of the multiple camp subject positions Hartigan values.

But is identity fluid only during such moments? And, does masquerade remake a previously secure identity or point more generally toward a fluidity constitutive of identity? At least since Lacan's incendiary remarks (in "The Meaning of the Phallus") about lesbians wearing "the mask . . . to dominate the identifications through which refusals of love are resolved" — that is, as an imaginary conquest over their rejection from heterosexual love — the topic of masquerade has been important for gender studies (quoted in Butler's *Gender Trouble* 49). In Judith Butler's well-known reading of Lacan (and of Joan Riviere's 1929 article "Womanliness as a Masquerade"), masquerade becomes not merely a condition of womanliness (as Riviere would have it) but the basic condition of performative identity. O'Hara's relation to such questions clearly comes from a very different register of language. Still, his take on the relation between the self and the larger collectivities that make it legible (in "In Memory of My Feelings" and elsewhere) does suggest an attempt to activate the gap between identities — not to bemoan this space as loss or as symptom. Nor is it clear that a masquerade or an incognito for O'Hara (or for Hartigan) is simply a remapping of a previously secure identity. "In Memory of My Feelings" seems to indicate the opposite.

Certainly Hartigan's work was important for O'Hara's thinking on these topics. Writing about her painting, O'Hara comes to emphasize both functional (rather than foundational) identity and heterogeneity as sources of value. In his essay "Nature and New Painting" (whose broader goal is a defense of a neofigurative turn O'Hara locates in Rivers, Elaine de Kooning, Freilicher, and Hartigan),[68] he writes that Hartigan

> had found that the great, beautiful and solitary aim of abstract painting was not hers, she could not give enough to that art. Essentially a painter of heterogeneous pictures which bring together wildly discordant images through insight into their functional relationship (their "being together in the world"), her method is seen in bold relief next [to] an abstract painter like Philip Guston, for instance, whose varied periods of explorations culminate in the pure, unified and perfect silence of his present work. From Miss Hartigan's early work to her latest one notes the progress of inclusion, a continual effort to put more into the picture without sacrificing the clarity she loves in Matisse nor subduing the noise of the desperate changes she perceives in the world around her.[69] (SS 45)

The idea of a functional relationship, here grounded in the existentialist language of "being together in the world," is what governs, through metonymic links, the production of heterogeneity and noise — two valued effects in O'Hara's formulation.[70] O'Hara's emphasis on heterogeneity indicates pleasure not merely with the variety of objects from the world that can make their way onto a Hartigan canvas but also with the range of handling methods whose effects work against the idea of a signature style, something many critics have noted even more of Freilicher's paintings. The struggle among such working modes can be one source of "noise," as can a kind of unanticipated and uncontrolled bleed from context into artwork. Functionality, however, suggests more than simple contiguity; it indicates also the force of a causality, one that, as in mathematical functions, can be unidirectional or mutually dependent.

By 1954 Hartigan had been through several dysfunctional relationships, two of them mediated by marriage. Robert Mattison, in his monograph on

Grace Hartigan, Grand Street Brides, *1954; oil on canvas, 72 x 102 in. Whitney Museum of American Art, New York. Photo: Geoffrey Clements. © Grace Hartigan.*

Hartigan, suggests a context for her painting *Grand Street Brides*: "Since 1949 Hartigan's studio had been on the Lower East Side, an area where marriage was extremely important and arranged brides were often brought from Europe. Nearby Grand Street featured rows and rows of bridal shops, their windows filled with mannequins" (34). Like *Masquerade*, *Grand Street Brides* is importantly linked to photography. Hartigan had Walter Silver take a series of photos of the bridal shops. In January 1954 Hartigan writes in her journal that she "passed by a store window jammed full of mannequins in cheap white lace bridal gowns with a seated figure in bilious violet maid of honor dress. It would make a marvelous picture, a kind of modern court scene" (Mattison 33). The ceremony of marriage is like a modern court scene because it sloppily appropriates the authority of court display to authenticate the institution. In seeking the associations of court power to overcode everyday life, the spectacle of marriage becomes a union without "grace."

Walter Silver, photograph for Grand Street Brides, 1954. *© Estate of Walter Silver.*

O'Hara suggests that the painted brides "face without bitterness the glassy shallowness of American life which is their showcase" (SS 45). This is a reference at once to the actual shallow space of the display window, the implicit shallowness of the painting, and to the surprisingly positive facial expressions of the mannequins. The brides are "showcased" only in the institutional act of marriage: presumably, as lower-class immigrant women of the New York 1950s, they will not have many other moments in the limelight. Internally, the painting also works to showcase three of the six brides by bathing them in color, as if they were under varied but highly saturated spotlights, while three other brides, primarily in black and white, become an intermediate phase of the painting's backdrop, the showcase's back wall. That the brides all look out at the viewer and not at each other suggests that they present a repertoire of purchasable attributes — the success of the marriage (its microcommunity-to-be) thus becoming dependant upon the stylistic flair of the ceremony itself. It is in this sense that marriage becomes, in Hartigan's painting, a co-opted form of social linkage.

O'Hara's remarks about Hartigan's work suggest both a shared interest in "noise" and heterogeneity and a concern with the structures and institutions of social linkage. Though the phrase *functional relationship* is undoubtedly abstract enough to take on nearly infinite meanings, I want to suggest that, whether fully consciously or not, O'Hara and Hartigan in the mid 1950s both imagined the social world as a site of functional relationships, a site in which the shifting subject positions they valued were produced as a function of contexts rather than as a product of innate psychological traits or universally binding identifications. Like O'Hara's inquiry in "In Memory of My Feelings," Hartigan's paintings deal both with the play of identities within masquerade and with the specter of marriage as a kind of co-opted, commercially mediated, social unity. Perhaps the final measure of Hartigan's involvement in a critique of the ideology of kinship is the fact that in 1960, when she was again married, her psychoanalyst convinced her that her relationship to O'Hara was destructive to her marriage. Several accounts suggest that this is what precipitated her move to Baltimore.[71]

Though O'Hara's bond to Hartigan was afamilial, it was nonetheless characterized by an extreme investment in her success. Grace Hartigan, one could say, was one of the initially obscure proper names that O'Hara attempts to code with meaning, to canonize. Despite the gender displacements inherent in O'Hara's singing the praises of his "muses" with his poetry, from the perspective of the art world this canonization seems continuous with the more monumental and masculine forms of canonization that O'Hara's writing generally attempts to unsettle.[72] O'Hara's status at MoMA positioned him as a privileged viewer of Hartigan's work. When Alfred Barr purchased Hartigan's *Persian Jacket* in 1953 from the Tibor De Nagy Gallery, O'Hara was at MoMA's front desk and could call Hartigan (who had no idea of the purchase) to report Barr's unloading the piece from a taxi. Later, when the painting was installed in O'Hara's office at MoMA, he would write Hartigan to tell her about it: "[We] now have your *Persian Jacket* in our office. As you know, we get a chance to choose something from the Collections whenever it is not on exhibition, so now we have you and a lovely early Miró (the ochre still-life kind, beautifully painted). Your painting looks marvelous after all this time, the trip to India left it fresh as ever, and people have been poking in to look at it all day yesterday. When you're in the building you can come up and look it over if you'd like" (Archive December 20, 1957).

The year of this letter — 1957 — O'Hara selected the American paintings for the Sao Paulo Bienal, in which Hartigan was included. More important, under the direction of Dorothy C. Miller, O'Hara helped to organize the higher-profile 1958–59 exhibition *New American Painting*, which also included Hartigan. O'Hara traveled with this exhibition to Paris in September 1959.[73] Such institutional backing separates the name Grace Hartigan from many of the other names O'Hara tries to recode in his writing. The self-consciously minor canonization achieved in poetry by a shifting pantheon of obscure names now gets underwritten by the Museum of Modern Art.[74] It *is* within his power substantially to affect the public reception of the name Grace Hartigan.[75] At the same time, whatever effect O'Hara had certainly was not transmitted by the veiled reference to "Grace" in the center of "In Memory of My Feelings."

Instead, the power of this poem resides in its attempt, in dealing with an excess of events and feelings, to think about subjectivity outside of its more normative explanatory contexts. The poem's larger movement through familial, world-historical, national, and ultimately afamilial social structures can be understood in relation to the more daily poetry of afamilial intimacy in O'Hara's other work — the "I do this; I do that" poems. It is in this sense that "In Memory of My Feelings" is a metacommunal poem, one that demonstrates how coterie in O'Hara's work can describe a conscious attempt to think through competing social frameworks and not merely a symptomatic effect of writing for one's friends. While the poem values an afamilial social structure, it does not freeze a group of readers as an idealized audience; even section 4 is positioned in between the kinds of intimacy associated successively with Jane and Grace. When O'Hara does thematize internalized figures of audience, his practice works (as I argued in chapter 2) less to contain poems within these figures' imagined reception, within a static sense of coterie in its pejorative sense, than to stage a dialog between an immediate audience and set of expanding reception frameworks that extend into literary history — and into the world beyond his control.

As "In Memory of My Feelings" suggests, O'Hara sought to create a context for writing in which the fluid subject and gender positions he valued could take on a socially embedded set of meanings. Such a context, what the writers and artists in O'Hara's New York circle actually created, was not simply a support group for queer writers or an aesthetic or social consensus. For O'Hara, subject positions enacted in writing would not be stable abstractions of a unified psyche (what the New Critics would call "personae") bringing insight *to* an abstract readership. Instead, the writing self comes *from* that community as well; its legibility emerges, in part, from the world of proper names inside the poems. "In Memory of My Feelings" bears a crucial relationship to this process, then, because it positions constructed, afamilial relationships as an alternative to more organic structures of community like the family and the nation: selves become legible within social frameworks that seek to explain the self and its feelings. And yet these explanatory frameworks each pressure and condition the self that emerges from them, hunted or haunted by the norms that inhere in narrating life through them. This inflection is precisely what makes such frameworks seem partial and unsatisfactory, what keeps the poem moving from one to the next. In considering O'Hara's poem "Commercial Variations," chapter 4 will elaborate on O'Hara's thinking about the nature of national stories of justification and the relation between microcommunities and nations. By shifting the focus to the larger question of the nation, I hope also to indicate further why and how, at its extreme moments, identification could come to be a violent and imperial relation to a world of exotic sites of affect.

4 COMBATIVE NAMES
MAYAKOVSKY AND PASTERNAK IN THE AMERICAN 1950S

O Boris Pasternak, it may be silly
to call to you, so tall in the Urals, but your voice
cleans our world, clearer to us than the hospital:
you sound above the factory's ambitious gargle.
Poetry is as useful as a machine!
— Frank O'Hara, "Memorial Day 1950"

Detroit's damp bars, the excess of affection
on the couch near an open window or a Bauhaus
fire escape, the lazy regions of stars, all
are strangers. Like Mayakovsky read on steps
of cool marble
— Frank O'Hara, "Ann Arbor Variations"

I had never read any Mayakovsky, but Frank turned me on to him and I'm always indebted to him because that opened my interest in Russian poetry. . . . He turned me on to the open public voice, especially the suicidal desperation of 'At the top of my voice.' It's a great classic. You see Mayakovsky wasn't printed in America, as Neruda was not printed in those days, for being commies. It was a blackout.
— Allen Ginsberg, interview with Brad Gooch

For those Americans who cared about Russian modernism in the 1950s, the question of just which version of it one was looking at, or could look at, loomed large. Between Alfred Barr's 1928 article "The LEF and Soviet Art" and Camilla Gray's 1962 *The Russian Experiment in Art, 1863–1922*, little scholarship was available on Russian art of the early twentieth century, especially that after the 1917 revolution.[1] By the mid-1950s, Barr's early enthusiasm about LEF — a word "formed from two Russian words meaning left front" (Barr 138) — had been replaced by the far more cautious stance he maintained as MoMA director during the height of the Cold War: Gabo and Pevsner came to represent the politically unthreatening Soviet modernism that could be dispensed to the United States. And while attention was lavished on them, little was known about such artists as Tatlin, Malevich, Rodchenko, and El Lissitzky—all of whom enjoy far stronger reputations today.

This now well-known art-historical story has, perhaps, a less-known literary parallel in the reception histories of Mayakovsky and Pasternak. Frequently read as a claim about the inevitability of a Stalin within any Communist experiment, Pasternak's 1958 novel *Doctor Zhivago* became an enormous international success. Whether or not such readings were convincing or should be extended as critiques of the ambitions of Communism, Pasternak became an international Cold War figure. At the same time, little was known of Mayakovsky — and this because he was taken, when he was available at all, as an ideological dupe, a propagandist for the Soviet state. Each suffered from caricature, and it was the instrumental uses of these differing caricatures that in the 1950s determined the uneven nature of two writers' receptions in the United States. The ideologically charged concept of freedom extracted from Pasternak can be taken as a parallel to the similarly instrumental idea of freedom that was culled from readings of American Abstract Expressionists and then broadcast internationally.

Since his time at Harvard in the late 1940s, O'Hara had been intensely interested in Pasternak and Mayakovsky. Consider his April 8, 1957, letter to Larry Rivers: "I have a new book of Russian poetry from 1917 to 1955 !!! yes, I'll loan it to you as soon as I've finished stealing from it. There are some great new translations (well, the poems are or seem to be) of Pasternak and Mayakovsky" (Archive). But even by the early 1950s, the proper name of each had, as my epigraphs for this chapter indicate, made a theatrical entrance into O'Hara's poetry. As with most names in O'Hara's writing, these proper names were charged with complex and multiple functions. The apostrophe to Pasternak in "Memorial Day," for instance, imagines a temporary link across the Cold War. As such, it presents the problems of audience and community that I have considered thus far in a very different way: here the question is not (as in "Biotherm," for instance) the relation between an intimate, second-person audience nested in the foreground and everyone else in the background. "Memorial Day" was written the year after NATO had come into being and just months after China, fresh from ousting Chiang Kai-shek, had signed a mutual defense treaty with the Soviet Union. Including Pasternak with a battery of implicitly influential Modernists (Picasso, Ernst, Klee, Apollinaire, Auden, Rimbaud, and Stein), the poem — like many to follow that would expand this dialog with Pasternak and create one with Mayakovsky as well — incorporates Russian modernism (and later explicitly Soviet modernism) within O'Hara's field of precedents at a time when such an association was politically risky. Moreover, O'Hara's apostrophe initiates a mode of intertextual connection and of implied audience that complicates the models of audience I have thus far been developing.

Critics have understood O'Hara's interest in Russian literature and music alternatively as sites for romantic identifications or as tonal fields from which O'Hara's poetry borrows. In the translator Paul Schmidt's brief note on the subject, O'Hara's Russia was "a Russia full of snow and tears" (H 194). For Marjorie Perloff, a more technical comparison between O'Hara and Mayakovsky makes the Russian a point of reference for O'Hara's "rapid transitions from lyricism to buffoonery" (P 137–38). Though such transitions exist in O'Hara, and though he did write seven poems titled "On Rachmaninoff's Birthday," O'Hara's dedicating "Second Avenue," his longest, most complicated poem, to "Vladimir Mayakovsky" (whose work at the time was largely unavailable to American audiences because of his status as *the* national poet of Soviet Communism) in 1953 seems a slightly more charged, even combative, enterprise than these accounts would suggest.[2]

Part of what becomes charged in their relationship is O'Hara's modification of Mayakovsky's apostrophes to cities and countries. The place to witness this transformation is in O'Hara's 1952 poem "Commercial Variations," a poem which, not accidentally, is also concerned with the rise of American art after World War II, with the story that Serge Guilbaut would narrate as *How New York Stole the Idea of Modern Art*. But for Guilbaut, as I mentioned in my introduction, O'Hara is part of the *problem* — one of those who added to the "miles of pages filled by friends, promoters and admirers of the abstract artists" and who thereby obscured the "link between art and politics, particularly between abstract expressionism and the ideology of the Cold War" (9). O'Hara's friendship and promotion were, however, not separate from his attempt to explore these links between abstract expressionism and the Cold War. In characterizing the links O'Hara makes to these Russian Modernists, this chapter will also turn to his art writing and consider "Commercial Variations" as a heretical and extreme account of the rise of post–WWII American art in New York (a topic that was fundamental to those writing art criticism in America in the 1950s). Most narratives of this rise were intertwined, of course, with the larger problem of explaining New York's increasing control of American cultural life and the vastly expanded postwar international power of the United States. New York's escalating role as a spectacle of culture was, for many, understood in some essential relation to the United States' new international position.[3]

Frequently undercutting spectacular rhetorics of cultural achievement, O'Hara was institutionally positioned, nonetheless, as a guide to New York's culture. Beginning in December 1951, he worked at the front desk of MoMA, applying for the position, according to some accounts, because of his enthusiasm for the Matisse retrospective organized by Alfred Barr.[4] In his early years working at the front desk, O'Hara of course was not connected to institutional decisions. He could talk to friends on the phone, read poetry, and revisit the shows. After being promoted to front-desk manager in March 1953, O'Hara resigned from MoMA in January 1954.[5] Exactly a year after leaving, O'Hara returned, now as a special assistant in the International Program under Porter McCray, who in turn worked under Nelson Rockefeller, who had begun funding the program with a five-year grant from the Rockefeller Brothers Fund in 1953.[6] It was not until May 1957 — almost a year after his return from Cambridge — that O'Hara began to select paintings for exhibitions. From here on, O'Hara's downtown-art-world authority, which he had already been accruing since 1952 through his talks at (and association with the members of) the Club and his reviews for *Art News*, began to register in his daily work at MoMA.[7] O'Hara's responsibilities grew exponentially, and he became a kind of ambassador of abstract expressionism, making frequent trips to Europe for MoMA, installing exhibitions, and giving talks.

Before O'Hara actually selected paintings, however, he wrote grant letters. These are worth looking at, in part because they required O'Hara to sketch the international situation of American art to potential funders. Consider, for instance, his October 16, 1956, letter to the Ford Foundation.[8]

> The image of the United States held by nations abroad is surprisingly similar all over the world, differing in degree rather than in kind according to whether the respective country is well disposed toward America or otherwise. In general, our technical achievements are highly regarded. On a cultural level, we are known best and most favorably by our literature, with which foreign countries frequently show a surprising and varied familiarity. Hawthorne, Melville, Poe and Whitman among 19th-century authors, Lewis, Dreiser, Hemingway and Faulkner among the 20th, are apparently especially well-known figures.
>
> While the best of our films are also recognized as a distinctive American contribution, on the whole we are apt to be judged unfavorably by the far more numerous run-of the-mill films. Other factors which have contributed largely to the formation of an unfavorable stereotype of America and Americans and a general undervaluing of our cultural standards are

> advertising and mass media. In contrast to these elements producing positive and negative reactions, our achievements in the visual arts have been virtually unknown abroad up until the past few years.[9]

O'Hara then appeals to the foundation's benevolence by explaining that "in attempting to counteract the prevailing impression of complete sterility in the visual arts, the United States is at a considerable disadvantage" because the U.S. government, unlike most, has no tradition of funding international "cultural activities." He then cites the five-year Rockefeller Fund as a significant gesture "to rectify this situation." Since 1953 it has, he writes,

> sent 35 exhibitions to 22 countries abroad and enabled 80 exhibitions from other countries to be presented to the American public. These exhibitions have been warmly welcomed, and in one sense, the program has been all too successful, for it has resulted in increasing requests for further shows from areas that have thus begun to be familiar with American art, and equally urgent requests from areas to which such exhibitions have not yet been sent. These demands[10] far outstrip the present capacity of existing government and private organizations to fulfill. . . .
>
> On the evidence of the reactions to the initial efforts of the Museum's International program, it is apparent that an extensive program of this sort in the field of American art would provide a particularly effective means of presenting certain aspects of American culture that are little known or frequently misunderstood abroad, and could also do much to correct the distorted picture of the United States that has been so harmful to our entire pattern of official and informal international relations. (October 16, 1956, Frank O'Hara papers, MoMa Archives, NY)

Four and a half years earlier, in April 1952, O'Hara had already confronted the problem of correcting "the distorted picture of the United States" — but from a significantly less official perspective. In 1952 O'Hara was unconstrained institutionally; his only ties to the New York Art world were his still-tentative link to the Club and his friendships with painters. O'Hara was undergoing the first phase of his enthusiasm for the city. Unlike his later museum catalogs for MoMA, this early account of American painting takes pleasure in America's status as an art-world parvenu.[11] Rather than seek to convince readers of the legitimacy of America's new art-world power, O'Hara brings in the languages of opera spectacle and machine politics to figure New York's odd status and power in the new global art world. Addressed directly through a series of apostrophes, New York becomes a queeny, decadent figure given the pleasure of watching a new form of masculine, gestural art spring up in its midst. However, if O'Hara's were merely a deflation of the new art, his account would be far less interesting. "Commercial Variations" represents a limit condition within O'Hara's story of abstract expressionism: though his later narratives sublimate this far more, O'Hara consistently identifies painting with a spectacle of masculine agency, with a Hollywood grandiosity — at once according respect to and deflating the massive subjectivities involved. The style of O'Hara's address to these subjectivities and to New York will, as we will see, return us to the character of O'Hara's dialog with Russian modernism.

This chapter, then, seeks to show how O'Hara's early attempts to imagine critical and historical terms for the situation of American art in the 1950s, apostrophizing both the city and the country more generally, are interwoven both with intertextual links to, and attempts to establish dialog with, Russian writing from the 1910s to the 1950s. What a subject is, which modes of address are open to it, and which kinds of freedom underlie it — ranging from political to sexual — are questions that O'Hara's connections to Russian literature continually bring up. To characterize this intertextual dialog, I will trace a genealogy of subjective freedom from Mayakovsky to O'Hara's "Commercial Variations," to the international spectacle of Pasternak's *Doctor Zhivago*, and finally to Allen Ginsberg's writings on Cuba in the early 1960s. In forging links to the other side of the Cold War, O'Hara works to revise the erotic economy of the Mayakovsky of the 1920s and disassociate the Pasternak of *Doctor Zhivago* from the American Right.

But as I make these links, the asserted context of O'Hara's writing shifts scales radically. The imagined space of coterie now becomes international. To account for this shift I will first need to expand my consideration of how proper names relate to models of audience. This process will be aided, I hope, first by a rough mapping of the "world" of O'Hara's names and then by a brief turn to the work of the poet Jack Spicer (1925–1965), an almost-exact contemporary of O'Hara.

Unlike the referential project of using names to relate the present to the deep space of literary history (as O'Hara does in "Biotherm," for instance), there is also a more strictly synchronic moment to the problem of how one understands names in O'Hara. Synchronic names produce temporary spatial constructions around O'Hara's poetry, shifting anchors to an implied empirical reality that is also, possibly, a reality of readers. Still, names need not document literal readers; nor is a finalized or indisputable picture of this network possible — both because such a picture would become impossibly intertwined at any single point (as we will see) and because positions shift throughout O'Hara's writing. But it may be helpful, nonetheless, to sketch what one might imagine as some of the various (and overlapping) scales of audience and reception implied by O'Hara's names. From center to periphery, one might choose the following categories and examples: boyfriends (Larry Rivers, Joe, Vincent), "muses" (Bunny Lang, Grace Hartigan, and Jane Freilicher), New York poets (Ashbery, Koch, Guest, Schuyler, and later Bill Berkson), New York painters (Willem and Elaine de Kooning, Kline, Pollock, Jasper Johns, Mike Goldberg, Norman Bluhm, John Button, Joan Mitchell, and Alfred Leslie), non–"New York School" New York writers (Ginsberg, Corso, John Wieners, LeRoi Jones/Amiri Baraka, and Edwin Denby), the New York art establishment (Charles Egan, Sidney Janis, and Betty Parsons), and other American poets (Robert Frost, William Carlos Williams, Wallace Stevens, Charles Olson, and Gary Snyder). There are also, of course, a few more categories: dancers, singers, conductors, jazz musicians, local and national politicians, military figures, classical composers, art historians, Hollywood stars, and stars of European cinema. Heuristic perhaps, this list immediately produces taxonomic aporias, like the fact that most of O'Hara's "muses," many of his closest friends, and some lovers, are also painters. My point, however, is less to fix names in categories than to show how the names situate O'Hara's writing within shifting concepts of space, audience, and authority. As they expand beyond the continental United States, O'Hara's name networks evoke a French modernism in poetry and prose (Apollinaire, Reverdy, Char, Cocteau, Colette, Butor, Genet, and Gide), a European modern art context (Picasso, Schwitters, Mondrian, Matta, Matisse, Léger, Ernst, Dubuffet, Duchamp, and Albers), and a few players on the world political stage (de Gaulle, Khrushchev, Eisenhower, JFK, and Jackie O, of course). It is in this broader context that one should consider O'Hara's sustained connection to Mayakovsky and Pasternak, a connection that links O'Hara to the Russias of both the 1910s and the 1950s.

One might compare the complex social space brought into being by O'Hara's use of proper names to the dedications and translations of Jack Spicer's 1957 book *After Lorca*, as described by Ellingham and Killian:

> Spicer's dedicatees make up a formidable range of muses: several of them were students in his Magic Workshop (Helen Adam, George Stanley, Ebbe Borregaard, Bob Connor); some of them were old friends from Berkeley (Pat Wilson, Donald Allen, Robin Blaser); some were

> former "boy-friends" (Richard Rummonds, Graham Mackintosh, Allen Joyce). One of them was a child of only three or four, Nate Hardin, the son of his old Berkeley friend, Sam Hardin. Several were new acquaintances, bar poets whom Spicer met at The Place thanks to John Ryan. Some of them were the actors with whom Duncan was working on *Medea Part II* — Erik Weir and Anne Simone. (103)

If Spicer's dedications thus enact an imaged social space in a slice of time, synchronically, *After Lorca* also creates an extremely complex and playful version of intertextual dialog, historically or diachronically, with Lorca — one in which the excuse of "translation" only partly masks both invented poems and radical changes in Lorca's meaning. The book, in fact, begins with an introductory letter supposedly written by *Lorca* (who died in 1936) about Spicer's book.

> It must be made clear at the start that these poems are not translations. In even the most literal of them Mr. Spicer seems to derive pleasure in inserting or substituting one or two words which completely change the mood and often the meaning of the poem as I had written it. More often he takes one of my poems and adjoins to half of it another half of his own, giving rather the effect of an unwilling centaur. . . . Finally there are an almost equal number of poems that I did not write at all (one supposes that they must be his) executed in a somewhat fanciful imitation of my early style.[12]

After continuing on about the problem of telling which poem belongs to which category, "Lorca" then admits to "sending Mr. Spicer several poems written after my death which he has also translated and included here" (ibid.). The provenance of these, Lorca feels, will be even more difficult to decide.[13] Finally, "Lorca" concludes by commenting on the uses Spicer made of him in correspondence — the sense in which their "exchange" (imaginary to begin with) was blotted out by the younger poet's desire to hear himself speak through his letters to an important poet: "The letters are another problem. When Mr. Spicer began sending them to me a few months ago, I recognized immediately the 'programmatic letter,' — the letter one poet writes to another not in any effort to communicate with him, but rather as a young man whispers his secrets to a scarecrow, knowing that his young lady is in the distance listening" (ibid.).

Though obviously playful, Spicer's metatranslation project and the letters engage the mechanisms of literary history more explicitly and theoretically than does O'Hara. As *After Lorca* continues, it also comes to analyze explicitly the shifting functions of a small audience of friends for one's poetry. In a letter explaining to Lorca "why I dedicate each of our poems to someone," Spicer writes that "My fellow poets (those I showed poetry to ten years ago) are as little interested in my poetry as I am in theirs. We both compare the poems shown (unfavorably, of course) with the poems we were writing ten years ago when we could learn from each other" (*Collected Books* 38).

Though not addressed as directly by O'Hara, similar audience dynamics still seem to have been at work in the New York School. Consider, for instance, Larry Rivers's remarks about his relationship with John Ashbery and his other poet friends:

> By 1962 John had exchanged his Ivy League jacket for a Parisian model with no inner pockets for the poems he used to pull out at a moment's notice. The necessity of friends' opinions about our work had diminished. By this time, we had both developed an audience outside our friends. In the early years of our artistic development we spent a lot of time showing our work to friends and seeing and hearing theirs. It was part of our reason for getting together. Who were we painting or writing for? Well, for our friends, and history. Who was looking over our shoulders as we worked, adjusting our aesthetics? The whole New York art world! But it didn't know it. So the time we spent showing our work to one another was reduced and formalized into exhibitions and publications.[14]

Like Spicer, Rivers identifies the practical need for an intimate audience with the early phase of a career, or rather, of his generation of the New York School. At this early point one writes for a split audience. Rivers seems to have understood his correspondence with O'Hara in similar terms: "From 1950 on, Frank and I wrote stacks of letters to each other. We wrote as if the committee that decides who goes down in history was looking over our shoulders at them. We kept every letter" (232). For Rivers, these letters are at once self-constituting gestures of authorship among a group of peers and pleasurable gifts.[15] If this effect of the letters operates within the present, another component operates — according to Rivers — by allowing the writer who writes letters (or the artist who draws) to establish through these quasi-traditional practices "the credentials of an artist of the past." Which suggests self-constitution is now occurring in a vertical or diachronic way. Certainly we see both of these dynamics in playful, extreme, and revelatory form in Spicer's *After Lorca*, where a historical ground emerges through Spicer's ventriloquized letters to Lorca and a contemporary through the dedications.[16]

If the proper names in O'Hara's poems and the dedications and intertextual letters in Spicer's all work to spatialize the circuits of poetry's consumption, turning the lyric subject into an uncharacteristically social variable, this effect might seem to depend upon proper names evoking a consistent set of public identities. But as I argued in chapter 1, philosophers of language have stumbled on precisely this point. To encounter obscure proper names in O'Hara is to produce the "meaning" of Joe LeSueur or Bunny Lang contextually, independent of a fixed body of public knowledge. Proper names in O'Hara could therefore be said to achieve two seemingly opposite, though central, effects. On the one hand, through their reference to an empirical world of identities, careers, and potential sites of reception, they thematize writerly production as importantly inflected by its positions within social and historical networks. On the other hand, when O'Hara includes unknown names or seems to appropriate the meaning of a known one, he dispels the illusion that we share a fixed set of attributes or associations that a proper name would evoke. O'Hara's proper names produce a fiction of stability, of empirical bedrock, and at the same time an opening to radical uncertainty about the reference field implied or contained in a name. As I argued in chapter two, O'Hara (unlike Ezra Pound in particular) stages the proper name's entrance into poetic discourse as a site of contested, appropriated, tactically wielded meaning — meaning whose contingency announces itself from the outset. Thus, when Mayakovsky and Pasternak appear in O'Hara's poems and essays in the 1950s, these proper names at once provocatively assert an international, trans–Cold War context for O'Hara's writing *and* begin an inquiry into what and how these proper names mean.

As a proper name, Mayakvosky enters O'Hara's writing in 1950 in the poem "Ann Arbor Variations," quoted in my epigraph. From the beginning, O'Hara uses Mayakovsky as a sort of bridge between a relatively private world of desire — "the excess of affection" that takes place in "damp bars" and "on the couch near an open window" — and a public world of either monumental or modernist architecture, with its "cool marble" or "Bauhaus / fire escapes." This technique parallels his use of Pasternak at the time, whose lyricism can "sound above the factory's ambitious gargle. / Poetry is as useful as a machine" (*CP* 18). But in "A Postcard for Boris Pasternak," written in October 1952, O'Hara renders explicit the Cold War cultural barriers that stand in the way of an easy identification with the Russian author:

> But all we love and are grows different, weeps,
> lying in the tender arms of our gigantic continents.
> You cannot know the Prussian lather of the suburbs
> here, nor I the bad blood in the crouching Urals;
> yours is the barren forest of the haunted patriot
> whose birds fly south when his breath writhes cold,
> highwayman out of bullets above the timber line,
> ambitious in poor country, athletic in snow.
>
> Dear Master, as time pushes us toward the abyss
> that's sharp as a sledge hammer, let always
> your prayer be perverse and gratuitous, a
> volcano in the lengthening bandyleg of truth
> (CP 113)

Composed in a rhetoric and vocabulary register that demonstrate the influence of a not-quite-digested surrealism — "let always / your prayer be perverse and gratuitous" — the passage imagines (and literally constructs) the intertextual moment of connection between the two poets as a form of resistance to a Cold War abyss that would instrumentalize poetry as it travels as a unit of commerce between countries. Alone in a Soviet Union abandoned by Mayakovsky (through his suicide) and by so many other writers and artists in their move to the West in the 1920s, Pasternak occupies "the barren forest of the haunted patriot / whose birds fly south when his breath writhes cold."[17] Though knowledge of the quotidian world of the Cold War "other" across the abyss is incomplete (Pasternak will never know "the Prussian lather of the suburbs," nor O'Hara "the bad blood in the crouching Urals"), O'Hara asks Pasternak, here as "Dear Master," to remain perverse and gratuitous — not to harness his writing, presumably, to the machine of Stalinist Soviet realism. O'Hara's last line then figures a trans–Cold War "truth" as a body stretched, bandylegged (or bowlegged), between the Soviet Union and the United States, one leg in each country — the distance between the two "lengthening." The anal or penile "volcano" thus becomes an inversion of the atomic bomb, a bodily explosion that pries writing loose from its instrumental grasp by institutional legs on both sides. With the publication of *Doctor Zhivago*, Pasternak will seem not "perverse and gratuitous" enough.

Because Mayakovsky died in 1930, the terms of O'Hara's engagement with the writer are, of course, quite different. Like Pasternak, Mayakovsky enters O'Hara's poetry at charged moments. Written over the spring and summer of 1954, parts of O'Hara's poem "Mayakovsky" (cited already in chapter 1) were conceived initially as a response to O'Hara's recent breakup with Larry Rivers. According to Brad Gooch, it was James Schuyler who, "inspired by the well-thumbed copy of Mayakovsky's poems lying on O'Hara's desk" (G 254), suggested the name "Mayakovsky" for the finished poem. As in "Ann Arbor Variations," O'Hara ties Mayakvosky to a crisis in desire. The poem begins:

My heart's aflutter!
I am standing in the bath tub
crying. Mother, mother
who am I? If he
will just come back once
and kiss me on the face
his coarse hair brush
my temple, it's throbbing!

then I can put on my clothes
I guess, and walk the streets.
(CP 201)

This kind of theatrical "I" undergoing larger-than-life crises is certainly one of the features that would have attracted O'Hara to Mayakovsky's writing. The odd status of Mayakovsky's biography within his writing is well described by Svetlana Boym, who claims that "Mayakovsky wished to motivate his life poetically, presenting it as a series of metaphorical knots in a single design, creating a biography in which each everyday occurrence is written as something significant and signifying" (142). For both O'Hara and Mayakovsky, these knots often create slippage between life and text and among versions of the self. Such a theatrical crisis of the self is precisely what O'Hara's "Mayakovsky" stages, its last section containing these lines — "Now I am quietly waiting for / the catastrophe of my personality / to seem beautiful again, / and interesting, and modern" (CP 202) — and concluding with these: "It may be the coldest day of / the year, what does he think of / that? I mean, what do I? And if I do, / perhaps I am myself again" (ibid.).

But the most important entrance of Mayakovsky's name into O'Hara's poetry is certainly in the dedication of the 1953 "Second Avenue," which occurs over a previous, cancelled dedication to Willem de Kooning. Why did O'Hara cancel the de Kooning dedication, and think of Mayakovsky as a substitute? What do the two have in common? One central point of reference in this tangle of questions is Robert Rauschenberg's now-famous *Erased de Kooning Drawing* (of the same year), which critics usually read as an initiatory gesture for the young artist. For Rauschenberg, erasing de Kooning represents another of the many literalizations in his career: a struggle with — an attempt to "erase" — a dominant precedent becomes an actual erasure. Rauschenberg materializes the language in which art criticism occurs such that his "work" consists of making de Kooning "invisible."[18] Like Rauschenberg's, O'Hara's erasure does not represent a simple negation of de Kooning, who remains a central figure for both Rauschenberg and O'Hara. De Kooning in 1953 was at the pinnacle of his success — the most cosmopolitan representative of the then-ascendant abstract expressionism. Sociable and articulate, de Kooning — unlike Pollock — was also not homophobic.[19] In fact, each act of erasure carefully *preserves* de Kooning: for Rauschenberg, in the authority of the more-established artist's name, which becomes a function of Rauschenberg's work; for O'Hara, in his "[Notes on *Second Avenue*]," written several years later, in which he both compares de Kooning and Mayakovsky as inspirations and identifies part of the poem as "a little description of a de Kooning WOMAN which I'd seen recently at his studio" (CP 497):[20] "Where Mayakovsky and de Kooning come in, is that they both have done works as big as cities where the life in the work is autonomous (not about actual city life) and yet similar: Mayakovsky: 'Lenin,' '150,000,000,' 'Eiffel Tower,' etc.; de Kooning: 'Asheville,' 'Excavation,' 'Gansevoort Street,' etc." (CP 497). O'Hara thus links Mayakovsky and de Kooning through enormous, ambitious scale and a renunciation of strict mimesis for different forms of "autonomous" enactment — a kind of life (inside art) that is not purely dependent on empirical life.[21] While I will discuss O'Hara's relation to de Kooning and Rauschenberg in chapters 5 and 6, I want to stress here the use O'Hara makes of Mayakovsky as a writer of epic, urban work full of complex enactments. Part of this enactment comes from the odd nature of Mayakovsky's apostrophes. Perhaps *the* poet of the new urban center, of the antipastoral in early-twentieth-century European poetry, Mayakovsky's frequent apostrophes to massive inanimate entities (Moscow, the sun, etc.) threatricalize and dramatize the "I," tending to work paradoxically both toward allegories of revolutionary power and toward denaturalizing poetic language.[22] In "An Amazing Adventure of Vladimir Mayakovsky," for instance, an apostrophe to the sun causes the sun to come down and have tea with the speaker. This moment is, first, an allegory for the would-be unlimited powers of enactment within a revolutionary language at work changing the world. At the same time, apostrophes generally—and especially an apostrophe like " 'Get down, you loafer!' / to the sun / I yelled with all my might" (*Selected Verse* 80)—tend to highlight the rhetorical, conventional aspects of poetic language.[23] Here as elsewhere, Mayakovsky denaturalizes verse language, showing its rhetorical seams, deploying it for quotidian, clearly "interested," purposes.[24] Picking up on this foregrounding of rhetoric, Viktor Shklovsky, the great theorist of estrangement, suggests that Mayakovsky's writing produces a joltingly active readerly experience: "Mayakovsky's images . . . make noise, shift levels. His metaphors are contradictory, and the currents of his poetry are of differing temperatures" (89). Apostrophe's scale elisions are part of Mayakovsky's wider technique of expanding subjectivity.[25] "Excessive personification and depersonalization become closely interwoven," Svetlana Boym argues, "and the poet's self-metaphorizing 'I' turns into a discontinuous series of personae, in which it is impossible to distinguish between mask and face, cloth and skin" (143). In "The Cloud in Trousers," Mayakovsky writes, "I feel / my 'I' / is much too small for me. / Stubbornly a body pushes out of me" (*Selected Verse* 71).[26]

Still, Mayakovsky carefully controls the erotic economy called into play by such scale shifts. Consider his "Paris (Chatting with the Eiffel Tower)," which, as I mentioned before, O'Hara cites as an inspiration:[27]

I await the appointed hour
when,
dodging the cops,
through thick
fog
comes the Eiffel Tower
to meet me,
a Bolshevik,
"They'll spot you,
psst,
don't shuffle so!"
The guillotine-moon breeds fear.

"Now listen
to me!"
(On tiptoe
I whisper
in her
radio ear)
"I've been busy
propagandizing.
Every building is with us,
But we
need you!
Will you head the uprising?
We'll vote you leader
if you agree.
Such a fine piece of engineering
rotting here
in Apollinaire moods!
Not for you
is the Paris
of bleary
bards,
stockbrokers,
Moulin Rouge nudes."
(*Selected Verse* 87–88)

In this revolutionary tryst with the Eiffel Tower, the speaker seeks to co-opt the symbol of French national subjectivity. The tower, of course, comes to the poet. As leader of the material world of Paris, the Eiffel Tower is the necessary, inevitable figurehead of the revolution in which the material objects of daily life — bridges, subways, buildings — will take the lead. The tower must leave Paris not merely because of French "stockbrokers" but, more specifically, because Parisian lifestyle suffers from an Apollinairean decadence that seems to Mayakovsky the antithesis to the tower's clean, rational basis in the world of technology and engineering — the world of production.[28]

In "How to Make Verse," Mayakovsky claims that "Our chief and unrelenting hatred comes crashing down on the sentimental-critical philistines: on those who see the greatness of poetry of the past in the fact that they, too, have loved, as Onegin loved Tatyana (souls in harmony!), because they too have an understanding of the poets (they learned them at school!), because iambics caress their ears. We abhor this foolish pandemonium because it creates around the difficult and important craft of poetry an atmosphere of sexual transport and swooning" (18). Though Mayakovsky powerfully attacks the logic involved in using identification as a source of authenticity, in the second part of the passage he relies on the strange, puritanical suggestion that the erotics of reading will subvert or sap revolutionary energy.[29] For New York School poets, precisely what poetry's relation to an erotic economy might be was a central question. Many actively revised the models of desire encoded in the modernist writers by whom they were otherwise most influenced. O'Hara's revisions of Apollinaire are, as I argued in chapter 2, a case in point. And it is this kind of revision — now of Mayakovsky's apostrophe poems — that I suggest we hear in a number of O'Hara's poems.

O'Hara's "A True Account of Talking to the Sun at Fire Island" is at once a self-conscious construction of genealogical links to Mayakovsky and a seemingly passive repetition of the previous poet's work.

> The sun woke me this morning loud
> and clear, saying "Hey! I've been
> trying to wake you up for fifteen
> minutes. Don't be so rude, you are
> only the second poet I've ever chosen
> to speak to personally
>
>   so why
> aren't you more attentive? If I could
> burn you through the window I would
> to wake you up. I can't hang around
> here all day."
>
>   "Sorry, Sun, I stayed
> up late last night talking to Hal."
>
> "When I woke up Mayakovsky he was
> a lot more prompt"
> (CP 306)

Though critics have often read stagy passivity and potentially mocking repetition — in Warhol's *Piss Painting*, Rauschenberg's *Factum* series, and Johns's *In Memory of My Feelings (Frank O'Hara)* — as a codedly queer mode of postmodern appropriation, the level at which such gestures enact a politics remains unclear: if we take a critique of *a priori* heterosexual agency as a point of departure, do the micropolitics of gender ever merge with the macropolitics of nationalism or class?[30] In O'Hara's case, in fact, sleeping late — not being "prompt" — might be taken to pun, self-mockingly, on the less dramatic political and historical situation in which O'Hara might be awakened for action — the American 1950s. Still, if Mayakovsky's poetry plays a very different social function, O'Hara's repetition should be understood not simply as a farce.[31] Not only do Mayakovsky's borrowed techniques mean something different in the America of the 1950s, not only does their simple appearance — like the appearance of Mayakovsky's proper name — suggest a more international, politically self-conscious model of poetry than was operative in 1952, but, on top of this, O'Hara manages to combine his reading of theatrical subjectivity with a move toward a less restricted economy of desire.[32]

Many of these questions come together in O'Hara's "Commercial Variations" — a poem that, apostrophizing New York City, provides a thumbnail sketch of the rise of abstract expressionism within a still-hostile, provincial context. All of this occurs, moreover, within a campy celebration of a queer, decadent New York that has just begun to admire the virility of gestural abstraction. The poem begins:

> "When you're ready to sell your diamonds
> it's time to go to the Empire State Building"
> and jump into the 30s like they did in 1929.
> Those were desperate days too, but I'd no more
> give up our silver mine, Belle, just because gold
> has become the world standard look, than all
> your grey hairs, beloved New York from whence
> all the loathsome sirens don't call. They would like
> to take you away from me wouldn't they? now that the fever's
> got me and there're rumors of a Rush in California
> and pine fields in Massachusetts as yet unindustrialized.
> (CP 85)

From the perspective of New York (the center of a triumphant America in 1952), selling its diamonds — at once currency and display — exchanging the most glamorous form of its wealth for a conventional one, would be like jumping backward, in a gesture that mimics the suicide leaps of broken stock-market investors of 1929 into the depressed 1930s. Pictured as a desperate, rich, and allegorical character in need of a wise confidant, what makes New York a candidate for a dramatic suicide is an anxiety about the source of its wealth; the apostropher must reassure the city that its fallen origins — a “silver mine” when “gold / has become the world's standard look” — are an asset rather than a liability. The United States's abandonment of the gold standard as a response to the Depression in 1933 here becomes an occasion to celebrate the more contingent, less naturalized value of silver, which is in turn used as a figure for New York's situation as a kind of parvenu cultural capital after World War II. This is the reason that the strutting bosses of Tammany's political machinery of the 1890s, who operated “before one hated to seem too cocky or too ritzy” can, later in the poem, be understood as correctives to New York's current anxiety.

This plea for power to display itself theatrically rather than rationalize or authenticate its origins, as well as this technique of collapsing the level of the subject onto that of the city or nation, are both echoed throughout O'Hara's other writings on American art in the 1950s. In “Commercial Variations,” this collapse occurs not merely through a scale-bending apostrophe but more specifically through O'Hara's superimposition of an autobiographical scene of adolescent gay sexuality onto the drama of New York.

> Belle of Old New York
> your desperation will never open in *La Forza del Destino*
> which was my father's favorite opera when he tried to jump
> out a window on New Year's Eve in 1940, thirty days
> before I ditched the stable boy who gave me the diamonds
> I'm turning in today for a little freedom to travel.
> (CP 86–87)

The poem's last lines build a complex set of links among selling diamonds, New York's potential jump from the Empire State Building, O'Hara's father's attempted suicide in 1940, and a “stable boy who gave me the diamonds.” The narrative of sex with a stable boy is an out gay intertext — “no *sasha* mine, / and an adolescent taken in hay / above horses” (CP 322) — running among many of O'Hara's poems.[33] Not merely a matter of personal iconography, the narrative works in this context to appropriate the city's significance at the level of the subject. As the city pines for an authentic, secure narrative of its formation, the subject takes this search up at its own scale by projecting a defining sexual moment that becomes a kind of mock-pastoral past.

But throughout the poem the theatricality of such projections tends to undercut their would-be pathos. Terms associated with opera and ballet (The Metropolitan Opera Company, *Carmen*, *William Tell*, *Erwartung*, *La*

Forza del Destino and Zinka Milanov) create a thematics of theatricality and campy excess organized around a queer New York, called in the first stanza "Sodom-on-Hudson."[34] Opera terms and New York icons — the Empire State Building, the Museum of Modern Art — set New York against the rest of the country not merely by virtue of its elevated culture, but more specifically through the gendered origins of its wealth. Clearing pine forests in unindustrialized Massachusetts and getting rich quickly in the California Gold Rush evoke historical mythologies of American wealth — masculinized, produced through hard labor — to which an effeminate New York, an heiress to a silver mine, no longer has access. This campy subtext emerges again as New York becomes Belle, with whom the confidant/speaker carries on a Hollywood exchange: "They would like / to take you away from me wouldn't they?" Still, the tonal shifts and the disruptive work of names operate in tandem with a serious inquiry into the nature of New York's new power.

As the poem continues, O'Hara seems to sketch a humorous contrast between the generally low level of art-historical knowledge in America and the particular ambitions of recent abstract New York painting. But just which aesthetic position is truly unhistorical and vulgar, and whether these terms are simple pejoratives, gets complicated in what follows.

> As the glassy fencing of sunrise in a fish market
> cries out its Americanism and jingoes and jolts daily
> over the icebergs of our historically wispy possum-drowsy
> lack of antiquity, we know that art must be vulgar to say
> "Never may the dame claim to be warm to the exact,
> nor the suburban community amount to anything in any way
> that is not a pursuit of the purple vices artsy-craftsy,
> the loom in the sitting room where reading is only aloud
> and illustrative of campfire meetings beside the Out Doors
> where everyone feels as ill at ease as sea-food."
> (CP 86)

We seem to begin in a kitsch genre painting — an Americana depiction of fish markets that Barnett Newman or Clement Greenberg would describe as "buckeye."[35] Here the quotidian sunrises do not melt the "icebergs of our historically wispy possum-drowsy / lack of antiquity." That is, though such painting is concerned with the temporality of daily conditions, its own representational mode engages history neither retrospectively (perhaps, implicitly, an impossibility in America) nor by situating itself as work that could have been done only in the present, only as a product of modernism. It is from within this tableau that "art" must make its short speech. Prefaced by "we know that art must be vulgar to say," this section turns slippery insofar as what is vulgar is not simply this degraded Americana context from which a more ambitious art must emerge. Instead, it is in part the quality and perhaps the force of negation necessary for some other form of art to emerge.[36] The first line of this impacted manifesto, then, is accordingly delivered in the tone of a hood for whom the artistic muse has become a dame gone cold to the "exact," the verisimilitude, perhaps, of the sentimental realism depicted above. The familiar history of abstract expressionism would have it that only the "buckeye" hickdom in which this passage begins is truly vulgar.[37] When O'Hara suggests that, on the contrary, such vulgarity *persists* in serious art, he seems to be anticipating T. J. Clark's recent suggestion that we understand abstract expressionism above all as vulgar.

But the fit is not that exact. Though both O'Hara and Clark understand *freedom* as a deeply implicated term, this leads to different understandings of vulgarity. For O'Hara, vulgarity is less a matter of an ascendant bourgeoisie achieving its own version of interiority in art (though it *is* this to an extent) than a spectacle of subjectivity (usually masculine) inventing and reinventing itself, gesturally, within a Hollywood set that projects a kitschy existential ambience. O'Hara's readings of Pollock and de Kooning, as we will see in chapter 5, revel in the excessive, melodramatic qualities of a masculine subjectivity pushing the limits of its "freedom." But that abstract expressionism merges with Hollywood fantasies is not, in O'Hara, simply a reason to dismiss the painting (and clearly, for Clark vulgarity is not a reason to dismiss abstract expressionism either): it is, instead, a way of allowing for self-consciousness, internal distanciation, and also a queer appropriation of masculine gesture within what otherwise appears (and has appeared throughout the history of writing on abstract expressionism) a smothering rhetoric of earnest, heterosexual angst. This, at least, is O'Hara's most extreme account of abstract expressionism, quite distinct from the one he cultivated as a more mild-mannered MoMA docent in his catalog essays.

Still, what is extreme about "Commercial Variations" is less any precise description of abstract expressionist practices and effects (this will come soon after in the next years) than a picture of the cultural conditions in which the painting makes its rise — a picture of the America of 1952, able to mint its own silver and eager to justify the authority of this currency through available American mythologies. This is why O'Hara imagines a moment in which potential threats available through reading are managed or co-opted by paternal education: "reading is only aloud / and illustrative of campfire meetings beside the Out Doors." Reading becomes a specifically illustrative (rather than a speculative) project, ideologically transmitting myths about the American "Out Doors." Folding this moment back into the first stanza, one might guess that what gets read by Father is not just the rule of a normative Nature (at odds with "Sodom-on-Hudson") but also mythic accounts of clearing forests and enduring the harshness of the West to profit from the natural riches of gold — narratives that justify and naturalize American wealth. Clearly O'Hara seeks to resist this kind of justification. But in constructing an account of how New York stole the idea of modern art from Paris, he also resists Serge Guilbaut's indignation at this "theft." To do so he stages instead the emergence of internationally acknowledged abstract painting in a triumphant post–WWII America and in New York's access to new cultural currency that it has the power to mint in its own "silver mine." O'Hara suggests, moreover, that we read this painting (preliminarily at least, at this moment of its emergence in 1952) not as a sublimated cultural achievement but as a messy, bumptious, and theatrical assertion of values whose status as art cannot be understood apart from its negation of an ignorant and incredibly powerful suburban cultural ideology that could easily swallow it up. ("You cannot know the Prussian lather of the suburbs" [CP 113], he had apostrophized to Boris Pasternak.)

But even this cynical account, the poem acknowledges, becomes a kind of interested history in itself: as the poem's alternative title ("V. on a Radio Commercial") suggests, any poem documenting the rise of American painting could itself be understood as a "Radio Commercial" or even a "Commercial Variation." O'Hara writes from within a cultural and historical situation, his titles imply, that tends to fold his own account back, symptomatically, into the moment it would profess to report upon. If "Commercial Variations" is, in O'Hara's own playful way, a self-conscious enactment of the interestedness of historical writing (especially that done by the victors), it is also an odd revision of the social functions of apostrophes to cities or countries O'Hara seems to associate with the Mayakovsky of the 1920s. Rather than call out for self-sacrifice and moral self-regulation, O'Hara doubles back, I think consciously, on this early moment of modernist subject production and torques it in almost the opposite direction. In the New York of 1952 it is only a turn toward the theatrical groundlessness of "Sodom-on-Hudson" — a culture of performance and unregulated desire — that can disrupt the naturalizing myths of American legitimacy and justification generated by the suburban hegemonic culture of the great "Out Doors." Of eroticism entering the space of reading, Mayakovsky had said, to repeat, "We abhor this foolish pandemonium because it creates around the difficult and important craft of poetry an atmosphere of sexual transport and swooning." By 1952, New Criticism had produced an American mythology of the "difficult and important craft of poetry" that was abhorrent to O'Hara and Ashbery. More important — though O'Hara would certainly not consciously distance himself from Mayakovsky's high ambitions — in the America of 1952, "foolish pandemonium" and "sexual transport and swooning" came to seem workable (or perhaps simply the only available) strategies of resistance. And it was in these same terms, very often, that O'Hara would come to understand the cultural achievements of abstract expressionism.

During a poetry reading of several New York and Beat poets, a drunken, homophobic Jack Kerouac began heckling O'Hara: "You're ruining American poetry." This is the macho "yatter" LeRoi Jones/Amiri Baraka contrasted with O'Hara's "grace." If graceful, O'Hara's response, according to Brad Gooch, is anything but kind: "[T]hat's more than you've ever done for it" (G 322–24). To take O'Hara's comment seriously — to imagine that he is *right* — would be to accept not only poetry's need for a new relation to and model of desire (not found in Kerouac) but also to see O'Hara's deformations at the level of the writing subject as part of this necessary "ruining" — a ruining that here extends to straight accounts of abstract expressionism and disinterested historiography. As O'Hara writes, "I know what I love / and know what must be trodden under foot to be vindicated / and glorified and praised: Belle of Old New York" (CP 86).

In the terms provided by "Commercial Variations," ruining or treading under would not simply be a matter of negating jingoistic art and paternal education in order to celebrate a secure subject of gay identity politics. Instead, these thematic levels are inextricably bound to destablilizations both of poetic subjectivity's normative scale — lyricism — and of an art history based on disinterested historical documentation. Describing his authorial relation to Manhattan in writing his now-famous "retrospective manifesto of manhattanism," *Delirious New York*, Rem Koolhaas also happens to peg O'Hara's ambition in "Commercial Variations": "Movie stars who have led adventure-packed lives are often too egocentric to discover patterns, too inarticulate to express intentions, too restless to record or remember events. Ghostwriters do it for them. In the same way *I was Manhattan's ghostwriter*" (11).

• • •

If in the early 1950s the mention of Mayakovsky called to mind the Russia of the 1920s, by the late 1950s the mention of Pasternak might have evoked the contemporary American Right. In his 1959 poem "For Bob Rauschenberg," O'Hara mentions in passing, "I despise my love for Pasternak" (*CP* 322). The reason to despise such a love, or at least to question its basis — as O'Hara did — was the reception that *Doctor Zhivago* was getting in the United States and in the West generally. O'Hara's 1959 essay "About Zhivago and His Poems" is a response to this reception. But before taking up the essay, I must first sketch how the idea of "Pasternak" achieved a utility for Western Cold War rhetoric. To do this I want to consider an instance of how the Soviet Union was mapped by the West that will illuminate both *Doctor Zhivago's* reception history and, more specifically, why and how Pasternak's biography suddenly became important in the late 1950s.

When the Nazis rolled into Russia in 1941, the disorganized Russians in the town of Smolensk were not able to destroy their suburban archive. Fifty files comprising about two hundred thousand pages were taken back to Germany. Ultimately, after the United States gained control of the archive in the aftermath of World War II, it was the Americans of the 1950s for whom these documents held the most fascination and importance. In 1958 Merle Fainsod, commissioned by the Rand Corporation, published a report on the archive, *Smolensk under Soviet Rule*. This report, introducing many previously unknown details of quotidian life in Soviet Russia, presented a sociological analog to the "revelation" that Pasternak's *Doctor Zhivago* was thought to have given the literary world.[38] In Fainsod's words, "To immerse oneself in the story of Smolensk is to capture the 'feel' and texture of Soviet life — the constant pressure from the center for ever greater production and the difficulty of transmitting this pressure down to the grass roots; the struggle of ordinary people to survive at the barest margin of subsistence" (13). Though America in the 1950s witnessed the publication of numerous books on Soviet politics, economics, and social life, the singularity of Fainsod's account is how its "evidence" replicates a realist literary structure: oppression becomes palpable by being grounded in mundane, quotidian experience.

The immersion in Smolensk that Fainsod offers is available, of course, only through the proxy of the narrator, who becomes the selector of specific themes, such as "the struggle of ordinary people." As a reader of individual desires through documents, as a collator of these desires into larger trends and attitudes, the narrator can ventriloquize an omniscient voice of generalized wisdom. This wisdom's larger frame of reference is, perhaps predictably, that of a representative American, a supposedly free voice speaking from a country without ideology about a country in which there is no escape from ideology. "Much of what the Archive contains," Fainsod continues, "is not unknown to us on the basis of scattered reports and reminiscences of former Soviet citizens who have fled their native land. But the difficulty of verifying the testimony of refugees has led many cautious scholars to treat their stories with circumspection and to ask for supporting documentary evidence which most refugees were in no position to supply. Not the least of the values of the Archive is that it provides such documentation on an unparalleled scale" (ibid.).

Whereas the Smolensk archive ties testimony to the dream of unequivocal documentary evidence, *Doctor Zhivago* links testimony to literary reputation, to the name. Pasternak's international status constructs him as one of those refugees who, though also lacking documentary evidence, can nonetheless be trusted. Like *Doctor Zhivago*, Fainsod's *Smolensk under Soviet Rule* also had thc appeal of being wrested violently from a Soviet Union that wanted to control its own self-representation. In both cases — at least in the Right's (and the disillusioned Left's) reading of Pasternak — the subject is the human toll that must inevitably accompany Communism, what Fainsod calls "the tension of living in a society in which human beings were means and not ends" (13). For Fainsod, there is little difference between the Russia of the 1920s and the Russia of the 1950s. The New Economic Policy (1921–1928) becomes merely the precursor to an inevitable Stalin. This attempt to link Communism inevitably to Stalinist oppression is the underlying task, the rhetorical struggle, of the text — the reason, also, that the unit of significance must be the individual, whose autonomy and experience is inevitably disturbed under attempts at radical collectivity.

Pasternak as individual, as a tragic biography, was an important theme in his reception history. In 1959, for instance, the German author Gerd Ruge published *Pasternak: A Pictorial Biography*. Working backward from Pasternak's having won the Nobel Prize, the book constructs a "man of culture" within what we are supposed to assume is an otherwise largely barren postrevolutionary Russia. Ruge therefore stresses Pasternak's ties

Uncredited photograph of Boris Pasternak.

Uncredited photograph of Boris Pasternak.

to prerevolutionary culture in Odessa, to the production of painting, music, and literature now impossible in the city (8). Combining drawings of Rilke, Tolstoy, Rachmaninoff, and Scriabin done by Leonid Pasternak, the writer's father, with photographs of Boris Pasternak, the text also works to humanize the author — to tie his writing to a tactile, enticing image-repertoire. The dramatic profile of Pasternak's head now becomes a symbol of his tragic recalcitrance. Because readers in the West have so little information about writers in the Soviet Union, it seems crucial that Pasternak come alive to his Western audience — that he be dissociated from Soviet ideological apparatuses and models of collective subjectivity — and be represented not as a Soviet but as a "human."[39]

The assumption that all literature was dead, merely propaganda, in the Soviet Union between the Revolution and the publication of *Doctor Zhivago* is another important subtext in Pasternak's reception. The very issue of the *Evergreen Review* in which O'Hara's essay appears begins with a full-page ad for *Doctor Zhivago* with a black-and-white photograph of the distinguished-looking author. In the ad, Ernest Simmons claims that the novel "at last revives the noble tradition of the Russian past that literature is the conscience of the nation." Another critic writes that "the Soviet Union's greatest poet dares to tell the truth about life in that country over the past 50 years."[40] Such sweeping claims allow critics to avoid the more difficult issue of how so much experimental literature — in the 1920s especially — managed to affirm the Revolution in ways that did not reduce the problem of reality. Mayakovsky, Shklovsky, Khlebnikov, Esenin, and the early Pasternak, therefore, are *not* the real conscience of the nation. Pasternak's less experimental and more explicitly critical work is figured, then, in terms of a return to a vital but suppressed tradition.[41] Obviously, suppression was an all-too-real fact under Stalin (who died in 1953) and well after. But Pasternak's reception nonetheless demonstrates how the starker fact of Stalinist literary politics could be remotivated to gloss over the more complicated problem of understanding the early period of post-Revolutionary literature — the Soviet writing from the early 1920s that was at once formally inventive and socially radical.

O'Hara's immediate response to the fact that Pasternak had been awarded but would probably not be able to accept the Nobel Prize was to cable the Soviet author.[42] In a sense, this gesture simply literalizes the work that proper names often perform in O'Hara's poems. Kenneth Koch writes of the cable that "Frank felt it was very important that we not only applaud [Pasternak's] getting the prize but that we let him know that there were

Hailed internationally as a great work of art and as *the* literary event of 1958, this is the celebrated novel whose publication was forbidden in Russia.

Doctor Zhivago

By BORIS PASTERNAK

In *Doctor Zhivago*, a book crowded with scenes and with people of unforgettable impact, the Soviet Union's greatest poet dares to tell the truth about life in that country over the past 50 years. "Anyone looking for adventures, the interweaving of plots, the imprint of historical events will find all these in this novel. It is a book born out of the depths of pain and love, nourished at the very roots of human liberty. And the presage of freedom on which it majestically ends is only its final harmony."
—NICOLA CHIAROMONTE, *Partisan Review*

"One of the major works of this century."
— BABETTE DEUTSCH

"In the grand old manner, a literary event is once again a political event, a social event, and a source of pride in man's creativity." — ALFRED KAZIN

"A composite, powerful book with few parallels in modern European literature — an historical novel in the sense that Tolstoy's *War and Peace* is one."
— ALBERTO MORAVIA

"At last revives the noble tradition of the Russian past that literature is the conscience of the nation." — ERNEST J. SIMMONS

$5.00, now at your bookstore
PANTHEON

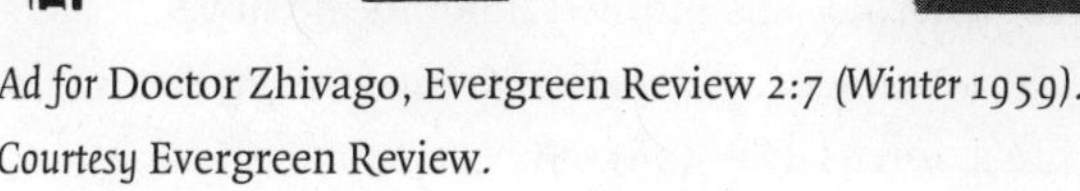

Ad for Doctor Zhivago, Evergreen Review 2:7 (Winter 1959).
Courtesy Evergreen Review.

poets in America who loved his early work, not just *Doctor Zhivago*. . . . We sent it off and I felt like an angel or like an airplane. I felt that life was much bigger. Frank did that all the time for everybody. . . . It was before any poet we knew except Allen Ginsberg was interested in real politics" (G 316). Koch's figures of an angel and an airplane articulate wonder at this gesture's ability to transcend and then redescribe space, to make life bigger. For Koch, moreover, this redescription pushes poetry into what is for him a new zone of real politics. But if the cable asserted an international connection among writers, the terms of this connection demanded more precise definition. As the West argued about how to place *Doctor Zhivago* in a history of the Soviet Union's self-representation, in his winter 1959 article in *Evergreen Review*, O'Hara praised Pasternak in order to *keep* him in the revolutionary tradition of Mayakovsky. Engaging negative response from the Left in France, O'Hara claimed, "I cannot agree with Elsa Triolet when she recently attacked Pasternak for having betrayed Mayakovsky in writing *Dr. Zhivago*" (CP 502). Instead, following Pasternak's own writing on Mayakovsky, O'Hara suggests that Mayakovsky's Romantic concept of poetic subjectivity works toward a questionable atomism and independence from intersubjective experience. Noting that Pasternak has defined the Romantic model as a poet who "imagines himself the measure of life and pays for this with his life" (CP 503), O'Hara claims that "outside the legend, the Romantic scheme is false. The poet who is its foundation, is inconceivable without the nonpoets who must bring him into relief, because this poet is not a living personality absorbed in the study of moral knowledge, but a visual-biographical 'emblem,' demanding a background to make his contours visible" (ibid.).

For Pasternak and O'Hara, while subjectivity in Mayakovsky may shift scales disruptively, it remains essentially atomistic: the fragmentation to which Shklovsky alludes would be not so much intersubjective as entropic or explosive. This atomism keeps subjectivity from being fully historical, from being affected by others. The process of becoming historical, of enacting influence intersubjectively, is for O'Hara central to *Doctor Zhivago*: "In the post-epilogue book of poems we find that Zhivago has not written the poems he wanted to, nor the poems we expected. . . . in the course of creating the poems he has become not the mirror of the life we know, but the instrument of its perceptions, hitherto veiled. This is the major expression of meaning which Pasternak has implied often in the novel proper. The human individual is the subject of historical events, not vice versa; he is the repository of life's force" (CP 506). Such an enactment allows

O'Hara to value the obligation that Pasternak argues a poet must have toward the potentially transformative events of life. For Pasternak, writing's relation to such transformations, like its relation to politics, is not something one simply chooses a priori. A poet's subjectivity is produced historically: "events require his participation to occur" (CP 507). According to O'Hara, Pasternak's stance is "not at all a counterrevolutionary attitude based on an intellectual-aristocratic system. It has not to do with a predilection for 'culture.' The lesson comes from life" (CP 501). And this lesson is not simply one of the failed revolution: "[I]f Pasternak is saying that the 1917 Revolution failed, he must feel that the West never even made an attempt" (ibid.). Pasternak's work suggests a reconceptualization of social life not simply from the position of capitalism's inevitability.

At the same time — in this essay, in his poems, and in his art essays — O'Hara demonstrates an awareness of how quickly and easily a discourse of the supposedly objective realities of life can blur into one of "freedom" and become an ideological tool. If *Doctor Zhivago* enacts a process of historical imprinting of subjectivity by having Zhivago's poems turn out to be different from those he would like to have written, despite O'Hara's attempt to highlight the force of this discrepancy as a saving grace, the novel's reception is also structured on a historically inflected displacement. As the ads and blurbs suggest, Cold War politics turn the proper name *Pasternak* into a tragic plea for freedom from within the Soviet Union.

In its very attempt to complicate this process, O'Hara's own essay must struggle against a similar appropriation. As it appears in *Evergreen Review*, opposite its last page is a cartoon depicting Castro in a hammock whose posts are gagged and bound military officers.[43] This caricatured lack of freedom, which works toward American nationalistic ends, provides — through proximity — a kind of false summary of O'Hara's article, of his take on Pasternak.

It is because, as the above examples suggest, one can lose a struggle to appropriate the semantic backing of a proper name that O'Hara can write to Joan Mitchell, in his 1958 poem "Far from the Porte des Lilas and the Rue Pergolèse," of the "danger of being Pasternakesque" (CP 311).[44] I will take up this poem in the context of O'Hara's poetry to painters in chapter 5; here I want to emphasize merely the fact that O'Hara links the problem of being Pasternakesque — the problem, by fall 1958, of having one's pleas for freedom appropriated by Cold War rhetorical systems — with the difficulty of situating abstract painting within a single or binding interpretive framework. Because of the political utility of the concept of freedom, Pasternak's

Political cartoon opposite the last page of O'Hara's "About Zhivago and His Poems," Evergreen Review *2:7 (Winter 1959). Courtesy* Evergreen Review.

co-option casts a shadow across both Mitchell's and O'Hara's attempts to create and value spontaneous action. And yet this poem ends with movement between continents, just as "Commercial Variations" ends with the city/speaker "turning in" diamonds "for a little freedom to travel" (*CP* 87).

It's unclear, of course, just how far literal freedom of movement might stand in for the larger metaphysical freedom that is the burden of the writing and painting under consideration. What is clearer, generally, is that freedom in O'Hara becomes a highly self-conscious and theatrical proposition. If O'Hara proposes a wider concept of sexual freedom than was possible for Mayakovsky (or Apollinaire or Breton), he is also suspicious of just how subversive this expanded economy of desire might be within the America of the 1950s. As "Commercial Variations" suggests, rallying around an expanded concept of theatrical desire holds promise not as a revolutionary strategy, nor as the first stage in the struggle for total freedom, but, more humbly, as a tactic for disrupting myths of a wholesome, homogeneous, heterosexual America justified in its post–WWII world domination and happy to be striking out onto its own fledgling examples of high, serious art. It is also in this context of challenging a neat picture of American art and culture in 1952 that I have suggested we read O'Hara's dialog with Mayakovsky and Pasternak. Whereas in many O'Hara poems the problems of reference and audience arise from the proper names of a set of intimate friends, O'Hara's dialog with Russian authors represents the other extreme of his odd effect of anatomizing the audience structures in which his work might possibly traffic. The term *coterie* might seem to make little sense at this scale and with these authors — personally unknown to O'Hara. Still, the "intimacy" O'Hara appropriates with the ideas of Mayakovsky and Pasternak (through sustained and heated reference), as well as the social implications of this intimacy, can be taken to link this strange phenomenon to the larger problems I have been analyzing under the rubric of coterie.[45]

The names Pasternak and Mayakovsky seem to project out from O'Hara's poems, asking to be related to Joe and Bunny and Kenneth Koch but also offering no easy means for such a connection. Though the same could be said for names of the dead or the spatially remote in O'Hara, the problem is obviously more intense in the case of Pasternak, frozen on the other side of the Cold War, alienated from the country he had committed to staying in after the Revolution. To tie Pasternak back to Mayakovsky and to give both of them important positions within his writing of the 1950s was, for O'Hara, a way to imagine a form of dialog with Russian modernism that would at once expand its possibilities and not contain its social implications into a neat, speaker-oriented atomism. As the examples of Mayakovsky and Pasternak suggest, O'Hara's poetry makes consistent and conspicuous use of the proper name as a way to map what one might think of as the social syntaxes by which names are grouped together or separated, weighed, judged, and circulated in everyday usage.

• • •

As one of this chapter's epigraphs indicated, Allen Ginsberg learned about Mayakvosky from Frank O'Hara. Ginsberg tells us, "I had never read any Mayakovsky, but Frank turned me on to him and I'm always indebted to him because that opened my interest in Russian poetry. . . . You see Mayakovsky wasn't printed in American, as Neruda was not printed in those days, for being commies. It was a blackout" (G 318). Like O'Hara, Ginsberg also positioned the embattled Cold War concept of freedom as a fundamental site of inquiry in his poetry and his life. Ginsberg's

Camilla McGrath, photograph of Frank O'Hara (right) and Allen Ginsberg. © Camilla McGrath.

1961 "Prose Contribution to the Cuban Revolution" is a letter written to Donald Allen from Greece and intended for Allen's forthcoming *Poetics of the New American Poetry*, a companion volume of theory to the influential *The New American Poetry* of 1960. In this letter, Ginsberg wonders if "a vast human-teeming world 'democratically' [can] regulate itself at all in future with the kind of communications mechanism this present known & used consciousness has available? How escape rigidification and stasis of consciousness when man's mind is only words and these words and their images are flashed on every brain continuously by the interconnected networks of radio television newspapers wire services speeches decrees laws telephone books manuscripts? How escape centralized control of Reality of the masses by the few who want and can take power?" (342). The letter includes accounts of recent homosexual encounters in Greece and the impending sense that the "I" will become less legible as a category; it also refers to earlier, formative mystical and drug experiences and to the equally formative context of friendship and love with Burroughs and Kerouac that shaped Ginsberg's poetry (by 1961 the three were a kind of coterie of Beat heroes). But most important, Ginsberg's letter, simply by *being* a letter and offering this explicitly personal account of the development of his writing, also enacts a claim about his poetics as exploring new seams between his life and his art. Like O'Hara's act of staging audience figures inside his poems, Ginsberg takes such a tactic even further by asking us to overhear his private letter in the social/literary space brought into being by the anthology. Moreover, Ginsberg explicitly frames this autobiographical sketch in a kind of challenging support of the Cuban Revolution. If the revolution is in the service of human liberation — which Ginbserg unequivocally supports — can it accept the type of subjectivity developed in Ginsberg's letter? Or will this version of revolution, as Ginsberg suspects, want to mold such a subject into a more galvanized, heterosexual, non-drug-taking, nonmystical citizen?

Paralleling the claims made by Ashbery and O'Hara about the modernism they at once loved and wanted to expand — that of Breton, Apollinaire, and Mayakovsky, all in varying degrees — Ginsberg gives this problem an immediate, contemporary face in the Cuban Revolution:

> No revolution can succeed if it continues the puritanical censorship of consciousness imposed on the world by Russia and America. Succeed in what? Succeed in liberating the masses from domination by secret Monopolists of communication.

> I'm NOT down on the Cubans or anti their revolution, it's just that it's important to make it clear *in advance, in front*, what I feel about life. Big statements saying Viva Fidel are/ would be/ meaningless and just 2-dimensional politics. (344)

Seven years later, in 1966, Ginsberg actually traveled to Cuba. As Michael Schumacher (one of Ginbserg's biographers) tells us, the poet's attention turned to Cuba's treatment of countercultural factions: "A special police group known as Lacra Social was cracking down on homosexuals and the Cuban version of beatniks, know as *los infermos* ('the sick'). People in the arts — particularly members of a local theater group — were harassed, intimidated, and called fairies."[46] As Ginsberg made connections with these communities and spoke out repeatedly against their treatment, he became an increasing annoyance to the Cuban government.

In the early 1960s, some of these qualified senses of Cold War freedom also entered Ginsberg's and O'Hara's relationship more directly. In a March 13, 1961, poem called "Vincent and I Inaugurate a Movie Theatre" (not published in O'Hara's lifetime), O'Hara's ties to Ginsberg get intertwined with the politics of Hollywood, American news services, and queer life inside theaters.

> Now that the Charles Theatre has opened
> it looks like we're going to have some wonderful times
> Allen and Peter, why are you going away
> our country's black and white past spread out
> before us is no time to spread out over India
> like last night in the busy balcony I see
> your smoky images before the smoky screen
> everyone smoking, Bogard, Bacall and her advanced sister
> and Hepburn too tense to smoke but MacMurray rich enough
> relaxed and ugly, poor Alice Adams so in-pushed and out
> in the clear exposition of AP American or Associated
> Paranoia and Allen and I getting depressed and angry
> becoming again the male version of wallflower or wallpaper
> (CP 399–400)

For O'Hara, Hollywood seems to provide the occasion for analyzing the production of consciousness in the United States — an analysis Ginsberg seeks, at least in part, through the idea of a retreat to other cultures, like India. Here, Alice Adams's limited subject position (in an unidentified

Plate 1. *Grace Hartigan,* Masquerade, *1954; oil on canvas, 81 x 86 in. Art Institute of Chicago. Photo © Art Institute of Chicago. © Grace Hartigan.*

Plate 2. Jackson Pollock, Autumn Rhythm: Number 30, 1950; *oil on canvas*, 105 x 207 in.
Metropolitan Museum of Art, New York, George A. Hearn Fund, 1957.
Photo © 1998 Metropolitan Museum of Art.

Plate 3. Willem de Kooning, Rosy-Fingered Dawn at Louse Point, *1963; oil on canvas, 80 x 70 in. Stedelijk Museum, Amsterdam.*

Plate 4. Willem de Kooning, Easter Monday, 1955–1956; oil and newspaper transfer on canvas, 96 x 74 in. Metropolitan Museum of Art, New York, Rogers Fund, 1956.
Photo © 1983 Metropolitan Museum of Art.

Plate 5. Jackson Pollock, Number 29, 1950; *enamel, oil, aluminum paint, wire lathe mesh, string, colored glass, and pebbles on quarter-inch glass, 48 x 72 in. National Gallery of Canada, Ottawa. Photo: National Gallery of Canada, Ottawa.*

Plate 6. Robert Rauschenberg, Allegory, 1959–1960; *combine painting: oil, paper, fabric, printer paper, wood, and umbrella on three canvases and metal, sand, and glue on mirrored panel, 72 1/4 x 114 1/2 x 132 in. Museum Ludwig, Cologne, Ludwig donation.* © Robert Rauschenberg/licensed by VAGA, New York.

Plate 7. Robert Rauschenberg, Charlene, 1954; combine painting: oil, charcoal, paper, fabric, newspaper, wood, plastic, mirror, and metal on four Homosote panels, mounted on wood, with electric light, 89 x 112 x 3 1/2 in. Stedelijk Museum, Amsterdam. © Robert Rauschenberg/licensed by VAGA, New York.

Plate 8. Robert Rauschenberg, Untitled, 1954; *front and back views of combine painting: oil, pencil, crayon, paper, canvas, fabric, newspaper, photographs, wood, glass, mirror, tin, cork, and found painting, with pair of painted leather shoes, dried grass, and Plymouth Rock hen, on wood structure mounted on five casters,* 86 1/2 x 37 x 26 1/4 in.

Museum of Contemporary Art, Los Angeles, Panza Collection. Photo: Paula Goldman.

film) seems to be a direct product of "American or Associated Paranoia." And it is this predictable limitation that upsets Ginsberg and O'Hara, turning them into "the male version of wallflower or wallpaper." As the poem continues,

> Vincent points out that when anything
> good happens the movie has just flicked over to fantasy
> only fantasy in all America can be good
> because all Alice Adams wanted was a nose
> just as long as any other girl's and a dress
> just as rustly and mind just as empty so America
> could fill it with checks and flags and invitations
> (CP 400)

In fact, O'Hara consistently associated Ginsberg with the concept of fantasy — not, it seems, simply in the sense of poetic reverie or dreams, but rather fantasy in the more utopian and critical sense of what it is actually possible to imagine; and this as a spur to the conceptual and social limitations of the present — in this poem associated symptomatically with the limitations on American consciousness imposed by the engines of mainstream American culture — from Hollywood to AP. To wrest freedom from Hollywood, as O'Hara seems intent upon doing, is both to read it against the grain (as Vincent does in the poem) and to treat the theater space itself as a space of social and sexual pleasures (as O'Hara does famously in his poem "Ave Maria") — pleasures whose indulgence the films themselves often acknowledge only through the category of fantasy.[47]

O'Hara returned to these linkages among Ginsberg, film and fantasy in his 1964 poem "Fantasy" (first published in *Lunch Poems*) and "dedicated to the health of Allen Ginsberg." Written in O'Hara's late, more collagelike fashion, the poem interweaves scenes of quotidian conversation with a dyspeptic Ginsberg ("two aspirins a vitamin C tablet and some baking soda / should do the trick, that's practically an / Alka / Seltzer. Allen come out of the bathroom / and take it" [CP 488]) and a range of Hollywoodesque scenarios taken, as Jim Elledge informs us, "from the 1943 anti-Nazi romance/ adventure film *Northern Pursuit*."[48] The poem goes from "down down went the grim / grey submarine under the 'cold' ice" to "I am the only spy left / in Canada, / but just because I'm alone in the snow / doesn't necessarily mean I'm a Nazi" (CP 488). The poem's ending falsely summarizes this fragmentary internal scenario in the manner of a Hollywood conclusion.

Allen,
are you feeling any better? Yes, I'm crazy about
Helmut Dantine
but I'm glad that Canada will remain
free. Just free, that's all, never argue with the movies.
(ibid.)

5 PROXIMITY'S PLEA
O'HARA'S ART WRITING

[Jackson Pollock's #12, 1952] is a big, brassy gigolo of a painting; for the first time the aluminum paint looks like money, and the color is that of the sunset in a technicolor Western.
— *Frank O'Hara,* Jackson Pollock

democracy is joined
by stunning collapsible savages
— *Frank O'Hara, "Ode to Willem de Kooning"*

Both in critical studies, like his 1959 book *Jackson Pollock*, and in his poems, such as "Second Avenue," "Ode to Willem de Kooning," and "Far from the Porte des Lilas and the Rue Pergolèse," O'Hara's writing famously blurs the line between poetry and criticism. Rather than draw out the critical implications of these extreme characterizations of Pollock and de Kooning, however, art critics have tended to dismiss O'Hara simply for pushing criticism toward poetry. Here, in its hybrid state, such writing falls into Clement Greenberg's hated category of "pseudo poetry" (4:144) and Michael Fried's despised "'poetic' appreciation" (*Art and Objecthood* 3). That O'Hara's critical prose is poetic is certainly a more common observation than the converse claim that his poetry is critical. This is because the assertion that a form of discourse operates critically tends to draw a reasonable question about the terms of this operation, whereas the claim that writing is poetic generally does not. From either side of the equation, though, critics have been less interested in characterizing how and why poetry interacts with other disciplines in O'Hara's work and in what the terms of this interaction might be than in attacking or celebrating the very *fact* that it does.[1] Thus, for postmodern critics reacting against Greenberg and Fried, the literal merging of poetry and painting or printmaking in O'Hara's collaborations with such artists as Grace Hartigan, Larry Rivers, and Jasper Johns has been framed as a subversion of Greenberg's and Fried's pivotal late-modernist stances against interdisciplinarity. Insofar as disciplinary

Jackson Pollock, Number 12, 1952; *oil on canvas,* 101 *7/8 x* 89 *in. Private collection, New York.*

specificity becomes modernism's last rallying cry, O'Hara, because he welcomes the interaction of text and image, gets understood as proto-postmodernist. But what remains contemporary about O'Hara is less the fact of interdisciplinarity than the special functions it takes on in his work, which have everything to do with his excessive and strange descriptions of Pollock and de Kooning.

Not surprisingly, Clement Greenberg was one of the first to attack O'Hara's criticism, understanding its "pseudo poetry" in the context of

Larry Rivers, Portrait of Frank O'Hara, 1953; *oil on canvas*, 54 x 40 *in.* © *Estate of Larry Rivers/licensed by VAGA, New York.*

Harold Rosenberg's popularization of a loosely existentialist art-critical lexicon. Like Michael Fried's later attack on the "'poetic' appreciation" he took to be characteristic of the writing at *Art News*, Greenberg's objections are worth looking at more closely, I think, because tracking the two critics' efforts to separate art criticism from a category they designate and dismiss as poetry can help to reframe their attempts to articulate the goals and boundaries of modernist art criticism in the 1950s and 1960s. In proposing critical terms for abstract expressionism and delimiting interpretive frameworks for reading gestural abstraction in particular, both single out poetic criticism as the primary threat to the legibility of a modernist art-critical vocabulary. Poetry emerges, then, not merely as one among many species of interdisciplinarity threatening art criticism but as a more fundamental hybridization and consequent weakening of *writing itself*. For Greenberg and Fried, it is as if at the very moment that language needed to remain most concrete, substantial, and self-evident in order to account for abstraction in art, poetic criticism began to reveal, even to highlight, not only language's own fundamental abstraction but also a kind of basic permeability between the lexical components, the vocabularies, supposedly proper to any single discipline. In O'Hara's writing on art, this permeability of vocabularies does not mark the obliteration of reference, or the process of becoming *like* the abstract paintings under consideration, so much as the proliferation of reference. To put it another way, rather than merely mimicking abstraction, O'Hara's poems involved with painting can be read as experimental modes of *criticism* in which proliferating discursive registers operate as possible locations for imagining the effects and implications of painterly gesture. Greenberg and Fried saw this proliferation of contexts under the sign of poetry as the irresponsible negation of the basic requirement that art criticism be a rigorous vocation necessitating a specialized, limited vocabulary. By contrast, O'Hara's practice of using poetry to superimpose and inflect a broad range of interpretive contexts might be seen as an aggressively nonprofessional alternative to the narrowing range of social and cultural implication afforded by the emerging language of professional formalism. What operates critically in O'Hara's approach is his attempt to find terms for abstract expressionism's exaltation of male energy, interiority, and spontaneous wildness and the relation these values bear to post–WWII American culture more broadly.[2] The effort to consider these frequently disturbing features of abstract expressionism takes O'Hara not only into Hollywood's powerful cultural imaginary but also toward the instrumental uses that rhetorics of American freedom were beginning to have both domestically and internationally during the Cold War. In these ways, O'Hara imagined frames for abstract expressionism's evocation of wildness and spontaneity — an evocation explicitly bound to the more sinister side of America's position of world domination after World War II — which anticipate those that emerged only in the late 1960s and early 1970s with the revisionist critiques of Max Kozloff and Serge Guilbaut.[3]

But unlike Kozloff and Guilbaut, O'Hara did not dismiss abstract expressionism because of its increasingly instrumental role as one of the

American state's main advertisements for democratic freedom. Perhaps as a result, the critical components of O'Hara's poetry have not entered the discourse of 1950s art history. Instead, because of his position in MoMA's International Program during the heyday of abstract expressionism, O'Hara has been understood as an uncritical, institutionally compromised promoter — one who, in addition to writing a series of MoMA catalogs, was also close friends with several of the major abstract expressionist painters, especially de Kooning. As I mentioned earlier, Serge Guilbaut is the art critic who attacks O'Hara's politics most directly. O'Hara's uncritical praise has rendered those other critics "determined to see art in its original context and to reestablish the link between art and politics, particularly between abstract expressionism and the ideology of the Cold War . . . [isolated] voices . . . in the wilderness" (Guilbaut 9).[4] But despite O'Hara's enthusiasm for (and both his social and professional proximity to) many of the abstract expressionist painters, it is in fact his awareness of the ideological functions played by a notion of critics or painters operating in the "wilderness" that, I will argue, complicates Guilbaut's claims.

Still, this awareness emerges more actively in O'Hara's poetry than in his art criticism, which does at moments suggest the more heroic account of abstract expressionism Guilbaut distrusts. Consider, for instance, the terms of this passage on Robert Motherwell:

> [W]hile the other protesting artistic voices of the time were bound by figuration and overt symbolism, the abstract expressionists chose the open road of personal responsibility, naked nerve-ends and possible hubris, and this separated them from the surrealists, the Mexican school and the American social realists. Belief in their personal and ethical responses saved them from aestheticism on the one hand and programmatic contortion on the other. Abstract expressionism for the first time in American painting insisted upon artistic identity. This, of course, is what made abstract expressionism so threatening to other contemporaneous tendencies then, and even now. (*Robert Motherwell* 10)

In this account, "personal and ethical responses" and "artistic identity" operate independent of the larger forces of co-option. The fact that O'Hara's MoMA catalogs at times slip into this more heroic tone (as well as intimating the language of museum pluralism and universal humanism) might tempt one to claim that O'Hara was only willing to "vend astringency off-hours" (*CP* 139) in his poetry. But such a model of public complicity (in essays) and private resistance (in poetry) is ultimately misleading, both because O'Hara was a well-known and well-published poet and because the intimate, unrestrainedly enthusiastic quality of his art essays is one of their most remarked features. Certainly this was the case with O'Hara's account of Jackson Pollock, which was singled out for criticism by Greenberg. Thus the relationships in O'Hara among privacy and publicity, resistance and complicity, and poetry and prose are in fact complexly intertwined.

In O'Hara's writing, the collapsing boundaries between disciplines parallels what was perceived, to many readers' anxiety, as a collapsing erotic or social space: His "'poetic' appreciation" is frequently an intense affective response to the works of his friends and lovers. The common charge that O'Hara was a coterie poet takes on a special meaning in the context of his art writing. No longer is it a matter of a reader being confronted by the names of obscure friends or seemingly private jokes. Instead, the implication of inappropriate closeness fundamental to charges of coterie becomes a matter of lacking critical distance in relation to art; in "Second Avenue," for instance, O'Hara writes of merging erotically with painters and paintings: "I sacrifice my brilliant dryness" . . . "my elegant distinction" (*CP* 141). Even for his many friends, O'Hara's appearance as an unqualified insider in the art world is a frequent concern. "He was not an historian or a scholar," John Button writes. "Although his knowledge of art was large and his spirit larger still, in the end he had to rely more on his own fine sensibility than on professional skills" (H 42). Similarly, Waldo Rasmussen notes, "In the early years Frank was under suspicion as a gifted amateur. He didn't have the credentials of art history training or a long museum apprenticeship to support his claim to direct exhibitions. His very closeness to the artists was questioned as a danger to critical objectivity" (H 86). As Rasmussen suggests, this anxiety about accreditation was necessarily linked to questions about O'Hara's lack of distance from his subjects. "Frank's contribution in both jobs [*Art News* and MoMA] was substantial," writes Irving Sandler, continuing as follows:

> [S]uch was his taste and knowledge of art, but what was really important about his public role was that it augmented his private role, that of the friend of artists. He had the ability to focus in on someone he liked so intensely that the one could only feel like Frank's best friend — and he had the generosity to have had dozens of close attachments, as Larry Rivers said. His attention was of vital significance to artists, literally sus-

> taining them. Morton Feldman wrote that "what really matters is to have someone like Frank O'Hara standing behind you. That's what keeps you going. Without that your life in art is not worth a damn." (H 78)

As this account suggests, O'Hara's practice as a critic blurs the distinctions between participation and commentary, and, moreover, it involves a whole realm of operations and effects that would seem to escape all critical frameworks save the memoir. While it would certainly be wrong to saddle Greenberg or Fried with a naïve belief in objectivity (both are explicit on this), in O'Hara's art writing this question comes up earlier, almost as a precondition for entering the writing. Thus, to enter is also to come to grips with a kind of referential density that rapidly shifts registers and frequently seems to involve both contingent experience and intimate personal knowledge of the artists.[5]

In O'Hara, the very idea of social and professional proximity, of the overly close relationship to one's audience fundamental to charges of coterie, comes to take on several new and more disruptive senses. First of all, the affective ties of social proximity get foregrounded as a kind of antiprofessionalism — an outing, so to speak, of investments in persons and aesthetic projects. Still, identifications and bonds are proof neither of simple complicity nor of privileged understanding. Emphasizing such ties works instead to implicate the viewer in O'Hara's poems as subject to the same desires for problematic forms of alterity that painting might provide. Another sense of proximity, however, emerges in O'Hara's attempt to trace how painting goes about pursing these ends and how this process interfaces with a viewer. Here, proximity is a matter of the line-to-line movement among analogies that produce interpretive contexts: the more localized formal association between a de Kooning gesture and "a bus" crashing "into a milk truck," for instance, is juxtaposed with a larger social equation in which these same gestures function as a culture's "stunning collapsible savages," thereby suggesting a mode of alterity against (or perhaps *through*) which "democracy is joined" (CP 285). The paratactic, proximate arrangement of such critical registers in O'Hara makes syntactic connections among these registers a largely nominal, specific project that must be taken up on a clause-to-clause level. Subordination and development exist but only as functions of individual poems, not as aspects of a redeployable critical lexicon. If this stance results in an antiprofessionalism in which the authority of a single critical discourse gets subsumed in a rapid movement from context to context, O'Hara's poems also suggest ways that this very movement itself might operate as a new way to picture abstraction within a more socially informed framework than was available to 1950s critics.

O'Hara actually believed that painters like de Kooning, Pollock, and Joan Mitchell held out temporary radical possibilities, but he recognized that their wild energies were in the process of being quickly recuperated by a more normalizing concept of culture.[6] His painting poems imagine complex economies of these processes at work, occurring in real time, from disjunctive poetic line to line, frequently shifting interpretive registers. O'Hara was thus a writer interested in interdisciplinarity before it became a rallying point for postmodernism. It is in part because O'Hara viewed abstract expressionism from aesthetic and social paradigms more closely identifiable with movements in art criticism which came after his death in 1966 that his writings on 1950s art have not been fully accounted for.

Many critics who identify themselves with postmodernism understand abstract expressionism as a last bastion of suspect metaphysics, one involving both a rhetoric of self-presence and a problematic attempt to identify with primitive cultures. Though O'Hara certainly had some sympathy for such ambitions in, say, de Kooning and Pollock, his own writing, including his criticism of these artists, tends to recode these terms. Consistently, for instance, he deflects the rhetoric of expressive interiority: "they have painted the ceiling in my heart / and put in a new light fixture" (*CP* 333). Moreover, he operates within an interdisciplinary interpretive framework that, as I have noted, was expressly attacked by abstract expressionism's most famous critics. Yet O'Hara identifies himself primarily with that movement. His interdisciplinarity is therefore not simply a matter of having championed work that collapsed disciplinary boundaries (Rauschenberg's, Joe Brainard's, and Jasper Johns's) but perhaps more importantly a matter of his own poetry having enacted this collapse. Before turning to his poetry, however, I must first consider Clement Greenberg's debate with Harold Rosenberg to give a sense of how O'Hara's writing interacts with the field of 1950s and 1960s art criticism.

In seeking to pry the reception of abstract expressionism away from the influential description offered by Harold Rosenberg in his 1952 article "The American Action Painters" (in Rosenberg's *Tradition of the New*), Greenberg's 1962 essay "How Art Writing Earns Its Bad Name" singles out a turn toward poetry as the most dangerous trap for art criticism.[7] After quoting what he takes to be self-evidently absurd sentences from Bryan Robertson and Thomas Hess, Greenberg turns to a passage in

Jackson Pollock, The Deep, 1953; oil and enamel on canvas, 86 3/4 x 59 1/8 in. Musée National d'Art Moderne, Centre de Création Industrielle, Centre Georges Pompidou, Paris. Donated by the Menil Foundation, Houston.

which O'Hara describes Pollock's *The Deep* as a "scornful, technical masterpiece, like the *Olympia* of Manet . . . one of the most provocative images of our time, an abyss of glamour encroached upon by a flood of innocence" (*Collected Essays and Criticism* 4:144). Though the sentence does sound absurd in Greenberg's brief quotation, what he excises from the passage is a larger claim that Pollock's late works provide a drama of wild, affective energies undergoing a kind of neutralizing framing: "a world of sentiment implied, but denied; a map of sensual freedom, fenced; a careening licentiousness, guarded by eight totems native to its origin" (*Jackson Pollock* 31). Later I will return to O'Hara's account of Pollock; for now, I only want to examine Greenberg's response to such writing:

> What is there about art writing that encourages this sort of thing? What is there in the people who read art writing that makes them tolerate it? Why is art writing the only kind of writing in English that has lent itself to Existentialist and Phenomenological rhetoric? What is there about modern art itself that leads minds like Herbert Read's and Harold Rosenberg's astray? The answer is not one, I think, that reflects on modern art. It has to do with the speed with which modernist painting and sculpture have outrun the common categories of art criticism, invalidating them not only for the present or future but also for the past. (This has not been a revolution; it has been a clarification.) The widening gap between art and discourse solicits, as such widenings will, perversions and abortions of discourse: pseudo-description, pseudo-narrative, pseudo-exposition, pseudo-history, pseudo-philosophy, pseudo-psychology, and — worst of all — pseudo poetry. (4:144)

What will first strike readers familiar with critiques of Greenberg is the rhetoric of immanence he uses to drive an absolute wedge between the would-be inherent facts and properties of modern art and its various misunderstandings.[8] These failed interpretive regimes are doubly "pseudo": Having strayed beyond their own disciplines, they now belong neither there *nor* in art criticism. Far from pursing what should be the obvious task of helping "to entrench" a discourse "more firmly in its area of competence" (4:85), interdisciplinary criticism, especially poetic criticism, capitalizes upon an unpoliced gap separating art from its explanation.[9]

But what, precisely, are the "poetic" terms in Rosenberg's criticism, and how do they relate to O'Hara? First, Rosenberg's account of gestural abstraction famously develops along loosely existentialist terms: "[T]he canvas began to appear to one American painter after another as an arena in which to act — rather than as a space in which to reproduce, re-design, analyze or 'express' an object, actual or imagined. What was to go onto the canvas was not a picture but an event" (*Tradition* 25). In order to defend this characterization of painting as event and canvas as arena, Rosenberg also evoked a rapid-fire movement among interpretive contexts characteristic of much poetic language, citing the "multiple existence which a painting now enjoys in separation from its physical body: its ghostly presence through reproduction in books and magazines that carry it *as picture* far from its durable being of paint and canvas; the intellectual character it takes on from the interpretations inevitably tacked on it by critics, art historians, psychiatrists, philosophers of culture; its role in the political rivalries of states and factions and in the educational activities of international institutions; the power of transformation it wields over its creator through the energy it accumulates on its passage though the social orbit" (*Tradition* preface).

Rosenberg's attempts to multiply possible interpretive contexts for painting might thus be read against Greenberg's increasing reluctance to make leaps from paintings to cultural contexts. Yet for Rosenberg, such proliferation can only operate so long as painting forever avoids an engagement with politics, an alliance he understands to have been proved impossible by the failures of social realism and regionalism. In his account, paintings must also be seen independently of their formal interrelations within art history, since pursuing these initiates a "burlesque" in which "artists vanish, and paintings spring from one another with the help of no other generating principle than whatever 'law of development' the critic happens to have on hand" (*Anxious Object* 43). Because abstract expressionism has "broken down every distinction between art and life," Rosenberg reasons, "it follows that anything is relevant to it. Anything that has to do with action — psychology, philosophy, history, mythology, hero worship. Anything but art criticism" (*Tradition* 28). As he proliferates these contexts, Rosenberg also responds directly to Greenberg's earlier attack:

> No doubt bad sociology and bad psychology are bad and have nothing to do with art, as they have nothing to do with society or with real individuals. . . . But the net effect of deleting from the interpretation of the work the signs pointing to the artist's situation and his emotional conclusions about it is to substitute for an appreciation of the crisis-dynamic of contemporary painting an arid professionalism that is a caricature of the estheticism of a half a century ago. The radical experience of confrontation, of impasse, of purging, is soaked up in expertise

> about technical variations on earlier styles and masters. . . . An art that had radically detached itself from social objectives is recaptured as a social resource. (*Anxious Object* 42)

Rosenberg was thus careful to frame art's extension into a social world as a matter of the alienated, individual psyche reaching tentative forms of expression against larger structures of collectivity. As many of O'Hara's comments suggest, he was intrigued by Rosenberg's characterization of the gestural moment-to-moment attention in abstract expressionist canvases as a matter of expressive, cathartic events or actions; still, what counted as the context in which one would later read these gestures was, for O'Hara, a much broader question.

Consider, for instance, O'Hara's 1958 poem "Far from the Porte des Lilas and the Rue Pergolèse," written to the painter Joan Mitchell in Paris that September, while O'Hara was in town to help out with both MoMA's traveling Jackson Pollock exhibition and *The New American Painting* — the two historic exhibitions that played the largest role in winning the European public over toward abstract expressionism.[10]

> Ah Joan!   there
> you are
> surrounded by paintings
> as in another century you would be wearing lipstick
> (which you wear at night to be old-fashioned, of it!
>   with it!   out!
>
> and the danger of being Proustian
> and the danger of being Pasternakesque
> and the cops outside the BALAJO frisking Algerians
> who'd been quietly playing "surf" with their
>   knuckles
>
> gee, if I don't stop being so futuristic Elsa Triolet
>   will be after me!
>
> a dream of immense sadness peers through me
> as if I were an action poem that couldn't write
> and I am leaving for another continent which is the
>   same as this one
> goodby
> (CP 311)

Though its first and last lines frame it as an occasional poem (in effect saying good-bye), inside the poem a scene of Mitchell surrounded by paintings collapses into something much stranger. By linking painting and personal accoutrement — "surrounded by paintings" as "wearing lipstick" — O'Hara puns back to, and genders, Rosenberg's claim that "a painting that is an act is inseparable from the biography of the artist" (*Tradition* 27). But for O'Hara this "act" operates within a larger and more socially motivated context: an initial attempt to explain the shifting status of lipstick for a woman "action painter" of the late 1950s opens, through the prepositional hiccups "of it! / with it!" onto a complicated, interwoven world of subtexts that never close the first, single parenthesis. Breaking the original syntax, the second stanza simply lists a series of "dangers" that, in 1958, threaten to overcode any attempt to value the gestural act as an instance of freedom. Possible interpretive sites spin by without accruing detail: aesthetic freedom in Proust; political freedom in Pasternak; the lack of social freedom for Algerians in Paris; the waning of cultural alterity in the wake of increasing post–WWII American imperialism: "I am leaving for another continent which is the / same as this one." And it is in part the paratactic arrangement of these clearly disparate types of "danger" that, implicitly, calls forth the imaginary wrath of Elsa Triolet, figured as a Stalinist critic who would be threatened by such unexplained discrepancies, by such "abstraction."

In evoking Boris Pasternak, O'Hara is nodding, as I argued in chapter 4, to attempts by Western powers to use the criticism of the Soviet Union within Pasternak's *Doctor Zhivago* as a wholesale condemnation of Communism. Because of the political utility the term *freedom* was coming to have in such debates, Pasternak's co-option casts a shadow across both Mitchell's and O'Hara's attempts to create and value spontaneous action. Larger forces here frame the processes "of confrontation, of impasse, of purging" that Rosenberg values. Densely packed with disjunctive sites in which to imagine gesture, the poem is less a reading of any one of Mitchell's canvases than a claim about the larger contexts that valuations of action, spontaneity, and freedom evoke in the fall of 1958.

In poems such as "Second Avenue," which I will consider below, O'Hara develops these contexts more thoroughly. Still, this type of poetic structure, in itself, can be considered as an argument within the context of 1950s and 1960s art criticism. That such poems did operate at least in part within the world of art criticism is evidenced by the fact that O'Hara actually did publish poems, and not merely critical essays, in *Art News*: his

"After Courbet" ran in the January 1958 issue; O'Hara also included one of his poems in his 1959 Pollock catalog (he also cites Michael McClure's "Ode to Jackson Pollock" in the catalog's bibliography).

And poetry's disruptive incursions into art criticism did not go unnoticed. In fact, the attempt to respond to such trespasses can be read as the formative moment in Michael Fried's career, a moment that gets bound up, eventually, with interdisciplinarity and postmodernity more generally. In a recent retrospective essay, Fried frames the arc of his career precisely as a reaction to what Greenberg has called "pseudo poetry," attaching this style more specifically to *Art News*[11] (the journal for which O'Hara worked between 1953 and 1955, along with New York poets Barbara Guest, James Schuyler, and John Ashbery): "Greenberg's verbally austere and intellectually rigorous yet passionately engaged criticism was at the farthest pole from the low-grade existentialist rhetoric and 'poetic' appreciation that characterized most of the writing in *Art News*, the leading magazine of contemporary art of the mid- and late 1950s, and it says a lot about what Stella, Bannard, and I already thought and felt about painting that Greenberg was the only art critic we valued and wanted to read" (3).

This view of poetry's uneasy relation to art criticism emerges as far back as Fried's 1965 "Three American Painters" (reprinted in Fried's *Art and Objecthood*), in which he explains that while "men like R. P. Blackmur, John Crowe Ransom, Allen Tate," had been around to give modernist poetry "the criticism it deserved," modern art has had to wait for Greenberg (and implicitly for Fried himself) to become its New Critics. This is because "the job of writing about art has tended to pass by default to men and women who are in no way qualified for their profession" (213–14). Central among these are the poets writing for *Art News* in the 1950s and early 1960s, whose very connection to a second discipline renders them structurally similar to the Minimalists, whom Fried will attack for eliding the difference between art and a second discipline (in this case theater) in his famous polemic of 1967, "Art and Objecthood" (also reprinted in Fried's 1998 book *Art and Objecthood*).

In this essay, there are objects in whose company we achieve self-presentness (Morris Louis paintings) and those that keep us company and are thus merely present (Tony Smith cubes). Though Fried insists that his related opposition between theatricality and absorption applies only to his historical account of eighteenth- and nineteenth-century French painting, his use of the term *theater* in "Art and Objecthood" has helped to bring the idea of theatricality (as a negative term allied with *presence*) into the debates surrounding the article; in his words, "*What lies* between *the arts is theater*" (164). Thus, theatricality has come to mean both an object's self-consciousness, which blocks access to a beholder's experience of uninterrupted self-presentness, and an art object's reliance on interdisciplinarity.

Fried's advocacy of presentness and absorption in the work of artists like Morris Louis, Frank Stella, Kenneth Noland, and Anthony Caro functioned for years as a foil by which critics advocating literal presence and theatricality in works by, say, Robert Rauschenberg, Robert Smithson, Vito Acconci, or Cindy Sherman, could claim to move beyond formalism and modernism.[12] In an essay to which we will return, Stephen Melville carefully demonstrates the ways that critics have simply reversed rather than explored Fried's opposition. If the rhetoric of subversion and clean historical breakage in early postmodern art theory now seems as dated as Fried's own last stand, this is in part because critics have not admitted the extent to which models of art-critical discourse, and not merely art objects, were at stake in the debate.

From this perspective then, the graphically distinct, italicized autobiographical sidebars and lyrical asides that theatricalize a text like Rosalind Krauss's *The Optical Unconscious* (situating Greenberg and Fried as foes, *again*, at this metalevel of the book's enacted interdisciplinarity) are only a recent chapter in this struggle.[13] Obviously a broad range of practices long predate Krauss's polemical use of writerly theatricality. Robert Smithson's essays from the late 1960s and early 1970s are certainly a high point within the genre.[14] But in the immediate aftermath of Rosenberg's 1952 "The American Action Painters," it is Frank O'Hara's painting poems concerned with abstract expressionism that shed the most light on Greenberg's (and later Fried's) concerns. Had Greenberg taken these poems seriously as a discourse, they might have served even more aptly as evidence of the poetic problem Rosenberg had unleashed. Which is to say that poetry's position at the top of the list — "worst of all," in Greenberg's string of hyphenated failures — is no accident. But beyond the simple muddying of thought, which poetic criticism could certainly be, O'Hara's was, in its strongest instances, also a challenge to art criticism's attempt to set up a proper, professional domain and method of inquiry.

It is in this context that I want to turn to O'Hara's poem "Second Avenue," which has occupied an important though vexing position within O'Hara's canon since its composition during the spring of 1953. Both contemporary readers and later critics have disagreed about its importance. All have accepted, however, that the poem is deeply involved with abstract expressionism and that it represents O'Hara at his most extreme. Here is how Brad Gooch describes the genesis of the poem: "During March and April [of 1953] O'Hara wrote his longest poem, the eleven-part 478-line 'Second Avenue,' the culmination of his accelerating desire to use a kind of automatic writing to match the epic scale and grandeur built by accident and subconscious connections in Abstract Expressionist painting, aleatory music, and French Surrealist catalogue poems. O'Hara worked on 'Second Avenue' mostly in Larry Rivers' plaster garden studio overlooking Second Avenue between Seventh and Eighth streets" (G 233).[15]

In 1956, when he was preparing the manuscript that would be *Meditations in an Emergency* for Grove Press, O'Hara wrote to editor Barney Rosset that "Second Avenue" was his favorite poem but that he anticipated it wouldn't be included in the collection because of its "four letter words" (Archive February 19, 1956). Aside from references to abstract expressionism and surrealism and the literal connection to Second Avenue, criticism — both positive and negative — has been able to say little about the poem. Marjorie Perloff's treatment is indicative of the frustration many readers seem to have experienced. Claiming that the poem is "too variable," Perloff cites some passages she calls "documentary" and then says that "they don't quite seem to belong in the same poem" (P 71–72) that contains a more abstract, syntactically ambiguous depiction of a de Kooning painting. "One is, in short, hard put," Perloff concludes "to find any line of development in *Second Avenue*; individual sections appear in no particular sequence; scenes and images are juxtaposed without a view of their place in the larger scheme" (P 72).[16] It does not take O'Hara's claim that his notes on the poem are "not explanatory of the meaning which I don't think can be paraphrased" (CP 495) to establish that the poem, like the painting that inspires it, actively resists summary. But at the same time, "Second Avenue," in its invention of multiple and seemingly conflicting analogical languages for painting and experience more broadly, registers deep interest in the problem of how one talks about objects that are not summarizable. And it is in this regard that the poem gives us models for analogical languages that might in turn be used on it, ones which provide a "line of development" that Perloff misses amid the poem's heterogeneity. Perloff's reading suggests that the poem's first three lines are a sort of throwaway, a quotation from another, more formalized poetic discourse that the poem then problematizes in the second stanza. But the poem's first lines are in fact central to its development of proximity as a mode, as a plea, even: "Quips and players, seeming to vend astringency off-hours / celebrate diced excesses and sardonics, mixing pleasures, / as if proximity were staring at the margin of a plea" (CP 139).[17] What a reader of "Second Avenue" encounters first off is a string of proximate vocabularies — both literary and quotidian — juxtaposed, abraded, combined into an overcharged whole that highlights gaps and discontinuities between the poem's "diced excesses."[18] It is in part the lack of a recognizable speaker in this world that led to negative reactions.[19] In addition to the literary language of surrealism, evoked throughout the first sections by phrases such as "Grappling with images of toothpaste falling on guitar strings" (CP 140), O'Hara makes nods toward psychoanalysis (with scare-quoted "couch" and "ears") and existentialism ("getting-out — of-bedness") (ibid.). At the same time, lines like "And it's very exciting to be an old friend / of Verlaine and he has his problems, divine dust bag" (CP 145) introduce a colloquial, more American tone that, in its self-reflexive borrowing, distances the poem from a strict homage to surrealism. The poem's heterogeneity becomes most apparent, though, as it begins to slip into radically flat narrative techniques somewhere between the nouveau roman and the pulp novel:

> The mountains had trembled, quivering as if about to withdraw,
> and where the ships had lined up on the frontier waiting for
> the first gunshot, a young girl lunched on aspergum. A cow
> belched. The sun went up. Later in the day Steven farted.
> He dropped his torpedo into the bathtub. Flowers. Relativity.
> (CP 146)

Such affectless descriptions exist side by side with insertions from a more traditional autobiographical language — "I met Joe, his hair pale as the eyes of fields of maize / in August, at the gallery, he said you're the first Creon / of 1953, congrats" (CP 143) — and with a kind of homemade Hollywood aesthetic in which O'Hara's friends get to act in odd, seemingly plotless Westerns.

> Joe LeSueur,
> the handsome Captain who smuggles Danish perfumes, tied up
> at the arroyo and with thunderous hooves swam across a causeway
> to make the Honest Dollar. In Pasadena they are calling
> "Higho, Silver!" but in the High Sierras they just shoot
> movie after movie. Who is "they"? The Westerners, of course,
> the tans. Didn't you ever want to be a cowboy, buster?
> (CP 144)

There are pop culture icons, "Marilyn Monroe. / Can one's lips be 'more' or 'less' sensual?" (*CP* 147); moments of New York daily life, "Taxicabs whistling by" (*CP* 148);[20] descriptions of paintings, finished and in process, "spasmodically obliterated with loaves of greasy white paint" (*CP* 149); snatches of art criticism, in which a painting might be "decorative as a Mayan idol too well understood / to be beautiful" (*CP* 141); and oblique conversation identified as taking place in painting studios, "Your feet are more beautiful than your father's, I think, / does that upset you?" (*CP* 147).

The "proximity" of these shifting and overlapping vocabularies in "Second Avenue," framed as languages for registering experience — "diced excesses and sardonics, mixing pleasures" — is the poem's operative mode, its argument or "plea."[21] But before jumping to these larger thematic levels, it is important to consider the microlinguistic levels in which O'Hara makes the proximity of constitutive vocabularies into a plea. The first three words — "Quips and players" (*CP* 139) — present an asymmetry that the poem explores throughout: a "quip" (a remark whose connotations extend from clever wit through sarcasm to taunts or gibes) would relate more directly to a "play" (the verbal mechanism that would bring a quip into being) than to a "player," who is perhaps the "I" of the quip, the one who might "vend astringency off-hours." But the grammatical positioning of a "quip" as that which vends such astringency produces a disruption in the first line (the "er" of player) and introduces the poem's tendency to complicate the distinction between poetry based on the conscious thoughts of a self-present poetic persona and that based on the contingent sound relationships within a preexisting vocabulary.

Just as the phrase "quips and players" does not resolve into the speech-based, verbal property of a poetic persona who would preexist discourse, so the proliferation of disparate models of "I/You" speaking situations in the poem's first section ("you, like all heretics, penetrate my glacial immodesty, / and I am a nun trembling before the microphone" [*CP* 140]) works to destabilize the would-be tonal and psychological unity out of which a reader would project a speaker. Though the fiction of immediate speech persists through the many first- and second-person constructions, the absurdity of tying these instances to empirical speakers produces a humorous gap that O'Hara exploits throughout. These types of sabotage are usually written off by critics as characteristic of O'Hara's juvenilia.[22] Even John Ashbery, who was deeply impressed by O'Hara from the start, suggested that the increasing incorporation of vernacular language worked "to ventilate the concentrated Surrealist imagery of poems like

'Hatred,' 'Easter' and 'Second Avenue' "(*CP* x).[23] But O'Hara himself was willing to debate the potential values of the type of overstuffed, claustrophobic vocabularies he employs in poems like "Second Avenue." Responding to Harry Roskolenko's negative review, in *Poetry* magazine, of Kenneth Koch's 1954 book *Poems*, O'Hara quotes the critical attack, seeking to turn its charge into an asset: " 'Mr. Koch, it seems, has a rare combination of words rattling about in his skull, but it is difficult to call any of his word combinations the bric-a-brac of poetry' " (SS 59). O'Hara continues: "It is amusing to think of the number of gifted (even great!) poets my epigraph applies to. Though I am in total disagreement with the rest of Mr. Roskolenko's review of *Poems* by Kenneth Koch . . . he has hit on something here; these very original poems have little to do with the restful and pleasant bric-a-brac he seems to prefer" (ibid.). One might link O'Hara's cultivation of "a rare combination of words rattling about in [one's] skull" to the "diced excesses" in "Second Avenue": Both are "staring at the margin of a plea" against "the restful and pleasant bric-a-brac" of 1950s academic poetry.

One of the central preexisting vocabularies O'Hara makes use of in "Second Avenue" is painters' talk. That the speech patterns, vocabularies, and favorite tropes of painters and critics were an important point of departure for O'Hara is borne out throughout his writing. "Franz Kline Talking," for example, reproduces an improvisatory ramble by Kline through Western art from Rembrandt to de Kooning, Turner to Cézanne, weaving in remarks by borscht circuit comedians, theses on community and imitation, and winding up with the following flourish:[24]

> Some painters talking about painting are like a lot of kids dancing at a prom. An hour later you're too shy to get out on the floor.
>
> Hell, half the world wants to be like Thoreau at Walden worrying about the noise of traffic on the way to Boston; the other half use up their lives being part of that noise. I like the second half. Right?
>
> To be right is the most terrific personal state that nobody is interested in. (SS 94)

O'Hara's writing on Kline, Motherwell, and Larry Rivers as well as his remarks about de Kooning all emphasize the verbal atmospheres that these artists create in dialog.[25] "I insist on immediacy, passion and tenderness, being-ness as such, sheer presence, objectivity, true invention and true resolution, light, the unexpected, direct colors" reads a Motherwell quote in an article in which O'Hara has already mentioned that if the artist

Larry Rivers, The Burial, 1952; *oil on canvas, 60 x 108 in. Fort Wayne Art School and Museum, Fort Wayne, Indiana. © Estate of Larry Rivers/licensed by VAGA, New York.*

"finds you thinking right, or if you have a really fresh idea, he acts as if you had just given him a present he'd been longing for" (SS 176). O'Hara's use of artists' languages might be understood within Claude Lévi-Strauss's opposition between the bricoleur (who arranges given materials, speaking "through the medium of things" [*Savage Mind* 21]), and the scientist (who seeks to fabricate his intellectual materials from scratch) — a position we could attribute to Greenberg. But O'Hara's difference from Greenberg here is also a matter of ethics. If for Greenberg the inevitable gap between the formal materiality of painting and the world of descriptive languages presents an ethical dilemma, allowing for "abortions and perversion of discourse," for O'Hara this gap is less a crisis that needs to be policed than a potentially generative space fundamental to language, whether it be describing painting or not. Phrases produce interpretive frameworks; the best do so unexpectedly, shifting quickly among viewpoints and seeming to energize the field of possibility around a painting. "The single most important event in [Larry Rivers's] artistic career," O'Hara remarks in "Larry Rivers: A Memoir," "was when de Kooning said that his painting was like pressing your face into wet grass" (CP 513). This fascination with disparate, nonprofessional aesthetic vocabularies activates O'Hara's painting poems, shifting the primary frame of reference from description of the paintings themselves to the discursive raw materials in which they circulate. By allowing these vocabularies to shape his poems, O'Hara moves toward modes of hybridization and proliferation that are diametrically opposed to the narrowing lexical range Greenberg and Fried imagined as the cure to a threatened art criticism of the 1950s and 1960s.

Though in his notes to "Second Avenue" O'Hara mentions "studio visits" to several painters — Grace Hartigan, Larry Rivers, and de Kooning — these sections bleed imperceptibly into the rest of the poem, which seems, in fact, consistently concerned with painting.[26] O'Hara overlaps specifically aesthetic, painterly experience with everyday life as one way of imagining the world brought into being by abstraction. His technique, however, is more specifically inflected than the familiar idea (reiterated in Rosenberg's "The American Action Painters"; see Rosenberg *Tradition of the New* 23–29) about art and life becoming one: the poem not only produces a confusion between what is inside and outside a frame, but this conflation often becomes specifically bound up with a mutual dependence between the exotic and the urban, the sophisticated and the wild, the foreign and the domestic. The turn to painting seems to occur most visibly in the section 3, which begins: "And must I express the science of legendary elegies / consummate on the Clarissas of puma and gnu and wildebeest? / Blue negroes on the verge of a true foreignness / escape nevertheless the chromaticism of occidental death / by traffic" (*CP* 141).

If we accept for a moment that the "science of legendary elegies" might have to do with the abstract, gestural painting that O'Hara explicitly evokes in his notes to the poem, then many of the excessive, revealing features Greenberg and Fried would have hated are in place. We could, in fact, read this passage as a literalization of Harold Rosenberg's desire for contextual proliferation transposed into poetry. So much so that, rather than "poetic" art criticism, this is art-critical poetry. What is actually critical in this passage — critical in a way that Fried in particular tended not to allow — is a social framework into which one can imagine gestural painting's pursuit of "true foreignness." Wildness, here, cannot be separated from its cultural functions.

Beginning with the then still almost-fresh figure of the action painter, the passage reads his "action" within several economies of self-consciousness and cultural exhaustion: his wildness is the lettered alterity of "Clarissas of

Jackson Pollock, Guardians of the Secret, *1943; oil on canvas, 48 1/8 x 75 3/8 in. San Francisco Museum of Modern Art, Albert M. Bender Collection. © Pollock-Krasner Foundation/Artists Rights Society (ARS), New York.*

puma," whose raw materials for producing foreignness effects — perhaps the primitivist motifs of "blue negroes" in Matisse or Picasso — are on the verge of "occidental death."[27] In the process of being replaced by modes of abstraction that themselves *enact* this alterity rather than represent it, the motif now belongs to an earlier chapter of the occident's quest for self-defining otherness. That "occidental death" would occur "by traffic" points to a process in which a specifically urban artistic culture tries on and gradually exhausts a succession of "wild" forms.[28]

After lines that read almost as a parody of abstract expressionist angst — "the true tillers of the spirit / whose strangeness crushes in the only possible embrace, / is like splintering and pulling and draining the tooth / of the world" (*CP* 141) — O'Hara contextualizes this as a "longing to be modern and sheltered and different / and insane and decorative as a Mayan idol too well understood / to be beautiful" (ibid.). Writing in 1959 of the central abstract section of Pollock's 1943 *Guardians of the Secret*, O'Hara suggests a parallel narrative of the search for vanishing wildness that he has already evoked in "Second Avenue": "After exploring [totemic figures] with great authority and finality . . . Pollock in the following years seems to move directly into the 'secret' " (*Jackson Pollock* 21). Perhaps by the time Pollock tries on the language of totems, its alterity is "too well understood" (CP 141) for it to remain wild or "insane" (ibid.), especially given the lineage of Picasso and other European abstract painters. This dilemma leads to a prototypically modernist question about objects of mimesis — "Can roses be charming?" — and this description: "As the sluice / pours forth its granular flayings a new cloud rises / and interplanetary driftings become simply initiatory gifts / like the circumcision of a black horse."

If Pollock is also evoked by the previous question about "true foreignness," he seems to enter more concretely here. Pollock of course painted a picture called *Circumcision*. Moreover, "granular flayings" poured out of a "sluice" certainly suggests, if not his actual drip technique, then the sort of effect the drips attain in a painting such as *Autumn Rhythm: Number 30, 1950* (plate 2). This association quickly extends toward the "new cloud" of "interplanetary driftings," which simultaneously evokes the clichéd vision of nuclear explosion behind so many accounts of abstract expressionism, the new elevated position of American art within the world, and Pollock's own status as an international (if not interplanetary) "event." How one gets entangled in this event seems to be the question of the next lines:

> the appeasement, frieze-style,
> of undulant spiritual contamination, to which sainthood
> I sacrifice my brilliant dryness, it had been my devoir
> and my elegant distinction, a luminous enlacement
> of the people through the bars of the zoo, the never fading.
> (CP 141)

Greenberg had already argued that one of Pollock's achievements was to question the naturalness of the easel by forcing paintings to suggest architectural friezes. O'Hara takes this idea a step further by suggesting the specific architecture of the zoo, a site where wildness gets demonstrated and framed and where, in the poem, the viewer undergoes a "luminous enlacement," a collapsing of both aesthetic and erotic distance: "I sacrifice my brilliant dryness."[29] In O'Hara's notes on the poem, "dryness" is associated with a kind of distance from involvement.[30] By constructing Pollock's "wild" affect as a site for unconscious erotic and aesthetic projections, O'Hara can be taken as one of the first to hear the terms of Greenberg's characterization of Pollock as "American and rougher and more brutal [than Picasso], but . . . also completer" (2: 125).[31] Here, Greenberg's often-remarked intense libidinal identification with Pollock seemed to burst through the imposed "verbal austerity" that he projected as a sublimatory grid. O'Hara's interest in, or openness toward, these breakdowns in distance (especially in these early poems) is also a measure of his distance from the rhetoric of professionalism.

> My spirit is clouded, as it was in Tierra del Fuego,
> and if the monsters who twirl on their toes like fiery wagons
> cannot dismiss the oceanographer of a capricious promptness
> which is more ethical than dismal, my heart
> will break through to casualness and appear in windows
> on Main Streets, "more vulgar but they love more than he
> hates, as the apples turn straightway into balloons
> and burst."
> (CP 141–42)

Comparing current states of complicity and impasse ("My spirit is clouded") to similar states within a prior space of cultural alterity ("Tierra del Fuego"), the passage tracks a kind of wild, uncontrollable energy—"the monsters who twirl on their toes like fiery wagons." Such energy is perhaps bound up with the unconscious, should we be willing to take the oceanographer as a humorous figure for the action painter probing the unknown depths of his subjectivity, doing so with an impulse "more ethical than dismal." The struggle to transcend the clouded spirit and achieve what O'Hara calls in Pollock "spiritual clarity" (*Jackson Pollock* 21) would, paradoxically, allow the "I" to "break through to casualness and appear in windows on Main Streets." The process of wild energy moving through alterity thus gets reabsorbed by culture as product, a process which again evokes O'Hara's 1959 description of Pollock's painting: "a world of sentiment implied, but denied; a map of sensual freedom, fenced; a careening licentiousness, guarded by eight totems native to its origin." It is in this sense that the rapid-fire proliferation of coded geographic regions might be taken as an analog for tracking the affective implications of a painterly gesture along this route. But the goal is not a mere marveling at painting's ability to evoke a dialectical succession of these imaginative regions — desert to sea, wild locations to main streets, heart to rhetoric. Instead, the struggle to "break through to casualness and appear in windows / on Main Streets" suggests a process like that evoked by "Clarissas of Puma," in which spontaneity or wildness gets framed, contained, and contextualized.[32] Even this excessive, multidirectional poetic language begins to inscribe the effects within a structure of instrumental cultural oppositions.

Still, if casualness and impulse are already saturated or coded, this coding happens at different cultural rates, a fact that seems to explain O'Hara's attraction to abstract expressionism in the early 1950s as a zone of comparative wildness. Though "Second Avenue" imagines various ways that the new painting is already being and has been recuperated to the ends of culture, the process is, for O'Hara, incomplete and inconsistent and therefore active and engaging — worth sacrificing one's "elegant distinction" in order to get involved, to get wet, and to suffer "luminous enlacement / through the bars of the zoo." The "newspapers of a sediment" (*CP* 139) have not quite dried. And this is why it is abstract expressionism and not psychoanalysis or existentialist philosophy or more familiar poetry that emerges as the central site of affect for O'Hara — why the poem proceeds through these others to get to painting, to the "science of legendary elegies."

As I have said, Pollock is not the only abstract expressionist painter to appear in "Second Avenue." Still, Willem de Kooning does not arrive until section 8, after the poem has cooled down, aired itself out with a great deal more flat narration. Unlike the passages I've just discussed, O'Hara clearly identifies the section on de Kooning: "Oh, I forgot to excerpt something else, a little description of a de Kooning WOMAN which I'd seen at his studio" (*CP* 497). After quoting from his poem, O'Hara adds, "Actually, I am rather inaccurate about the above, since it is a woman I saw leaning out a window on Second Avenue with her arms on a pillow, but the way it's done is influenced by de K's woman (whom he thinks of, he once said, as 'living' on 14th St.)" (ibid.). A "quip" of de Kooning's noted by Richard Shiff helps to frame the verbal world that O'Hara might have associated with the resurgence of figuration in de Kooning's *Woman* series in the 1950s. To a remark by Clement Greenberg that "it's impossible to paint a face," de Kooning is said to have replied, "That's right, and it's impossible not to."[33] Whereas Greenberg speaks the language of historical imperative, de Kooning shifts the framework inside his response, seeming to agree with the historical point and then to allow for its contradiction by the fact, presumably, that one always either recognizes faciality in abstraction or reproduces it unconsciously. Though we have no record of whether O'Hara heard this comment, the simultaneous respect and subversion it demonstrates, as well as its complex punning, are typical of his own relation to Greenberg. The passage of "Second Avenue" that O'Hara identifies with de Kooning runs as follows:

Willem de Kooning, Woman I, 1950–1952; oil on canvas, 75 7/8 x 58 in. Museum of Modern Art, New York.

You remained for me a green Buick of sighs, o Gladstone!
and your wife Trina, how like a yellow pillow on a sill
in the many-windowed dusk where the air is compartmented!
her red lips of Hollywood, soft as a Titian and as tender,
her gray face which refrains from thrusting aside the mane
of your languorous black smells, the hand crushed by her chin,
and that slumberland of dark cutaneous lines which reels
under the burden of her many-darkly-hued corpulence of linen
and satin bushes, is like a lone rose with the sky behind it.
A yellow rose. Valentine's Day.
(CP 147)

Similar to O'Hara's remark about the "aluminum paint" in Pollock's # 12, 1952 looking "like money" and the color being that of the "sunset in a technicolor Western," here the lips of *Woman 1* are the "red lips of Hollywood." In "Favorite Paintings in the Metropolitan" (1961), O'Hara will write that "Richard Burton / waves through de Kooning the / Wild West rides up out of the Pollock" (CP 423). Whereas the association between Pollock and Hollywood wildness emerges more gradually, O'Hara seems to process de Kooning's angst and violence through this link from the start.[34] In "Second Avenue," this stance allows O'Hara to reverse the violence of de Kooning's disfiguring gaze so that the painter's hand gets crushed by the woman's chin. The Hollywood framework also allows O'Hara to recuperate camp humor that viewers might otherwise find lacking or insufficient.[35] Thus he can frame this tawdry, squalid scene — complete with a reference to "Trina," the battered wife in Frank Norris's novel *McTeague* — with "A yellow rose. Valentine's Day." The American violence of de Kooning's *Woman* takes its position next to Buicks, Gladstones, and film sequences interpolated from Westerns — "Higho, Silver!" — rewritten into flat avant-garde scenarios.[36]

The paratactic rhetoric of "Second Avenue" here allows for a set of crucial substitutions. First, O'Hara's experience along Second Avenue can substitute for a de Kooning painting, and second, the Hollywood excess of the painting can become equivalent to invented scenes that employ (and deform) the logic of the Western, substituting his friend Joe LeSueur for the protagonist. If nothing else, this strategy allows O'Hara to place what was for many the very particular violence of de Kooning's *Woman* series within a far larger cultural condition. Certainly O'Hara's interest in this aspect of de Kooning's (and Pollock's) work finds no analog in Michael

Fried's criticism: "[M]odernist art in this century," Fried writes as a preface to a treatment of these two painters, "finished what society in the nineteenth began: the alienation of the artist from the general preoccupations of the culture in which he is embedded, and the prizing loose of art itself from the concerns, aims, and ideals of that culture" (*Art and Objecthood* 217).

In the beginning of section 10, "Second Avenue" circles back on de Kooning explicitly.

> The silence that lasted for a quarter century. All
> the babies were born blue. They called him "Al" and "Horseballs"
> in kindergarten, he had an autocratic straw face like a dark
> in a de Kooning where the torrent has subsided at the very center
> of classicism, it can be many whirlpools in a gun battle
> or each individual pang in the "last mile" of electrodes, so
> totally unlike xmas tree ornaments that you wonder, uhmmm?
> what the bourgeoisie is thinking of. Trench coat. Broken strap.
> Pseudo-aggressive as the wife of a psychiatrist. Beating off.
> Banging off. It is delicately thorough in laying its leaden sneer
> Down in Brettschneider's Funeral Home. You'll say I'm supper,
> naturally, but one is distinguished by the newspapers of the lips.
> (CP 148–49)

Again the art-historical register — "where a torrent has subsided at the very center of classicism" — meets Hollywood, or at least the mythology of American violence, deep inside the rhetorical folds of a long sentence, where the subsided torrent "can be many whirlpools in a gun battle." Conjoined over a comma, the two discourses are introduced without hypotactic ceremony. "Al" and "Horseballs" look on. And while the bourgeoisie might, O'Hara imagines, prefer a decorative painterly language similar to "xmas tree ornaments," they seem, somehow, to be behind de Kooning in all of his ugliness and newness — which sort of makes him "Al" or "Horesballs" miraculously doing okay at the party when the conversation turns to art history and patronage.

Though I have been able to account for only a small portion of the poem's 478 lines, I hope to have indicated a "line of development," a kind of reading protocol by which "proximity . . . staring at the margin of a plea" can begin to make sense both of the poem's general organization, its interest in contingent vocabularies as terrains of experience, and more specifically of O'Hara's reading of abstract expressionism within the poem as a site of affect that gives rise to, and sits at the center of, this barrage of proximate experiential vocabularies. Rather than operating simply as a catalog of juxtaposed language materials, these vocabularies, as they emerge out of surrealism and existentialism and meet flat narration and Hollywood scenarios at the occasion of American abstract painting, allow O'Hara to literalize Harold Rosenberg's idea of tracking a painterly gesture through a culture's incomplete process of familiarizing and instrumentalizing that gesture's "wild" energies. O'Hara reads such a recuperative process as part of the deepest logic of any attempt at artistic wildness. Yet his reading is far from bleak: naïvely or not, he figures the incomplete process of culture's recuperation of abstract expressionism, in 1953, as an occasion for linguistic celebration. Analogies emerge out of a disjunctive, paratactic poetic language that features an encyclopedic and humorous range of discontinuous stylistic registers. O'Hara's painting poems present, therefore, a special kind of interdisciplinarity, or what Michael Fried would call "theatricality"; not merely merging two disciplines, they instead initiate almost infinite substitutions among discourses in their rapid, line-to-line attempt to imagine contexts for painting. It is for this reason that they seem, and are, antiprofessional.

• • •

Unlike Pollock, who remained a distant, admired acquaintance for O'Hara, de Kooning, whom O'Hara met in 1952, became a good friend — all the way until O'Hara's accidental death after being hit by a jeep on Fire Island in 1966 (de Kooning came from East Hampton to visit at the hospital in Mastic Beach before O'Hara died).[37] "I liked him immediately," de Kooning remarked about O'Hara, "he was so bright. Right away he was at the center of things, and he did not bulldoze."[38] O'Hara, in turn, locates painters like de Kooning not only as offering inspiration but as central *readers* of the poetry he, Koch, Guest, Schuyler, and Ashbery were writing in the 1950s: "for most of us non-academic, and indeed non-literary poets in the sense of the American scene at the time, the painters were the only generous audience for our poetry, and most of us read first publicly in art galleries or at The Club" (SS 169). De Kooning was definitely a reader of O'Hara's work. J. H. Prynne speculates, in fact, that O'Hara's 1957 "Ode to Willem de Kooning" may have inspired de Kooning's *Rosy-Fingered Dawn at Louse Point* of 1963 (see plate 3).[39] Certainly O'Hara was influenced by de Kooning in different ways over their long relationship. O'Hara's ode, for instance, provides a radically different reading of de Kooning from that offered in "Second Avenue." Partly this may be a function of de Kooning's own shift from the *Woman* series to the more abstract and often landscape-format works of the mid- to late 1950s, two of which, *Gotham News* and *Easter Monday* (plate 4), are mentioned explicitly in the poem.[40]

O'Hara's ode imagines de Kooning's art practice, in what starts out in familiar abstract expressionist terms, as a form of exemplary choice: the painter's decisiveness becomes a foil against which the poet can register his own "lapse of nerve" (*CP* 283), his implicitly uneven attempt to "seize upon greatness" (*CP* 284). De Kooning's exemplarity, however, carries with it the prohibition against imitation: the painter does not imitate nature and (therefore) the poet should not imitate the painter. Though de Kooning offers "generosity and / lavishness of spirit" (ibid.), representing de Kooning's actual qualities would make the poet "inimitably weak / and picturesque, my self" (ibid.). Where, then, does this leave the poet in his attempts to write a poem "about" or at least "to" de Kooning? This dilemma points in two directions — one formal, one thematic. Formally it accounts, I think, for the poem's active, variable experimentation with visual prosody. Thematically de Kooning's problematic exemplarity seems to lead toward a historical consideration of the social and even political forms and functions of radical individuality. As in "In Memory of My Feelings," O'Hara moves from a fragmented present, experienced as a crisis, toward a kind of research or genealogical background. Whereas in "In Memory of My Feelings" this background involves comparing the different social logics that characterize the family, the nation, and world history as identity-producing frameworks, here we get a classical precedent: the pathos of Homeric epic as it dovetails into Athenian democracy. The forms of individuality imagined in this context give rise to the last section's depiction of dawn (moving theatrically across broken poetic lines) as a moment of radical choice and to several lines that encode a view of abstract expressionism's relation to contemporary American democratic processes.

In a talk given to the world of New York painters at The Club in 1952, O'Hara distinguished *form* in poetry from *design*, conceptualizing the latter in terms of what is now called visual prosody. In his epigraph, O'Hara uses a dictionary definition of *design* to stress its potential political and rhetorical functions: "a plan . . . as a design for a revolution; also a preliminary intellectual conception, as of a poem or an argument" (*SS* 30). By reminding his audience of these connotations, O'Hara connects contemporary interest in visual prosody to its special, overtly political status in futurism, Dadaism, and Russian constructivism. This broad connection leads into the senses in which writers come to appropriate forms of design as their signature styles: "When you think of e. e. cummings, in whose work design is very important, you think immediately of his identifying characteristics, and what you are thinking of is design" (ibid.); finally, O'Hara notes "how many contemporary poets emphasize the visual rather than the spoken organization of the poem" (ibid.).

I stress these points because though O'Hara focuses in his "Ode to Willem de Kooning" on the powers and possibilities of radical individuation, this interest does not translate into a speech-based poetics that might be taken as a more immediate poetic analog. Instead, O'Hara again (oddly?) associates de Kooning with modernist Russian poets: whereas this happened in "Second Avenue" through substituting Mayakovsky for de Kooning in the dedication, here it happens, slightly less directly, through O'Hara's interest in the radical, nonpersonal powers of design.[41]

O'Hara's ode is one of his most overtly designed poems. The poem's first lines work to establish the varying stanzaic structures as semantically overdetermined units within a poem "on" the connotations of pure forms.

> Before the sunrise
> where the black begins
>
> an enormous city
> is sending up its shutters
>
> and just before the last lapse of never which I am already sorry for,
> that friends describe as "just this once" in a temporary hell, I hope
>
> I try to seize upon greatness
> which is available to me
>
> through generosity and
> lavishness of spirit, yours
>
> not to be inimitably weak
> and picturesque, my self
>
> but to be standing clearly
> alone in the orange wind
>
> while our days tumble and rant through Gotham and the Easter narrows
> and I have not courage to convict myself of cowardice or care
> (CP 284)

The more traditionally poetic and depersonalized images of the first four lines must struggle against the longer lines of prosy "confession" — as if the poem's first lines were an attempt to wring independent poetic gestures out of their personalized, degraded condition in prose. To read in such a way is not to claim that the poem is like a painting but that the rhetorical emphasis on gestures within painting provides a set of figures through which one might seek semantic importance in the relation of isolated "strokes" or figures to more continuous surfaces or grounds in the stanzaic structure of the page.[42]

In the last lines of the first section, O'Hara depicts de Kooning as counteracting inertia without progressing in some teleological development of art, one of the "men / who lead us not forward or backward, but on as we must go on / out into the mesmerized world / of inanimate voices like traffic / noises, hewing a clearing / in the crowded abyss of the West" (*CP* 284). Is New York now the West, a new frontier? Such a conflation (similar ones operate in "Second Avenue") allows a nationalist discourse of freedom and expansion to vanish at the same point as a quotidian urban one, as if the first were its hidden, simultaneous condition of possibility.

Seeming to follow the concluding line of section 1 into "the crowded abyss of the West," section 2 conducts this search not horizontally or spatially toward America's West but vertically or temporally in a historical direction by looking into the origins of Western civilization. In doing so the section briefly abandons design for a more normative formal arrangement of three stanzas of continuously justified short lines. Within these taut lines, O'Hara finds a tautness in de Kooning's landscape horizons, which is in turn an ethical tautness: "while we walk on to a horizon / line that's beautifully keen, / precarious and doesn't sag / beneath our variable weight" (ibid.). De Kooning's heroic enactment of the dawn light conditions of Gotham and Sag Harbor have as their not-so-distant condition of possibility the dawn of the West: "In this dawn as in the first / it's the Homeric rose, its scent / that leads us up the rocky path" (*CP* 284–85).

Relating a description of dawn activities in book 2 of *The Odyssey* both to de Kooning's *Rosy-Fingered Dawn at Louse Point* and to O'Hara's ode, J. H. Prynne links Homeric daylight "with the public business of managing sexual appetite, managing great wars and petty lusts, through the rhetorically dense medium and the heroic devices of a grandly embattled literary notion of the public sphere" (41).[43] But for Prynne, in O'Hara's poem at least, this "public sphere" remains tenuous, as the individual values of ethos threaten to overtake the collective values of pathos. While "the uttering position" of O'Hara's middle-section Greek interlude "is still overtly collective: the *we* and *us* of a tragic chorus, and not the I of solitary advantage," afterwards ethos, "the force for personal action and its potential fate" (49), overtakes pathos. For Prynne this involves a "premature fatalism" (50) — a "deeply heroic dismay which focuses" O'Hara's "admiration for the painter's struggle with the classical past and its violent finality" (49).

But I sense considerably less loss and nostalgia in O'Hara's poem. Though it is suffused with heroic, individual struggle, such struggle is not simply belated. Dawn's powers of annihilation seem to construct a temporary space of wide possibility, one associated with a kind of nominalism that is easily accommodated within democracy.[44]

> Dawn must always recur
> to blot out stars and the terrible systems
> of belief
> Dawn, which dries out the web so the wind can blow it,
> spider and all, away
> Dawn,
> erasing blindness from an eye inflamed,
> reaching for its
> morning cigarette in Promethean inflection
> after the blames
> and desperate conclusions of the dark
> where messages were intercepted
> by an ignorant horde of thoughts
> and all simplicities perished in desire
> (*CP* 285)

Dawn would be a moment beyond reactivity, a relatively public moment beyond the private "blames / and desperate conclusions of the dark." Violence here seems to have less to do with a tragic loss than with a surplus of possibility, given to us in what follows in a set of images that (perhaps breaking the first section's desire not to imitate de Kooning) suggest a material world encoded in each active brush stroke.

> A bus crashes into a milk truck
> and the girl goes skating up the avenue
> with streaming hair
> roaring through fluttering newspapers
> and their Athenian contradictions
> for democracy is joined
> with stunning collapsible savages, all natural and relaxed and free
> (ibid.)

Willem de Kooning, Gotham News, *1955; oil, enamel, charcoal, and newspaper transfer on canvas, 69 x 79 in. Albright-Knox Art Gallery, Buffalo, New York, gift of Seymour H. Knox, 1955.*

This roaring is the roaring of gesture, which literally takes place — in both de Kooning's *Gotham News* and *Easter Monday* (see plate 4) — against sections of painted backgrounds in which newspapers, used initially to keep pigment wet, began to transfer themselves onto the paint. One such transfer, at the bottom right of *Easter Monday*, preserves an "advertisement for *Alexander the Great* in CinemaScope";[45] though the effect may have been accidental, Richard Burton's rushing into battle with his spear and shield begs to be seen now as an analogy for the abstract expressionist's channeling his reserves of wildness in order to merge his corporeal gestures with the field of his own canvas, paintbrush and palette raised. Even if O'Hara hadn't written elsewhere that "Richard Burton / waves through de Kooning" (*CP* 423),

Willem de Kooning, detail of Easter Monday *(see plate 4).*

it would be impossible to imagine that O'Hara didn't notice this detail. In fact, Burton seems to wave through O'Hara's references in the ode to "stunning collapsible savages," "Athenian contradictions," and "fluttering newspapers."[46] Ultimately the poem's climactic section imagines the contradictory and savage world of these gestures — "crashes," "skating," "roaring," "streaming," and "fluttering" — not merely as the experiential thrill of unexpected, violent combinations within the wet surface, so often emphasized in de Kooning's painting, but finally as a discourse about how "democracy is joined." That this joining is done "with stunning collapsible savages" works to link the rhetoric of wildness specifically associated with abstract expressionism with a wider discourse on democracy.

But how, exactly, are canvases "stunning collapsible savages"? How does democracy make use of the savage? First, similar to many critical accounts of abstract expressionism (like Serge Guilbaut's), painting's "savagery" might be understood as its possibility of radical individuation, of an infinite freedom without obstruction. In this moment, painting's wildness becomes an instrumental advertisement for what democracy allows and is not afraid of — in O'Hara's figure, both stunning in its sudden effect and collapsible in the way that urban billboards are. But at the same time, this radical individuation can also operate as a sort of threatening unconscious to the logic of democracy. By this I mean not merely the violence endemic to imperialism — the savage pleasures of which provide an advertisement for a "democracy" that dares not speak its name and also bind democratic subjects together against the "savage" populations on the fringes of this process. Rather, inasmuch as the poem thematizes New York as the scene of these "Athenian contradictions," perhaps one might understand "stunning collapsible savages" as the images of unchecked and violent desire through which the state reminds its citizens of its necessary, protective role. Savagery here would be the disturbing consequence of *too much freedom*.

And thus democracy must at once advertise and regulate freedom. The tension between these two poles is visible throughout the history of democratic discourse, present even in the "Athenian contradictions" that seem to cause the first Delphic oracle, "Know thyself," to check the atomistic potential latent in its dictum with the second, "Nothing in excess," which suggests a radically different language of external control.[47] Given both O'Hara's previous consideration of the cultural functions of wildness in "Second Avenue" and the centrality of these concerns to "Ode to Willem de Kooning," I do not think it is excessive or arbitrary to see "stunning collapsible savages" as a crucial pivot for O'Hara's ideas about painting's relation to how "democracy is joined." O'Hara's phrase suggests, moreover, that because the complex and sometimes instrumental message of painting's savagery is "collapsible," it can be usefully redeployed — the boards of a canvas merging with the scaffolding of a city billboard. Savagery's being "stunning" thus marks an affective response both to painterly aesthetics and to the popular cultural world of attention-grabbing signage that operates within and contributes toward an overpacked urban world of distractions.

O'Hara's poetry on abstract expressionism collapses two discursive scales by using the psychologically and formally more finite world of the individual canvas to open out to the larger structures of cultural fantasy that make these effects legible in the first place. The very structure of viewing in O'Hara is thus a kind of *mise-en-scène* in which one's entrance into a painting's abstract, gestural world often winds up immanently reinscribing the larger problems of the outside world from which one has exited. Far from an infinite power of atomistic individuality, wildness reenters the discussion in a variety of qualified, reframed, or historicized postures. This struggle between wildness and its uses is not simply the story of internal ethical turmoil popularized by Rosenberg. It is rather a struggle better identified at the level of reception, at the level of cultural recuperation of painting's central experiential terms — wildness, foreignness, and freedom — which seem bound to temporal or historical cycles of exhaustion but which, in O'Hara, often hold out temporary utopian possibility. O'Hara's best poems to painters thus neither seek to preserve paintings from the larger discourses in which they are bound up nor do they try simply to see canvases as excessive examples of this co-option. Instead, the possibility of co-option inheres in the best moments of fantasy projected by the paintings, rendering the viewer's excessive and self-conscious pleasure slightly campy. O'Hara's art poetry suggests that the simultaneous logics developing through sequences of overdetermined lines can register the mutual inscriptions that structure viewing. It is this effect that allows his work to be read as a significant moment in 1950s art criticism, one whose refusal to stick to a single story helps us, in retrospect, to imagine the sublimations that went along with the process of formalizing so-called formalist art criticism. The inappropriately "close," rapid-fire quality of O'Hara's art writing also suggests why it lacks canonical status and is read primarily as documenting the " 'poetic' appreciation" of someone inside a coterie.

If O'Hara's art writing does seem to emerge out of the " 'poetic' appreciation" that Greenberg and Fried associate with *Art News* and even the specific Rosenbergian vocabulary, O'Hara — by allowing art history, politics, and popular culture into a painting's possible discursive sphere — develops Rosenberg's vague schema of "Action Painting" into a far more concrete world of interwoven cultural implications. The project of placing O'Hara's art writing, then, is not a matter of separating or elevating it from Fried's charge but of formulating the kinds of articulateness poetry could achieve in its best instances in the 1950s. O'Hara ultimately imagines a form of viewing which — unlike Rosenberg's and even more unlike Greenberg's and Fried's — links abstract expressionism not merely to the forms of existentialism that had gripped so many imaginations but to the popular culture of Buicks and Gladstones, Hollywood subjectivity, and daily life in post–WWII American urban centers. Moreover, O'Hara sketches a way to understand this pipeline between abstract expressionism and popular culture as a matter of an ascendant post–WWII American culture straining after, and quickly exhausting, forms of wildness and foreignness.

O'Hara suggested this process as early as his 1951 poem "A Terrestrial Cuckoo," which, in its depiction of post–WWII American artists in search of the exotic amid a world thoroughly controlled and disenchanted by America, figures a trip down the Essequibo as a kind of Disneyland "tropical paradise" ride "in our canoe of war-surplus gondola parts" (*CP* 62). Sensing that the scene is a kind of *tromp l'oeil* paradise, the speaker later asks, "Are there people nearby? And postcards?" (ibid.). The United States has become, after World War II, "A Terrestrial Cuckoo," a nation that colonizes territory by placing its eggs in other nests, a practice that leads to the waning of "true foreignness" and to the half-upset and faux naïve question: "Oh Jane, is there no more frontier?" (ibid.).

6 COTERIE AND ALLEGORY
RAUSCHENBERG'S RAW MATERIALS

If [Morris] Louis is a recovery and repetition of Pollock, so also is Rauschenberg — the two possibilities are entwined in one another, are each other's condition of possibility. But it is through Rauschenberg that the story of painting's confusion with and dependence on the theater is narrated, and it is Rauschenberg's work that seems increasingly capable of standing as emblem — hinge — for the past decades.

— Stephen Melville, "Notes on the Reemergence of Allegory"

What an amazing identity Number 29 *[see plate 5] must have! — like that of a human being. More than any other work of Pollock, it points to a new and as yet imponderable esthetic. It points to a world a young experimentalist like Allan Kaprow, who has written on Pollock in another vein, is searching for, and it is the world where the recent works of Robert Rauschenberg must find their emotional comfort. Other paintings of Pollock contain time, our own era with valuable elements of other eras revalued, but* Number 29 *is a work of the future; it is waiting.*

— Frank O'Hara, Jackson Pollock

If it is to hold its own against the tendency to absorption, the allegorical must constantly unfold in new and surprising ways.

— Walter Benjamin, The Origin of German Tragic Drama

It is customary, as I myself have done in the last three chapters, to pair O'Hara with abstract expressionist and neofigurative painters of the 1950s. And yet O'Hara worked at MoMA until his death in 1966 and was widely involved with other artists. This chapter first makes a case study of one such relationship, his early advocacy of Robert Rauschenberg, before considering O'Hara in the context of 1960s art and its polemics.

Though O'Hara's writing on Rauschenberg begins in the mid-1950s, ultimately it speaks very closely to late-1960s debates — especially to Michael Fried's endlessly generative critique of interdisciplinary in "Art and Objecthood." In this chapter, however, Fried will come into play not as a critic of discipline-merging poetic criticism but rather as the foil against which would-be postmodern concepts of allegory emerged. Rauschenberg, of course, was fundamental to such a concept of allegory. At least since Craig Owens's 1980 article, "The Allegorical Impulse: Toward a Theory of Postmodernism" (in Owens's book *Beyond Recognition*), the idea of Rauschenberg as an allegorist has been at the center of numerous versions of postmodernism in art. And if debates about postmodernism in art have cooled a bit over the past decade, it may be in part because the concept of postmodern allegory at their core can now be safely situated as a familiar brand of semiotics. Fragmentary and limited in scope, O'Hara's writings on Rauschenberg nonetheless suggest a compellingly different tack — one in which Rauschenberg's allegorical qualities are, finally, neither purely textual nor entirely material and in which the code of the subject can enter without collapsing the discussion into iconography.

A revived interest in allegory can be traced from Walter Benjamin through Paul de Man and to a series of debates that took place in a number of periodicals, especially *October*, in the early 1980s.[1] An indication of the perceived stakes of these debates at the time can be found in Marcia Tucker's foreword to the 1987 anthology of artists' writings, *Blasted Allegories*, in which she proposes two central functions for this new understanding of allegory. Confronted with the prospect of uniting such disparate artists and writers as John Baldessari, David Salle, Adrian Piper, Dan Graham, Jenny Holzer, Matt Mullican, and Cecilia Vicuña, Tucker suggests, first, that they "leave us with no single style, no unity of purpose, nothing — other than the allegorical 'impulse,' if it can be extended so far as to encompass the myriad viewpoints presented here — that can be fixed or categorized definitively" (viii). Whether such an impulse can actually link these practices is an open question for Tucker and for us. But that allegory should even be suggested as the potential template for such connections is telling of allegory's then-ascending critical value. This valuation stems from Tucker's second claim, that an allegorical sensibility separates these artists from earlier, implicitly modernist or symbolist, sensibilities. If an "allegorical impulse" now seems an increasingly impossible marker of periodization, it is partly because, throughout these debates, such a sensibility tended to be defined in terms of broad surveys of artists (as was the case in Craig Owens's article).[2] Still, the interest in allegory did have several productive effects.

For Owens, recent art challenged the traditional notion that symbol is an organic, internal mode of figuration and allegory an external, artificial one. "Allegory can no longer be condemned," he writes, "as something merely appended to the work of art, for it is revealed as a structural possibility inherent in every work" (74). Implicitly calling into question the distinction between interpretive modes and objects "in themselves," Owens's two-part article popularized a version of postmodern allegory among art historians. For Owens, allegorical effects tend to operate as forms of epistemological negation within semiotic frameworks. And Owens compellingly articulates the interpretive blockages characteristic of many recent allegorical practices; but he also treats these blockages as finalized effects so as to sever allegorical practices from the possibility of their participation in wider semantic contexts — especially social and institutional frameworks that were a very conscious concern of many so-called allegorical artists.[3]

Owens's rhetorical position now seems characteristic of an early moment within the dissemination of poststructuralism within art history in which the pursuit of "meaning," in any of its forms, was the outmoded goal of the iconographer. To make a space for semiotics and deconstruction was to demonstrate the naïve empiricism, positivism, or tyrannical drive toward totalization latent in interpretive models based on meaning. Given that these symptoms *did* structure much art history and criticism at the time, one can understand Owens's desire to reconfigure the field. But in uncoupling interpretation from outmoded concepts like iconography, with its part-by-part accumulation of meaning, Owens positioned allegory as a concept that could only deliver consistent and contained effects like equalization or dissociation. Allegory thus remained stranded at this early phase of the struggle between semiotics and traditional art history.[4] This is especially so insofar as we take Rauschenberg, as Owens does, as the initial moment of a would-be postmodern allegory, a practice that mushrooms into the "allegorical impulse" with which Tucker organizes her survey.

Writing in the late 70s and early 1980s, Owens bases his account of this impulse on a reading of Paul de Man's early work, which foregrounded epistemological struggles between allegory and symbol, or grammar and rhetoric, as a primary discourse on interpretive recuperation that must precede any "thematic" reading.[5] "Allegory," de Man writes, "names the rhetorical process by which the literary text moves from a phenomenal, world-oriented to a grammatical, language-oriented direction."[6] But de Man's later work, especially *Aesthetic Ideology*, developed a complicated (and counterintuitive) concept of materiality that intertwines itself, for many of de Man's critics, with its sometimes opposite — phenomenality.[7] This is significant for Owens inasmuch as he would appeal to de Man for a final move from one category to the other. "The allegorical discourse that characterizes postmodernism," Owens writes, "is a direct consequence of its preoccupation with reading. It is not surprising, then, that we should encounter Robert Rauschenberg, on the threshold of postmodernism, executing works which transform our experience of art from a visual to a textual encounter, and entitling these works *Obelisk, Rebus, Allegory*" (74).

Owens was obviously right to highlight the textual component of Rauschenberg's work. But his account suggests that the materiality of Rauschenberg's combines (his three-dimensional works from the mid-1950s to the early 1960s that combine painting and sculpture and often include a wide variety of both found objects and collage materials) operates only as a catapult toward what becomes, eventually, a purely textual experience. Owens tells us little about the character of this textual encounter except that it is frustrating:

> [I]t remains impossible to read a Rauschenberg if by reading we mean the extraction from a text of a coherent, monological message. All attempts to decipher his works testify only to their own failure, for the fragmentary, piecemeal combination of images that initially impels reading is also what blocks it, erects an impenetrable barrier to its course. Rauschenberg thus confounds the attitude toward reading as an unproblematic activity — which persists, as we know, under the dubious banner "iconography" in art-critical and art-historical discourse, which are thereby paralyzed when confronted with his work and with postmodernism in general (76).

Certainly the negative moment in this passage has been confirmed by the conspicuous failures of a number of traditional iconographic readings of Rauschenberg that have occurred mostly since Owens's article.[8] Still, Owens's passage leads one to wonder precisely how to proceed with a combine piece — a question he takes up only briefly in a reading of Rauschenberg's *Allegory* (see plate 9).[9] After an extended quotation from de Man's well-known deconstructive reading of Yeats's poem "Among School Children," Owens cites the de Manian model of irresolvable conflicts between literalness and figuration and grammar and rhetoric, claiming that as one superimposes the three major allegories of the piece — thematization of consciousness as a dump; the dump as a space beyond recuperation, a space of death; and the ill-repute allegory has fallen into — one is left with a version of postmodern allegory, representative in its "fundamental illegibility." Still, *Allegory*, with its lack of specific photographic references, is not quite representative of Rauschenberg, whose photographic references tend to combine registers of information — from the mute and indecipherable to the seemingly autobiographical and the culturally mass-produced.

Insofar as he highlights a "fundamental illegibility," Owens also follows Rosalind Krauss's 1974 reading of Rauschenberg's *Small Rebus*, a piece with a significantly wider semantic range at the level of explicit collage referentiality. "In the particular way that Rauschenberg enforced a part-by-part, image-by-image reading of his work, he guaranteed that the experience of it would share with language some of its character of discourse," Krauss writes in "Rauschenberg and the Materialized Image." "The encounter with one image after another would, that is, demand an attention to a kind of temporal unfolding that was like that of hearing or reading a sentence. And though the syntactic connections between Rauschenberg's images never have the grammatical logic of a known language, they implied that the modality of discursiveness was one aspect of the artist's medium" (37). In reading Rauschenberg, Krauss recognizes both the necessity and limitation of a concept of temporally unfolding language, which, though highlighting sequential effects, lacks a binding syntax for visual juxtaposition.[10] The heterogeneity among the objects juxtaposed does, however, allow Krauss to claim for it a kind of binding immanence: "[B]y never transcending the material world, the image is unambiguously identified with that material world — arising from within it rather than beyond it" ("Image" 40). Rauschenberg's images signify materiality and then stop signifying. The effect of Rauschenberg's work is thus strangely homogeneous, since no matter what the nature of the juxtaposition, the effect will always be to turn the image into an equivalent material object or thing. "Because each image is given the same level of density as an object," Krauss says, "one is struck not by their multivalence as signs, but rather by their sameness as things. Within the space of *Small Rebus*, that is, they all seem to take on an equal degree of density. They share an equal thickness in terms of their presence to experience. Thus the viewer of the work is struck by the fact that the surface of this painting is a place, or locale, where this kind of equalization can happen" ("Image" 40–41).

If rendering images equivalent or giving them the material qualities of things is an important effect in Rauschenberg (one I will consider below), Krauss does not demonstrate why such an effect should be understood as a formal telos, an equalizing end to signification that would forestall all further interpretation based on juxtaposition and render all of his pieces

Robert Rauschenberg, Small Rebus, *1956; combine painting, 35 x 46 in. Museum of Contemporary Art, Los Angeles, Panza Collection.*

"essentially dissociative."[11] And yet art historians who (understandably) want to position themselves against the iconographic readings of Rauschenberg continue to accept this basic principle of Krauss's interpretation. Branden Joseph, for instance, in what is otherwise one of the best recent accounts of the artist, claims that "Rauschenberg's work . . . shows little or no construction of meaning out of the juxtaposition out of [its] parts" (138).[12] But if Rauschenberg's combines trouble interpretation, if they include vast amounts of texts (both literally and in titles and puns) only to complicate the juxtaposition of images by proliferating and materially embedding them, the result is not a simple denial of meaning. Rather, Rauschenberg's work produces meaning through its very oscillation between materiality and textuality — though this meaning is anything but thematic or iconographic. And in as much as Rauschenberg's work will sit stably within neither category, it is perhaps even *more* de Manian than Owens acknowledges.[13] Jonathan Culler touches on such an understanding of allegory when he describes it as "the mode which recognizes the impossibility of fusing the empirical and the eternal and thus demystifies the symbolic relation by stressing the separateness of the two levels, the impossibility of bringing them together except momentarily and against a background of disassociation, and the importance of protecting each level and the potential link between them by making it arbitrary. Only allegory can make the connection in a self-conscious and demystified way" (*Structuralist Poetics* 230).

Understanding allegory not as an essential dissociation but as a mode that stages the contingency of links, competition, and even mutual inscription between two registers of interpretation allows the term metacritical and demystifying roles. It is in this sense that reading a coterie, too, could be figured as an allegorical enterprise, since such a reading presents the problem of understanding at once a rhetorical mode *and* a historically inflected collection of proper names and events. There is no simple synthesis. And yet coterie repeatedly stages the collision between these registers, just as allegory stages a collision between the empirical and the textual, the material and the phenomenal. Like allegory, coterie is an impossible hinge.

O'Hara's links to Rauschenberg extend, however, well beyond these morphological parallels. In fact, O'Hara was Rauschenberg's first positive critic. Moreover, O'Hara's 1955 review of and 1959 poem to the artist suggest a point of departure for an allegorical reading of Rauschenberg that is quite different from the kind of allegory pursued by Owens and Krauss. After extrapolating a number of concepts and attitudes from these O'Hara pieces about Rauschenberg, I will explore them further later in the chapter, by taking up a reading of Rauschenberg's 1954 combine *Untitled*.[14]

Though O'Hara was undoubtedly closer to many other artists, there is an odd parallel between his own career and Rauschenberg's.[15] Both central to versions of postmodernism, their works have often seemed to embarrass criticism by their casualness, literalness, and extraordinarily specific reference systems. Both, moreover, have usually been seen in relation to a close friend or boyfriend within the discipline (Johns/Ashbery), whose work is taken to be more philosophically substantial. But beyond this parallel at the level of reception, their careers are more particularly intertwined. In January 1955, while Rauschenberg was still not trusted by critics, O'Hara wrote the first positive review — this one of Rauschenberg's December 1954–January 1955 show at the Egan Gallery in New York.[16] Along with many of the red paintings (including *Yoicks*, *Red Import* and several untitled ones), we know that early combines were included, among them *Collection* and possibly also *Charlene*.[17] As the first positive review of Rauschenberg, O'Hara's piece for *Art News* is worth looking at in full in conjunction with plate 7 and figure 25.

Robert Rauschenberg, Minutiae, 1954; combine painting: oil, paper, fabric, newspaper, wood, metal, and plastic, with mirror on string, on wood structure, 84 1/2 x 81 x 30 1/2 in. Created as a set for Merce Cunningham Dance Company's Minutiae. Collection of the artist.

> Bob Rauschenberg, *enfant terrible* of the New York School, is back again to even more brilliant effect — what he did to all-white and all-black in his last show and to nature painting with his controversial moss-dirt-and-ivy picture in the last Stable Annual, he tops in this show of blistering and at the same time poignant collages. Some of them seem practically room-size, and have various illuminations within them apart from their technical luminosity: bulbs flicker on and off, lights cast shadows, and lifting up a bit of pink gauze you stare out of the picture into your own magnified eye. He provides a means by which you, as well as he, can get "in" the painting. Doors open to reveal clearer images, or you can turn a huge wheel to change the effect at will. Many of the pieces are extrovert, reminiscent of his structure in the Merce Cunningham ballet *Minutiae*, but not all are so wildly ingenious: other pieces, including two sex organs (male and female) made from old red silk umbrellas, have a gentle and just passion for moving people. When you look back at the more ecstatic works they, too, have this quality not at all overshadowed by their brio. For all the baroque exuberance of the show, quieter pictures evidence a serious lyrical talent; simultaneously, in the big inventive pieces there is a big talent at play, creating its own occasions as a stage does. (*WW* 20)

In positioning Rauschenberg as the *enfant terrible* of the New York School, O'Hara suggests that this self-consciously disruptive relationship stems, in part, from a set of literalizations — moves by which the language of painting, particularly abstract expressionist painting, confronts itself *as* language within Rauschenberg's theatrical environments.[18] Punning on occupying the canvas, either as a painter or a viewer, Rauschenberg literalizes this absorptive space (immediately rendering it theatrical) so that "you, as well as he, can get 'in' the painting." But this pun on Pollock's famous remark points not to a move from materiality to text (as Owens suggests) nor from image to material (as Krauss claims).[19] Instead, Rauschenberg calls into being a supplementary verbal context that, operating alongside the substance of the combine, neither obliterates the object from which it emerged nor subsumes its own signification into a homogeneous effect. What gets materialized here is not so much any particular image but the larger discursive context in which painters paint. It is in this atmosphere of literalized verbal codes for painting that we read O'Hara's interest in their room-size scale (which would have been true of *Minutiae* and the combine *Untitled*) and his pun on their manufactured luminosity

Robert Rauschenberg, Monogram, 1955–1959; *combine painting: oil, paper, fabric, printed paper, printed reproductions, metal, wood, rubber shoe heel, and tennis balls on canvas, with oil on Angora goat and rubber tire, on wood platform mounted on four casters,* 42 x 63 1/4 x 64 1/2 in. *Moderna Museet, Stockholm.*

(*Charlene*, for instance, featured an electric light). The concept of a beholder's involvement gets further literalized both with the viewer's eye finding itself enlarged in a mirror behind gauze and with the idea of participation: one can "turn a huge wheel to change the effect at will," which may be a reference to the splayed umbrella that becomes a kind of wheel in the upper right corner of *Charlene*. When O'Hara concludes by telling us that "in the big inventive pieces there is a big talent at play, creating its own occasions as a stage does," he implies not merely that Rauschenberg's pieces are dramatic or theatrical but that this stage is a space on which the language of recent painting gets anatomized — its metaphysics of entry, illumination, movement, participation, and scale all splayed out within a built environment designed to highlight, though also to take pleasure in, the conventionality of these verbal adjuncts to the experience of viewing paintings.[20] This play will reach a new level with *Monogram* (which was not

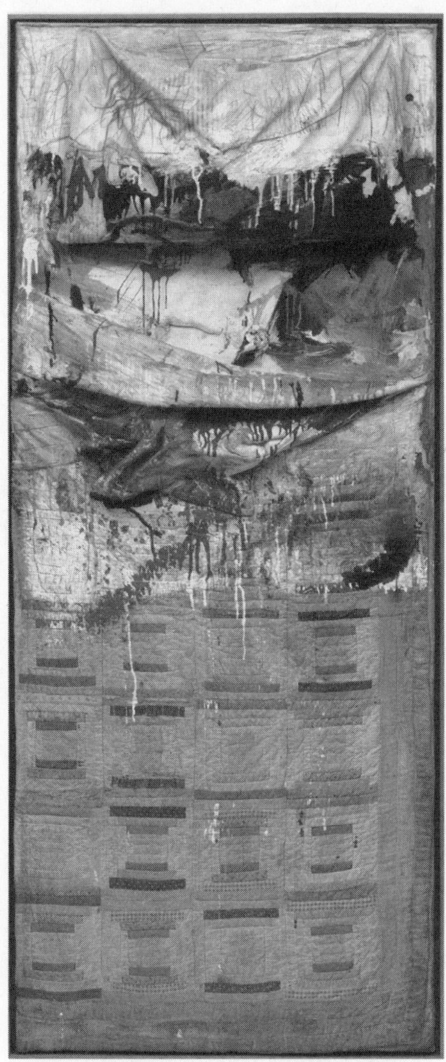

Robert Rauschenberg, Bed, 1955; combine painting: oil and pencil on pillow, quilt, and sheet, mounted on wood, 75 1/4 x 31 1/2 x 72 1/2 in. Museum of Modern Art, New York, gift of Leo Castelli in honor of Alfred H. Barr, Jr., 1989. Photo: Museum of Modern Art. © Robert Rauschenberg/licensed by VAGA, New York.

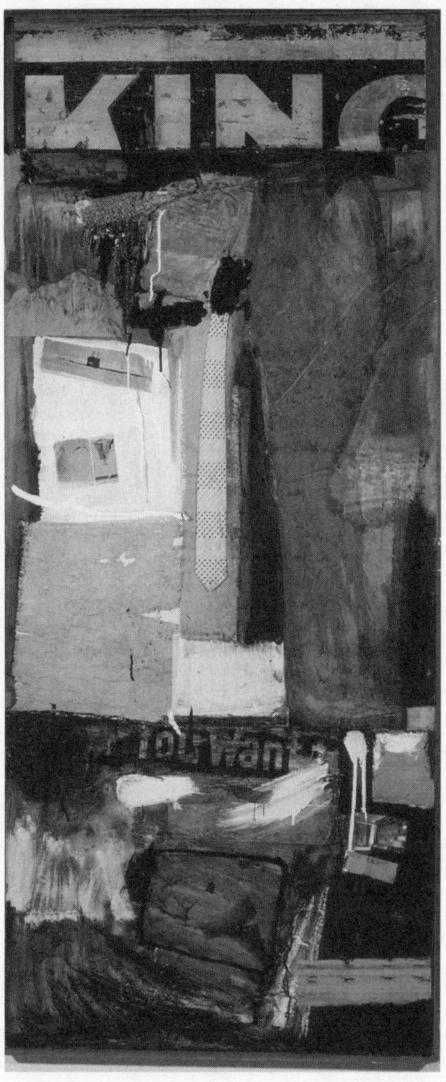

Robert Rauschenberg, Kickback, 1959; combine painting, 76 1/2 x 33 1/4 x 2 3/4 in. Museum of Contemporary Art, Los Angeles, Panza Collection. © Robert Rauschenberg/licensed by VAGA, New York.

finished until 1959 but was visible in Rauschenberg's studio as early as 1955), in which an Angora goat has come to replace the bestial or primal action painter getting "in" to his painting's field, a field that, now horizontal and strewn with wreckage, is more of an overgrown pasture.

O'Hara's positive take on Rauschenberg found little sympathy among New York art critics in the mid-1950s, and Rauschenberg did not have another solo show until 1958. Leo Steinberg's response to Rauschenberg's 1956 show at the Egan Gallery is typical: "On the merry works of Robert Rauschenberg the kindest comment I can make is that some of my friends, whose (other) judgments I respect, think it not out of place in an art exhibition. Presumably these 'combines' of elaborated whimsy, glue and chic will steal the show. Eulenspiegel is abroad again, and one must be patient" ("Month in Review" 46–47). By Rauschenberg's March 1958 show at the Castelli Gallery, there were more positive signs, though far from anything like the climate of approval that had met Jasper Johns's first show at Castelli that January.[21] Leo Steinberg came around to Rauschenberg,[22] and Leo Castelli bought *Bed*, though this was the only piece in the show that sold.[23] When he wrote his first review of Rauschenberg, O'Hara had comparatively little power in the art world. By 1959, however, O'Hara had — to repeat — been hired by MoMA as a special assistant in the International Program and was working under Porter McCray. O'Hara would be appointed assistant curator the following year. But already by 1959 he was selecting artists for international shows, and in fact, it was O'Hara who chose three Rauschenbergs[24] — *Bed*, *Thaw*, and *Kickback* — for *Documenta II: Kunst nach 1945*, in Kassel, West Germany, in 1959.[25] This was a pivotal moment in Rauschenberg's career: by the end of the year he would be included in Dorothy Miller's *Sixteen Americans*, a show of higher profile. On May 19, 1959, probably while he was reviewing work for the Documenta exhibition, O'Hara wrote "For Bob Rauschenberg" — a poem that provides a rich, early, and as yet unexamined account of what it might mean to read the artist allegorically.

> Yes, it's necessary, I'll do
> what you say, put everything
> aside but what is here. The frail
> instant needs us and the cautious
> breath, so easily drowned in Liszt
> or sucked out by a vulgar soprano.
> (CP 322)

O'Hara begins counterintuitively by finding in the work an invitation to a mode of thinking curiously related to Michael Fried's famous concept of absorption: successful occupation of the instant — grace, even — is seen as a function of complete attention to some given context without preconceived or overstated gestures. Such a context, what is "here," is implicitly the particular qualities of Rauschenberg's nonartistic materials rather than, for Fried, the "here" of a medium like painting's unique resources. Fried, as we will see, dismisses Rauschenberg for failing on these very grounds — for abandoning modernist painting and its "distinctions between works of art and other kinds of objects or occurrences in the world" (*Art and Objecthood* 259). But the kind of absorption O'Hara finds in Rauschenberg is itself illuminating with regard not merely to the Friedian model but also to Rauschenberg's own reception history.

To account for this deferral of absorption, for the narratives that inevitably come in to enact or describe presentness — to describe the replacement of access to a "now" or a "here" with deferred, temporal consciousness — is in one sense to invoke the now-familiar shift from a symbolic to an allegorical mode.[26] Such a shift has, as I mentioned at the outset, been proposed as a key to postmodernism, a key offered through Rauschenberg. For O'Hara, the earnest ambition of a kind of absorption — to "put everything / aside but what is here" — must from the beginning ward off a powerful set of distractions (such as Liszt and the "vulgar soprano") that thematize a failure to grasp the "frail / instant." But even in this statement of principle, a version of modernist immanence becomes an odd kind of intertextuality, a network of interwoven subtexts. The poem as a whole can be taken as a way of configuring this Rauschenbergian network — the salient features that simultaneously establish and undermine the immanence of "what is here." This project is implicitly initiated by a second-person interlocutor who calls out for one to pay attention: "Yes, it's necessary. I'll do / what you say." A moment of this conversation seems to precede the poem, which begins with the poet responding to the interlocutor as much as to the work; or, the work is itself an instance of this conversation, a mode of "discursiveness," as Rosalind Krauss noted in 1974 ("Image" 37). Which is to say that some dialog about the possible relations between quotidian objects and art is the poem's first concern, a concern that the poem deftly shifts back onto the objects, as if it emerged immanently from them though also spoken out loud.

By 1959 some of the objects O'Hara would have seen in Rauschenberg's work included men's button-down shirts and ties, paint-encrusted blankets, steel radial tires, embroidered fabrics, stuffed hens and goats, rickety wooden panels, dress shoes, splayed umbrellas, mirrors, and Pantone paint samples. O'Hara certainly calls our attention to the effects of Rauschenberg's raw materials — their ability to arrest a "frail / instant" and focus attention on "what is here"; but he does not see Rauschenberg's motivation of substance as a final and uniform effect. That is, the poem's uneven associative terrain — its mention of sexual history, music, literary history, and struggles against appropriation or institutional framing (all of which I'll get to) — testifies to an unevenness within Rauschenberg's effects. This interest in unevenness, in quite different kinds of articulateness within the combines, separates O'Hara's reading of Rauschenberg from those of many of the artist's critics from the 1950s to the present. And in 1959 there was still very little positive written about the artist.

To "put everything / aside" at that moment therefore also meant to hold in abeyance the quite large climate of negative critical opinion that might prejudice one against Rauschenberg: to experience the raw materials of Rauschenberg's combine pieces as raw materials was, in part, to *decontextualize* them from the noise of negative critical opinion that sought to overcode them — much as the "vulgar soprano" or the Liszt would distract one from the present. Rauschenberg's negative reception was only partly a function of a still-dominant abstract expressionism (dominant at least until 1962).[27] When critics weren't objecting to his reliance on textuality, they were disturbed by his seemingly anti-art stance (labeled "Neo-Dada" after 1958)[28] and/or troubled by the historical implications of a reengagement with modes of modernist negation. "[I]t is necessary," one critic complains of the 1951 show at Parsons, "to know the title of each painting before it takes on more than a formal meaning."[29] This attack can then be paired with Dore Ashton's reaction to Rauschenberg's 1953 show at the Stable Gallery: "Sick unto death of 'good painting,' Rauschenberg has decided that paintings have lives of their own." While Ashton also notices Rauschenberg's punning relationship to the language of art description (and history), such a stance is, for her, atomistic, childish, and ahistorical: "But isn't Rauschenberg's experience, his unique experience, like a small thorn in the hide of an elephant? Doesn't art require a hint of the banal, a hint of the social role of man to locate it in time and history."[30] James Fitzsimmons extends this view of Rauschenberg into the combine pieces, which he describes as "vast paste-ups of torn newspaper coated with black paint and hung as panels, edge to edge . . . Rauschenberg . . . working instinctively and with little structural sense, has produced a city-dump mural out of handmade debris." The problem is not a distaste for junk, Fitzsimmons says, but the belatedness of Rauschenberg's turn toward junk — compounded, again, by a reliance on the verbal: "No doubt the author of these contraptions could explain them, but whatever their metaphysical implications, how dull they seem 25 years after Dada, how much less amusing than Duchamp's *object trouvés* and Man Ray's *object inutiles*."[31]

Bracketing temporarily the historical time line onto which O'Hara situates the work, another sense of his attempt to "put everything / aside but what is here" seems to be directed against the charge that Rauschenberg's combines are undermined by their supplementary linguistic effects. But rather than demonstrate their nondiscursive immanence (their compellingness as instances of materiality), O'Hara punningly suggests that their discursiveness is simply immanent and not an external supplement. This play on Rauschenberg's relation to immanence is perhaps O'Hara's central gesture: O'Hara knows to "put everything / aside" is precisely what Rauschenberg — famous dabbler with urban detritus — has been charged with *not doing*, that this charge has generally come from within a version of modernism based on the rhetoric of immanence.[32] O'Hara must put the discourse of immanence aside in order to treat Rauschenberg immanently. So there is a sort of faux naïvete in O'Hara's absorption in "what is here" in Rauschenberg's pieces. It is a theatrical absorption.

Why should I hear music? I'm not
a pianist any more, and in truth
I despise my love for Pasternak,
born in Baltimore, no *sasha* mine,
and an adolescent taken in hay
above horses —
(CP 322)

Not distracted by a "vulgar soprano" or Liszt, we might dissolve ourselves musically into the "frail / instant" — insofar as O'Hara insists on music as part of the associative terrain — by imagining the prepared pianos and framed quotidian sounds of John Cage or the patterned, minimal note pulses of Morton Feldman, the two musicians with whom Rauschenberg was most closely associated.[33] But before any consideration of experimental music can move to particulars, we must switch tracks into literature (perhaps through the association of Pasternak's early musical training, which greatly attracted O'Hara). Again, instead of a reflection on Pasternak's writing "in itself," we glance off into fleeting references toward the contingent topics of sexual history (O'Hara's) and the fact that the American Right's warm reception of *Doctor Zhivago* has, by 1959, made it impossible still to love Pasternak. While I have already discussed these lines in chapter 4, I must here briefly relate them to the specific textual or associative picture of Rauschenberg they help to establish. First, Rauschenberg's work, like O'Hara's poems, seems to open up the question of sexual history — "no *sasha* mine / and an adolescent taken in hay / above horses" — not as a veiled central content (as more recent iconographers claim) but in the context of a wide variety of intertexts that operate on quite different discursive registers. O'Hara would have seen and recognized references to Rauschenberg's shared life with Cy Twombly and Jasper Johns in the combines — photographs of Johns, for instance, in the 1954 combine *Untitled*. And yet these intimate and autobiographical registers, especially when positioned against culture more broadly, easily lend themselves to co-option. This is the immediate logic of having the Pasternak reference precede the reference to sexual history, since in *Doctor Zhivago* a story about a struggle to achieve autonomous subjectivity has, beyond the intentions of the author, become a simplistic Cold War advertisement for the West.

Awkwardly intertwining public and private interpretive registers, O'Hara's poem also therefore stages the problem of coterie. It does so, moreover, not just within one temporal slice but diachronically as well.

> what should I be
> if not alone in pain, apart from
> the heavenly aspirations of
> Spenser and Keats and Ginsberg,
> who have a language that permits
> them truth and beauty, double-coin?
> exercise, recreations, drugs —
> (CP 322)

The family of attributes one might associate with each of the proper names in the poem is, of course, fluid and multiple. But in the context of debates about Rauschenberg's early work (to which O'Hara has already been alluding), we might associate the name Spenser with familiar charges against Spenserian allegory: that it imposes a supplementary verbal quality on depicted events and is thus overly discursive and that these conflicting levels of interpretation result in composite aesthetic experiences, or what Edwin Honig calls (from a more positive perspective) "fantastic amalgamations."[34] Pulled into the context of the artistic and cultural negations or destabilizations that were understood to link Rauschenberg to Neo-Dada,[35] one sense of the name Keats, then, would seem to be that of negative capability: "when man is capable of being in uncertainties, Mysteries, doubts, without any irritable reaching after fact & reason."[36] In his 1965 catalog *Three American Painters*, Michael Fried seeks to separate the "Neo-Dada figures such as John Cage, Jasper Johns, and Robert Rauschenberg" (who had recently called the work of art into question) from the ambitions of modernism:

> [A]t bottom, Dada in any of its manifestations and modernist painting are antithetical to one another. Where the former aspires to obliterate all distinctions between works of art and other kinds of objects or occurrences in the world, the latter has sought to isolate, assert, and work with what is essential to the art of painting at a given moment. It would, however, be mistaken to think of Dada — the most precious of movements — as opposed to art. Rather, Dada stands opposed to the notion of value or quality in art, and in that sense represents a reaction against the unprecedented demands modernist painting made of its practitioners. (*Art and Objecthood* 259)[37]

Fried's reading of Rauschenberg is worth considering here because, though it does not appear until six years after the poem, it dismisses Dada in a way that was common until recently: Dada operates not as a radical negation but as a weak cop-out, an evasion of the difficult demands of modernist paintings.[38] The problem is not negation or doubling back per se but doubling back on a mistake, on a negation of value. If we are right to hear Keats here as an emblem of negation, then certainly Allen Ginsberg's attack, in his 1956 *Howl*, on a hypostatized figure of oppressive rationality, Moloch, would follow from and update this project.[39] Thematizing a Beat coterie of resistant and often queer hipsters, Ginsberg seems to bring this genealogy into the present, where it can be mined not merely for Keats's "truth and beauty," but also for "exercise, recreations, drugs."

If the "Spenser and Keats and Ginsberg" trio is, for O'Hara, one of the exemplary instances of "what is here" in Rauschenberg, this is so not because Rauschenberg, in his discursiveness, is simply like these authors because he makes allusions to them, or shares precisely their own "heavenly aspirations." Though an identification with these aspirations has seemed to hold out the possibility of some transtemporal collectivity, O'Hara's poem ends by returning to the question of "what is here" (in

Rauschenberg but also in these aspirations), only to put its material certainty, its immanence, into greater doubt.

what
can heaven mean up, down, or sidewise
who knows what is happening to him,
what has happened and is here, a
paper rubbed against the heart
and still too moist to be framed.
(CP 322)

Linking back to the three poets' aspirations, which allow the speaker to avoid being "alone in pain," heaven here operates less as a theological future reward than as a question about the present possibility of social, literary, and erotic contact, about "what has happened and is here." Access to this potentially immanent experience in Rauschenberg's art would seem to be complicated still further by the spatial complexities ("what / can heaven mean up, down, or sideways") of his sculptural works and combines — especially the arrangement of collage elements and quotidian objects on multiple three-dimensional surfaces that can be seen from a variety of different angles and in many relations to each other.[40] O'Hara seems to come at these formulations about the slipperiness (or moistness) of immanence as a way to conceptualize the semantic range of Rauschenberg's notorious "raw materials." But it is not only umbrellas, shirts, or stuffed hens that he will not read "immanently." Rather, O'Hara's refusal to understand such objects as self-evidently mute material mirrors his resistance to interpreting Rauschenberg's collage elements as simply autobiographical — that is, as immanent to, or neatly framed within, the atomistic code of the subject.

If Rauschenberg's raw materials bear the traces of interiority, of a "paper rubbed against the heart," still they remain "too moist to be framed." O'Hara thus seems careful not to frame these effects of rawness and disruptive moistness as essentially subversive. They are, instead, temporarily so — temporarily because O'Hara implicitly imagines these practices within the history of art, within a series of institutional recuperations, so that Rauschenberg's grainy rawness can eventually become the de facto background for any MTV video. It is precisely in relation to such later recuperations that one might read Rauschenberg's famous statement — "Painting relates to both art and life. Neither can be made. (I try to act in that gap between the two.)" (see Kotz 7). This "gap" is

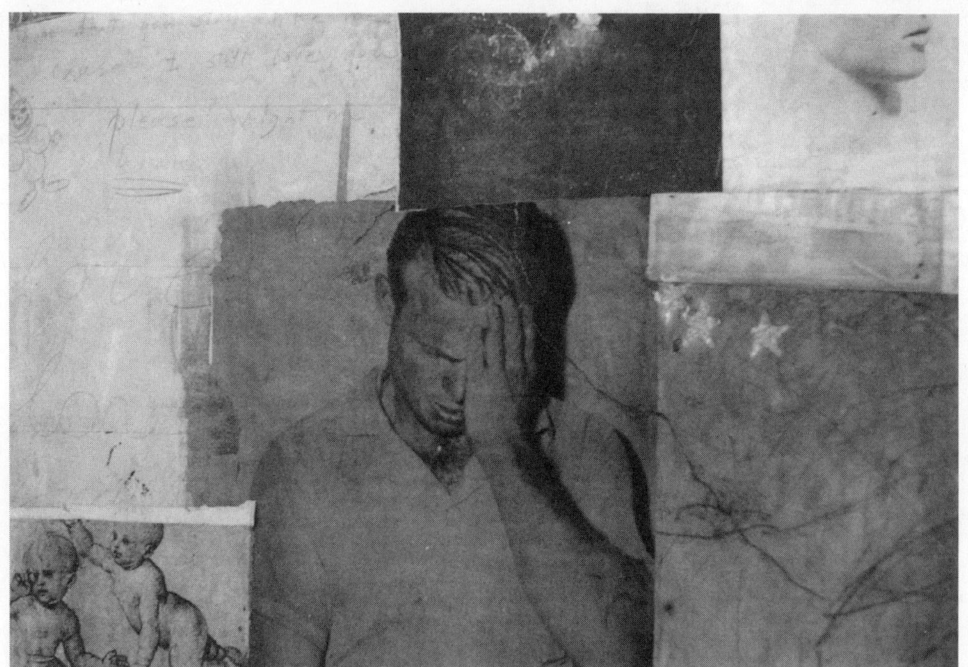

Robert Rauschenberg, detail of Untitled *(see plate 8).*

less spatial than temporal and historical — a gap separating an object "too moist to be framed" from its eventual framing.

• • •

Because O'Hara's insights on Rauschenberg are at once fragmentary and not closely bound to any single piece in a sustained way, the first part of this chapter seems to beg the question of precisely how, inside the works, immanence becomes semantically coded, how the code of the subject comes into contact with meanings outside it and how all of this might relate to allegory. In the period of the 1954–1955 Egan Gallery show, the combine *Untitled* (see plate 8) may be at once the most seemingly autobiographical and yet the most semantically various and unstable.[41] It is the kind of piece William Rubin seems to have in mind when he calls Rauschenberg's work "particular rather than archetypical" and at times "embarrassingly private" (26).[42]

But if the coterie qualities of *Untitled* might embarrass a viewer, this is not simply because the work neatly documents a private life. Not framed by a title providing a multivalent interpretive trope — like *Rebus*, *Interview*, *Allegory* or, from Rauschenbergs' silkscreens, *Express* or *Payload* — *Untitled* at once denies such a trope and, when it is referred to as *Untitled Combine ("Man with white shoes")*, attaches another more biographical one provisionally through parentheses.[43] Indeed, the very fact that there is uncertainty about whether the parenthetical phrase should be part of the title speaks to the piece's own concerns: do we read the combine without biographical presuppositions, or do we see it as relating primarily to a single human subject?[44] And as a freestanding three-dimensional framework at once containing literal objects (a hen and a pair of shoes) and plastered with collage material on several sides, the combine provides quite a bit to read.[45]

But before this reading can proceed to the particulars of text and collage, one is first struck by a series of larger-scale oscillations or plays between two-dimensional surfaces and literal objects. This play might be understood through O'Hara's remark that Rauschenberg "provides a means by which you, as well as he, can get 'in' the painting" — since a series of animal and human stand-ins evoke not merely the abstract expressionist notion of an artist merging himself with his canvas (or becoming animal in his act of composition), but also the task of a viewer being able to perform this merging vicariously in a later act of interpretation.[46] Such interpretation is further theatricalized by impossible analogies established between the hen or the shoes and the collage surface against which we read them (or behind which we eventually discover them). *Untitled* thus playfully literalizes the idea of "content" by shielding actual objects behind each of the two major collage fields, objects that pose themselves as delayed signifieds occupying actual rather than implied space (as if to enforce the comparative reality of their less legible messages).

Nor are the collage surfaces easily or consistently legible. The back surface, for instance, provides a painterly collage field, a sort of anthology of textures and mark-making techniques that includes newspapers, wrapping paper, comics, photographs, postcards, and drawings, as well as paint that appears to be squeezed directly from the tube and, in other sections, paint that is crusted and glommed onto the paper surfaces.

Overall, three major breaks in the surface disrupt the flatness of the visual field: part of an image of a face, a postcard of a river in Uniontown, Alabama, on the left, and a photo of a domestic interior in the lower right. Less visible are a photo of a building with frontal columns below and a sequence of comic strips in the upper right. The characteristic gesture here is the smear, which extends also to the photographs, as is not the case

Robert Rauschenberg, detail of Untitled *(see plate 8).*

Robert Rauschenberg, detail of Untitled *(see plate 8).*

Robert Rauschenberg, detail of Untitled *(see plate 8).*

on the front surface. A material conglomeration into or onto which spatial and narrative moments are either punctured or applied, this surface recalls the exuberant textures Rauschenberg had been experimenting with beginning with his black paintings but extending through his gold and the red paintings as well.[47] What punctures this material plane, what is allowed to register space on it, is the superimposition of nostalgic narratives of turn-of-the-century interiors or uncorrupted nature, sites of fantastic or projected completeness that resonate with the idealized function of the suited man on the front. As fictions of completeness, these images suggest the problems of the relation between raw material and narrative conclusions that the front of the combine develops more fully.

But it is the front upper surface that provides the greatest density of collage material. As one begins to sort out the types of material presented here, rather than *Rebus* or *Allegory*, the more limited, less allusive figure of a scrapbook might, at first, come to mind. The detail and complexity of this material are greatest on the surface above and to the right of the standing man. The upper collage surface provides photographic images of children, embracing couples, and tombstones as well as newspaper scraps and actual drawings. But if we assume that our reading of the collage field should be governed by the figure of a subject in whom all of these images would be reconciled, whose kinship structures are somehow being diagramed, we must still reconcile this plane within the complicated whole of the piece.

Such a double reading might go, tentatively, as follows: within the main collage field, the landing parachute at the top might be taken to imply an origin, initiating a set of possible movements through the rest of the images, which could be seen to end with the photograph of a man with his head in his hands at the bottom of the section — Jasper Johns, in fact. Though variant paths might introduce new folds, the section could be construed as a narrative of subject formation, including origins (parents, landings, hens, childbirth), events (a Miss America contest, a marriage), and conclusions (tombstones, emotional crises). This genealogy would belong to the man in the white suit seen below, who, standing just off to the side, would seem to be its materialization or conclusion. But if *Untitled* seems to hold out the possibility of such a neat autobiographical reading, it also materializes or literalizes such a reading in disruptive ways that recall the relation between text and object, surface and sculpture, that I described earlier.

In the context of *Untitled*, Rosalind Krauss's 1974 reading of Rauschenberg's "materialization of images" now provides us a new point of departure. What has been materialized, what has become a mute and equivalent thing, in *Untitled*, however, is not only the collection of photographs and drawings pasted onto the wooden or fabric sculptural surfaces but the larger, though fragmentary, narratives they seem to encode.[48] Images and the larger narratives they suggest seem to have become things not because they disintegrate into Krauss's homogeneous material surface but because the meanings that emerge from that surface operate at a metanarrative rather than an autobiographical register.

It is significant to the piece's meanings, moreover, that the autobiographical subject, who will not quite be summarized by the collection of images (with the familial structures they seem to imply), is one who operates outside the reproductive logic of heterosexual narratives. Though the combine seems to provide all of the "raw materials" for constructing the image system or kinship relations of a normative life — wedding-anniversary announcements, photographs of family members, children's drawings, and a well-dressed male subject in whom all of these experiences would seem to be reconciled — yet this dandy cannot quite conclude the narrative because of two characteristic Rauschenberg puns, puns that, as O'Hara suggests in his review, destabilize the relationship between object and text, immanence and uncontainable recoding. The first offers the absent subject who would, but doesn't, "fit the shoes" left empty in the piece's back compartment. The second presents the hen as a parody of routinized, instrumentalized reproduction.

But *Untitled* is no simple allegory for the queer refusal of heterosexual narrative. If that refusal operates, *in potentia*, within the combine's raw material, the piece as a whole problematizes the narration of a self more broadly — both by proliferating visual information beyond the possibility of any neat recuperation and by collapsing distinctions between interior and exterior registers of discourse. Thus, one finds images of quiet lakes and quaint Victorian interiors Rauschenberg seems not to have visited next to discarded wrapping papers, paint-smeared fabrics, and encrusted comic-book fragments; reproductions of Leonardo da Vinci's cherubs next to original drawings by Cy Twombly, Jack Tworkov, and Rauschenberg's three-year-old son. In combining these materials, *Untitled* elaborates not so much *a* particular background as an intersubjective struggle among several, marked by evacuations, revisions, and impossible conclusions. In the years to come Rauschenberg will first move away from the code of the autobiographical toward appropriation in his combines, before turning to the silk-screening process to create an inventory of images that he can deploy in multiple combinations and iterations. But even at the early stage of *Untitled*, the autonomy of the would-be autobiographical image is under pressure. Though O'Hara does not present his own reading as explicitly allegorical, its mutual inscriptions of the interior and the exterior and of materiality and text suggest how it might be usefully positioned within Rauschenberg's later reception.

In suggesting that one register of Rauschenberg's allegorical effect involves the code of the subject, I want to stress that this flickering subject does not offer itself as a consolidated identity — one that might seek simply to replace the angst-ridden macho self of abstract expressionism. Instead, Rauschenberg confronts identity claims at a more foundational level, since his troubling raw material forces the discourse of subjectivity to engage its condition of possibility, its reliance on competing syntaxes and logics of organization to mobilize image pools that are themselves always threatening to become pools of things or rigidified narratives, to be, as O'Hara suggests, "drowned in Liszt / or sucked out by a vulgar soprano."

This articulate recalcitrance of raw material is characteristic, historically, of allegory. In his study of allegory in German *Trauerspiel*, Benjamin claims that "the language of the baroque is constantly convulsed by rebellion on the part of the elements which make it up" (*Origen* 207). This rebellion returns us to Michael Fried's disagreement with Rauschenberg's work. Defending his emphasis on "conviction" as a fundamental category in art history, Fried acknowledges that such a term

> invites inquiry into what might be called the politics of conviction, that is to say, the countless ways in which a person's deepest beliefs about art and even about the quality of specific works of art have been influenced, sometimes to the point of having been decisively shaped, by institutional factors that, traced to their limits, merge imperceptibly with the culture at large. In a particular instance this may result in the undermining of certain beliefs and their replacement by others (a state of no belief is impossible). But it doesn't follow merely from the recognition of influence, even powerful influence, that the original beliefs are not to be trusted. A host of institutional factors must have collaborated long ago to incline me to take Manet seriously; but I can no more imagine giving up my conviction about the greatness of his art than I can imagine losing interest in painting altogether. (Both events could happen and perhaps will, but if they do I will scarcely be the same person. Some convictions are part of one's identity.) ("How Modernism Works" 71)

The objections to this type of reasoning worked out initially within Marxism and later within cultural studies converge on the notion that ideology, or the influence of what Fried would call "institutions," works precisely by making institutionally produced effects seem natural and original and thus trustworthy. Obviously, Fried sets himself up for this type of critique; rather than play it out here, what seems important to note is that the problems of identity enacted by Rauschenberg's combine pieces provide a way to imagine Fried's claims about identity cast back into the very history Fried seeks to narrate. That is, it is important to Fried's history (though obviously something that cannot register *in* this history) that Rauschenberg renders the raw materials of identity recalcitrant, opaque, foreign: at the very moment Fried uses a claim about conviction being as fundamental as identity to separate the high modernism of Louis, Noland, Stella, and Caro from the degraded, supposedly antimodern work of what he calls the "Neo-Dada figures," Rauschenberg creates works that disrupt the foundational status of precisely this concept of identity. This is what Stephen Melville has in mind when, considering the status of the absorption/theatricality debate in the aftermath of "Art and Objecthood," he remarks that "[w]e are no more free to walk away from the complications imposed on criticism by an acknowledgement of its theatricality than Fried is to walk away from the complications imposed on the history of art by the persistence of a [Tony] Smith or a Rauschenberg" (72).

Melville thus attempts to deconstruct (rather than simply invert) Fried's absorption/theatricality distinction. In doing this Melville looks closely at Fried's writing, especially "Art and Objecthood," as a way to complicate its status as the last straw man of modernism.

> "Postmodernism" — insofar as it is characterized by its allegorical impulse — represents the freeing of painting from its prison of opticality as well as its recovery of subject matter beyond itself and the logic of its medium. But we do well to see how small a liberation this is. If it is true that the past fifteen or twenty years have seen the hegemony of the optical dismantled, it is still true also that "paintings are made to be beheld" — opticality is but one name for, interpretation of, this "primordial convention" (just as the literal construal of the medium is but one construal among others of the medium of painting).
>
> We cast "postmodernism" at a deeper level if we say that the allegorical impulse is one which would acknowledge explicitly the futility of trying to sort the "mere" from the "pure" — an impulse to embrace the heteronomy of painting. (80)

Understanding the allegorical impulse as a crisis between the mere and the pure is a useful way to avoid the reactivity and transcendence implicit in many theories of postmodernism. But unlike Steinberg, Crimp, Krauss, and others, Melville does not read individual artworks by Rauschenberg to explore just how they impose "complications . . . on the history of art." In a sense, then, my effort to relate Rauschenberg to the problems brought up by Frank O'Hara's writing has been an attempt to come at this issue from another angle, one that can account for an allegorical impulse that is neither iconographic nor fundamentally illegible.

Rauschenberg's practice of materializing images (and at times narratives) works not to produce a particular formal effect, the pure equalization that Krauss mentions, but to unsettle the relations among images, narratives, and identities more broadly. It is not that images can make a final jump to the pure status of things, but that the unarrestable slippage between the categories of things and images, like that between pure materiality and mere textuality (or vice versa), works in Rauschenberg to address the institutions and conventions of image reading that would render a subject legible or place an artwork within an art-historical category. This is perhaps the widest frame of reference in which Rauschenberg's allegorical effects register. It is characteristic of the "fabulous amalgamations" in the combines, however, that allegory operates both as a broad, abstract question about the institutional underpinnings of the subject and as a more specific question about the literal character of artistic language or the logic of historical recycling.

That the code of the subject (and its history) enters the allegorical amalgamation does not mean that this code simply subsumes all other codes. As in O'Hara, Rauschenberg stages interiority as a discourse on par with others. Rauschenberg's interiority has been a stumbling block to interpretation — having either stolen the show (in the iconographic readings) or been awkwardly ignored (in the semiotic readings) — in part because the conspicuous entrance of the subject has been understood as a departure from the would-be separate field of cultural appropriation in which Rauschenberg's allegorical, subversive practices were originally articulated. But it is at this impasse that the example of O'Hara and the problem of coterie can usefully expand one's understanding of Rauschenberg. O'Hara is significant to Rauschenberg's reception history, then, not merely for his early advocacy and for the allegorical possibilities encoded in "For Bob Rauschenberg." Instead, the larger questions in O'Hara's reception history — what one makes of the rhetoric of coterie, of the field of radically specific and unfamiliar proper names amid the more "public" cultural materials of O'Hara's *Collected Poems* — has immediate relevance for a reading of Rauschenberg. As in O'Hara's work, Rauschenberg's heterogeneity of raw materials stages a conflict between levels of reading not as an unfortunate side effect of careless excess but as a focused and articulate inquiry into the points of linkage among ostensibly separate discourses. Allegory is perhaps *the* mode in which to understand these links.

• • •

Since almost everyone in the two-department Janis show of new realists showed works based on the abstract-expressionists schema as individualized (for them*), or satirized, into an available mode of feeling for expression, it may be interesting to point out that the best works were those in which the connections between the originator of the idea, the off-shooter and the new-realizer were most clear. Art, these days, is everything, including Life, and these were also the best in the show: Oldenburg (Gaudi and Miró through Pollock), Dine (Barnett Newman through Jasper Johns and Bob Rauschenberg), Segal (Giacometti through Larry Rivers' sculptures of the late 50s), Rosenquist (Magritte through Motherwell).*

— Frank O'Hara, "Art Chronicle III"

The concerns that emerge out of Rauschenberg's reception history present one path from abstract expressionism through minimalism and into the more explicitly theatrical or interdisciplinary artwork of the 1970s and 1980s. In advocating an interdisciplinary critical stance that could shift interpretive registers quickly and in finding new ways to conceptualize the status of the subject in work that was not simply lyrical, O'Hara both anticipated and critiqued some of the main lines of postmodern criticism concerned with allegory. But understanding O'Hara solely as a forerunner of contemporary (or post-1967) art theory would be a mistake. In fact, his position within 1960s art discourse is far more complicated. Though O'Hara advocated for Rauschenberg, Johns, and Joe Brainard and included Claes Oldenburg, Lee Bontecou, John Chamberlain, Roy Lichtenstein, and a number of other artists more closely associated with pop art and minimalism in group exhibitions, O'Hara's curatorial and critical orientation remained importantly, and at times even defensively, tied to the first and second generation of abstract expressionist painters and to many sculptors who could be understood in relation to abstract expressionism, either by a direct analogy or through social milieu — from David Smith, Rueben Nakian, and George Spaventa to Tony Smith. Most of O'Hara's critical energies in the 1960s went into the large work of consolidating and critically constructing a version of the accomplishments of abstract expressionism — a project that was now getting under way in a more systematic and contentious way through a range of retrospectives (and their attendant catalogs), critical histories, and polemical essays. As museums began to mount major retrospectives, the question of what abstract expressionism *had been* became all the more pressing. In 1963 O'Hara helped with MoMA's traveling Franz Kline retrospective; in 1965 O'Hara curated a Robert Motherwell exhibition; in 1966, Rueben Nakian; and O'Hara was planning to curate similar and more important shows on Pollock and de Kooning — all at MoMA. At the same time O'Hara remained alive to shifts in the art world that were going on around him. And as a member of a museum that needed to promote the art of the 1960s — a curator/critic and *not* a historian — O'Hara had a professional stake in familiarizing himself with and supporting this newer art. After strong hesitations, we see O'Hara coming around to Warhol by 1965;[49] we see him supporting Claes Oldenburg, Joe Brainard, Al Held, and Ronald Bladen and rethinking the pivotal role of Tony Smith for the art of the 1960s. In his "Art Chronicles" (which he wrote — quickly, under deadline — for *Kulchur* magazine between 1962 and 1963), we see O'Hara suggesting historical models that might connect the New Realists, the pop artists, and a range of other at-that-point still slightly amorphous trajectories in contemporary art to readings of both abstract expressionism and European modernism before it. In his interviews, collaborations (especially those with Joe Brainard), poems, and catalog essays of the 1960s, O'Hara at once sought to consolidate the historical importance of the Abstract Expressionists and to build provisional links to the newer art of the 1960s, especially pop art, construing the present in such a way that it did not so much negate or radically transform the 1950s as extend and clarify it. Considering just how O'Hara dealt with these tensions, I now want to expand the framework from my reading of his relation to Rauschenberg and describe O'Hara's complex and wider participation in 1960s American art.

Histories of post–WWII American art frequently use both the increase in numbers of collectors and radical shifts in purchase prices for major paintings to give a picture of the development of an art market between the end of World War II and 1970.[50] Sidra Stich, for instance, notes that "major collectors numbered around two dozen in 1945, about two hundred in 1960, and over two thousand in 1970" (100). The expansion of this market was, of course, not only carefully monitored (and applauded) by institutions like the Museum of Modern Art (which had helped to bring it about) but also reflected in the museum's curatorial practices, themselves often models for other institutions. As a microcosm of these institutional shifts, consider a July 1963 memo O'Hara received at MoMA, a document concerned with the precise description of damaged artworks, called *Glossary of Terms Used in the Registrar's Records to Describe the Condition of Paintings.* The glossary divides damage into seven genres: friction, impact or pressure, heat or fire, liquids, accretion, vermin, and corrosive substances. Each genre then contains from two to seventeen species, glossed in short paragraphs. Subcategories of impact or pressure, for instance, are "age crack, chip, concentric cracking, crack, crease, cut, dent, dig, flattening, gouge, herring bone cracks, hole, pin hole, puncture, radial cracks, slash and tear." Fire or heat involves "burning, charring, cockle, dessication, fading or bleaching, parching, scorch, singe, smoke damage and sunburn" (Frank O'Hara papers, 9. MoMA Archives, NY).

While rigorous art conservation of course long predates the 1960s, it was nonetheless in the sixties that art conservation underwent its most drastic professionalization.[51] This development,[52] then, might be understood in relation to the relatively new situation of insuring exponentially more valuable paintings for their mobile roles within increasingly frequent international exhibitions.[53] At the same time, and arguably in part *in response* to the art world's (especially the museum world's) increasing emphasis on preserving pristine art objects, 1960s art inaugurates a wide range of attempts to downplay, transcend, or assault art's object status. From such a perspective Jackson Pollock would become an important precursor to 1960s art, not only because of what Allan Kaprow identified in 1958 as an attempt to extend the space of the painting "out into the room" (6) but also because of Pollock's (mis)treatment of the canvas itself: most of his paintings would count as suffering from two of the species of "liquids" damage (running and stain) and perhaps all species of the "accretion" genre — from efflorescence, fingerprints, foreign matter, runs, and smoke damage (possibly from cigarettes) to soiling, splashing, spotting, and staining.[54]

While Clement Greenberg and Michael Fried would attempt to recuperate this category of mark making based on pouring, dripping, and staining as central to late modernism, others began to see such methods as challenging or even negating the idea of an art object in a more fundamental sense. Many other "conditions" within the MoMA memo, for instance, could apply to the works of an artist like Robert Rauschenberg and his use of decay, foreign matter, age cracks, and frame rubs.[55] And it is in this sense that the memo might be read, inversely, as a kind of manifesto of 1960s art making, extending from the range of art now celebrated under the banner of the *informe* (the dirt- and decaying-metal-based early paintings of Rauschenberg; the *Ray Guns* of Claes Oldenburg, made of corroded pipes, bent nails, and soiled string; the torn, scratched, burnt, and generally assaulted objects of Piero Manzoni, Lucio Fontana, and Alberto Burri)[56] to the attempt to transcend or reject objects more generally in environments, happenings, earthworks,[57] and conceptualism.[58] To curate at MoMA in the 1960s — even only until 1966 — was to confront, from an institutional position concerned with the presentation and display of objects, a rapid sequence of new claims about art's status *as* an object.

O'Hara's broad curiosity (not to mention his institutional position) made it difficult to accept the kind of blanket condemnation of art's increasingly self-conscious object status that Michael Fried, for instance, would develop in his famous attack on minimalism in 1967, "Art and Objecthood." Already by 1965, though, Fried had laid most of the groundwork for this position in his exhibition at the Fogg Museum at Harvard, *Three American Painters*, which argued a historical trajectory from Jackson Pollock into the color-field painters of the late 1950s and early 1960s — Morris Louis, Jules Olitski, and Frank Stella (who was also celebrated by the Minimalists). While O'Hara might have been sympathetic to a historical scheme that kept Jackson Pollock at the center of contemporary art practice in 1965 and thus denied the historical centrality of both pop art and minimalism, the limited sphere of this practice in color-field painting was a problem.[59] Moreover, Fried's new characterization of Pollock presented clear threats to O'Hara's: it helped to tilt the artist's reception away from the Rosenbergian, *Art News* idea of action painting (which O'Hara had deformed into his own stranger, more extreme reading practice) and toward a more Greenbergian language. The result was that by the mid- to late 1960s the most critically compelling and powerful celebration of (an albeit reduced canon of) abstract expressionism (and its would-be continuation in color-field painting) became aligned with Greenberg's and Fried's polemics about formal criticism. Where, then, did this leave O'Hara?

The overly easy answer to this question is to align O'Hara with the account of abstract expressionism beginning to be offered at the time by his friend, Irving Sandler, whom O'Hara in 1959 had called "the balayeur des artistes" (*CP* 329).[60] The reason for this alignment would be Sandler's attempt to identify himself against formal criticism and with the abstract expressionists themselves, a position which recalls the charges that O'Hara was a coterie critic, a critic biased by his social and professional proximity to his would-be subjects. In his 1970 book, *The Triumph of American Painting: A*

History of Abstract Expressionism, Sandler claims: "Firsthand contacts with most of the leading figures of the movement have, hopefully, made it possible for this book to reflect 'the sympathy of a man who stands in the midst and sees like one within, not like one without, like a native, not like an alien,' to cite Woodrow Wilson's conception of the historian's role" (1). And though Sandler will admit that the tangle of viewpoints of those involved makes pleasing all of the participants impossible,[61] he will nonetheless react to Greenberg and Fried's formalist account by asserting the diametrically opposed concept of content:

> A statement by Mark Rothko sums up the Abstract Expressionists' antipathy to formalist aesthetics: "I would sooner confer anthropomorphic attributes upon a stone than dehumanize the slightest possibility of consciousness." Formalists have countered by asserting that statements concerning content and artistic intention are too subjective to be dealt with objectively. Nevertheless, poetic insights, no matter how private, can be true revelations and can be checked against the evidence of the picture surface, verified, as it were, or at least made comprehensible. (2)

But it is here at the concept of the poetic, paradoxically, where Sandler begins to part ways with O'Hara. Sandler accepts Greenberg and Fried's division between the formal and the poetic and merely attempts to recuperate the poetic as the realm of the subjective and the private — of *content* aligned firmly and finally against *formalism*. The long-caricatured polar extreme of pure formalism — as an interpretive position somehow blind to content (which of course neither Greenberg nor Fried supported) — is certainly more familiar than its opposite, the poetic. What is interesting to remark here is the way that the poetic could stand in as a kind of metaphysics of content, of pure meaning. Presented as such it is no wonder that the poetic has had a long list of detractors — stretching from Greenberg and Fried to Benjamin Buchloch and James Meyer. But just as art historians have been moving away from the use of formalism as a convenient straw man, so they might want to rethink the idea of the poetic as a pure metaphysics of content. Certainly the main lines of avant-garde poetry bear no relation to this caricature of the poetic. And as we have seen in O'Hara, the concept operates neither as a transcendental category of content nor as an exclusively private domain.[62] If in responding to 1950s art O'Hara used a poetic mode to link the supposedly personal gestures of abstract expressionism, tentatively and experimentally, both to popular culture and Cold

War politics, his response to the 1960s took a slightly different tack: in part because he had already understood the art of the 1950s in a wider social context, he could now take the New Realists, the Pop Artists, and the Minimalists less as representing a radical break than a transformed continuity — albeit one whose new contexts and associations still required the wide, discontinuous analogical structure of his poetic response.[63]

That O'Hara could embrace both David Smith and Tony Smith in the 1960s is a case in point.[64] Asked about the current state of American art in a 1965 interview with Edward Lucie-Smith, O'Hara cites sculpture in particular as the discipline in which "the most original work is being done right now" and, after mentioning the art of George Sugarman and Ronald Bladen, O'Hara claims that "people whose work has been perhaps a little neglected . . . are becoming much more assimilable. Say Barnett Newman and the sculptor and architect Tony Smith . . . whose ideas have been influencing people for several years, but no one really looked at his work. . . . And now, because of these younger people, it is possible to find people who are interested enough to investigate Tony Smith's work and his ideas in a much more tangible way. Before it seemed to be like theory. . . . Suddenly it has become a reality" (SS 20). Tony Smith had of course been at the center of Michael Fried's polemic against minimalism.[65] Troubled by the way that Smith's practices (especially his famous ride along the unfinished New Jersey Turnpike) had framed a seemingly nonartistic and nonrepeatable experience as art, the reality of Smith's influence on younger artists was for Fried all too real.[66] As a sculptor, moreover, Smith produced "presences" rather than allowing a viewer an experience of self-presence. This lurking anthropomorphism was a feature that Fried extended to minimalism as a whole — and one that was thought to separate the movement from the work of the previous generation, especially David Smith. O'Hara undercut Fried's historical scheme not merely by advocating for *both* David and Tony Smith, but also by identifying with the works of David Smith in terms of theatrical presence: "The best of the current sculptures didn't make me feel I wanted to *have* one, they made me feel I wanted to *be* one" (SS 125).

O'Hara, though, does not simply locate an anthropomorphism in David Smith's sculpture; rather, he playfully psychologizes these "presences," rendering them theatrical to a degree even Fried could not have anticipated: "They look severe and dashing. . . . they are the sort of people who are about to walk away because you just aren't as interesting as they are, but they're not quite mean enough to do it" (SS 122). As in O'Hara's

David Smith, Tanktotem IX, 1960; *steel, painted blue, white, and red, 90 3/4 x 30 3/4 x 24 1/8 in. Estate of David Smith.*

Tony Smith, The Elevens Are Up, 1963; *painted plywood mock-up, two units, each 8 x 2 x 8 ft.*
Installed at Paula Cooper Gallery, New York, 1985 (subsequently destroyed).

excessive account of the contexts conjured by gestural abstraction, this depiction of David Smith's sculptures is simultaneously admiring and playfully at odds with the emerging attempts to limit the domain and vocabulary of formal description. The painted surface of Smith's new sculptures "give a velvety texture . . . like the iron hand in the velvet glove" (SS 121). The theatricality of O'Hara's account has to do, however, not merely with the *identities* of the pieces but more importantly with their *interactions* — both among themselves and with the landscape. Smith's exterior sculptures at Bolton Landing, his home and studio near Lake George in northern New York, O'Hara compares to "people who are waiting admittance to a formal reception" (ibid.).[67] O'Hara then goes on to consider the contextual effects of being able "to see a cow or a pony in the same perspective as one of the *Ziggurats*" (ibid.). Again, as with the question of sculpture suggesting a presence, a being, rather than offering a viewer an experience of presentness, it was this shift from the sculpture to its context against which late modernist critics like Fried held out; and they held out by *opposing* David Smith in particular to Tony Smith.

When O'Hara turned to Tony Smith, then, it was perhaps not surprising that he stressed his links to abstract expressionism rather than posing him as a threateningly alien sensibility (and even as the antithesis of art), as Michael Fried had. In fact, part of O'Hara's attraction to Tony Smith may have had to do with understanding Smith as a figure who could synthesize generational conflicts:[68] Smith's social milieu had been that of the Abstract Expressionists, and he had shared the aesthetic ambitions of Still, Rothko, and Newman in particular. At the same time, Smith was taken up by the younger generation of Minimalists — especially Robert Morris.[69] Considering Smith's conflicting relations to his contemporaries, the Abstract Expressionists, and the younger generation of Minimalists who celebrated his work, Robert Storr claims that "Smith retained all the basic attitudes of his contemporaries despite the fact that he was breaking new ground in circumstantial alliance with his juniors. . . . But Smith wanted what the minimalists categorically rejected, a sculpture that was symbolically charged with an unsentimental but unmistakable humanism, a sculpture in which platonic forms were imbued with life force" (27–28). And it may have been this last feature, coupled with Smith's "romantic attachment to art as a heroic enterprise" (34), that especially endeared him to O'Hara. For despite what he says in the interview about Smith's importance to younger artists, it was not Smith's importance to minimalism, for instance, that captured O'Hara's attention. In fact, O'Hara's curatorial practice at MoMA in the 1960s downplayed the Minimalists.

ModernSculpture USA (which O'Hara produced under Rene d'Harnoncourt[70] in 1965 for the Rodin Museum in Paris) was an exhibition that could have registered Minimalism as a new movement but pointedly did not. Composed largely of figurative, assemblage, and gesturally abstract sculpture, O'Hara's and d'Harnoncourt's selections included Nakian, Louise Nevelson, Isamu Noguchi, David Smith, Mark DeSuvero, Louise Bourgeois, and Joseph Cornell.[71] And though the exhibition also included Claes Oldenburg, Lee Bontecou, and John Chamberlain (all of whom came to be included in Donald Judd's minimalist pantheon, for example), it was also possible to understand these three sculptors in more figurative and expressivist terms. Chamberlain's undulating metal surfaces could be seen not as an assault on constructivist transparency of structure but as sculptural analogies for de Kooningesque gestures; Bontecou's works not as "exceptionally single" specific objects that present "no field in which the structure or the image occurs . . . no supporting context"[72] but as sculptural explorations of the existential void. And so on.[73] The point is not simply that O'Hara understood all sculpture of the 1960s within his own sometimes-prototheatrical lexicon of abstract expressionism but rather that the expansion of terms was gradual and tended to take place in close dialog with the art of the 1950s. This desire to keep such a dialog in place may explain the exclusion of Donald Judd, Carl Andre, Dan Flavin, Robert Morris, and Robert Smithson from *ModernSculpture USA*.[74]

Another reason O'Hara may have remained cool to the Minimalists is that, although he appreciated noncompositional music like that of Cage and Feldman, he does not seem to have allowed a space in art for the kinds of noncomposition pursued, for instance, by artists like Donald Judd (in his specific objects) and Robert Morris (in his gestalts).[75] Consider O'Hara's 1960 catalog on Helen Frankenthaler, in which the resistance to composition immediately becomes an endorsement of the unconscious: "One of the crucial decisions for the contemporary artist, representing a great conflict in temperament, is the very question of conscious composition, whether to 'make the picture' or 'let it happen.' Cubism says one thing and Surrealism the other, both influences persisting in a variety of interpretations and guises. Each has its pitfalls, the one dry formalism, the other a complete mess."[76]

O'Hara's response to pop art was equally complicated, partial, and mediated. Early on, O'Hara's connection to the movement occurred

Claes Oldenburg, Floor Burger, *1962; canvas filled with foam rubber and cardboard boxes, painted with latex and Liquitex, 52 x 84 in. Art Gallery of Ontario, Toronto, purchased in 1967. Photo: AGO/Sean Weaver. © Claes Oldenburg and Coosje van Bruggen.*

primarily through Oldenburg, whom he tended to define against Warhol. Thus, while O'Hara's initial take on Warhol was lukewarm (and he famously resisted having his portrait done by Warhol),[77] O'Hara could find in Oldenburg a transmutation of the everyday that maintained a complex, ironic, and humorous relationship to the art of the 1950s. Calling Oldenburg's 1961 storefront installation *The Store* "the best thing since L. L. Bean," O'Hara goes on to suggest that the artist "actually does what is most often claimed wrongly in catalog blurbs: transform his materials into something magical and strange. If Red Grooms is the poet of this tendency and Jim Dine the realist, then Oldenburg is the magician" (*AC* 9). But, as O'Hara will add in a 1963 "Art Chronicle," this magic is in no way mystical:[78] "With the perverse charms of Gulliver and of Alice-in-Wonderland, Oldenburg makes one feel almost hysterically present, alert, summoned to the party" (SS 142).[79] As most later critics will agree, Oldenburg achieves his special brand of theatricality — his gesture of casting attention toward the viewer's surroundings — through shifts in scale, ones that O'Hara then links to the body. But whereas Rosalind Krauss, for instance, will point to softness as the device that, working in tandem with scale shifts, draws out analogies between the viewer's body and the objects presented, O'Hara will understand the bodily aspect of Oldenburg's practice primarily as a consequence of the artist's rendering abstraction seemingly edible, consumable, and even "delicious":[80] "[P]art of Oldenburg's vivacity consists in the satiric employment of 'delicious' abstract paint-techniques to render delicious desserts and snacks and in the suave monumentalizing (his huge cloth pieces have zippers) of contemporary American Bread and Wine and Pants, but I think there is more to it than that. At any rate there is nothing chichi or wall-eyed in his work, an unusually positive quality for an artist working in this general tendency to have right now" (SS 142).

Such a stance will allow O'Hara at once to keep Oldenburg in dialog with the 1950s and to distinguish him from Warhol — who is presumably both "chichi" and "wall-eyed." But if — at least until 1965 — O'Hara was careful in his art criticism to distance himself from pop-art strategies and affects associated with Warhol, O'Hara had in his poetry begun a more direct experimentation with at least two of the major genres newly revitalized by pop art: the comic book and illustration.

This experimentation happened especially in his collaborations with the artist Joe Brainard, who had moved to New York from Tulsa, Oklahoma, in 1961 and was already a close friend of poets Ron Padgett and Ted Berrigan.[81] O'Hara supported Brainard early on, buying several pieces before Brainard had a gallery.[82] Brainard describes his collaboration with O'Hara in his classic "I remember" form: "I remember collaborating with Frank O'Hara. It was easy. Or so it seemed. Mostly they were cartoons. I would do the drawing first and then he would fill in the balloons instantly. On the spot. Sharp and funny and very frank" (H 168).

This on-the-spot quality is clear in the result. Though they present some of the main pop techniques — comics and illustration (coupled with lower-level collage) — they use hand-drawn captions that insist on spontaneous expressivity, even when the captions are oblique and tangential, as they typically are. "Have you seen Doctor Strangelove yet? It's really quite articulate, very fine," says a top-hat-wearing dragonfly perched on a bee on the stalk below, this against a repetitive Christmasy backdrop of rotund Santas, mistletoe, and serenading horn players in silhouette. These collaborations tend to use the language of illustration against itself

Joe Brainard, Red Rydler and Dog (from C Comics 1), c. 1964; collaboration with Frank O'Hara: ink on paper, two sheets, each 14 x 8 1/2 in. Collection of Pat and Ron Padgett.

— presenting many of advertising's visual rhetorics of condensation and focus only to undercut them by additional material and elliptical captions. O'Hara called his collaborations a "cartoon revival."[83]

While most of the collages are single image, O'Hara and Brainard also did several multi-image cartoons. *Red Rydler and Dog*, for instance, was first published in *C Comics* in 1964: in it, the two turn the visual stereotypes of cowboy masculinity into a brief narrative about a cowboy who lost his dog (always drawn with a scrawled out face) and "developed a bad habit of writing mash notes to other cowboys." At one point the note writer seems to have stolen the clothes of a gang of queer wranglers. There is a scuffle, a gunfight, a definitive whistle blowing, and the appearance of a cute young Indian boy — all promising and not quite delivering closure.[84] Like

O'Hara's recoding of abstract expressionism into a Wild West or Hollywood spectacle, here he and Brainard seem interested in the cowboy as a figure of excessive, theatrical masculinity, one that easily flips over into a queer role.[85] What is important to stress about O'Hara's collaborations with Brainard, then, is not merely that they gave O'Hara an arena to work out a new relation to some of the main techniques of pop art — or that they reintroduced narrative into art (this had already been a component in his collaborations with Larry Rivers, Grace Hartigan, and Norman Bluhm) — but more specifically that *Red Rydler* took as its framework the world of the cowboy cartoon, in which adolescent boys are offered versions of clearly defined (and formed) masculinity exemplifying itself in brief narrative vignettes. In deforming and "queering" these narratives, Brainard and O'Hara used their collaborative methods to situate themselves as the first level of audience, O'Hara responding quickly to the offered sketch and Brainard in turn watching his piece get recoded by O'Hara's text. This coterie structure — an overheard private joke about cowboy masculinity (now released into public) between two gay men — is thus slightly different from the coterie structure of a poem like "Biotherm," in which the humor generated by deformed cultural materials is not framed within one primary register.

The practice of playfully nesting a smaller, more intimate audience within an ostensibly more public document also entered O'Hara's work at MoMA in the 1960s. Here, in O'Hara's catalogs for MoMA, one could certainly consider the dedications or acknowledgments to painters, as well as the nods to the cultural work of his friends or his specially formed genealogies of precursors.[86] But because it more directly takes up both the institutional power of MoMA itself, and O'Hara's position within the institution, I want to close by looking at another document, which has as yet gone unconsidered in the O'Hara literature. On April 8, 1965, as O'Hara was promoted from assistant curator to curator, he wrote a job description that was given to his boss in the International Program, Waldo Rasmussen, who was also O'Hara's close friend and former lover. Though in some sense performing its function as a thorough account of his responsibilities, the letter is also a parody of a job description, since it enumerates both a string of tasks that any team of a dozen workers could never perform and a Byzantine structure of social expectations — stated and not — in which these tasks are embedded. As such, the description undoubtedly reflects O'Hara's decade of experience of having performed these functions already. More importantly though, the letter offers this impossible picture of what the two curators in fact do as a kind of gift from one to the next. Consider first O'Hara's account of the steps "direction of an exhibition usually includes":

> conception of nature of exhibition; discussion of feasibility and desirability within the general program; formulation of exhibition proposal (after investigation of possibility of available works) for presentation to program committee, in collaboration with the Director of the Department; selection of works, most often in consultation with the artists, and/or dealers involved, and also the principal lenders; formulation of loan request letters, and phone calls where lender is recalcitrant in replying; first-hand knowledge of condition of loans, along with the exhibition assistant, for reassurance (or contradiction) of lenders; preliminary plans for, or actual installation of, exhibition (especially for international exhibitions); writing of introductions;[87] consultation on catalogs; approval of press release and choice of photographs for publicity; frequently, attendance at one or more openings, which includes checking of condition of works and advice on installation; occasional meetings with the press in respect to the given exhibition; supervision of incidental correspondence with lenders in respect to their loans; first-hand knowledge, with exhibition assistant, of condition of loans before return; drafting of thank you letter; consultation on any insurance claims or complications attendant on return of loans; selection or approval of press reviews to be sent to artists and lenders; minor, but time-consuming follow-ups, such as purchase requests from exhibition, return of borrowed color plates and/or negatives (frequently retained by other institutions), and miscellaneous inquiries. (April 8, 1965, Frank O'Hara papers, 18. MoMA Archives, NY)

The breathless paratactic tonality of this paragraph operates as a linguistic analogy for the experience of undertaking the barrage of simultaneous, overlapping, and distracting jobs involved in seeing through an exhibition — particular and demanding jobs that seem to hide under the more generalized veneer of being a curator. Overseeing such exhibitions that originate at MoMA, in fact, is only the first of seven such areas of more or less time-consuming responsibility involved in O'Hara's job. Consider his explanation of the requirements of organizing visiting exhibitions, for instance, which begins with

> consultation with director and exhibition assistant on conception of show and my role in it (whether selection of certain elements or artists, advice on selection, or merely coordination of requests and special

services, such as additional research, discussions with artists and dealers or phone calls to reluctant lenders); frequently investigations of artists and works which will not be in the show but should be covered as background is involved, and sometimes leads to the inclusion of works previously unknown or ignored; recording with exhibition assistant of status of loan requests and responses and notification to director of refusals so that alternatives may be requested; examination of works when they arrive and when they are dispersed. (ibid.)

Such exhibitions (item 2 of his list) involve "also, in general most of the duties outlined in 1 above, because the director in cases like this usually leaves all the 'organizing' details to me and the exhibition assistant." Item 2 thus initiates a kind of infinite regress: as a result of outside directors' shirking what O'Hara implies should be their responsibilities, organizing visiting exhibitions not only adds a whole new category of tasks, but re-involves all of item 1. The list then continues, mentioning meetings with MoMA staff outside of the area of exhibition activities, keeping up with galleries,[88] domestic travel, and foreign travel before concluding with attendance at special events, which O'Hara describes as a matter of "[a]ttending openings, dinners, cocktail parties and studios because of interest, but more frequently because someone has lent, will lend, has done us favors, is involved in one or another program, and WANTS YOU TO BE THERE, for whatever reason, seldom made plain except in the direst of circumstances, like a favor back, getting into a show they've heard about, or more frequently getting a friend or protegé into said show" (ibid.). In attending such events, it is for O'Hara the *unstated* desires or assumptions circulating within the social situation that are the most important, the most pressing. At once performing and parodying its function, O'Hara's letter as a whole, then, could be said to derive its humor precisely from inventorying the parallel assumptions that underlie his employment at MoMA and from offering this inventory to his friend Rasmussen, who is equally subject to MoMA's vast, unspoken needs. In this sense, O'Hara's letter also parallels many of the concerns of his poetry, concerns I have been trying to address under the umbrella problem of coterie: like his poems the letter is addressed to (but not solely for) a second person who is part of the same social formation whose shifting logic the letter anatomizes.

That O'Hara's internal correspondence at MoMA mirrors some of the concerns of his poetry is no surprise. Still, while O'Hara's responsibilities at MoMA increased over the course of the early 1960s, as he oversaw more and more retrospectives of Abstract Expressionists and was asked to take on an increasingly public role for the museum, his poetry production — especially after the great FYI poems of 1961 and 1962 — clearly declined. At the same time, after the sudden rise to prominence of pop art in 1962, O'Hara was forced to negotiate in his art writing the very changed terrain of the New York art world. If ultimately his writing anticipates many of the concerns of the post-1967 interdisciplinary art world, the world lamented in Michael Fried's "Art and Objecthood," O'Hara nonetheless does not resemble the major critics of late modernism — from Donald Judd and Robert Morris to Robert Smithson or Rosalind Krauss. Though advocating theatricality — both in the sense of mixing genres and in the sense of treating artworks as anthropomorphic presences — and a kind of contextual bleed between objects and their contexts, O'Hara's playful and fragmentary art writing stages its advocacy of 1960s artists — be they Tony Smith, Claes Oldenburg, Joe Brainard, or even Andy Warhol — against the historical grid of abstract expressionism, whose language is seen as allowing for the new modifications, which in turn clarify and extend its contributions, even if ironically. It was this kind of historical understanding that allowed O'Hara to mount the major MoMA retrospectives of abstract expressionist painters in the 1960s and yet, with significant ties to younger artists operating in the 1960s, manage to steer clear of simple nostalgia or reaction.

CONCLUSION

My consideration of O'Hara's art writing over chapters 3 through 6 has entailed a gradual shift of orientation for this book as a whole. We have moved away from a poetry of proper names toward modes of experimental art writing that motivate models of kinship in slightly different ways. In his work on Robert Rauschenberg's combines and Grace Hartigan's paintings, O'Hara seems to be dealing with how selves emerge from various constitutive social contexts. But in his writings on more abstract painters like de Kooning, Pollock, or Joan Mitchell, O'Hara seems instead to be considering how the material traces of a "self" thematized in gestural painting can be related back to social and cultural contexts. To speak of kinship here would seem to evoke, as I suggested in chapter 6, a more distant and analogical sense — one of possible links among interpretive discourses that critics usually take pains to keep separate. And if Greenberg and Fried do treat poetry's intrusion into the field as a fundamental threat to the legibility of art history as an enterprise (and implicitly to art historians as a group), still a few more words about kinship may be in order here.

We are now in a position to remark on an important and very basic continuity in O'Hara's thought. He is famously attracted to immediacy. But what links all of the writings we have been considering is a process of denaturalizing the field of attributes one associates with seemingly immediate markers or marks: the meaning of a proper name, painterly gesture, or collage configuration. The phantom immanence of the proper name might thus be considered along a continuum with the seeming immediacy of gestural painting and supposedly autobiographical collage: would-be markers or designators in language behave instead as wild signs; seemingly emphatic and particular marks by painters that would index private psychic states instead keep escaping into the more public fantasies and nightmares of popular culture (especially Hollywood) and the Cold War; or, what appears to be the visual proof of a self and its history in collage keeps turning in on the syntactical codes by which such a self has been educed, mingling with other selves and with culture more broadly. It is the gradually destabilized rhetoric of immediacy that guides each of these processes — the vanishing of secured immanence.

Proper names are, of course, literal mechanisms in kinship structures. But it is also true that in O'Hara this literal, immediate quality — what seems to make proper names more substantial than other words — has been everywhere pushed and pulled, motivated and destabilized. This is what makes "Cornkind," "Poem (The rich cubicle's enclosure)," "Biotherm," "In Memory of My Feelings," and many of O'Hara's other poems into such rich considerations and enactments of social relations. O'Hara's model of coterie operates as an experimental kinship structure precisely through this denaturalizing of the name — both because names in the present undergo a radical shifting of attributes and because a similar version of this fluidity happens in the appropriations of cultural and literary history. And, as I argued in chapter 2, it is through these appropriations that the shifting circle contextualizes or performatively grounds itself.

Still, what separates coterie, conceived as such from a range of denaturalizing critical tools (allegory, ideology or mythology critique, the discourse of contingency in philosophy), is that coterie is of course also a form of sociality, a logic that allows for actual (if shifting) group formations. Its negative critical moment is in a sense lived positively in its practice. Indeed we first spot coterie because the textual signs of it seem to correspond to an all-too-real empirical social phenomenon. This is why I have stressed O'Hara's reception history, for in many ways the actual basis of coterie *depends upon* the kinds of reaction that are there instantiated. Someone needs to notice — and take exception. Otherwise one just has a circle or a community. And if these terms, too, grow only stranger the closer we look at them, still their ontology does not depend on a breach of would-be public canons of reference or of earnestly proclaimed standards within the literary and art-historical fields.

But here we reach one aspect of the limits of our ability to theorize coterie in general rather than historicize actual coteries. I mentioned in the introduction that asking negative critics of coteries to explain their theories of appropriate reference would give us one kind of history of how the literary field has been defined at different moments. If one function of coterie writing is thus a critique of assumptions about the securely public sphere and its various opposites, this very critique will necessarily operate differently in response to shifting definitions of these concepts — in response to different *real* conditions. Not all of these responses are equally compelling. If coterie works emerge as such only through objections raised against them, this constitutive act should not be taken, in itself, to bestow subversive value. That is, the most compelling coterie works invent forms and devices for actively anatomizing their social moment. And this is why unknown poets who still produce "I do this; I do that" poems, or who use names much as O'Hara did, cannot be assured of any radical effect. And yet, because the family, the school, the job, the political party, and the nation persist as the given frames for both an understanding of the self and for social activity, and because the term *friends* would often seem to designate an almost accidental social formation, stripped of intentionality and form, the violent negation of these former categories that coterie calls into being retains some transhistorical traction — even if the actual mechanism by which this negation occurs remains fluid. To have rejected these categories and offended an upholder of "public" norms in art or literature is something.

O'Hara's negations are not those of a situationist or 1970s punk. However great these responses remain, O'Hara's writing is more subtle, generous, and playful. These are among its most enduring and attractive qualities. But these effects emerge not only from the isolated sentiments of his seemingly speech-based and immediate lines. One grasps them best through the special joy evoked by *The Collected Poems* as an entirety, where the daily mapping and enacting of social formations and the constant reshuffling of cultural monuments expand, page by page, into a fragmentary and quotidian epic of urban life. Here O'Hara's conspicuous immediacy begins to project into an almost-infinite network of pasts and futures. Here O'Hara's often-celebrated lyrical self begins to merge with the anatomized occasions and social formations that make it legible.

NOTES

INTRODUCTION

1. O'Hara's first chapbook, *A City Winter and Other Poems*, was published by the Tibor de Nagy Gallery in 1952. His other main books — *Meditations in an Emergency*, *Second Avenue*, *Odes*, *Lunch Poems*, and *Love Poems (Tentative Title)* — appeared between 1957 and 1965.
2. This review is reprinted in *Frank O'Hara: To Be True to a City*, ed. Jim Elledge (1990), 39.
3. Perloff accounts for this especially in her first chapter, "The Aesthetic of Attention" (P). The first two chapters of James E. B. Breslin's *From Modern to Contemporary: American Poetry, 1945–1965* discuss the institutionalization of midcentury American modernism. Breslin's chapter 8 then describes in more detail how O'Hara "broke from the canonical orthodoxies of the fifties" (210).
4. Frank O'Hara Archive, June 26, 1956 (Dodd Center, University of Connecticut, Storrs). By far the majority of O'Hara's letters quoted in this study come from this collection (referenced hereafter parenthetically as Archive), which was assembled by Donald Allen as a "Selected Letters" but remains unpublished.
5. In their 1981 article "Rational Geomancy: A Realignment of Kinships," Steve McCaffery and bp Nichol present an alternative to the historical paradigm underpinning most avant-gardes (in which major art is produced solely through a struggle with the recent past). In arguing for an expanded reference field, or what they call a "macrosyntax," the two authors explicitly construct this field around a model of experimental kinship. See *Rational Geomancy: The Kids of the Book Machine* 153–57.
6. But in calling coterie a literary device, I do not mean to imply that O'Hara retains intentional command of all coterie effects in his work. At moments I will treat the problem of coterie as a symptom of his reception history.
7. In "Warhol Paints History, or Race in America," Anne Wagner suggests one of many ways of reading Warhol beyond his own intentionality. She argues that "when Warhol spoke of painting 'the dogs in Birmingham' — when he painted *Race Riot* [1963], in other words — he declared through his words' omissions his historical *parti pris*. What is omitted? Exactly what is present in each picture. White male master, black male victim: the standard drama of race. Though these characters are his paintings' actors, they are also its givens, its unconscious, you might say. They take over the painted image, somewhat against its will" (111). Another important reading of Warhol that complicates the kind of interiority Wolf claims is Hal Foster's "Death in American."

8. Steven Clay and Rodney Phillips's *A Secret Location on the Lower East Side: Adventures in Writing, 1960–1980* is one of the more successful and inventive recent versions of this archival work that stresses the particulars of a literary community. The book documents small, experimental presses in the United States over this twenty-year period by combining statements from the presses' editors with factual information, bibliographies, and an introduction. Drawing extensively on the techniques of oral biography, Lewis Ellingham and Kevin Killian's *Poet Be Like God: Jack Spicer and the San Francisco Renaissance* is another successful "documentary" account of a poetry community.
9. See also Claude Lefort, *Democracy and Political Theory* and *The Making of Political Identities*, ed. Ernesto Laclau.
10. Two good examples are Lyn Hejinian's *The Language of Inquiry* and *Aerial 8: Barrett Watten*, ed. Rod Smith. Two important articles on the question of community for the Language writers are Alan Golding's chapter "'Provisionally complicit resistance': Language Writing and the Institution(s) of Poetry" in his *From Outlaw to Classic: Canons in American Poetry* and Andrew Ross's discussion with Barrett Watten, "Reinventing Community: A Symposium on/with Language Poets," in which Ross argues that the Language writers "came to recognize that an integral component of the poetics which they were developing had to do with examining the everyday social relations which underpinned the production, distribution and reception of their work" (Smith *Aerial* 8, 188).
11. The symptoms of this struggle with the New York School in the person of Berrigan are on the surface and should be read in the context of Watten's 1983 obituary for Berrigan, "After Ted," in which Watten claims alternately that "Berrigan's purpose is often to be unreachable and inevitable . . . causing the desiring reader to weep with vexation while admiring the intellect in the lines" (a charge that could also be made against O'Hara) and that "Berrigan's reading of *The Sonnets* at Langton Street [in San Francisco] contained some of the greatest verbal moments in American language" (Smith *Aerial* 8, 106). Watten also claims that "Berrigan's death was not exactly Mayakovsky's suicide, which likewise was intended to give greater markedness to the work. But it was literary, prefigured every step of the way, and it can be criticized as a work" (ibid.).
12. This article appears in Smith *Aerial* 8, 32–38.
13. This field — the kinds of claims about O'Hara, and the language used to make them — can be experienced most decisively in *Homage to Frank O'Hara*, a collection of short and generally informal essays by O'Hara's friends and coworkers at MoMA, including Bill Berkson and Joe LeSueur (who edited the collection) as well as John Ashbery, Morton Feldman, Kenneth Koch, Joe LeSueur, Waldo Rasmussen, and Renee Neu. My claim that these essays (the book includes poems too) set the terms for a kind of identification with

O'Hara should not be taken as a dismissal; I take up the terms of this rich and frustrating book throughout this study.

14. In *The Romantic Ideology* McGann argues that "the scholarship and criticism of Romanticism and its works are dominated by a Romantic ideology, by an uncritical absorption of Romanticism's own self-representations" (1).
15. Hazel Smith's *Hyperscapes in the Poetry of Frank O'Hara: Difference / Homosexuality / Topography* and William Watkin's *In the Process of Poetry: The New York School and the Avant-Garde* both represent a shift away from anecdote and memoir toward theory. Both, however, tend to offer broad inventories of possible links between New York School writing and theory rather than sustained arguments about those links.
16. Though Guilbaut's book has been important in both questioning the terms of abstract expressionism's reception and in providing the means by which further materialist critiques can proceed, he arrives at this reductive picture of O'Hara for three reasons. First, Guilbaut is so suspicious of the premises around which he believes abstract expressionist paintings to be organized that he refuses to interpret specific canvases; he writes off all detailed analysis, like O'Hara's *Jackson Pollock*, as mere formalism. (Though Guilbaut does not mention the book, it was O'Hara's best known writing on abstract expressionism.) Second, Guilbaut, like many historians, does not consider poetry to contribute meaningfully to an art historical or political discourse. Therefore the more impacted, difficult thought that occurs in O'Hara's poems is either disregarded or understood as so much more mere advocacy. Finally, questions involving gender that O'Hara addresses to abstract expressionism and to American culture more broadly do not seem to register to Guilbaut as political questions. This is less a fault of Guilbaut's book, whose scale of concern is admittedly different, than a measure of the effect of queer theory over the last twenty-five years.
17. While many of the poets and poetry critics who constitute the referential field of the first half of my study — for instance, Marjorie Perloff, Barrett Watten, Charles Bernstein, and Bill Berkson — are familiar with the writings of these art historians, the knowledge (or, one could say, interest) is generally not reciprocal.
18. According to Bois and Krauss, "Bataille's tastes in art are not in question here. Rather, with regard to the *informe*, it is a matter instead of locating certain operations that brush modernism against the grain, and of doing so without countering modernism's formal certainties by means of the more reassuring and naive certainties of meaning. On the contrary, these operations split off modernism, insulting the very opposition between form and content — which is itself formal, arising as it does from a binary logic — declaring it null and void" (16).
19. Buchloh writes: "It is clear that, for postwar Germany in particular, the type

of factually specific memory that Haacke constructs is not very appealing. What the dominant forces in contemporary German culture seem to prefer is work that ostentatiously mourns the political barbarism of the Nazi past. Apparently, Germans can afford to applaud the sublime and polyvalent (or merely politically obscurantist?) poetic meditations and pictorial reconciliations of work by Beuys and Kiefer" (*Neo-Avantgarde and Culture Industry* 205).

20. In his essay "Nomads: Figures of Travel in Contemporary Art," Meyers claims that "the first nomadism is lyrical — a mobility thematized as a random and poetic interaction with the objects and spaces of everyday life . . . the second nomadism is critical" (Coles 11). Examples of the former are Gabriel Orozco and Rirkrit Tiravanija; of the second, Renée Green and Christian Philipp Müller.

1. NOMINAL FAMILIES

1. It is of course worth distinguishing between Pound and Eliot, as I will continue to do in chapter 2, which takes up Pound explicitly. To most poets in the early 1950s, despite Pound's more explicitly deplorable politics, he was a more appealing, because more marginal, figure. Even to liberals like Williams, Ginsberg, Zukofsky, and Olson, Pound could be understood as an antiauthoritarian poet.
2. In his *Languages of Liberation: The Social Text in Contemporary American Poetry*, Walter Kalaidjian argues that the opposition between the New Critics and the range of antiacademic poetics, including O'Hara's, represented in Donald Allen's 1960 *The New American Poetry* is "highly suspect" on the grounds that *both branches* of postwar American poetry retreated from a "dialog with contemporary culture in favor of the author's private lyricism" (Kalaidjian 4). Though Kalaidjian's book provides a useful and broad account of the institutionalization of postwar lyricism, the suggestion that O'Hara is part of a retreat from a possible dialog with contemporary culture is a misreading I will challenge throughout this study.
3. We might contrast O'Hara here with Ashbery, who also cultivates an eccentric genealogy but tends to leave explicit references to it out of his poems. At the same time, Ashbery was also willing to produce a critical book, *Other Traditions*, about his favorite obscure authors — John Clare, Thomas Lovell Beddoes, Raymond Roussel, John Wheelwright, Laura Riding, and David Schubert — each of whom receives a chapter.
4. For good accounts of canon formation in American poetry, see Jed Rasula's *The American Poetry Wax Museum: Reality Effects, 1940–1990* and Alan Golding's *From Outlaw to Classic: Canons in American Poetry*. Golding, for instance, makes his case for how canonization occurs by arguing both against what he claims is an overstated view of institutional control in Eagleton and others and against the poet-centered view of canonization in Vendler, Kenner, and espe-

cially Bloom. The limitation of a model of poets canonizing poets is that critics do not "question from where the later poet derives his or her putative power to canonize" (57). To contest Vendler's claim that poets always respond to other poets at the level of style, Golding demonstrates that John Berryman's "responds to [Ann] Bradstreet's social and historical situation" (59). Ultimately, Golding understands canonization as a matter of individual agency that can attain long-term effects only through "institutional mediation" (57). For an account of these two books, see my "Book Review," from which the above formulations are taken (403–9).

5. I asked Ashbery about O'Hara's attraction to working within a close literary circle or coterie, and his response tellingly differentiates the two writers: "I never really had that urge. Or maybe I was just a wallflower. I remember before I went to France and I would occasionally go to the Cedar Bar and be introduced *yet again* to the famous artists for whom I was a person who was always tagging along with O'Hara. But he really relished that ambience, which was the closest thing then (and I would imagine now) to French literary café life. And then when I came back once in 1963 he had this party for me with all the young poets he had met — I think they were all men, Berrigan, Joe Brainard, Tony Towle, Jim Brodey, Bill Berkson, Stephen Holden — who were gravitating to him. . . . They obviously really worshipped him as a figure, and Frank got tremendous energy out of this" (interview with the author April 21, 2003).

6. O'Hara's project of revaluation might be usefully contrasted with the three-part schema of "major," "minor," and "personal" literature that Eliot develops in his essay collection *On Poetry and Poets*, specifically in "What Is Minor Poetry?" While Eliot does allow for fluidity between major and minor, he considers the final category as quarantined and private. According to Eliot, the danger of defining minor poetry would be the fiction that we could settle the distinction definitively and finally: "Then if we tried to make out two lists, one of the major and one of the minor poets in English literature, we should find that we agreed about a few poets for each list, that there would be more about whom we should differ, and that no two people would produce quite the same lists: and what then would be the use of our definition?" (*On Poetry and Poets* 34). As critics have noted, the category of minor literature allows Eliot to depersonalize his revision of the canon. Cultivating interest in thoroughly recognized but not highly valued writers like Dryden or the Metaphysical poets allowed Eliot to find in them an antidote to the supposed excesses of the major poets with whom he disagreed (Milton or the Romantics, for instance) without making this revaluation seem to turn on the doctrinal and political objections Eliot himself, famously and personally, had against these so-called major writers. What is less familiar about Eliot's revaluation, though, is the status accorded his third category of valuation in "What Is Minor Poetry?"

These are what Eliot calls "personal affections for the work of some poet of no great historical importance." Of this category, Eliot writes: "I should suspect that the person who only liked the poets whom the history books agree to be the most important, was probably no more than a conscientious student, bringing very little of himself to his appreciations. This poet may not be very important, you should say defiantly, but his work is good for me" (*On Poetry and Poets* 37–38). By containing this sub-minor poetry in a personal poetic sphere below the threshold of "historical importance," Eliot's framework suggests that debate or influential revaluation can only occur within the major/minor axis. But it is of course by activating this third term that O'Hara not only revalues individual authors but also calls into question the assumptions of a literary historical model like Eliot's.

7. Here we should recall the remarks of Pearl K. Bell, Raymond Roseliep, and Gilbert Sorrentino quoted in the introduction. Consider also, by way of slight contrast, Robert Creeley's thoughts about O'Hara's model of audience. Asked by John Sinclair in 1966 why he first started a magazine, Creeley responds: "It's the dissatisfaction with the social occasion of writing. Not that we didn't like it, we didn't have a background for it. You see, aspects of the *kind* of writing and its people do continue very actively in Kenneth Koch's and Frank O'Hara's work on the one hand, or in Donald Hall's work — Hall was also at Harvard — they continued in the *social* situation of writers. Not that they were the less writers, but they had a use of it socially that we didn't have" (Creeley 61).
8. David Lehman's *The Last Avant-Garde: The Making of the New York School of Poets* returns to earlier mythic accounts of O'Hara, whom he sees as "the hero, the great animateur, the catalyst of the New York School" (72).
9. Perloff's stance here seems related to Charles Altieri's earlier account of names in O'Hara's works. For Altieri, in a reading almost diametrically opposed to Geoff Ward's, names mark the impossibility of identifying with the details of other people's lives: "[O'Hara's] texture of proper names gives each person and detail an identity, but in no way do the names help the reader understand anything about what has been named. To know a lunch counter is called Juliet's Corner or a person O'Hara expects to meet is named Norman is rather a reminder for the reader that the specific details of another's life can appear only as momentary fragments, insisting through their particularity on his alienation from any inner reality they might possess" (*Enlarging the Temple* 111).
10. Symbolism in "The Rhetoric of Temporality" is not simply a mode of figurative language but an initial stage in an epistemological struggle. See de Man, *Blindness and Insight*, 206–7.
11. The terms of Charles Altieri's judgment of O'Hara in *Enlarging the Temple* are similar: "His influence and popularity are considerably greater than his

achievement" (198). For Altieri, O'Hara's failure is a philosophical one. Unsuccessfully engaging a dialectic between alienation and presence, O'Hara insists on the temporary, diversionary rewards of a continuous stream of details severed from their potential symbolic roles.

12. *The Oxford English Dictionary*, 2d ed. (1989), s.v. "Coterie."
13. In English poetry, references to "cots" persists into the early nineteenth century, most interestingly in the work of John Clare.
14. Though Peter Bürger's *Theory of the Avant-Garde* highlights this process more directly, Renato Poggioli's *The Theory of the Avant-Garde* also suggests the ways in which radical practices can get co-opted as stylistic sheen. O'Hara was a student of Poggioli at Harvard.
15. Ashbery's *Turandot and Other Poems*, which included four drawings by Jane Freilicher, was published in 1953 by the Tibor de Nagy Gallery, which had also put out O'Hara's *A City Winter* the year before.
16. Claiming that their work was marginal is, of course, different from claiming that this work *represented* marginalized identities. Considering the functions of marginality for late-nineteenth-century French avant-garde painters in his *The Painting of Modern Life*, T. J. Clark argues that Manet and others adopted "an aesthetic of the unfixed and unfinished, an art which declared that the modern was the marginal, and that the truth of perception lay in staying on the surface of things and making do with ambiguity" (47). The increasing emphasis put on enactment (rather than depiction) is crucial to a history of the uses of the rhetoric of marginality.
17. For a rich cross-section of debates on the meanings and uses of "context" for the New Historicists, see *The New Historicism*, ed. H. Aram Veeser.
18. Contextual loss, it is important to stress, can happen both spatially and temporally. As "The Triple Fool" suggests, one could have read Donne "out of context" in his own period, much as one necessarily must do so, to an extent, now. Similarly, some early readers of O'Hara felt that what they lacked was not a reconstruction of some referential world but spatial and or social access to this world in the present (as in Creeley's remarks, quoted earlier). This response oddly pries the problem of context out of its typically historicist framework, though of course, as we move away from the moment at which such a response was possible — the almost-recent past of the 1950s and early 1960s — the problem of O'Hara's context again assumes the more familiar temporal or historical guise.
19. After establishing the group's membership, Kors demonstrates that previous accounts of the coterie had been inaccurate in picturing them as a uniform group of atheists whose gatherings involved work on collective projects, like the encyclopedia.
20. A good account of this is the chapter "Ideology and Canonical Form" in John Guillory's *Cultural Capital: The Problem of Literary Canon Formation*.

21. Here it would not be enough (as in Marotti's account of Donne) to understand the problem of coterie as a matter of reestablishing the immediate reception context so as to supply a range of information about "Adieu's" characters, which might in turn frame its thematized ambivalancies ironically against O'Hara's budding career. What the poem attempts to "canonize" is not merely an experience but a constellation of proper names; these constellations shift, however, from poem to poem.
22. Though Eliot, more than Pound, acknowledges local contingencies of literary value, he carefully frames these within a larger picture of culture that reinscribes natural hierarchies, both literary and social.
23. Whereas Lévi-Strauss understands kinship structures as predicated on the incest taboo, Judith Butler sees them as based on a prior ban on homosexuality, thereby suggesting an even more fundamental role for reproduction within the system. In *The Elementary Structures of Kinship*, for instance, Lévi-Strauss argues that "[t]he *fact of being a rule*, completely independent of its modalities, is indeed the very essence of the incest prohibition. If nature leaves marriage to chance and the arbitrary, it is impossible for culture not to introduce some sort of order where there is none. The prime rôle of culture is to ensure the group's existence as a group, and consequently, in this domain as in all others, to replace chance by organization. The prohibition of incest is a certain form, and even highly varied forms, of intervention. But it is intervention over and above anything else; even more exactly, it is *the* intervention" (32). In *Gender Trouble*, Butler takes up kinship structure not through Lévi-Strauss directly but through Freud: "Although Freud does not explicitly argue in its favor, it would appear that the taboo against homosexuality must *precede* the heterosexual incest taboo; the taboo against homosexuality in effect creates the heterosexual 'dispositions' by which the Oedipal conflict becomes possible" (64).
24. See Saul Kripke, *Naming and Necessity*, 31. See also John Lyons, *Semantics*, 215–23.
25. Kripke argues against a proper name's necessity at two levels: first, a name itself refers to someone who might not have had any of the qualities that he or she had; second, when we refer to that name, we do not necessarily refer to any essential qualities, any fixed set of the features, that she or he did in fact have. Kripke establishes that no single piece of career property can always be called to mind through a reference to a person. His examples are famous figures with two roughly equal résumé lines — Benjamin Franklin (postmaster or inventor of bifocals) and Aristotle (student of Socrates or teacher of Alexander).
26. O'Hara evidently liked this poem quite a bit. He said as much in a March 26, 1964, letter to Lawrence Ferlinghetti about the publication of *Lunch Poems*: "How great that you like Cornkind, it makes me feel that we know each other

better than either of us ever suspected" (Papers, Bancroft Library, University of California, Berkeley).

27. In a chapter on Robert Duncan's and Jack Spicer's versions of community, Maria Damon claims that "rather than a predictable, narrowing transformation from two to one (two lovers producing one child), which projects one life into the future in linear trajectory, the results of homosexual union, uncementable in offspring, are indeterminate and potentially limitless. The results often consist in shared knowledge, which is then further shared in widening concentric circles" (149). While I agree with much of Damon's analysis, it is not clear why knowledge would not be a possible result of a heterosexual union. Nor are *predictable* and *linear* the most accurate terms for what can be constricting about heterosexual reproduction and its narratives. Elsewhere in the chapter, Damon's insights correspond more closely to the logic of "Cornkind": "In the paradigm of same sex reproductive connections, people cannot be replicated, only touched or taught, in transitory encounters where repercussions are paradoxically timeless" (150).

28. Still, as debates within anthropology have suggested, the relation between the logic of proper names and domination or violence is far from clear. Discussing proper names in his book *Tristes Tropiques*, Claude Lévi-Strauss suggests that "the primary function of written communication is to commit slavery" (299). That proper names cannot be uttered in many societies is a proof of their strategic position in politicized systems of designation: names, even in speech, presuppose the designatory power, the parceling of property, that Lévi-Strauss links to writing in general. For Jacques Derrida, however, this "violence" must be located several stages earlier; names are always already improper: "the proper name has never been, as the unique appellation reserved for the presence of a unique being, anything but the original myth of a transparent legibility" (109). What cancels the proper name's would-be positive, designatory moment is not merely the relational, systematic nature of kinship structures but the differential classifications upon which language itself is based. Derrida sees prohibitions on naming treated by Lévi-Strauss, therefore, not as evidence about the violence of writing but as effects of a preexistent "arch-writing" within supposedly "illiterate" societies. The violence of designation does not emerge with writing but preexists it.

29. O'Hara took up an avuncular pedagogical relationship not only with New York School Poets but with friends as well. Consider, for instance, this October 29, 1962, letter to Larry Rivers about Rivers's son Steve, in high school at the time: "Anyhow I just sent him some books which he thought he'd like to dip into as the library up there was pretty dull and academic (he told me he intended to improve it for future generations before he left), so I dished him up some W. C. Williams, LeRoi Jones, Diane Di Prima, David Schubert, and

even Joel Oppenheimer and a couple of other very avant-garde looking pamphlets which should keep the kids either burping or scorning for a week or so" (Archive).

30. In addition to the first generation of New York School Poets (excluding Guest), the 1970 *Anthology of New York Poets*, edited by Ron Padgett and David Shapiro and dedicated to O'Hara, included Clark Coolidge, Kenward Elmslie, Ted Berrigan, Harry Mathews, Tony Towle, Tom Clark, Tom Veitch, Lewis Mac Adams, Frank Lima, John Giorno, Joe Ceravolo, Jim Brodey, John Perreault, Bill Berkson, Michael Brownstein, Ed Sanders, Peter Schjeldahl, Aram Saroyan, Ron Padgett, Dick Gallup, Bernadette Mayer, Edwin Denby, and David Shapiro. The only woman included was Mayer; it thus left out Barbara Guest, Anne Waldman, Alice Notley, Diane Di Prima, Maureen Owen, and many others.

31. In his *Memoir 1960–1963* Tony Towle notes the anthology's impact: "While browsing in a bookstore on MacDougal Street, I came across Donald M. Allen's *New American Poetry 1945–1960*, published by Grove Press. . . . I realized that, expensive or not, I had to have this book. It promised revelation" (31).

32. Two poets who were at first baffled or annoyed by the O'Hara sections in the Allen anthology but later influenced are Ted Greenwald and Lewis Warsh. In "Frank O'Hara: A Personal Memoir," Greenwald recalls his first impressions: "while I was still living at home and going to school, my friend Lorenzo [Thomas] . . . had told me I ought to take a look at the poems of Frank O'Hara, they were really terrific, particularly, 'Why I Am Not a Painter.' . . . I read and reread the poem, and some of the other poems, but except for a dopey and nasty marginal note I made about the probable sexuality of the poet . . . nothing sank in" (*H* 180). By contrast, Greenwald mentions the 1964 special issue of *Audit* devoted to O'Hara as the text that caught his attention. Lewis Warsh had a similar first reaction: "I must admit that in my first reading of the *New American Poetry* anthology the poets in the New York School section interested me the least. . . . [They] sounded a bit too formal and rhetorical to me, too on the surface — Frank O'Hara, most confusing of all, since he was formal and colloquial almost in the same breath — I wasn't ready for it" (xx–xxi). Running between spring 1966 and spring 1969, six issues total of the magazine *Angel Hair* appeared, which included most of the poets loosely associated with the second-generation New York School (as well as other poets) and first-generation New York School Poets. Issue 6, for instance, included eleven previously unpublished poems by O'Hara.

33. What writers testify to is also some quality that was off the page. "I wrote in a diary not long ago," Joe Brainard confesses "that 'If I have a hero it is Frank O'Hara.' I do. And it is Frank. Because Frank really lived life. Which, as you know, is not easy. You can get hurt that way. It's very time consuming" (*H* 168).

34. Koch also wrote about his teaching at all levels. His pedagogical books cover college students, children, and nursing-home residents. These books are *Making Your Own Days: The Pleasures of Reading and Writing Poetry* (1998); *Wishes, Lies and Dreams: Teaching Children to Write Poetry* (1970); *Rose, Where Did You Get That Red? Teaching Great Poetry to Children* (1973); and *I Never Told Anybody: Teaching Poetry in a Nursing Home* (1977).
35. Towle says this of Koch: "Kenneth was already established as a professor at Columbia University, one learned, so he certainly didn't need to teach at the New School to supplement his income. Eventually I understood that he was giving these workshops to *engage the interest*, one might say, of poets who weren't taking the undergraduate curriculum at Columbia — like myself" (52).
36. Brad Gooch includes remarks from Tony Towle that substantiate this: "He was the opposite of Kenneth as a teacher. He was very generous in allowing the students to speak, perhaps too much so. What he would have to say would have been a lot more interesting than what a lot of the students had to say. He was that way to a fault. He was self-effacing. Whereas Kenneth was very didactic" (G 400).
37. Towle's account substantiates this: "I had taken Frank O'Hara's and Kenneth Koch's recently ended poetry workshops at the New School, and it seemed that O'Hara was becoming a personal friend" (12).
38. According to Gooch (377–437), O'Hara was involved with Brodey and Brainard in particular among younger writers and artists.
39. Tony Towle's account of coming to know Berrigan in the 1960s helps to draw out this contrast: "My lack of literary education was a sensitive point and Ted had found it. He quickly took the line that, not only had I not read enough in general, but I was socializing with poets whose work I should be home studying. . . . There was no question that Ted had read a *lot* more poetry than I had. He had discovered O'Hara, Koch, and Ashbery — and James Schuyler — on his own a couple of years before, and had been single-minded in searching out their often hard-to-come-by publications and read them assiduously. He was perhaps the foremost scholar on the New York School and now he was ready to join it" (90).
40. Consider the following revelatory anecdote about Berrigan told by Stephen Rodefer: "Once at a party at the Berkeley Poetry Conference in 1965 (at Dave Haselwood's I think) it seemed both wonderful and astonishing that he accepted without a blink a copy of Frank O'Hara's *Lunch Poems*, only just published, from Victor Coleman, would Ted sign it. And unflinchingly, immediately, he did, much obliged" ("Strange" 145).
41. Berrigan's friends emphasized his connection with O'Hara in the essays included in *Nice to See You: Homage to Ted Berrigan*, ed. Waldman. Ron Padgett writes this in "On the Sonnets": "In a sense, some of *The Sonnets* had already

been written. Many of the lines he used were from previous poems of his, or from translations or mistranslations he'd done. Some were entire poems he had written as far back as the fall of 1961. . . . Some lines were 'lifted' out of poems by John Ashbery, Kenneth Koch, and Frank O'Hara, or from Ted's immediate friends, such as Dick Gallup, Joe Brainard, and me. It was of course not a question of plagiarization — a term that sent us into spasms of laughter — it was a matter of using 'found' lines to create an entirely different work, and the intentions were, if I may use such a word here, noble" ("On the Sonnets" 9–10).

42. To speak of Berrigan being "more bohemian" is not merely a matter of his more direct link to downtown Manhattan counterculture but also of his lower-middle-class background, which afforded less institutional support and access to power than O'Hara had. Berrigan appears sometimes to have been understood by the first generation of New York School Poets (and to have understood himself, sometimes playfully) as wild, green, and slightly unrefined. Berrigan seems to be playing this role, for instance, in "The Chicago Report" (a letter from Berrigan to Ron Padgett describing a three-day trip to Chicago in the late 1960s). In it, Berrigan is told by Paul Carroll that Kenneth Koch (for whom Berrigan is looking) is "at giant millionaire's party no bums allowed" ("Chicago Report" 29). Berrigan eventually manages to get in to the party and describes his meeting with Koch as follows: "K is broadly grinning and executing some kind of ritzy penguin hops. The music stops. We attack Kenneth. He says, Com'stai! Andiamo! Sacre bleu! Pastafazol! etc, and throws his arms around me. I say, 'Where's the pussy?'" ("Chicago Report" 30). Later, after Koch is insulted by the millionaire host, Mr. Arkadin, Berrigan intervenes: "I say, let's go find him and kick his ass, Kenneth" ("Chicago Report" 32).

43. In *All Poets Welcome: The Lower East Side Poetry Scene in the 1960s*, Daniel Kane writes, "The consistent intertextual references by Second-Generation New York School poets to poems written by First-Generation poets are so preponderant that a single poem by Frank O'Hara found itself recycled in literally dozens of other texts" (113).

44. Shapiro claims that Berrigan's writing demonstrates "the theme of friendship more than romantic love" and connects this to the cultivation of milieu in the work. Shapiro notes that Berrigan "often played the role of a summer savage from Oklahoma, then would speak didactically about his love for Shaw and Whitehead" ("On a Poet" 225).

45. Anne Waldman also writes of the importance of community and ties it to O'Hara: "Some writers need to be nurtured in small groups; others work very well in isolation. Personally, I was happy to be in a community of New York writers. I was reading a lot of John Ashbery, Frank O'Hara, a lot of other New York Poets. Being from the area, I guess I was identifying with their

states of mind, rather than the particulars. . . . O'Hara was very freeing because he presents details of his personal life, throws his friends into poems, what he's eating, reading, seeing. Poems I was writing from my apartment on St. Mark's Place were like that" ("Interview" 267).

46. Alice Notley, *Margaret and Dusty*, 21–22.
47. Directing itself to an intimate second-person audience and populating itself with proper names and quotidian details, Bernadette Mayer's book *The Desires of Mothers to Please Other in Letters* (written 1979–80, published 1994) might be read as a related extension of ideas central to O'Hara and his legacy. As in the case of Alice Notley, Mayer's writing is in no sense simply an afterlife of O'Hara. In particular, Mayer's early books — *Memory* (1971), *Moving* (1975), and *Studying Hunger* (1976) — are far more procedural, serial, and antisubjective than O'Hara's writing. For many commentators, Mayer became a New York School writer only later in her career, after her more radical experimental period. For an account of Mayer's relation to the New York School, see my "Faulting Description: Clark Coolidge, Bernadette Mayer and the Site of Scientific Authority" (in *Never Get Famous: Essays on New York Poetry beyond "The New York School,"* ed. Daniel Kane).

2. COMPARATIVE COTERIES

1. I realize that limiting my account of O'Hara's dialog with modernist precedents to literature and painting (which the second half of the study will consider) gives a somewhat incomplete picture. Certainly he had long-term engagements with music, film, ballet, and dance as well. Perloff and Gooch each provide useful overviews of O'Hara's interdisciplinary interests. For specific accounts of O'Hara's involvement with music, one can consult Morton Feldman and Ned Rorem's articles (in *Homage*) as well as O'Hara's own essays "About Ben Weber" and "New Directions in Music: Morton Feldman" (in *Standing Still*, ed. Donald Allen). For essays on O'Hara's relation to film, see Epstein and Elledge.
2. The full range of this admiration and its general effects on O'Hara's writing have been well documented by Marjorie Perloff. As a preface to more detailed investigations, she notes that "with the exception of Auden, whom he considered an American poet anyway, and the early Dylan Thomas, the poetic landscape of modern Britain struck O'Hara as excessively conventional and tame; it could not, in any case, compete with the Germany of Rilke, the Russia of Mayakovsky and Pasternak, the Spain of Lorca — and certainly not with France" (P 34). James Breslin, on the other hand, does an especially good job with O'Hara's relationship to the more academic midcentury modernism.
3. A good example of this reoccupation and transformation comes in a June 25, 1954 letter to Fairfield Porter, in which O'Hara collides gay cruising with a

self-deprecatory dressing-down of the Baudelairean dandy: "My activities lately indicate that soon JA [John Ashbery] will be forced to give over the title Larry assigned him 'Last of the Gay Blades' to me — but then John should rest this summer anyway. Baudelaire had the funds to be a dandy but the most I can manage is to be a petit boulevardier" (Archive).

4. With some exceptions, I treat each writer selectively over roughly one decade of significant work, bound closely to models of the artistic group: Apollinaire in the 1910s, surrealism in the 1920s, Auden in the 1930s, and Pound in the 1940s and early 1950s.
5. Even when O'Hara advocated heterosexual reproduction, the terms of his advocacy could challenge the family. When Diane di Prima, for instance, decided to have the child she had conceived with Amiri Baraka (then LeRoi Jones, who was married to Hettie Jones), O'Hara supported what was generally understood as a scandalous decision: "Nearly everyone thought I was behaving badly. . . . Only Frank O'Hara and his friends tended to see all this in a larger or more remote context — as if we were nineteenth-century artists in Paris, or somewhere where these things happened" (*Di Prima* 275).
6. Gooch rightly notes this poem as the model for O'Hara's "Poem Read at Joan Mitchell's" (293).
7. Gooch includes Freilicher's response: "The poem was very nice, but somehow I felt there was a certain resignation in the tone" (ibid.).
8. The singular status of surrealism derives in part from the limited information about Russian constructivism available to American writers of the 1940s and 1950s; I take up this question in chapter 4.
9. In his July 4, 1939, talk, "The College of Sociology," Bataille dealt with Caillois's accusations of mysticism against the College with the atypical move (among avant-garde collectives) of preferring "to speak against the background of a disagreement rather than on terms accusing him, perhaps, through misinterpretation." Similarly, he responded to Michel Leiris's claims that the College lacked sociological rigor and was becoming not, as it had hoped, a "moral community" but a "clique" (Bataille 354–5) only by registering being "hurt to see Leiris reproach us" (Bataille 335) and not in any way by condemning him.
10. Consider by way of contrast the conclusion to a 1969 Situationist text, "The Latest Exclusions," that explains why the British Situationists T. J. Clark, Christopher Gray, and Donald Nicholson-Smith were kicked out: "It will be noted that for nearly two years there have been no other exclusions. We must admit that this notable success is not entirely due to the real elevation of consciousness and coherent radicality of individuals in the present revolutionary period. It is also due to the fact that the SI [Situationist International], applying with increasing rigor its previous decisions on the preliminary examination of those wanting to join it, has during this same period refused

some fifty or sixty requests for admission: which has spared us an equal number of exclusions" (Knabb 294).

11. There were daily required meetings (for which one could not arrive late) whose topic was controlled by Breton. Members spoke of these as "communion" and of Breton during this time, in the words of one banished Surrealist (Ribermont-Dessaignes), as a "poor-man's Stalin" (Polizzotti 311, 317).
12. In his *A Boatload of Madmen: Surrealism and the American Avant-Garde, 1920–1950*, Dickran Tashjian describes how Ford used the language of liberation in Breton's *First Manifesto* as a grounds to challenge Breton's views on homosexuality (171).
13. Still, according to Ashbery, American surrealism had little effect on O'Hara, who turned instead to French poetry and American painting: "Except for some rather pale Surrealist poetry written in England and America during the 1930s, and an occasional maverick poet like John Wheelwright or Laura Riding; except for Hart Crane in his vatic moments and the more abandoned side of Dylan Thomas and the early Auden, there was nothing like a basis for the kind of freedom of expression the Frank instinctively needed" (*CP* viii).
14. See "The Heritage of Dada and Surrealism" in *Reported Sightings* (199). Ashbery continues: "[René Crevel's] suicide a few days after a notorious row between Breton and Ilya Ehrenburg (who with his customary finesse had qualified the Surrealist movement as 'pederastic'), at the time of an international Communist cultural congress in Paris from which the Surrealists were excluded, was a blow to Surrealism and to literature. Though Maurice Nadeau in his *The History of Surrealism* avoids linking Crevel's suicide to this incident and calls it an act of 'attempted affirmation' (of the irrational, apparently), it seems obvious that Crevel must have felt like an exile in the promised land he helped to discover" (6).
15. Speaking of his theatrical collaborations with artists at Artists' Theater in New York, O'Hara says, "The painters who collaborated with us, like Alfred [Leslie] and Larry Rivers and Grace Hartigan and Jane Freilicher, and Elaine de Kooning and Nell Blaine, they got the script and saw it as a theatrical event 'Transcript of USA: Poetry: Frank O'Hara'" (H 215).
16. Of the consciousness of French book arts, from cubism through surrealism, that underlay his own collaborations with O'Hara, Larry Rivers says, "We were grown up . . . but we wanted to taste that special lollipop Picasso, Matisse, Miró, Apollinaire, Éluard and Aragon had tasted and find out what it was like" (G 298).
17. These collaborations are taken up by Perloff (75–112) and also by Russell Ferguson throughout his *In Memory of My Feelings: Frank O'Hara and American Art*.
18. To produce *Stones* with Rivers (1957), O'Hara worked directly on a lithography stone over multiple sessions. His *Poem-Paintings* with Bluhm (1960) also

occurred over multiple sessions; here they worked on paper, and the pieces were generated, they said, by music.

19. Though itself apparently written in an equal hurry, John Perreault's 1967 review of *Poem-Paintings* suggests that for O'Hara (whom he describes as "a friend of the painters") a form of sociality is fundamental to the collaborations: "Norman Bluhm and Frank O'Hara dashed off this frolicsome, meaningful, beautiful collection of poem-paintings back in 1960, all in one short frenzy of creativity that must have been like two collaborating Zen monks in a zany dance of the seasons."
20. In his introduction to O'Hara's *Collected Poems*, Ashbery says it is these limits that led O'Hara toward American art, especially abstract expressionist painting, as a model for process poetry (CP vii–xi).
21. Norman Page's *Auden and Isherwood: The Berlin Years* offers a largely biographical sketch of the two authors' milieu, the just barely underground queer culture in Berlin in the late 1920s and early 1930s.
22. In *Later Auden* Edward Mendelson explains how this happened and mentions that Auden "chose a line from Firbank as the epigraph to *The Age of Anxiety*" . . . before being persuaded by Theodore Spenser to drop it, eventually restating it as the epigraph to one section, "The Masque" (284). It is worth noting, however, the moralizing language with which Auden contains Firbank's humor: "The fact that Firbank's novels are so funny is proof that he never lets us forget the contradiction between life as it is and life as we should like it to be, for it is the impossibility of that contradiction which makes us laugh" (ibid.).
23. Not only is gossip a sign of a friendly person's interest in other people and "the greatest safety value to the emotions that exists," but "gossip is creative. All art is based on gossip—that is to say, on observing and telling" (Auden *Prose* 428).
24. For Mendelson, *The Orators* "is an account of everything a group ought not to be. . . . Auden began it as a deliberately negative vision of groups, but as he worked on it, and after he published it, he came to recognize that he had favored his negative vision more than he thought, and not simply because he could find no alternative" (*Early Auden* 93–94).
25. Auden's transition affected not only the later but the earlier work as well, since it was after his more conservative transformation that he edited his major poetry collections. For an account of this process, see Joseph Warren Beach, *The Making of the Auden Canon*.
26. By 1964 Auden had edited editions of Kierkegaard, Goethe, Baudelaire, Van Gogh, Henry James, Ernst Toller, and Frederick Rolfe as well as numerous anthologies, including collections of Norse verse, Elizabethan poetry, Elizabethan music, light verse, and aphorisms.
27. Mentioning *The Orators* by name, Brad Gooch confirms the importance of the book in his discussion of O'Hara's role in teaching younger poets (G 365).

28. "*The Orators* is Auden's only published work that is virtually impenetrable without certain keys. He freely gave those keys to readers who bothered to ask — the book's meaning was never, as some unhappy critics imagine, reserved for Auden's friends, who were as puzzled as anyone — but the keys cannot possibly be deduced from the text alone" (Mendelson *Early Auden* 96–97).
29. This poem was not published in O'Hara's lifetime and did not make it into either O'Hara's selected or collected editions. It is instead part of his posthumous collection, *Frank O'Hara: Poems Retrieved*.
30. Bob Perelman describes well the complex intertwining of Pound's appeal and repulsiveness for readers: "Pound at various points was writing an epic, saving the Constitution, constructing the Confucian-Fascist blueprint for the Salò Republic, and building 'the city of Dioce whose terraces are the colour of stars.' In other words . . . distinctions between the literary and extraliterary become difficult to draw: the supreme social importance of a highly specialized conception of literature is the spur that drives him out into public space. There is a continuous contradictoriness built into Pound's notion of the genius that makes all the details of his writing fall into the charged and problematic place from which they continue to pose crucial questions about politics, aesthetics, and ethics. What gives the best of Pound's writing its power cannot be dissociated from the worst of it" (*Trouble* 30–31).
31. For an indication of this influence one can consult *Pound/Zukofsky: Selected Letters of Erza Pound and Louis Zukofsky*, ed. Barry Ahearn.
32. See *Charles Olson and Ezra Pound: An Encounter at St. Elizabeths*, ed. Catherine Seelye. On Ginsberg, see Tytell 312, 336–37.
33. For an account of O'Hara's activities at The Club, see Gooch (214–17).
34. This is to say also that the discrepancy between O'Hara's remarks at The Club and his poem can be understood as more than simple hypocrisy or lack of nerve. The question of how one separated the early Pound from the Pound of St. Elizabeths was tricky — probably something that was not quite addressable in a short talk. And O'Hara's decision not to publish "Poem (The rich cubicle's enclosure)" may have been a result of his initial uncertainty about his own reactions to *The Pisan Cantos*. On the other hand, the poet also refers to himself as one of a group of "bung-hole blowers" — a term one doesn't often find in print in 1952.
35. For an account of how, in *The Pisan Cantos*, "Pound's investment in a poetics of tropological stability, of fixed address and proper names, survives the fall of Mussolini and the collapse of the fascist dream," see Paul Morrison's *The Poetics of Fascism: Ezra Pound, T. S. Eliot, Paul de Man* (36).
36. Though he probably did not know the precise conditions of Pound's incarceration at St. Elizabeths, O'Hara knew the crucial fact that Pound was being

contained — that his space was limited and restricted, its boundaries enforced through locks and the threat of violence.

37. There were many whose defense of Pound's right to write offensively did not follow from a theory of the separation of the aesthetic and the political. Even one of his most conservative supporters, Archibald MacLeish, could argue that Pound's views were simply incoherent and misinformed rather than subsumed within the would-be autonomy of poetic discourse: "What will save him, if anything, is the fact that no jury on earth could think this kind of drivel would influence anybody to do anything, anywhere, at any time. . . . Poor old Ezra! Treason is a little too serious and a little too dignified a crime for a man who has made such an incredible ass of himself, and accomplished so little in the process" (Carpenter 699).
38. One might read this moment against Marjorie Perloff's claim that Pound "provides the impetus for the stress on precision that we meet in contemporary poetics" (*Poetic License* 124).
39. Michael Bernstein cites four criteria for epic: first, that it provide "models of exemplary conduct (both good and bad)"; second, that "within the fiction of the poem, the dominant, locatable source of narration will not be a particular individual (the poet), but rather the voice of the community's heritage 'telling itself'"; third, that "the proper audience of epic is not the *individual* in his absolute inwardness but the *citizen* as participant in a collective linguistic and social nexus"; finally, that "the epic . . . must contain both clearly recognizable models of 'the good' and an applicable technique, methodology, or behavior pattern by which that good can be concretely realized and imitated" (14).
40. Instead, the uneven dynamics of authority become far more of a question within the critical history: first, whether to include less-known members of the group (like Kenward Elmslie, Harry Mathews, and Edwin Denby), and second, how to deal with the discrepancy in levels of critical attention even among the more-established members. While a great amount of scholarship has focused on Ashbery and a fairly large amount on O'Hara, far less exists on Schuyler and Koch and almost none on Guest, who (though clearly a member in a way that is at least disputable, with Elmslie, Mathews, and Denby) is often left out of histories of the New York School poets. I explore these questions further in "Poet as Action Figure: The New York School Out of History" (*Arshile* 11), a review of David Lehmans's *The Last Avant-Garde: The Making of the New York School of Poets.*
41. These include O'Hara's posthumously published collection of critical writing, *Standing Still and Walking in New York*, along with the collection of essays and remarks on O'Hara edited by Bill Berkson and Joe LeSueur, *Homage to Frank O'Hara*. More recently, Kenneth Koch's *Making Your Own Days* reflects on New York School poetics. Ashbery's introduction to *The Collected Poems of*

Frank O'Hara is another important document, along with several of the essays in Ashbery's selected art writing (see *Reported Sightings*, ed. David Bergman). To some extent it is the art writing of the New York writers that is closest to a poetics. Insofar as this is the case, one can also read O'Hara's *Art Chronicles*, and *What's With Modern Art?* (his reviews for *Art News*), James Schuyler's *Selected Art Writings*, and Barbara Guest's *Dürer at the Window: Reflections on Art* as works of New York School poetics.

42. Describing the role of community for the Language writers, Lyn Hejinian, for instance, accords the term a variety of self-conscious and theorizable functions that can distinguish it from its more familiar guise as support group: "The community creates the context in which the work's happening happens. It does so by generating ideas and work that might not have come into being otherwise, and, in the best sense, by challenging everyone involved. In this last respect, a community presents a more difficult milieu than that of the support group. To be simultaneously permissive and rigorous is the challenging task that a highly functional community must attempt" (*Language of Inquiry* 35).
43. In chapter 3, I consider O'Hara and his circle in relation to the theorizations of community produced by Paul Goodman, whom O'Hara read in the early 1950s.
44. For a more recent version of this same charge, see Hilton Als's "Frank Appraisal" (1999).
45. In fact, O'Hara did not start writing art reviews until 1953, and he did not work at the Museum of Modern Art in any other capacity than at the front desk until 1955. At very few points is his critical practice closely allied to Greenberg's. O'Hara's 1954 essay "Nature and New Painting" (SS) is an explicit response to Greenberg's 1949 essay "The Role of Nature in Modern Painting" (*Collected Essays and Criticism* vol. 2).
46. Aside from the suggestion that Greenberg's support for the group was tied to his relationship with Frankenthaler, nothing about this is particularly damning. Even this kind of overlapping of alliances is a familiar art-historical story.
47. In retrospect, Hugh Kenner would have to be taken as the star among Pound's pupils who came "templar." Kenner's 1951 *The Poetry of Ezra Pound* (Kenner's Yale Ph.D. dissertation), is justifiably famous: as with Kenner's later books, it provides a concise and eloquent account of the processes involved in reading a modernist author while seeming to enact many of the formal properties of the poetry and prose he is discussing. For Kenner, it is because these processes are, or at least should be, strictly aesthetic that he could create a monumental public space for Pound within a developing discussion of modern American poetry while Pound remained incarcerated for promoting fascist politics. But Kenner's structural position as a political spin doctor, managing the public reputation of a difficult client, emerges

openly in the book; comparing what he calls Flaubert's plotless fiction to Pound's plotless epic, Kenner parenthetically bemoans, "Pound's veneer is in the same way incomparable (in places; if he would only stop shoving his muttering fanatic's face through those lyric pages!)" (246). Rather than treat the relation between Pound's poetics of discretion or precision and this fanaticism, Kenner's frustrated aside ultimately disconnects the two.

48. Though O'Hara had significantly less institutional power in literature than he did in art, his writing career was similarly aided by John Bernard Myers, who published his and Ashbery's first books. While O'Hara's reputation as a poet became quite large, he did not edit, award grants, or write very much poetry criticism.

49. Marjorie Perloff suggests that this passage is one of a series of literary parodies in "Biotherm" — in this case of Pound's *Usura* canto (P 177).

50. Bill Berkson explained *FYI* to Don Allen: "FYI comes from the typical heading for office memorandums — 'For Your Information' — which was also the title of *Newsweek* magazine's 'house organ,' a little offset journal of employee gossip distributed weekly. I had worked at *Newsweek* the summers 1956–7 and told Frank about it & he picked up on 'F.Y.I.'" (P 172).

51. Michael Bernstein usefully summarizes Pound's view of economics: "[A]ny detailed study of an entire economic structure is fundamentally uncongenial to Pound: he seeks out individual malefactors primarily because, with their removal, he is certain that the general problems will also be resolved. . . . '[E]nemies' . . . are rarely seen as representatives of a historically created social class acting within a particular economic structure: they are only parasitic and dangerous individuals carrying out the same fiscal conspiracy against the common weal throughout history" (64).

52. Berkson wrote this essay (which also includes a glossary) for a deluxe art-book edition of the poem with lithographs by Jim Dine, published by Arion Press in San Francisco in 1990.

53. Geoff Ward nicely describes this effect in O'Hara through a comparison with Byron: "[I]n both cases, not only does a window giving onto deep-space, a refusal to relinquish metaphysics, shimmer in the margins, but a perpetual reverse reading becomes necessary whereby margin becomes mirage, where deep becomes layered becoming deep again, where metaphysics and nihilism seem not so much opposed as latent in each other" (47). In "Biotherm," "deep space" is less one of lyrical subjectivism than of cultural history.

54. Approaching this same question with his characteristic and funny understatement, Joe Brainard remarks that, "If Frank O'Hara liked a movie one day that didn't necessarily mean that he would like it the next day" (H 167).

55. Charles Altieri cites Wordsworth's line — "A truth that is its own testimony" — as a goal for what he describes as Pound's practice of using quotations and translations to construct an expressive certitude that would not be

reliant on a witness. "Testimony requires witnesses — a fact that led Romantic poets to project the values that poems could assert in terms of audience figures defined within the poem" (*Painterly Abstraction* 311).

56. "Individually [many of the] passages," Perloff continues, "may seem to be pure slapstick, but the remarkable thing about 'Biotherm' is that, as in a sophisticated orchestral composition, everything casually mentioned is picked up somewhere later in the poem in an altered context" (P 177).
57. Gooch sees the poem as part of a narrative of seduction: "Back in the city O'Hara managed to draw out his feelings for Berkson by returning to work on 'Biotherm,' a long poem he had begun on August 26 to present to Berkson for his birthday but kept in the typewriter until January 23 when he finished it. . . . 'Biotherm' was filled with winks and digs meant for Berkson alone. It was a work of complex courtship. But between many of its lines were complaints of frustration — a frustration on which O'Hara perversely fed" (382–84).
58. Though Perloff emphasizes thematic unity and repetition of obscure references as a way to transcend what appears to be a disturbing particularity, she still locates Berkson as the poem's privileged and ultimate reader at the core of the work: "Biotherm" contains "brief reminders that the poem's variations radiate from a center which is the loving relationship between Frank and Bill, and which is epitomized by the line 'pretty rose preserved in biotherm.' . . . What the poem preserves in 'biotherm' *in order to entertain his friend* is a dazzling array of memories and inventions" (P 175 [italics mine]).

3. IN MEMORY OF MY FEELINGS

1. Goodman breaks the early-century avant-garde into naturalism; 1920s experimentalism, which he calls "the revolution of the word"; and socially committed writing of the 1930s.
2. This is true despite the fact that Goodman was one of the very few out gay writers in the early 1950s. In this text, he less identifies himself as gay than suggests a sort of moral openness to homosexuality by distancing himself from what he assumes to be the audience's judgment on a scene in Genet, in which a character is "honorably glorying in a masochistic idolatry for a Nazi soldier occupying Paris, with whom he happily performs what the audience will consider the ugliest possible sexual act" (373).
3. Typically, Olson proposes not a simple advocacy but a complex transformation of Goodman, linking "Goethe, by way of Paul Goodman's article" to two other coordinates: "The NY Times, as, journalism obeying modernism, & becoming the documentation of the day anywhere: all the news . . ." and (3) "The CANTOS as, one man's attempt to poise, all culture, to see, what modicum is, usable, out of, the welter" (in Butterick *Complete Correspondence* 7: 74–75).

4. Many critics have remarked on the gendered aspects of Olson's and Creeley's writings. In his book *Black Chant: Languages of African-American Postmodernism*, Aldon Lynn Nielsen, however, links such claims to the problems both of avant-garde production and of coterie specifically: "It is likely that the reason so few formally avant-garde poems by black women were in print in the 1950s and early 1960s is the same reason so few poems by women were to be found in the magazines and anthologies published by the Beat and Black Mountain groups. The coteries of avant-garde poetry in America were largely operated as male enclaves, even when, as in the case of *Yugen*, one of the coeditors was a woman" (161).
5. Libbie Rifkin writes that "Olson and Creeley's 'polis' — expanded, publicized, granted a small operating budget — appeared to function most ideally on the epistolary page where it began" (58).
6. This dynamic she sees gradually transformed into *The Black Mountain Review*, which she characterizes as "a coterie publication" because it drew "its contributors from Creeley's expatriate community, Black Mountain students past and present, and scattered *Origin* regulars" (57).
7. Davie complains more generally about *The New American Poetry* that "Allen's sadly indiscriminate anthology, which came out in 1960, was the means by which the so-called Black Mountain group of poets came to be recognized as . . . a feature of the Anglo-American literary scene" (217).
8. Commenting on the circle that Spicer and Duncan were part of at Berkeley, Maria Damon notes another precedent for their model of community: the two poets had studied with Ernst Kantorowicz, who had previously been "a member of the 'George-kreis,' the small and elite circle that formed around the gay German poet Stefan George. Duncan, Spicer, and Blaser formed their own 'kreis' modeled on George's and adopted his theory that the poet was a 'priest-king whose duty was to guard and pass on the essence of the cultural heritage,' not seeking a large public but '[addressing] himself . . . to disciples' and '[endowing] words with mystical properties'" (153). Despite basing his circle on what she calls an "elitist George coterie" (159), Damon finds that "Spicer's praxis concerning community could be quite radical" (ibid.), in part because he rejected identity as the sole criterion of belonging, pushing the concept of community into the writing itself: "poetic language comes to constitute the true domain of their sexual and political community" (143). At the same time, "Spicer's increasingly embittered and sparse lines reflect his ambivalence about membership in a cultural and social ghetto on the verge of breaking into political visibility" (ibid).
9. Joe LeSueur described the O'Hara-Spicer relationship as follows: "Frank represented a very urbane and (to Jack, I believe) a campy kind of poetry, or maybe he felt it was a little effete . . . but I do remember Jack not much liking Frank's work. . . . And Frank, though he could see that Jack had talent,

wasn't very attracted to his poetry. Then, too, Frank was used to winning people over, and Jack simply would not be won over by him. And as I've suggested, they were a little competitive, Frank representing N.Y. and Jack being the champion of the Bay Area poets" (Ellingham and Killian 65).

10. Ellingham and Killian report Earl McGrath's take on the poet's competition: "'O'Hara and Spicer were too much alike. . . . Their enthusiasm, their interest in the young. Basically, they were both doing the same thing, which was trying to run their friends' lives: what they should be doing, what they should be thinking, reading, writing, so forth and so on. Jack was a little bit more censorious than Frank — it was always like a pep talk with Frank, you know, but with Jack it was always like a scolding. I was always so worried, I could make the wrong move, I could go the wrong direction, to listen to him. He was a very kind person, but a bit of a crab'" (64).
11. At the time, Goodman was a fairly important figure in the New York literary scene. Relating him to New York School interest in coterie, John Bernard Myers writes that Goodman "was concerned with such libertarian notions as 'mutual aid' and what he called 'communitas'" (*Tracking the Marvelous* 30). The notion of "mutual aid" was of course most famously articulated by Peter Kropotkin in *Mutual Aid: A Factor of Evolution*.
12. Nor did O'Hara share Goodman's sense that the writer of occasional poetry was writing simply to or about the names featured in his writing. As I argued in chapter 2, intimate reference tends to operate in O'Hara as an internal reception framework that comes into contact with other more impersonal and abstract reception frameworks.
13. On top of the theoretical differences between the two writers, there was the more practical matter of Goodman's social manner. When O'Hara got to New York, he discovered that Goodman "insisted on holding court and on being surrounded by young writers as disciples" (G 201), demanding, like Pound, to be understood as the center of information and taste.
14. In 1951 the Hopwood judges were three established poets — Karl Shapiro (who was O'Hara's biggest supporter), Louis Untermeyer, and Peter Viereck. Only seven manuscripts, however, were submitted that year.
15. O'Hara's relation to French writing has been a tricky issue for much O'Hara criticism. Though New York School writers like Koch and Ashbery often celebrate O'Hara's transformations of surrealism, contemporary critics have used his involvement with surrealism as a way to write off what they take to be the immaturity of his early work. The contrast, for both Perloff and Breslin, is one between the manners of the early work and the more authentic emotions of the latter. Though O'Hara's work no doubt transforms itself between, say, 1950 and 1956, the mannered effects of a poem from 1952 like "Poem (The rich cubicle's enclosure)" underlie its emotional impact and its powers of critique (as I argue in chapter 2). Thus, if O'Hara's aesthetic does

shift in the early 1950s, the opposition between manners and emotions may not be the most accurate way to chart the movement. In the next two chapters I will consider two other early poems, "Commercial Variations" and "Second Avenue."

16. In a letter from Cambridge to Kenneth Koch in April 1956, O'Hara writes: "We have met a talented poet up here name of John Wieners, whose work we [referring to himself and Bunny Lang] both like. I wish I'd some to send you but I sent it to Barbara, John Myers and Daisy at Jimmy's suggestion, since he's never been published — you might keep this information one from the other so if they like it they'll each have a sense of discovery, not that it really matters." (Archive)
17. One indication of this connection is the fact that O'Hara was the only New York School writer to be included in *The Portable Beat Reader*, edited by Ann Charters. The anthology includes four O'Hara poems: "Les Luths," "Post the Lake Poets Ballad," "Personal Poem," and "The Day Lady Died." In the introduction to O'Hara's section, Charters quotes Bill Berkson on O'Hara's relation to the Beats: "O'Hara's most obvious distinction from the Beat aesthetic was a socioeconomic one. While espousing much the same poetry tradition and many similar personal attitudes, O'Hara went neither 'on the road' nor, indeed, on any programmatic quest; he was skeptical of almost all the publicized Beat paraphernalia — psychedelics, jazz, pronouncements on prosody, activist politics, occult or formal religious studies" (399). The one point I would disagree with in this inventory is "activist politics"; the skepticism is more Berkson's than O'Hara's.
18. Ginsberg testifies to O'Hara's ability to win converts for the Beats: "I remember Richard Howard was [in 1958] a young critic, or poet, I had known since Columbia. As far as poetics in those days he and John Hollander were more or less academic so-called rightniks. I said, 'Well Frank O'Hara thinks Wieners is great.' He said, 'Well anything Frank O'Hara says is true'" (G 319).
19. In a July 10, 1957, letter to the Kochs, O'Hara writes this: "I recently saw Allen Ginsberg here on his way to Europe and liked him enormously! He also sent me his *Howl* book which I also liked enormously! Beat that. I think he's gotten *very good*. What do you think?" (Archive).
20. The December 7, 1961, letter also explains why O'Hara has given Wieners Ashbery's address: "I saw John Wieners last Sunday for a little while and he looked very well and feels much better and is writing again. He was pleased that you have mentioned him to me and I gave him your address so he could send something for the magazine, which he promised to do. I felt that that would be better, since you are interested in his work and I don't know how Jimmy feels about it" (Archive).
21. In "Prose Contribution to Cuban Revolution," Ginsberg writes, "Now Bill

and Jack were my monsters . . . that is they were the broad funny minds in which I recognized the sense of life, through whose eyes I saw" (335).

22. In one of many such statements, Ginsberg claims that "Corso's contribution to the whole thing was that the line was a unit of thought, so to speak, which is something I follow" (*Improvised Poetics* 4).

23. Here is one of Ginsberg's many comments: "People take us too seriously & not seriously enough — nobody interested in what *we* mean — just a lot of bad journalism about beatniks parading itself as highclass criticism in what are taken by the mob to be the great journals of the intellect. The ignorance of the technical accomplishment & spiritual interest is disgusting. How often have I seen my work related to Fearing & Sandburg, proletarian literature, the 1930's — by people who don't *connect* my long line with my own obvious reading: Crane's 'Atlantis,' Lorca's *Poet in NY*, Biblical structures, psalms & lamentations, Shelley's high buildups, Apollinaire, Artaud, Mayakovsky, Pound, Williams & the American metrical tradition, the new tradition of measure" ("'When the Mode of the Music Changes the Walls of the City Shake'" 326–27).

24. In a January 27, 1957, letter to Kenneth Koch O'Hara writes: "As a result of reading *Howl* recently I have written two little meditations which are so quiet as to be absolutely vaporous and as indecisive stylistically as the orchestral part of a Chopin piano concerto played by itself. It's like one of those missing solo recordings where the reader has to supply everything on his 88 key home set. I'm calling it Play-a-Part-Poetry" (Archive).

25. It is important to remember, though, that these poems are separated by a year and a half from the string of related poems O'Hara wrote in the summer of 1959: "All that Gas," "The Day Lady Died," "Rhapsody," "Adieu," "Joe's Jacket," "Personal Poem," and "Poem (Khrushchev is coming on the right day!)" In the meantime, O'Hara experimented with the ode, writing "Ode to Joy," "Ode on Lust," "Ode to Willem de Kooning," "Ode to Michael Goldberg ('s Birth and Other Births)," "Ode (to Joseph LeSueur) on the Arrow that Flieth by Day," "Ode on Causality," "Ode: Salute to the French Negro Poets," and "Two Russian Exiles: An Ode." The temporality of these odes is often that of the past as an illumination of the present, though the Joe LeSueur ode is an interesting exception.

26. Though the poem is dated June 27–July 1, 1956, it derives from a twenty-line poem, in short five-line stanzas with a refrain of "What land is this, so free?," written June 17, 1955. I consider the relation between the 1955 and 1956 poems later in this chapter. In 1960, "In Memory of My Feelings" reached an even wider audience when it was included in Donald Allen's famous anthology, *The New American Poetry*. Allen includes this composition and publication history in *The Collected Poems* (538).

27. O'Hara's choice to frame the poem with these likenesses recalls Whitman's attempt to see grass not so much as *an* analogy but as a producer of analogies.

Section 6 of "Song of Myself" begins thus: "A child said *What is the grass?* fetching it to me with full hands; / How could I answer the child? I do not know what it is any / more than he" (*Leaves of Grass* 33). In section 6 Whitman develops a complex, open set of analogies for grass that the poem never exhausts. Though I will pursue a few of O'Hara's links to Whitman, this is a topic whose full elaboration would require a separate essay.

28. In asserting this, I want to challenge Marjorie Perloff's claim that "O'Hara unifies his kaleidoscopic vision by repeating certain key images. . . . In the 'midst' of all 'these ruses' is the serpent, who stands here for the poet's true self— the self that must triumph if he is to become an artist" (P 142).
29. Daniel Cottom, in his "'Getting it': Ashbery and the Avant-Garde of Everyday Language," calls the "it" whose routine function Ashbery estranges the "transporting coherence crucially involved in communication" (3).
30. Such summary is at once a threat from the outside (the social world) and internally determined by the poem's own rhetoric, its need for self-framing, for summary at the beginning and end of sections. While in other O'Hara poems this problem is explicitly thematized as a pronoun, often an "it" or a "that," which must but cannot summarize an entire section, here the reduction tends to take place in an image that stands tentatively as an impossible summary of the experiential world that has generated it. (A good example of this problem in O'Hara's other poems is the disengaged "that" from the second stanza of "Poem (The rich cubicle's enclosure)" which, as I argued in chapter 2, highlights the impossibility of summarizing the various strands of the first stanza at the same time as it pokes fun at Ezra Pound's desire to eradicate ambiguity.) In the conclusion of section 1, the complicated proliferation of selves, each figured as a snake — linked at times to races and journeys into the sky — comes together tentatively in the figure of a medusa: "My transparent selves / flail about like vipers in a pail, writhing and hissing / without panic, with a certain justice of response / and presently the aquiline serpent comes to resemble the Medusa" (*CP* 253). Here and elsewhere, the threat of stasis finds its most extreme form in stone monumentality, what will later be defined as art, which doubles as a form of "dead" writing. In this image the multiple vipers depicted in section 1 become a medusa, whose decoding inevitably creates such stasis. What has allowed the vipers to coalesce into a legible figure has in turn rendered this legibility the condition of stasis.
31. According to O'Hara's roommate Joe LeSueur, O'Hara's last words to his mother — whose alcoholism had apparently endangered O'Hara's sister, Maureen — were, "Why don't you go fuck yourself!" (*Digressions* 229).
32. Like the conclusion to section 1, section 2's final passage works both to summarize the issues this section presents — to package them now as a question rather than as an image — and to highlight the impossibility of such a summary.

33. I discuss the relation between the anthropological categories of alliance and filiation in chapter 1 and in my conclusion.
34. The poet Tony Towle says this of the proper name "Jane" [Freilicher] in Kenneth Koch's and O'Hara's poems: "I had once thought that she was a shared rhetorical device ('Exactly, Jane . . .') but not only was she corporeal, but occupied an important position both with these poets and among a group of figurative painters as well" (57).
35. The range of O'Hara's early camp could include "A Poem in Envy of Cavalcanti" (*CP* 35), "A Pastoral Dialogue" (*CP* 60), "A Terrestrial Cuckoo" (*CP* 63), "A Mexican Guitar" (*CP* 71), and "Ashes on Saturday Afternoon" (*CP* 77).
36. Similarly, in his essay "Gay Language as Political Praxis: the Poetry of Frank O'Hara," Bruce Boone argues that in O'Hara a "coded gay language . . . expressed a need for self-preservation on the part of the gay community" and at the same time "had the effect of preventing the recognition of an oppositional content of gay speech, on the part of the dominant straight group" (59–93).
37. For a critique of the limitations of Ross's reading of O'Hara's "The Day Lady Died," see Marjorie Perloff's revised introduction to the 1997 reprint of her book *Frank O'Hara: Poet among Painters.*
38. Some of the most obvious thematic political moments include remarks on homophobia in "Biotherm," racism in "Far from the Porte des Lilas and the Rue Pergolèse," and nationalism in early poems like "Easter" and "Hatred." While O'Hara does make some explicit links between camp and "coping," the logic is less reactive than affirmative, as he writes in "Day and Night in 1952": "We do not know any more the exquisite manliness of all brutal acts because we are sissies and if we're not sissies we're unhappy and too busy. Be not discouraged by your own inept affection. I don't want any of you to be really unhappy, just camp it up a bit and whine, whineola, baby. I'm talking to you over there, isn't this damn thing working?" (*CP* 93).
39. *Sexual Dissidents* 308. As Dollimore notes, camp does not have one universal meaning, both because it is precisely a critique of universality and because the mode of that critique constantly changes.
40. In treating the peoples who clear the way for the modern German state, Hegel's rhetorical gestures suggest precisely this type of theatrical procession, with the precondition of entrance on the stage being a link in the teleology. Thus he can dismiss most of world history: "Yet this entire body of peoples [all of Eastern Europe] remains excluded from our consideration, because hitherto it has not appeared as an independent element in the series of phases that Reason has assumed in the World" (350).
41. Being "beneath these lives" echoes the lines that close section 1 — "love of the serpent! / I am underneath its leaves as the hunter crackles and pants" (CP 253).

42. For O'Hara, Whitman is one of only three American poets who are "better than the movies" (*CP* 498). Crane and Williams are the other two.
43. Fred Orton's reading of the submerged texts in Jasper Johns's early flag paintings suggests an important analogy: "The Stars and Stripes provide the structure for the textuality to operate within, but that structure has a relatively autonomous existence apart from the textuality as reading-matter. It provides the all-over context for the texts-as-jokes, but these seem to be indexed more to their lost original contexts and Johns' reasons for choosing them than they are to the flag. Something or someone is being played with, caricatured and snubbed — including, perhaps, the artist himself — but the flag of the United States survives relatively intact. Strongly prefigured, it seems not to be what is being made the figure of fun" (128). If Johns's camp "triviality" sits awkwardly inside the world of the flag, for O'Hara the awkward relation to the national context comes from camp referentiality exceeding itself, each reference becoming too important.
44. Like Perloff's reading, in which O'Hara's "actual biography . . . is subordinated to a series of hallucinatory visions and memories" but "the poet's true self" unifies O'Hara's "kaleidoscopic vision" (*P* 142), Alan Feldman also claims that a central, essential self is the project of the poem. His reading, however, has the advantage of situating autobiography as a discourse within the poem on par with all others: "The history of the self has no importance or validity in itself, but only as one of various kinds of materials that can be used in the poem." But then he goes on: "To rescue the essential self the poet makes works of art" (97).
45. In a transformation that thematizes the slippage between art and life, the first of the multiple identifications — "I am a Hittite in love with a horse" — leads later to "They look like gods, these whitemen, / and they are bringing me the horse I fell in love with on the frieze" (*CP* 256).
46. O'Hara's "After Courbet" is a significant, longer poem dedicated to another famous Communard.
47. Foucault suggests that, for the writer of farcical or parodic history, his object does not offer the covert masquerade sought by straight history, "the possibility of alternative identities, more individual and substantial than his own" (93). Instead, "The new historian, the genealogist, will know what to make of this masquerade. He will not be too serious to enjoy it; on the contrary, he will push the masquerade to the limit and prepare the great carnival of time where masks are constantly reappearing. No longer the identification of our faint individuality with the solid identities of the past, but our 'unrealization' through the excessive choice of identities — Frederick of Hohenstaufen, Caesar, Jesus, Dionysus, and probably Zarathustra" (93–94).
48. In her essay "How Am I to Become a Legend" Multu Konuk Blasing describes this moment as an "imperial self" that is "consuming all and

being consumed by all" (*Politics and Form* 61). This insight comes, however, in the context of an argument about how O'Hara's work, because it posits a continuity between subjectivity and culture, is strictly accommodationist. Such a view radically forecloses the social implications of O'Hara's work.

49. This is from Baraka's first book, *Preface to a Twenty Volume Suicide Note*, reprinted in *The Amiri Baraka/LeRoi Jones Reader* (12).
50. I consider O'Hara's relation to Kerouac in chapter 4.
51. For a more thorough treatment of O'Hara's relation to race, see Benjamin Friedlander's "Strange Fruit: O'Hara, Race and the Color of Time." Friedlander's ultimate claim that racial ambivalence should be understood as the basis of O'Hara's poetics is less persuasive than his subtle and insightful readings of the thematics of race in individual poems.
52. Fried's 1967 essay "Art and Objecthood" ends with the claim that "presentness is grace" (in *Art and Objecthood* 168); I take up Fried's writing in chapters 5 and 6.
53. Certainly, nonmaterialist terms persist in the later work. But they tend to be more thoroughly removed from white, and especially Christian, culture. See, for instance, Baraka and Fundi's *In Our Terribleness*, which considers the politics of fashion within African American urban ghettos.
54. For accounts of Baraka's involvement, see Werner Sollors, *Amiri Baraka/LeRoi Jones: The Quest for a "Populist Modernism"*; William J. Harris, *The Poetry and Poetics of Amiri Baraka: The Jazz Aesthetic*; and Lorenzo Thomas, *Extraordinary Measures: Afrocentric Modernism and Twentieth-Century American Poetry*.
55. For an account of O'Hara's complex relationship to Baraka, see Michael Magee's "Tribes of New York: Frank O'Hara, Amiri Baraka, and the Poetics of the Five Spot." Magee's article provides valuable new statements about O'Hara from Baraka, Berkson, and others and links up crucial points in O'Hara's and Baraka's writings of the early 1960s. I am not quite persuaded, however, by Magee's larger claims that "O'Hara . . . made African American cultural expression the prime mover behind the 'experimental attitude' of the American avant-garde" (701) and that for O'Hara "jazz was the most effective, the most persuasive, form of democratic symbolic action, and that American writers would do well to consider both its formal and social implications" (695). In a March 20, 1958, letter to Gregory Corso, O'Hara wrote about jazz: "I don't really get the jazz stimulus but it is probably what I get from painting and probably similar at least; that is, you can't be inside all the time it gets too boring and you can't afford to be bored with poetry so you take a secondary enthusiasm as the symbol of the first — for instance, I've noticed that what Kerouac and 'they' feel as the content of jazz in relation to their own work (aspirations), I feel about painting with the corresponding differences in aspiration, that is where one takes Bird for inspiration I would take Bill de Kooning: partly perhaps I feel that jazz is beautiful enough or too, but not

fierce enough, and where jazz is fleeting (in time) and therefore poignant, de K is final and therefore tragic. A question of the durably painful or the finally painful, but pain to endure must be slightly less powerful than that pain which is final? Masoch, well, what are you going to do? This may not be too interesting and I don't know whether I really believe it or not—but I do. Then also, I don't have to see what I admire while I'm writing and would rather not hear it, which seems unavoidable in the jazz milieu since even if they don't whistle while they work they read with it. Maybe I should try to give a reading somewhere in front of a Pollock or a de K. . . . hmmmm. Then it would just make me look more physically interesting, whereas jazz makes a poet (every 30 years) sound more poetically interesting. I guess my point is that painting doesn't intrude on poetry. What got me off onto this? 'You're imagined silence,' as Ashbery would say" (Papers Harry Ransom Library).

56. Baraka's suggestion is that this anarchy is an unconscious symptom rather than an articulated program. But consider, by way of contrast, a position like Jackson Mac Low's, taken from a 1975 talk on his own public readings of the 1960s: "(I began performing publicly in 1960.) Gradually, while doing public performances in the '60s, I came more & more to realize the degree to which this kind of performance was a model for a free anarchist society" ("Poetics of Change" 178).
57. In *A Secret Location on the Lower East Side: Adventures in Writing, 1960–1980*, Steven Clay and Rodney Phillips note that the *Floating Bear* started in February 1961 and that "twenty-five issues came out in the magazine's first two years" (75).
58. For a cultural account of the rise of the reading in New York, see Daniel Kane's *All Poets Welcome: The Lower East Side Poetry Scene in the 1960s.*
59. I give a number of examples of this process in chapter 1.
60. I consider Rauschenberg's statements in chapter 2 and his work in chapter 6.
61. It seems possible that the images of summoned devils and of the Atlantic, posed as they are in the play's last major speech, actually suggested the two Hartigan paintings of O'Hara mentioned in the poem. As we know, Hartigan was later to use a great deal of O'Hara's specific language in the canvases of *Oranges*. Whatever may have prompted the specific settings and titles for Hartigan's portraits of O'Hara, however, is less important to the present argument than the thematic and formal concerns brought up by Hartigan's paintings.
62. We will see this technique again in chapter 4 in "Commercial Variations."
63. My suggestion is not that the collapse of shepherds' speech into a text that marks itself as highly conventionalized writing (a pattern common to eclogues from Virgil to Spenser to O'Hara) is in itself subversive or singular. Instead, it is the selection of the eclogue as a mode, combined with the stage directions, that achieves the subversive effect with respect to rewriting the problem of Hartigan's identity.

64. O'Hara's *Try! Try!* and John Ashbery's *Everyman* were performed together in Cambridge at the newly formed Poets Theater in April 1951. Daniel Ellsberg's review for the *Harvard Crimson* suggests the strange relations these plays maintained with their audiences. Though Ellsberg is largely sympathetic, he says this of Ashbery: "The first play, by John Ashbery, showed typical defects. The lines occasionally gave hints of being good verse, but not of the sort whose meaning is apparent at one hearing." Then, of O'Hara, he writes that *Try! Try!* "was labeled on the program a 'noh play,' and we were handed some notes on the Noh Plays of Japan: 'The audience once dressed for them as if for a religious service in elaborate ceremonial robe. . . . The audience is supposed to know all the plays by heart.' Having put the modestly dressed audience on the defensive, the play earned the most appreciative reception of the evening" (SP 223).
65. Roland Barthes writes that "[f]or classical metaphysics, there was no disadvantage in 'dividing' the person. . . . quite the contrary, decked out in opposing terms, the person advanced like a good paradigm (*high/low, flesh/spirit, heaven/earth*); the parties to the conflict were reconciled in the establishment of a meaning: the meaning of Man. This is why, when we speak today of a divided subject, it is never to acknowledge his simple contradictions, his double postulations, etc.; it is a *diffraction* which is intended, a dispersion of energy in which there remains neither a central core nor a structure of meaning: I am not contradictory, I am dispersed" (*Barthes by Barthes* 143).
66. Hartigan claims also to have used "Daisy Aldan, Floriano Vecchi and Richard Miller" (H 30).
67. The table in front, which works to flatten space, and the contortions of Freilicher's dress and face appear to be overt borrowings from Picasso's *Les Demoiselles d'Avignon*, a painting to which both Hartigan and O'Hara allude in their comments on *Masquerade.* Hartigan, who was recommended to John Bernard Myers of Tibor by Clement Greenberg himself, was originally an abstract painter. By the mid-1950s, however, she not only painted from photographs but also included "historical" references ranging from obvious quotations of Matisse and Picasso to entire repaintings of Dürer, for example, in a gestural realist mode.
68. O'Hara begins by defining nature in historical terms: "And what does 'nature' mean in relation to painting? It depends on the historical period" (SS 41). The title of the essay appears to be an explicit reference to Clement Greenberg's 1949 essay "On the Role of Nature in Modernist Painting." And though O'Hara sees a different history of twentieth-century art from Greenberg's, one that allows for a greater simultaneity of relevant working modes at a single moment, O'Hara does not figure Greenberg's account (the way disagreeing critics will begin to fifteen years later) as a tyrannical dictum that must be subverted. While Russell Ferguson's catalog essay for *In Memory of*

My Feelings: Frank O'Hara and American Art valuably correlates O'Hara's writings to his collaborations, Ferguson's larger argument is simply that O'Hara was a pluralist, which fails to account both for the force of O'Hara's writing and for his more particular relation to Greenberg and Fried. I will take up these relations in my last three chapters.

69. Given O'Hara's other writings on Pollock and de Kooning especially (which we will turn to in chapter 5), a phrase like the "beautiful and solitary aim of abstract painting" is self-consciously excessive and yet not simply derogatory or ironic. One might account for the distancing this sentence achieves by thinking about O'Hara's parallel movement, in poetry, away from monumentality toward the occasional. From one point of view (call this Harold Rosenberg's), high abstract expressionism is the ultimate occasional art — painting as event. And yet this art is, in O'Hara's characterization, solitary. Perhaps this is so (O'Hara does not go into this problem here) insofar as its occasions cannot be intersubjective ones. The occasion of abstract painting lacks the sort of functional relationship Hartigan explores.
70. In fact this whole paragraph, as Blasing notes, is intimately related to O'Hara's own poetics (35–36).
71. The two made up briefly during the summer of 1966 just before O'Hara's death. Hartigan's painting *Frank O'Hara (1926–1966)* memorializes his death. See Mattison, 70.
72. As with his deflation (and queering) of the pastoral, O'Hara could be said to take a camp pleasure in hyperbolically overplaying the role of courtier sonneteer — an effect which becomes legible primarily across the broad range of his poetry. While one moment O'Hara sings the praises of his "muses," the next he relates a graphic homosexual encounter. Hartigan is O'Hara's last major female muse, Jane Freilicher and Bunny Lang having preceded her.
73. Gooch tells us that "Grace Hartigan also arrived with Robert Keene, a Southampton bookstore owner who was briefly her third husband, to bask in the publicity of 'The New American Painting'" (G 314).
74. Indeed, in his prose about Hartigan's painting, O'Hara's position grows dizzyingly complex because he is talking, in many cases, about paintings for which he himself posed.
75. To an extent, this same story can be told with a number of other artist friends, including Jane Freilicher, Larry Rivers, and Alfred Leslie. Though the institutional structure is quite different, one might argue that by the late 1950s or early 1960s O'Hara wielded enough power in the poetry world to affect the status of the names he included in his work.

4. COMBATIVE NAMES

1. Barr's account of his trip to Russia was first published in the winter 1978 issue of the journal *October* and later reprinted in the posthumously pub-

lished 1986 collection of his writings, *Defining Modern Art*, where "The LEF and Soviet Art" was also reprinted. Barr was aware of and encouraged Gray's book.

2. Waldo Rasmussen, O'Hara's colleague in the International Program at MoMA, remembers O'Hara wielding Mayakovsky as a "combative name" (interview with the author March 31, 2003).
3. The link between postwar international power and cultural status was not lost on prominent planners and political figures. Beginning in the 1920s, though with greater momentum after World War II, Robert Moses, for instance, reshaped New York in conscious dialog with Baron Haussmann's reconstruction of nineteenth-century Paris. Long before Moses's spectacular staging of the 1964 World's Fair in New York, he could write of Manhattan that "[o]ur museum guides, in three hours, can show visitors the arts and crafts of three thousand years, and the flora, fauna, feathers, furs and fins of all species which have enlivened biology since this revolving globe cooled sufficiently to support it" (76).
4. According to Brad Gooch, "when Barr's Matisse retrospective opened on November 14 [1951], O'Hara was so intent on viewing and reviewing the paintings that he applied for a job selling postcards, publications, and tickets at the Museum's front desk" (G 207).
5. In December 1953 he began writing reviews for *Art News*, a job he would continue until December 1955.
6. In April 1955 "O'Hara was promoted to a more permanent position as Administrative Assistant in the International Program" (G 257). This post he kept until December 1955, when he quit the job to take a six-month leave at the Poets Theatre in Cambridge. After coming back to MoMA during the summer of 1956, O'Hara's real responsibilities began in May 1957, when, according to Gooch, he was allowed "to select paintings to represent the United States in the Fourth Annual Art Exhibition of Japan, which opened in Tokyo in May 1957. For this exhibit of fifteen paintings by fifteen painters, O'Hara chose a mixture of second-generation Abstract Expressionist and figurative painters including Frankenthaler, Goldberg, Goodnough, Hartigan, Elaine de Kooning, Leslie, Mitchell, Pace, Parker, Resnick, and Rivers" (G 294), as well as Twombly, Diebenkorn, and Jan Muller — who had as yet had only a single one-person show each.
7. According to Gooch, O'Hara first visited the Club late in 1951; his first talk was on March 7, 1952, as part of "a fourth and final panel on 'Abstract Expressionism' titled 'A Group of Younger Artists' with Jane Freilicher, Grace Hartigan, Larry Rivers, Al Leslie, and Joan Mitchell, moderated by John Myers" (G 216). By the time O'Hara had a more permanent position at MoMA, his authority in the art world was already recognized: "At a panel at the Club on January 21 [1955] — less than three weeks after O'Hara began to

work for McCray — O'Hara's essay 'Nature and New Painting' (published with a drawing by Jane Freilicher in *Folder 3*) was discussed by a panel consisting of Alfred Barr, Jr., Clement Greenberg, and Hilton Kramer" (G 259).

8. The letter begins, strangely, by telling the Ford Foundation that "cultural interchange" should be understood as a response to "the need to affirm cultural values in an increasingly secular and mechanized era." But lest the foundation feel responsible for this condition, the letter then recasts culture "at a more competitive level," where cultural accomplishments have become recognized as "essential assets [attributes crossed out] whereby each nation seeks to maintain its prestige vis-a-vis its presumed allies or potential enemies" (Frank O'Hara papers 5. Museum of Modern Art Archives, New York; further references to this archive will be marked as MoMA).
9. O'Hara's letter goes on to suggest that the international perception of the United States as a consumer rather than a producer of culture has been exacerbated by the impossibility of seeing American art in Europe — a situation that was, of course, about to change dramatically, in part through the Museum of Modern Art's and thus O'Hara's efforts. "The widely known fact that American public and private collections have become storehouses of masterpieces from all over the world, and the activity of American museums in borrowing still other works of art from abroad for loan exhibitions, have perhaps led to the idea that America was a cultural vacuum which itself produced nothing. Such an impression on the part of the European public would indeed be hard to dispel, in view of the fact that even the major museums of Europe own practically no American works of art — Whistler's *Mother* in the Louvre and a Grandma Moses in Musée National d'Art moderne being all that Paris possesses, while London has no American work of art at all in the National gallery and but three in the Tate. Exhibitions of American art have likewise been almost unknown abroad until the past few years" (October 16, 1956, Frank O'Hara papers, 5. MoMA).
10. The word "requests" is crossed out.
11. While O'Hara's catalogs were not done under Alfred Barr directly, Barr was certainly a respected and influential figure within MoMA generally and for O'Hara specifically.
12. See *The Collected Books of Jack Spicer*, ed. Robin Blaser, 11.
13. "Lorca" goes on to complain that "[e]ven the most faithful student of my work will be hard put to decide what is and what is not García Lorca as, indeed, he would if he were to look into my present resting place. The analogy is impolite, but I fear the impoliteness is deserved" (ibid.).
14. Rivers, *What did I do? the Unauthorized Autobiography of Larry Rivers*, 218.
15. "If I made drawings to give myself the credentials of an artist of the past, Frank wrote letters to bolster his image as a writer, for himself as well as for those who received them. Let me not forget that it was also fun and natural

for Frank, who felt compelled to put down on paper as much of his thoughts and experiences as he could cram into any one week. His letters are an amazing surge of single-space enthusiasm; like all his friends, I was flattered to received them and careful to save them" (Rivers 238).

16. Spicer gets at the practical uses of intertextuality toward the end of the book, when he again addresses Lorca: "This is the last letter. The connection between us, which had been fading away with the summer, is now finally broken. I turn in anger and dissatisfaction to the things of my life and you return, a disembodied but contagious spirit, to the printed page. It is over, this intimate communion with the ghost of Garcia Lorca, and I wonder now how it was ever able to happen" (51).

17. Those who came to the West included Gabo and Pevsner, El Lissitzsky, Roman Jakobson, and Elsa Triolet.

18. De Kooning, of course, is said to have carefully selected a drawing that would be difficult to erase. See Walter Hopps, *Robert Rauschenberg*, 75.

19. John Bernard Myers, director of the Tibor de Nagy Gallery, claims that he introduced O'Hara to de Kooning during the summer of 1952 (*Tracking the Marvelous* 136).

20. One important effect that preserving de Kooning in the "Notes" has is to suggest that, since Mayakovsky had died in 1930, the attempt to represent quotidian life in the New York City of 1953 must turn either to painting or to the literature of different periods and different countries. I think this gesture can be seen as an attempt on O'Hara's part to distance himself from the institutionalized modernism of the followers of Eliot. In this vein, O'Hara writes, "only Whitman and Crane and Williams, of the Americans, are better than the movies" (*CP* 498).

21. See Hess's *Abstract Painting: Background and American Phase*, as well as his *Willem de Kooning*. Interpreting de Kooning's famous statement "I paint myself out of a picture," Hess claims that "[w]hen the artist is finished, the picture begins its own life" (*Willem de Kooning* 24). The bounds of this autonomous life, however, are more narrowly prescribed by Hess: "Once they are defined, de Kooning's shapes stand for themselves, retaining all their meanings and contradictions, but they are never letters in an alphabet from which words can be spelled" (*Willem de Kooning* 16). Though O'Hara never suggests that one simply "reads" a de Kooning, he does accord the paintings a discursivity that Hess denies.

22. For theorists like Paul de Man, allegory is the figurative mode most closely linked to demystification. In "The Rhetoric of Temporality," de Man argues that "[w]hereas the symbol postulates the possibility of an identity or identification, allegory designates primarily a distance in relation to its own origin, and, renouncing the nostalgia and the desire to coincide, it establishes its language in the void of this temporal difference. In so doing it prevents

the self from an illusory identification with the non-self, which is now fully, though painfully, recognized as a non-self" (*Blindness and Insight* 207). Mayakovsky's writing, far from suggesting the melancholic existential knowledge evoked by de Man, nonetheless stages identification in such excessive terms as to arrive at a similar demystification from a very different path.

23. If in Mayakovsky the poetic self becomes an unapologetic advocate of the Soviet state and its social project, it also self-consciously stages the rhetorical moment in such advocacy. For an account of how apostrophe embarrasses readers — forcing them to acknowledge their expectation that poetry will not theatricalize its own form of address — see Jonathan Culler, "Apostrophe," in *The Pursuit of Signs*.
24. Not surprisingly, Mayakovsky's editors tend to apologize for his soap jingles and directions for living in the Soviet state, which are usually omitted from anthologies. For example, in editing *The Bedbug and Selected Poetry*, one of the most widely accessible Mayakovsky collections, Patricia Blake chooses what she calls the more "lasting" or "literary" of Mayakovsky's works. Thus Blake places Mayakovsky's writing in a tradition of quasi-universal literary "experience" that his work explicitly undercuts by cultivating quotidian, temporally specific, and above all "rhetorical" concerns.
25. It was precisely this quality in Mayakovsky's work that made Leon Trotsky nervous: "Just as the ancient Greek was an anthropomorphist and naïvely thought of the forces of nature as resembling himself, so our poet is a Mayako-morphist and fills the squares, the streets and fields of the Revolution with his own personality. True, extremes meet. The universalization of one's own ego breaks down, to some extent, the limits of one's individuality, and brings one nearer to the collectivity — from the reverse end. But this is only true to a certain degree. The individualistic and Bohemian arrogance — in contrast, not to humility, which no one wants, but to a necessary sense of the measure of things — runs through everything written by Mayakovsky." See "Futurism" in Trotsky's *Literature and Revolution*, 149. Expanding can also mean fragmenting, as Shklovsky notes about Mayakovsky's theatrical performance: "The poet dissects himself on stage, holding himself between his fingers as a gambler holds his cards" (53).
26. In the chapter "On a Generation That Squandered Its Poets" in *Language and Literature*, Roman Jakobson describes this tendency as Mayakovsky's "infinitely varied theme" and goes on to call it a "[w]ariness with fixed and narrow confines, the urge to transcend static boundaries" (266–67).
27. O'Hara mentions the poem in his "[Notes on *Second Avenue*]" (*CP* 495).
28. The Russian "romance of production" is, as is well known, a consistent theme throughout the writing and film of the late teens and 1920s. Some of its highlights include Dziga Vertov's fantastic film *The Man with the Movie*

Camera and Viktor Shklovsky's *The Third Factory*. Shklovsky deals self-consciously and at times critically with Soviet Russia's emphasis on both material production and what we would now call "subject production."

29. Such a statement calls to mind, ironically, the rigid "sense of the measure of things" that Trotsky misses in Mayakovsky's work.
30. For a reading of Warhol in relation to Pollock, see Rosalind Krauss, *The Optical Unconscious*. For an account of Rauschenberg and Johns in relation to abstract expressionism, see Paul Schimmel's "The Faked Gesture: Pop Art and the New York School."
31. "Repetition belongs to humor and irony," writes Gilles Deleuze in *Difference and Repetition*: "[I]t is by nature transgression or exception, always revealing a singularity opposed to the particulars subsumed under laws, a universal opposed to the generalities which give rise to laws" (5). More recently, art historians have been given a psychoanalytic version of repetition as difference in Hal Foster's *The Return of the Real*. I will return to Deleuze's and Foster's concepts of repetition in chapter 6.
32. This reading of Mayakovsky was certainly shared by Allen Ginsberg, who, as my epigraph indicates, was introduced to Mayakovsky by O'Hara.
33. For instance, in "Oranges" (CP 5) this same event gets an extended treatment, the stable boy becoming "Pan."
34. This line recalls O'Hara's "Poem (The rich cubicle's enclosure)," directed against Pound, in which "Venice-on-Hudson" is linked to "bung-hole blowers" (PR 82). In each case New York's identity is appropriated, homosexualized, and then wielded against a hostile opponent.
35. Greenberg, in his famous essay "American-Type Painting" (*Collected Essays* vol. 2) elaborates on the genre in the context of a discussion of Clyfford Still. In *Farewell to an Idea: Episodes from a History of Modernism*, T. J. Clark offers an account of the function of the category of "buckeye" for Greenberg, linking it to Clark's own ideas about vulgarity, which I will consider below.
36. For T. J. Clark, abstract expressionism's "vulgarity" is both a condition of reception, part of the "object's existence in a particular social world," and a "telltale blemish, some atrociously visual quality" in the object itself (*Farewell* 376).
37. See, for example, Thomas Hess, *Abstract Painting: Background and American Phase* and Irving Sandler, *The Triumph of American Painting*.
38. Both Fainsod's and Pasternak's books should be seen in relation to Khrushchev's 1956 "secret speech," which historian James T. Patterson describes as an "amazing speech that Khrushchev gave to the 1,400-odd top Soviet officials who were attending the twentieth Congress of the Communist Party in Moscow in February 1956. Although the address was supposed to be secret, it soon leaked to the Russian people and to the West. Khrushchev attacked Stalin (his former boss and patron) as a paranoiac

tyrant who had inflicted purges, show trials, terror, forced labor camps, and mass executions on the people of his country. Khrushchev called for the de-Stalinization of the Soviet Union and eastern Europe, maintained that capitalism and communism were not incompatible, and seemed to welcome coexistence with the West" (Patterson 304).

39. Explaining Pasternak's relation to the revolution of 1905, Ruge suggests that "what Boris Pasternak must have felt in those days when, during one of the demonstrations, he received a blow from a nagika (the Cossack whip) was probably not so much the anger of the revolutionary as indignation at the harshness and inhumanity with which the demonstrators were treated" (20).
40. The writer is Nicola Chiaromonte of the *Partisan Review.*
41. Though *Evergreen Review* does print two translations of Mayakovsky in its September/October 1961 issue ("And You Think You Could?" and "Once More on Petersburg"), both are relatively tame.
42. O'Hara's sustained focus on the Soviet Union during this period is documented in the following poems, written between July 8, 1958, and September 17, 1959: "Fantasia (on Russian Verses) for Alfred Leslie" (*CP* 303), "A True Account of Talking to the Sun at Fire Island" (*CP* 306), "Far from the Porte des Lilas and the Rue Pergolèse" (*CP* 311), "Two Russian Exiles: An Ode" (*CP* 313), "On Rachmaninoff's Birthday (It is your 86th birthday)" (*CP* 321), "For Bob Rauschenberg" (*CP* 322), "Variations on Pasternak's 'Mein Liebchen, Was Willist du Noch Mehr?'" (*CP* 339), and "Poem (Khrushchev is coming on the right day!)" (*CP* 340).
43. While the November/December 1960 issue of *Evergreen Review* included a collective statement against French colonialism in Algeria (signed by, among many others, Simone de Beauvoir, Maurice Blanchot, André Breton, Michel Butor, Marguerite Duras, Michel Leiris, Alain Robbe-Grillet, Nathalie Sarraute, Jean-Paul Sartre, and Claude Simon), the magazine seems to have been more cautious, even patriotic, about American diplomacy.
44. The poem was written in Paris on Sept 17, 1958, after *Doctor Zhivago* was published but before the news of the Nobel Prize. Still, the reference to Triolet seems a clear indication that the struggles within the reception are already active.
45. "In general," Tony Towle writes, "Frank dealt with the all-time greats as if he had been at the dinner table with them the previous week, where there had been gossip, brilliant conversation, and plenty of drinks to go with dinner" (57).
46. Michael Schumacher, *Dharma Lion: A Biography of Allen Ginsberg*, 420. Ultimately, though, Ginsberg's more radical gesture of challenging postrevolutionary Cuba's sexual policies became wrapped up in his more symptomatically hippie stance of advocating drug use itself as a kind of politics. Asked by a reporter

what he would want to discuss with Castro, Ginsberg is said to have responded that he would not only question Cuba's leader about his country's abusive treatment of *los infermos* and homosexuals but he would ask Castro in addition "why marijuana was not legal in Cuba [and] propose that rather than executing opponents of the revolution and political terrorists, Cuba give these people magic mushrooms and innocuous jobs such as positions as elevator operators at the Havana Riviera Hotel" (421).

47. A good overview of O'Hara's relations to the movies is Andrew Epstein's "'I Want to be at Least as Alive as the Vulgar': Frank O'Hara's Poetry and the Cinema," in *The Scene of My Selves: New Work on New York School Poets*, eds. Diggory and Miller.
48. Jim Elledge, "'Never Argue with the Movies': Love and the Cinema in the Poetry of Frank O'Hara" (*To be True to a City* 356).

5. PROXIMITY'S PLEA

1. Rather than assume interdisciplinarity as an a priori value, I want to claim only its contextual effectiveness. In the context of O'Hara criticism, Jacques Debrot finds O'Hara's collaborations with artists valuable *because* of their interdisciplinarity, which he sees as a subversion of Fried's strictures. Though I agree that O'Hara's work should be read in relation to Fried, I think that, especially after forty years of interdisciplinary artwork dominating the art world, one must argue the specific functions and effects of an instance of interdisciplinary thought to establish its value. See Debrot's "Present, The Scene of My Selves, The Occasion of These Ruses: Frank O'Hara's Collaborations with Grace Hartigan, Larry Rivers and Jasper Johns."
2. "O'Hara displays," as Marjorie Perloff writes, "a certain ambivalence to the great Abstract Expressionists, an ambivalence which creates interesting tensions" (P 85). But rather than understand these tensions and ambivalences at a personal, aesthetic level, as Perloff does, one might relate them to the increasingly instrumental role American painting was coming to play in international politics. In O'Hara's poetry, abstract expressionism is a site, at once, of liberatory formal invention and self-conscious wildness that serves ideological purposes; imaginative models of affect *and* repressive national fantasies.
3. See Guilbaut's *How New York Stole the Idea of Modern Art* and Kozloff's, "American Painting during the Cold War" (first published in *Artforum*, May 1973, and reprinted in *Pollock and After*, ed. Frascina).
4. Even for critics interested in the New York School, though, O'Hara's art criticism tends to be considered only briefly, as in Fred Orton's otherwise excellent *Figuring Jasper Johns*, or treated simply as a pluralist, which oversimplifies O'Hara's relation to 1950s debates within art criticism. For this latter approach, see Russell Ferguson's *In Memory of My Feelings: Frank O'Hara and American Art*.

5. Published after my article version of this chapter appeared in *Qui Parle* 12:2 (2001), David LeHardy Sweet's book *Savage Sight/Constructed Noise: Poetic Adaptations of Painterly Techniques in the French and American Avant-Gardes* (2003), in his chapter on O'Hara, also emphasizes the importance of "proximity" in O'Hara's writing: "the big and the small, the serious and the trivial all entered the fabric of his poems by virtue of their accidental proximity to the poet" (30).
6. As early as his 1958 article "The Legacy of Jackson Pollock," Allan Kaprow could complain that Pollock's insights had already been institutionalized within the discipline of painting: "The act of painting, the new space, the personal mark that builds its own form and meaning, the endless tangle, the great scale, the new materials are by now clichés of college art departments. The innovations are accepted. They are becoming part of textbooks" (*Essays on the Blurring of Art and Life* 2). Kaprow is, of course, far from dismissing Pollock; he proposes instead that Pollock's real influence is now extending into the literally three-dimensional spaces of events and happenings.
7. Waldo Rasmussen, O'Hara's colleague at MoMA, described O'Hara's relation to Greenberg as "acute rivalry." Rasmussen continues: "Greenberg was so . . . not sermon on mount, because that's Christian, but a kind of Jewish prophet. Laying down the law. The tyranny of it. There was something about his ego that would have clashed like dynamite with Frank's. Because he had such a prophetlike character. And that's not Frank, and he would have fought that. And what I felt about Frank was more an allegiance to second-generation New York School artists [like Mike Goldberg]. But Greenberg did support artists that Frank liked — like Motherwell and Frankenthaler" (interview with the author March 31, 2003).
8. Perhaps the most influential critique of this aspect of Greenberg is Leo Steinberg's *Other Criteria: Confrontations with Twentieth-Century Art.*
9. Taking a traditional view of poetry, Greenberg separates it from the other hyphenated failures on his list: poetic criticism is not an abortion of discourse, but of "intuition and imagination" (4:85).
10. Kozloff dismissed the show in an early review: "Making much headway [in] England and Germany, less in France and Italy, the *New American Painting* . . . furnished out-of-date and over-simplified metaphors of the actual complexity of American experience" (116). Written a year after Kozloff's article, Eva Cockroft's essay "Abstract Expressionism, Weapon of the Cold War" gives a fuller account of MoMA's role in Cold War diplomacy, describing O'Hara's immediate boss, Porter McCray, as "a particularly powerful and effective man in the history of cultural imperialism" (127).
11. For a brief account of the relation of *Art News* to New York poets, see Bill Berkson's "Afterword" to O'Hara's *What's With Modern Art? Selected Short Reviews and Other Art Writings.*

12. See, for instance, Craig Owens, *Beyond Recognition: Representation, Power, and Culture*; Douglas Crimp, "On the Museum's Ruins"; Hal Foster, *Recodings: Art, Spectacle, Cultural Politics*; and Rosalind Krauss, *The Originality of the Avant-Garde and Other Modernist Myths*.
13. Krauss stages her own relation to Fried, Greenberg, and their creed as if she were an apostate Modernist, though one upon whom modernism's truly religious character flashed only in a [modernist?] epiphanic moment, of which the narrative contains many: "I remember reading Michael's last sentence — 'Presentness is grace' [from "Art and Objecthood"] — with a dizzying sense of disbelief." This same autobiographical interpolation concludes with her account of Fried telling Krauss that Ted Williams was, for Fried, Greenberg, and Frank Stella, the ideal modernist because Williams "sees faster than any other living human." "This was by way, of course, of inducting me onto the team, Michael's team, Frank's team, Greenberg's team, major players in the '60s formulation of modernism" (*Optical Unconscious* 6–7).
14. The classic examples are his essays "Entropy and the New Monuments," "A Tour of the Monuments of the Passaic, New Jersey," "The Spiral Jetty," and "Frederick Law Olmsted and the Dialectical Landscape," though all of Smithson's writing qualifies. See Smithson, *Collected Writings*, and my essay, "Smithson, Writer."
15. Only one section (section 9) of the poem's eleven parts was published before 1960, when the poem came out as a kind of chapbook published by Totem Press in New York. In this way it was a true coterie poem; Rivers, Ashbery, Koch, Hartigan, de Kooning, and many other of O'Hara's friends read it, but in manuscript form.
16. In its heterogeneous organization as well as its questioned position as possible juvenilia within the poet's oeuvre, "Second Avenue" resembles Kenneth Koch's *When the Sun Tries to Go On* (written as a poem in 1953, published initially in Alfred Leslie's *The Hasty Papers* in 1960 but not published as a book until 1969) and John Ashbery's difficult book, *The Tennis Court Oath*, especially its longest poem, "Europe," which also includes narrative elements, characters, and stylized accounts of travel, all within a highly variable surface. All three of these poems, moreover, have been important for contemporary experimental poets: that the first lines of "Second Avenue" are quoted in Ron Silliman's best-known poem *Tjanting* provides a central example. For an account of Silliman's use of O'Hara, see my article, "The Labor of Repetition: Silliman's 'Quips' and the Politics of Intertextuality." But while both "Second Avenue" and *The Tennis Court Oath* have been taken to mark an extreme phase for each poet of intertextual or interdisciplinary engagement with art, somehow the terms of this engagement have seemed far less clear to O'Hara's critics, who have generally shied away from the poem. On the other hand, John Shoptaw (in *On the Outside Looking Out: John Ashbery's Poetry*)

and David Shapiro (in *John Ashbery: An Introduction to the Poetry*) both provide thorough readings of "Europe."

17. Perloff writes, "No sooner does O'Hara provide us with this lyric model than he undercuts it" (P 70). She then quotes the first two lines of the next stanza: "This thoroughness whose traditions have become so reflective, / your distinction is merely a quill at the bottom of the sea" (CP 139). "Lines 4 and 5," she writes, "prick the balloon, as if to say, 'Oh, so you thought I was going to be *poetic*, did you?' But why be poetic when our 'traditions have become so reflective'? And what, after all, is the poet's pen but 'a quill at the bottom of the sea'?" (P 70–71). In order to produce the reading that the rest of the poem undermines the "aureate diction" (P 70) of these first lines, Perloff must claim that the "thoroughness whose traditions have become so reflective" is referring to what she understands as the poetic "quotation" above and not, as O'Hara claims in his notes, "the philosophical reduction of reality into a dealable-with system" (CP 495). Given that this is one of the very few lines, among the poem's 478 lines, for which O'Hara identifies a referent, I think it is safe to follow his lead — which means, then, that we would read the "This" of line 4 as unhinged from its immediate antecedent, a type of disjunction that occurs throughout "Second Avenue."
18. O'Hara's approach here might be usefully compared to that of Jackson Mac Low, who developed similar effects by using aleatory methods: "I realized by the later 50s that the events we single out as 'experiences of emotion' as against those we call 'sensations' occur as randomly as the sounds in a forest, & began to feel less difference between generating works systematically & recording emotional events" ("Museletter" 27).
19. My claim is not that substituting the category of the speaker with that of a generative vocabulary or language more generally is inherently valuable. There are bad versions of it. For instance, in his discussion of protofascism, Fredric Jameson argues about Wyndham Lewis's sentences: "the phrases, with their heterogeneous sources and references, are never completely subdued and mastered by the sentence as a larger unit" (*Fables of Aggression: Wyndham Lewis, the Modernist as Fascist* 71). Lewis cultivates this internal war of cliché fragments from mass culture as a figure, Jameson suggests, for the larger, necessarily violent set of reactionary cultural upheavals to come.
20. The manuscript of the poem, in Donald Allen's papers at the University of California, San Diego, in the Mandeville Special Collections, demonstrates how the substitutions in O'Hara's revisions brought the poem away from the empirical reality of the street toward a greater level of abstraction: "celebrate diced excesses on sidewalks" becomes "celebrate diced excesses and sardonics" (CP 139); "This thoroughfare whose traditions have become so reflective" becomes "This thoroughness whose traditions have become so reflective" (ibid.). Similarly, in section 3, the final version's clearly audible

pun, "occidental death / by traffic" (*CP* 141), does in fact emerge out of "accidental death," crossed out and substituted in the manuscript.

21. While one can identify, for instance, a sassy colloquial voice and languages of both fantastic literature and over simplistic narrative, it may not be possible to separate each of these into a distinct discursive register, ascribing each phrase to a vocabulary. One might claim that O'Hara "celebrate[s] diced excesses" by employing what Roman Jakobson in "Two Aspects of Language and Two Types of Aphasic disturbances" (*Language in Literature*) calls the metonymic axis of combination rather than the metaphoric axis of selection. But as both Jakobson and Roland Barthes (for whom metonymy is also very important) recognized, no aspect of a poem is purely paradigmatic or syntagmatic, metonymic or metaphoric, at all possible interpretive levels. Still, these distinctions retain force both as methods of specification and as the groundwork for tracking a significant shift away from metaphor in poetry since the 1950s.
22. Here is Breslin's critique of the early work: "O'Hara's early experiments with surrealism, in 'Oranges,' 'Easter,' and 'Second Avenue,' juxtapose the beautiful and the obscene, the natural and the mechanical, in ways that are more contrived than revelatory, as if bombastic French language games were a sufficient substitute for the current 'academic parlor game.' The linguistic difficulties posed by 'In Memory of My Feelings,' however, are generated by complex emotional substance and a dazzling stylistic variety" (242). Perloff's objections are similar: "By late 1953, then, all the necessary ingredients were present. . . . But after *Second Avenue* O'Hara learns to relate individual elements more intricately, to forge them into a coherent whole. And he now begins to put the 'straight Surrealism' behind him" (P 74).
23. One could claim that the later sections of the poem achieve a kind of "ventilation" by introducing a more colloquial — even, at times, narrative — tone. These sections are palpable breaks within the larger world of overcharged vocabulary and syntax.
24. In the windup to Kline's talk, O'Hara summarizes how abstract expressionism has made a specifically American experience possible: "The painters of this movement, so totally different from each other in aspect, so totally without the look of a school, have given us as Americans an art which for the first time in our history we can love and emulate, aspire to and understand, without provincial digression or prejudice. The Europeanization of our sensibilities has at last been exorcized as if by magic, an event of some violence which Henry James would have hailed as eagerly as Walt Whitman and which allows us as a nation to exist internationally" (SS 89).
25. This fascination runs throughout O'Hara's art criticism. See in particular "David Smith: The Color of Steel," "Franz Kline Talking," and "Larry Rivers: A Memoir" — all reprinted in *Standing Still and Walking in New York*.

26. In "Larry Rivers: A Memoir," O'Hara calls Greenberg "the discoverer," referring presumably to his critical role in finding gallery representation for talented young painters — including Rivers and Hartigan (*CP* 512).
27. In the chapter "The 'Primitive' Unconscious" (*Recodings*), Hal Foster attempts to separate the symptomatic model of primitivism from a more disruptive one he sees coming out of surrealism: "[T]he dissident surrealists (Bataille chief among them) present, if not a 'counterprimitivism' as such, then at least a model of how the otherness of the primitive might be thought disruptively, not recuperated abstractly" (200). In this latter model, "the primitive appeared less as a solution to western aesthetic problems than as a disruption of western solutions" (ibid.). Though one might also stress O'Hara's identification — not with Bataille specifically but with surrealist primitivism — I'm not sure that French surrealist primitivism presents a clear alternative to all the versions of primitivism circulating in the American 1940s and 1950s — in the self-conscious moments of some of the painters in particular.
28. As the passage continues, the painters themselves seem to remain marginal in O'Hara's account, subject only to "asphalt abuse which is precisely life / in these provinces printed everywhere with the flag 'Nobody'" (*CP* 141). For now, the American flag somehow enforces their anonymity (having yet to graft their gestures onto itself as proof of American freedom).
29. Michael Leja offers this description of Pollock's reception during the transition toward greater abstraction: "Web, entrapment, ensnaring — these are metaphors that will be courted increasingly as Pollock's handling of the figure-field dynamic proceeds. That which formerly made the figures now imprisons them. Pollock may have freed line from one manner of bounding form, but it does not necessarily become nonmimetic, 'pure' line (if such a thing is imaginable) as a result" (290).
30. O'Hara writes that what he calls the "verbal elements of the poem" (presumably those set pieces, like his studio visits, that can be clarified with references and paraphrased as vignettes) "are not too interesting to discuss although they are intended consciously to keep the surface of the poem high and dry, not wet, reflective and self-conscious" (*CP* 497).
31. The fact that Greenberg does use the word "completer" in other, non-American contexts (such as his essay "On the Role of Nature in Modern Painting") does not, I think, undercut the significance of its proximity to Pollock, whose classically laconic, American statements include lines like "I've knocked around some in California, some in Arizona. Never been to Europe" and, to the question of why he prefers New York to the West, "Living is keener, more demanding, more intense and expansive in New York than in the West." These are from Pollock's "Answers to a Questionnaire."
32. Greenberg himself was not immune to such insights. Consider, for exam-

ple, this passage from his review of de Kooning's first solo show in 1948: "The indeterminateness or ambiguity that characterizes some of de Kooning's pictures is caused, I believe, by his effort to suppress his facility. There is a deliberate renunciation of will in so far as it makes itself felt as skill, and there is also a refusal to work with ideas that are too clear. But at the same time this demands a considerable exertion of the will in a different context and a heightening of consciousness so that the artist will know when he is being truly spontaneous and when he is working only mechanically" (2: 229–30).

33. See Richard Schiff, "Water and Lipstick: De Kooning in Transition" in *Willem de Kooning: Paintings*, 34. Schiff also quotes several of de Kooning's remarks about the importance of the face both in his *Woman* paintings, and, less obviously, in his landscapes: "A picture to me is not geometric — it has a face" (44); "I cut out a lot of mouths [while working on the *Woman* series]. First of all, I felt everything ought to have a mouth. Maybe it was like a pun, maybe even sexual. . . . I put the mouth more or less in the place where it was supposed to be. It always turned out to be very beautiful and it helped me immensely to have the real thing. . . . it was something to hang on to" (40).

34. Picking up on this Hollywood strain within O'Hara's institutional work, Bill Berkson writes (to repeat a quote from chapter 2) that "In the actual organizing and mounting of exhibitions, Frank played out his feelings for MOMA as a site of composite grandeur, part salon of the *ancien regime*, part soundstage at Warner Brothers in the thirties" (*WW* 33).

35. Consider T. J. Clark's reading of Greenberg's well-known negative reaction to the *Woman* series: "What Greenberg was recoiling from, I think, is the way choosing Woman as his subject allowed de Kooning to extrude a quality of perception and handling that stood at the very heart of his aesthetic and fix it onto an Other, a scapegoat. . . . Greenberg drew back from this not, need I say it, out of concern at de Kooning's misogyny, but from an intuition that such splitting and projection would make it impossible for de Kooning's *painting* to go on sustaining the right pitch of tawdriness, ironic facility, overweening self-regard. I think he was right. Only when de Kooning found a way to have the vulgarity be his own again — or rather, to half-project it onto cliché landscape or townscape formats that were transparently mere props — did he regain the measure of meretriciousness his art needed. The male braggadocio, that is to say, had to be *unfocused* if he was to paint up a storm" (*Farewell* 393).

36. This take on high art's relation to mass culture is obviously quite different from Greenberg's. "In Greenberg's analysis," writes Thomas Crow, "mass culture is never left behind in modernist practice, but persists as a constant pressure on the artist, severely restricting creative 'freedom.' But the pressure is, of course, all in one direction — all repulsion, no attraction" (238).

37. See Gooch (463), who also notes that during the summer of 1966, while O'Hara was on Long Island, de Kooning "bicycled by, while O'Hara was trimming wisteria on a high ladder, to announce that he would finally agree to a retrospective at the Museum. 'If *you* do it, OK!' he said. The agreement was a coup, as de Kooning had refused such a show for years. He had dismissed retrospectives as obituaries" (G 452–53).
38. Quoted in Peter Schjeldahl, "Frank O'Hara: 'He Made Things & People Sacred'" (H 141).
39. See Prynne, *A Discourse on Willem de Kooning's "Rosy-Fingered Dawn at Louse Point"* (48).
40. *Gotham News* is in landscape format; *Easter Monday*, in portrait. But there is fluidity between these modes even within a single canvas: Prynne notes, for instance, that *Rosy-Fingered Dawn at Louse Point* has elements of both the landscape and the portrait and seems to have shifted its orientation during de Kooning's process several times (35).
41. O'Hara then uses the opportunity to talk about a topic as potentially tame as "shaped poems" to stress the radical genealogy underlying visual prosody, a genealogy that is, for O'Hara, about the relation between typographical experimentation and the limits of recognizable personalizing features.
42. For an account of how O'Hara's painting poetry disrupts the tradition of ekphrasis ("the use of literature to imitate a work of plastic art"), see Michael Davidson's 1983 essay "Ekphrasis and the Postmodern Painter Poem." Davidson writes, "In both O'Hara and Ashbery . . . a painting serves to trigger a series of reflections, the working-out of which depends upon semiotic and stylistic factors within the canvas. One of the things that this working out discovers is the uneasy status of the painting regarded as an object. In order to render the instability of this artifact, the poet becomes a reader of the painter's activity of signifying. This act of reading is never passive, never recuperative since its function is to produce a new text, not to re-capture the original in another medium. The poet who reads another work of art transforms his hermeneutic into performance, just as the reader of the poem participates among the various codes of the text to generate his own readings" (77).
43. This public sphere is, for Prynne, a launching ground for the "ethical sublime" (48). Employing an Aristotelian model in which "pathos is emotion as roused in the listener, and . . . ethos is 'moral character', as reflected in deliberate choice of actions and as developed into a habit of mind" (42), Prynne suggests that "the truncated, gestural citations of a tragic destiny" in O'Hara's poem "conjure with the outcomes of ethic narration but subsume all into a climax of belated, post-heroic pathos" (72).
44. In chapter 6 I will consider a similar space of nonappropriated potentiality that O'Hara attributes to Robert Rauschenberg, whose works are "too moist to be framed" (*CP* 322).

45. The text is transcribed in Harry Gaugh's *Willem de Kooning* (New York: Abbeville, 1983), 60.
46. I want to thank my student Michael Boguslavsky for calling my attention to the multiple senses of this detail.
47. If one actually knew oneself, wouldn't the abstract, transpersonal imperative against excess be superfluous? In *The Birth of Tragedy*, for instance, Nietzsche focuses on the impossible tension between these two moments in the oracle: "If we conceive of it all as imperative and mandatory, this apotheosis of individuation knows but one law — the individual, i.e., the delimiting of the boundaries of the individual, *measure* in the Hellenic sense. Apollo, as ethical deity, exacts measure of his disciples, and, to be able to maintain it, he requires self-knowledge. And so, side by side, with the aesthetic necessity for beauty, there occur the demands 'know thyself' and 'nothing in excess'" (46).

6. COTERIE AND ALLEGORY

1. See, for example, Paul de Man's *Allegories of Reading* and *Blindness and Insight*. Owens's two articles on allegory, which are reprinted in *Beyond Recognition*, appeared in 1980 in the spring and summer issues of *October*. See also Joel Fineman, "The Structure of Allegorical Desire," and Stephen Melville's essay "Notes on the Reemergence of Allegory," which is quoted in my epigraph. In the 1970s, though, the relation between allegory and the commodity, about which Walter Benjamin insisted, tended to drop out. Insofar as Hal Foster's *Return of the Real* deals with allegory, it is an attempt to reconnect this link.
2. The last chapter of Hal Foster's *Return of the Real* takes up this question by asking rhetorically, "Whatever Happened to Postmodernism?"
3. Though Owens does agree with Douglas Crimp that Rauschenberg's appropriation operates as a subversion of the paradigm of artistic ownership characteristic of the museum, Owens does not clarify the link between the "fundamental illegibility" he attributes to Rauschenberg's allegory and the institutional reflexivity that seems to emerge from this illegibility. See Crimp's "On the Museum's Ruins."
4. Benjamin Buchloch's "Allegorical Procedures: Appropriation and Montage in Contemporary Art" made the most concerted effort to consider the potential social implications of recent allegorical practices, offering readings of Dan Graham, Louis Lawler, Hans Haacke, Sherry Levine, Martha Rosler, and Dara Birnbaum. Though the article begins with an illustration of Rauschenberg's *Erased de Kooning Drawing* of 1953, Buchloch does not circle back to Rauschenberg's foundational status within this discourse except to claim in passing that Johns's and Rauschenberg's ambivalent stance toward the gestural and the handmade place them in a quite different, and implicitly more suspect, relation to expressivity from the later artists he champions. Rauschenberg's *Factum 1* and *Factum II* are "delicate constructs of compromise, refining gestural

definition and juxtaposing individualized painterly craftsmanship with seemingly anonymous mechanicity, compared to the radical epistemological crudity and seeming inexhaustible shock of the three-dimensional, unaltered Ready-made" (Buchloch 46–47).

5. To dispute de Man's claim is not to argue that some social real world, what he would call a "phenomenal world," exists beyond his view but that the rhetorical systems fundamental to allegory are already positions from which the crucial historical, social inflection of poetry and art can be registered. De Man, throughout his writing, proleptically engages the claim to move beyond formal questions. In "Semiology and Rhetoric" he claims that "[w]e speak as if, with the problems of literary form resolved once and forever, and with the techniques of structural analysis refined to near perfection, we could now move 'beyond formalism' towards the questions that really interest us and reap, at last, the fruits of the ascetic concentration on technique that prepared us for this decisive step" (*Allegories* 3).
6. The context is de Man's discussion, in his 1982 essay "Reading and History," of Walter Benjamin's concept of allegory; still, this quote works in the passage to speak beyond Benjamin (de Man *Resistance to Theory* 68).
7. T. J. Clark touches on this in an essay called "Phenomenality and Materiality in Cézanne": "No wonder we can never be sure where materiality ends and phenomenality begins. Each thrives interminably on the other's images and procedures. An account of matter will never be rigorous enough, or vivid enough, to seal itself against the other's metaphorical world" (99). J. Hillis Miller offers a theoretical overview of this problem in his essay "Paul de Man as Allergen": "[M]*ateriality* and its cognates occur in three related, ultimately more or less identical, registers in de Man: the materiality of history, the materiality of inscription, and the materiality of what the eye sees prior to perception and cognition. In all three of these registers . . . materiality is associated with notions of performative power and with what seems materiality's opposite, formalism. In all three modes of materiality, the ultimate paradox, allergenic idea, or unintelligibility is the claim or insinuation that materiality is not phenomenal, not open to the senses" (187–88).
8. In the iconographic version, one turns the wealth of detail inside a Rauschenberg combine, for instance, into a unified, though veiled, subtext — often homoerotic. While such subtexts do exist, they are not simply the end result of Rauschenberg's works: it is important that they be understood in relation to the remainders and excesses of meaning that Rauschenberg's work constantly produces. See Kenneth Bendiner, "Robert Rauschenberg's *Canyon*"; Jonathan Katz, "The Art of Code: Jasper Johns and Robert Rauschenberg"; and Laura Auricchio, "Lifting the Veil: Robert Rauschenberg's *Thirty-four Drawings for Dante's Interno* and the Commercial Homoerotic Imagery of 1950s America." In the semiotic readings, however, such remain-

ders and excesses themselves become the full story, as if meaning itself simply meant reduction and as if meaning were therefore simply a naïve and even an oppressive category.

9. Though they do not treat iconography as a matter of identity, Roni Feinstein's *Robert Rauschenberg: The Silkscreen Paintings, 1962–64* and Charles F. Stuckey's reading of *Rebus* ("Reading Rauschenberg") are no less positivistic.
10. In *Small Rebus* the very concept of a rebus depends upon difference among the elements contained. Even if the desire for the rebus phrase may be only a structural function, not dependent upon its actual arrival, such a desire must be pursued by an investigation of how differences within the piece signify.
11. In her more recent essay for Rauschenberg's 1997 Guggenheim retrospective, Krauss addresses the question of allegory directly. Echoing Douglas Crimp's "On the Museum's Ruins," she suggests that "[i]f allegory begins with the doubling of one text (or image) by another, Rauschenberg is clearly placing photography and (Renaissance) painting into such a reciprocal relationship" ("Perpetual Inventory" 218). Crimp sees Rauschenberg's "breakthrough" in terms of his help in what Crimp calls the "destruction of painting": "In the work of Rauschenberg photography began to conspire with painting in its own destruction" (53). In its ability to promote techniques of multiple, dispersed reproduction rather than those of singular, "aura"-based production, photography comes, for Crimp, to undermine the regressive politics of painting. Thus, in Rauschenberg's work, "notions of originality, authenticity and presence, essential to the ordered discourse of the museum are undermined" (ibid.).
12. Joseph also claims that "the images in Rauschenberg's Combines are ruins. They have been disembedded from their existence in a particular historical place and time, and as reproductions (or reproductions of reproductions), the images, even those of old master paintings, have been emptied of the integrity of their contents" (*Random Order: Robert Rauschenberg and the Neo-Avant-Garde* 136).
13. The attention given in art theory to dissociation and materiality is in some ways analogous to that brought to bear on what have (inaccurately) been called "nonsemantic" aspects of poetry: line breaks, acoustic patterns, and syntax. In both disciplines this shift has been part of an important movement to theorize elements within art and poetry that threaten modes of totalizing and universalizing hermeneutic inquiry. But this attention has often led to the position that merely noticing a disruptive component's ability to undermine a global hermeneutics is enough. Such readings, predictably enough, work to make meaning in any guise whatsoever, the oppressive burden from which criticism labors to liberate us. But in fact, the rigorous tools elaborated by versions of poststructuralist art and literary theory enable critics to focus on the nonmeaningful in more meaningful ways than ever

before. As Charles Bernstein has pointed out in his "Artifice of Absorption," (13) such extralexical effects in poetry are far from meaningless:

> the designation of the visual, acoustic,
> & syntactic elements of a poem as "meaningless",
> especially insofar as this is conceptualized as
> positive or liberating . . . is symptomatic of a desire to
> evade responsibility for meaning's total, &
> totalizing, reach; as if meaning was a husk
> that could be shucked off or a burden that could be
> bucked. Meaning is not a use value *as opposed to*
> some other kind of value, but more like valuation
> itself; & even to refuse value is a value & a sort
> of exchange.

When Bernstein speaks of "meaning's totalizing reach," he means not that meaning can be totalized but that signification stops nowhere amid the complex of effects produced by a poem (or a painting). Interested in and benefiting from a tradition of radical formalism, Bernstein seeks to apply such insights to a broader interpretive theory that describes and interrogates the marginal zones within difficult poetry without writing such areas off under generalized effects. In this sense, his project seems valuable to art theory as well.

14. Though this piece is sometimes titled *Untitled Combine ("Man with white shoes")*, I will refer to it by its original designation, *Untitled*.
15. O'Hara certainly wrote more about (and aligned himself more closely with) the Abstract Expressionists and the Gestural Realists who followed them, especially Hartigan and Rivers. Nor is O'Hara at the center of Rauschenberg's engagement with literature or poetry more specifically: when Rauschenberg turned most visibly to literature in the early 1960s it was to the canonical authority of Dante; later, he collaborated with Alain Robbe-Grillet from 1972 to 1978. Moreover, the trajectories of their careers are quite different: O'Hara's early death in 1966 at age 40 ensured his cult status; Rauschenberg has had a long career marked by several distinct phases — from combines to silkscreens to the international Rauschenberg Overseas Culture Interchange (ROCI) begun in 1985.
16. O'Hara's 1962 *Art Chronicle I* notes that "Rauschenberg had recently a very beautiful show at Castelli Gallery and one unprecedented to my knowledge. It began as a group show, and gradually more Rauschenbergs moved in, while others moved out amiably, as if to say, 'Okay, Bob, this turn seems right for you, so take it, maestro, from Bar R.' It was a beautiful show, and an event more interesting than many of the 'happenings' down town. The gallery kept changing the paintings, which gave an unusual urgency to gallery-going.

If I hadn't been lucky, I would have missed seeing *Blue Eagle*, a modern work which nobody should be deprived of" (SS 131).

17. See "Chronology" in Hopps and Davidson (554).
18. We gather from the above that O'Hara saw Rauschenberg's *Growing Painting* from 1953 (shown in January and February of 1954 at the Stable Gallery) and the Merce Cunningham performance *Minutiae* (at the Brooklyn Academy of Music), for which Rauschenberg did the backdrop (now a combine of the same name).
19. Pollock's classic statement was written with the help of Harold Rosenberg: "My painting does not come from the easel. I hardly ever stretch my canvas before painting. I prefer to tack the unstretched canvas to the hard wall or the floor. I need the resistance of a hard surface. On the floor I am more at ease. I feel nearer, more a part of the painting, since this way I can walk around it, work from the four sides and literally be *in* the painting. This is akin to the method of the Indian sand painters of the West." The article was originally published as "My Painting" in *Possibilities* 1 (Winter 1947–1948); see Naifeh and Smith (552).
20. Most of these comments apply far more readily to paintings like *Charlene* and *Collection* than they do to the more abstract red paintings.
21. Johns's show ran from January 20 to February 8, 1958; all but two paintings were sold by the close of the exhibition, including three to MoMA.
22. Here is Steinberg's May 1958 letter to *Arts Magazine*: "Two years ago, in these pages, I wrote a brief and, I hoped, somewhat scathing paragraph on what I called 'the merry work of Robert Rauschenberg.' 'Eulenspiegel,' I concluded, 'is abroad again, and one must be patient.' . . . These last four words are all right: the rest I regret. And I want to take this opportunity to say that Rauschenberg's latest show at Leo Castelli's seems to me to include two or three paintings of remarkable beauty" (9).
23. Rauschenberg's first museum sale would not come until early 1959, when Alan Solomon bought *Migration* for the Cornell University collection. Later that spring Rauschenberg exhibited in *Three* (along with Norman Bluhm and Jean Dubuffet) at the Castelli Gallery. Robert Scull offered to buy *Monogram* for MoMA but Alfred Barr declined.
24. Asked if he would have needed to argue the case for including these Rauschenbergs, O'Hara's colleague in the international program at MoMA, Waldo Rasmussen, told me, "Oh I would think so. And let's face it, Rauschenberg was a hell of a lot better artist than Mike Goldberg, and Johns too. It probably required finagling. One of the hard things was just the physicality of it because Rauschenberg's works aren't easy to ship around. But it just spoke so much for that time that you couldn't — if you were alive to what was happening in American art — not show them in an important exhibition like Documenta" (interview March 31, 2003).

25. Documenta II included 144 works by forty-four American artists. It also featured works by prominent European artists, among them Leger, Picasso, Matisse, Schwitters, Nolde, Rouault, Kandinsky, Mondrian, Beckman, Braque, Dubuffet, Bacon, and Ernst. Though O'Hara's papers at MoMA demonstrate that he helped with the selection of the American artists, he is not listed in the German catalog, which mentions only Porter McCray. Further references to the Frank O'Hara Papers at the Museum of Modern Art Library will be marked parenthetically as MoMA.
26. As Stephen Melville writes, "Allegory has its way of insisting on the problematic — on the uncertainty, at every moment, of the relation between a given present or claim to presence in narratives — stories and histories — by which it is traversed and in which it could figure" (81–82).
27. Clement Greenberg links abstract expressionism's downfall explicitly with the rise of Rauschenberg and Johns: "In the spring of 1962 there came the sudden collapse, market-wise and publicity-wise, of Abstract Expressionism as a collective manifestation. The fall of that year saw the equally suddenly triumph of Pop art, which, though deriving its vision from the art of Rauschenberg and especially Johns, is much more markedly opposed to painterly abstraction in its handling and general design" (4: 215).
28. The term was first applied to Jasper Johns but later extended to Rauschenberg and others. For an overview of the wider art-historical moment, see Susan Hapgood, *Neo-Dada: Redefining Art, 1958–62*.
29. See Cole (18).
30. See Ashton (21, 25); like Steinberg, Ashton will reverse her opinion on Rauschenberg.
31. See Fitzsimmons (33), who sees Rauschenberg and Twombly insisting (unsuccessfully) on new meanings in art practice: "There is a minimum of art and, consequently, of expression in the paintings which Cy Twombly and Robert Rauschenberg recently exhibited at The Stable Gallery. Patently earnest, intelligent young men, Twombly and Rauschenberg, like a great many other abstract expressionists, seem to feel that today not only painting — its appearance, its shapes and surfaces — but art, and the creative process itself must mean something they never meant before."
32. Rauschenberg's revaluing and archiving of refuse often became a source of humor among those in O'Hara's circle (most of whom, despite Rauschenberg's claims to the contrary, actually supported his art). In an October 1, 1960, letter to the painter John Button, for instance, Fairfield Porter writes: "We went often to the beach, where he [James Schuyler] practically never swam, but picked things up which he invested with a Rauschenbergian potential value" (in Spring 245). Similarly, in a letter the previous year to his son Laurence, Porter writes of cleaning up before a party: "[W]hen I said to mother I would like the mantlepieces cleared up, she remarked, 'That

mantlepiece is clean enough, or my name is not Bob Rauschenberg' (he [Rauschenberg] was at Larry's [Rivers], and therefore came)" (Spring 244). See also O'Hara's own remarks below about serving hors d'oeuvres on "little squares pulled off 1954 Rauschenbergs," mentioned in note 55.

33. Rauschenberg's collaborations with (and influence at the hands of) Cage are well documented; see, for example, the 1997 Guggenheim catalog and Kotz. Rauschenberg also did a performance with Feldman at the Stable Gallery during his 1955 show.

34. In mentioning Honig (from whom O'Hara took a course on allegory, at Harvard), my point is not to present a simple source for O'Hara's ideas but to suggest some formulations about the relation between allegory and both discursiveness and amalgamation with which O'Hara would have been familiar. Allegory is the "method that too easily lends itself to the abuse of discursiveness," writes Honig, in his 1959 treatment of Spenser in *Dark Conceit: The Making of Allegory*. Hand in hand with this discursiveness, as its positive value, come "fabulous amalgamations of national, classical and Biblical lore out of which the allegory grows." For Honig, Spenser creates "a new order and a new time — a permanent present where 'thinges forepaste'" (91, 96).

35. Until recently, such avant-garde repetitions had been understood either as numbing reiteration of the same (Fitzsimmons's remarks are typical here) or as an ineffective because of institutionalized repetition. An example of this is Peter Bürger's claim: "[T]he neo-avant-garde institutionalizes the *avant-garde as art* and thus negates genuinely avant-gardiste intentions. This is true independently of the consciousness artists have of their activity, that defines the social effects of works. Neo-avant-gardiste art is autonomous art in the full sense of the term, which means that it negates the avant-gardiste intention of returning art to the praxis of life" (58). Hal Foster, disagreeing with Bürger specifically, asks: "[R]*ather than cancel the project of the historical avant-garde, might the neo-avant-garde comprehend it for the first time?* . . . In art as in psychoanalysis, creative critique is *interminable*, and that is a good thing (at least in art)" (*Return of the Real* 15). This formulation concludes Foster's larger objection: "Bürger echoes the famous remark of Marx in *The Eighteenth Brumaire of Louis Bonaparte* (1852), mischievously attributed to Hegel, that all great events of world history occur twice, the first time as tragedy, the second time as farce. . . . This trope of tragedy followed by farce is seductive — its cynicism is a protective response to many historical ironies — but it hardly suffices as a theoretical model, let alone as a historical analysis. Yet it pervades attitudes toward contemporary art and culture, where it first *constructs* the contemporary as *post*historical, a simulacral world of failed repetitions and pathetic pastiches, and then *condemns* it as such from a mythical point of critical escape beyond it all. Ultimately *this* point is posthistorical, and its

perspective is most mythical where it purports to be most critical" (*Return of the Real* 14). Foster's championing of avant-garde repetition might thus be compared to Gilles Deleuze's claims in *Difference and Reptition*, which, oddly enough, end by citing Harold Rosenberg's essay "The Resurrected Romans" in *The Tradition of the New*: "Marx's theory of historical repetition, as it appears notably in *The Eighteenth Brumaire of Louis Bonaparte*, turns on the following principle which does not seem to have been sufficiently understood by historians: historical repetition is neither a matter of analogy nor a concept produced by the reflection of historians, but above all a condition of historical action itself. Harold Rosenberg illuminates this point in some fine pages: historical actors or agents can create only on the condition that they identify themselves with figures from the past. In this sense, history is theatre: 'their action became a spontaneous repetition of an old role. . . . It is the revolutionary crisis, the compelled striving for 'something entirely new,' that causes history to become veiled in myth'" (Deleuze 91).

36. Quoted from *Romantic Poetry and Prose*, eds. Harold Bloom and Lionel Trilling (New York: Oxford, 1973), 768.
37. This view of Dada was shared by O'Hara's professor at Harvard, Renato Poggioli, whose 1962 *The Theory of The Avant-Garde* preceded Bürger's now-better-known book by twelve years. According to Poggioli, "it was perhaps only in dadaism that the nihilistic tendency functioned as the primary, even solitary, psychic condition; there it took the form of an intransigent puerility, an extreme infantilism" (62).
38. Stephen Melville accounts for Fried's attempt to distance himself from Greenberg's claim that flatness is the "irreducible essence of pictorial art" by noting that "[t]he 'purity' that Fried thus surrenders with one hand is (almost) silently recovered with the other (and for those concerned with tracing the genealogy of a new allegorism it is far from irrelevant that the recuperating hand here is one concerned to fence the high serious art of Morris Louis off from the degenerate and theatrical flatbed tableaux of Robert Rauschenberg)" (62–63).
39. While one clearly wouldn't think of the breath units involved in Ginsberg's long anaphoric lines as cautious, they are certainly an attempt to ground language in the body's particularity, which linked him to Charles Olson's famous interest in breath: "If I hammer, if I recall in, and keep calling in, the breath, the breathing as distinguished from the hearing, it is for cause, it is to insist upon a part that breath plays in verse which has not (due, I think, to the smothering of the power of the line by too set a concept of foot) has not been sufficiently observed or practiced, but which has to be if verse is to advance to its proper force and place in the day, now, and ahead. I take it that PROJECTIVE VERSE teaches, is, this lesson, that the verse will only do in which a poet manages to register both the acquisition of his ear *and* the pres-

sures of his breath" (Olson 17). Olson's influential essay was originally published in 1950. In her article "Before Bed," Helen Molesworth ties what she sees as the bodily and particularly excremental project of Rauschenberg's early work to Olson's desire, expressed later in his essay "Proprioception," to "(re)attribute specific organs' emotional characteristics, such as desire to the heart, sympathy to the bowels" (72).

40. With the introduction of his idea of the flatbed picture plane, Leo Steinberg was the first to articulate this problem in a more systematic way: "[S]omething happened in painting around 1950 — most conspicuously . . . in the work of Robert Rauschenberg and Dubuffet. We can still hang their pictures — just as we take up maps and architectural plans, or nail a horseshoe to a wall for good luck. Yet the pictures no longer simulate vertical fields, but opaque flatbed horizontals. They no more depend on a head-to-toe correspondence with human posture than a newspaper does. The flatbed picture plane makes its symbolic allusion to hard surfaces such as tabletops, studio floors, charts, bulletin boards — any receptor surface on which objects are scattered, on which data is entered, on which information may be received, printed, impressed — whether coherently or in confusion. The picture of the last fifteen to twenty years insists on a radically new orientation, in which the printed surface is no longer the analogue of a visual experience of nature but of operational processes" (*Other Criteria* 84).

41. This work could be grouped among what O'Hara called the "big inventive pieces" of the 1955 show, though it is unclear if the piece was exhibited in the 1955 Egan Gallery exhibition. We do know that it appeared the next year in a show curated by Thomas Hess, which O'Hara (interested in Rauschenberg and close to Hess) almost definitely saw. Certainly he saw it while he was reviewing Rauschenberg's work for *Documenta II*.

42. Despite this, we see in the catalog to *Documenta II* that a William Rubin is listed as the owner of *Kickback* (now at LAMOLA), one of the three Rauschenbergs exhibited; *Documenta II: Kunst nach* 1945 V1: 338.

43. In his catalog essay "The Faked Gesture," Paul Schimmel develops this biographical reading as a combination between private life and personal art production: "*Untitled Combine ("Man with White Shoes")* (1955) is a history painting bringing together a chronology of Rauschenberg's own oeuvre ca. 1950–1954 and a nostalgic view of his friends and family while growing up in the South. Contained inside the multidimensional, freestanding painting is a black painting (ca. 1951), and a combination of a white painting (1951) over a dirt painting (1952) with his own white shoes and socks. There is an outside panel that is reminiscent of the first mature collage and painted works of around 1953. This brief history of Rauschenberg's art is juxtaposed with intimate mementos of his life" (31). Rauschenberg referred to this painting as "the first real combine painting" (Rose 58).

44. Kotz refers to the piece as *Untitled* but then titles her chapter on the combines "The Man with the White Shoes" (89, 85). The catalog for the 1997 retrospective at the Guggenheim also refers to the piece as *Untitled* and notes in the "Chronology" that the piece was completed in the fall of 1954 (554); it has often previously been dated as 1955. It is primarily the owner of the piece, the Los Angeles Museum of Contemporary Art (LAMOCA), that refers to it alternately as *Untitled Combine ("Man with White Shoes")* — in *Hand Painted Pop*, for instance — and *Untitled ("Man with White Shoes")* (in correspondence with the author). LAMOCA also continues to date the piece 1955.
45. Though it is usually depicted with its open bottom area (containing a stuffed hen and a photograph of a man in a white suit) toward the viewer, the piece operates in the round more than almost any of the other combines.
46. *Untitled* deals with the question of its own framing by viewers both by delaying a total apprehension and by establishing a complicated thematics of vision. O'Hara's remark (probably in reference to *Charlene)* about "lifting up a bit of pink gauze" and staring "out of the picture into your own magnified eye" pointed to Rauschenberg's self-conscious concern with viewers "recognizing themselves" in a work of art, with the artwork becoming a site for identifications and projections of a complete self. Insofar as *Untitled* thematizes bodies that might stand in for a viewer, both the well-dressed man, the dandy, who stares only at himself (removed from the main structure of the piece) and the empty shoes displace the idea of a subject completing the piece — a displacement that is enforced by the temporal problem of reading individual surfaces at the expense of a notion of the whole. On the back surface, the primary figure — a collage drawing of a head at the top center, directly under the shoes — is significantly cropped so as to exclude the eyes. Glances in the first collage surface avert the viewer and are primarily in profile, culminating with the photo of Johns full-on but downward-looking. The only figure who looks straight ahead is the suited man, whose status as part of the piece I have tried to problematize: he is, rather, a tentative conclusion that seems to be in bad faith and/or a stand-in for our activity. That is to say that theatricality, in the sense not merely of crossed genres (which happens throughout) but of direct, full-on glances at the viewer, happens only in this bracketed section of the piece, a section that suggests at once the impossible conclusion of the piece's narrative as a well-formed subject — the "content" that it can't deliver — and, analogously, the impossible reconciliation of the piece's project for the completed viewer regarding his reflection.
47. The overlapping of painterly surfaces and particular photographic images that occurs throughout the piece might be seen as a kind of embarrassing literalization of Harold Rosenberg's claim, mentioned in chapter 5, that an abstract expressionist canvas is "inseparable from the biography of the artist" (*Tradition* 27). Of course, when Rosenberg wrote this in 1952, he had

in mind as the realm of biography something more like the heroic shots Hans Namuth took of Jackson Pollock's process than the endlessly interpretable, possibly embarrassing, and finally equivocal raw material included in Rauschenberg's combine *Untitled*.

48. But it is not only the disjunction between the sculptural objects and the collage fields that leads us to the problem of reification. Rauschenberg also produces gaps in the syntax of his collage narrative, gaps that register both across images and objects as we try to connect one to another and inside individual images (at the level of expression) — as, for example, in the photograph of a troubled Johns (who had recently become Rauschenberg's boyfriend).

49. O'Hara mentions Warhol positively not only in his 1965 interview with Edward Lucie-Smith but also in his 1966 essay on Alex Katz.

50. Though the title of Clement Greenberg's April 30, 1961, article — "The Jackson Pollock Market Soars" — was chosen against Greenberg's will by the editors of the *New York Times Magazine*, the facts to which it referred were certainly true: "Another of his [Pollock's] oils, measuring a little over three by eight feet, was sold several months ago in New York for more than $100, 000" (4: 107).

51. In an interview about conservation techniques for the 1998 exhibition *Deep Storage: Collecting, Storing and Archiving Art*, conservator Elizabeth Lunning (from the Menil Collection) remarks that "self-awareness has increased considerably in the last two decades. This coincides with the emergence and maturation of a generation of conservators who were trained in the training programs that were established in the 1960s and 1970s; the evolution of conservation as a profession, with a Code of Ethics and standards that emphasize the need for good record keeping and documentation" ("Storage and Art over Time: A Conversation with a Conservator: Ingrid Schaffner talks to Elizabeth Lunning" 244).

52. As the values of the works in international exhibitions soared, MoMA curators like O'Hara were asked to become connoisseurs of damage — to master not only the memo's seven-part taxonomy of damage genres (say, friction gouges as distinct from impact or pressure gouges) but also distinctions between species within these larger genres: herring-bone from radial or concentric cracks; pin-hole fissures from worm holes; fly specks from standard fissures; scorches from singes, parching, sunburn, or general dessication.

53. Waldo Rasmussen, O'Hara's colleague in the International Program, was trained in conservation at the Portland Art Museum before coming to MoMA in 1954. Rasmussen notes, though, that O'Hara also wrote damage reports: "We all wrote damage reports. Anyone who was working that closely with the exhibitions did" (interview March 31, 2003).

54. Not as universally disruptive, artists like Helen Frankenthaler and Morris Louis would nonetheless follow directly in at least part of Pollock's antiarchival trajectory.

55. O'Hara himself picks up on this decaying, vintage quality of Rauschenberg's work in a May 9, 1960, letter to John Ashbery: "We got a note from Joan that she and Mario are arriving June 1st and what about dinner, so Vincent, Joe and I have all written in our little 1960 books that we dine with them that night! It is very pleasant to already have made a date for June, and it will give us time to marinate some bison ears in yoghurt and to prepare our favorite hors d'oeuvre-paste made of puréed lentils and snuff which takes WEEKS to make and is served on little squares pulled off 1954 Rauschenbergs" (Archive).

56. For a taxonomy of these practices, see *Formless: A User's Guide*, by Yve-Alain Bois and Rosalind Krauss. Oldenburg's *Ray Guns* are a particularly significant example here, in that he gathered them and displayed them in his meta-museum, the *Mouse Museum*. Bois refers to it: "The idea of the Mouse Museum emerged in 1965 but would not be achieved until 1972, for Documenta V, in Kassel, Germany. A selection of ray guns was presented in a special wing of Oldenburg's *Mouse Museum* . . . and decorously classified in various vitrines according to whether they had been made by the artist, simply altered by him, made by others, or only found (without being altered)" (Bois and Krauss 176–77). O'Hara knew and commented on these ray-guns. In "Art Chronicle III" he compares Oldenburg's guns to those of Niki de St. Phalle: "It is not the ray-gun of New York, with its humorous-Nihilistic overtones and Pogoesque sarcasm, but a gun with which to shoot into bags of pigment and thus 'enter' the work as a participant in its composition as you hit a sac of pigment and thus effect an alteration in the picture. What hath Pollock wrought?" (SS 142)

57. In the case of Smithson, there is both the move away from discrete, gallery-based objects and the insistence on entropic, disruptive activities, such as those in his *Asphalt Rundown* (1969) and his *Glue Pour* (1969).

58. Obviously, museums and galleries have long since made their peace with each of these practices.

59. David Shapiro confirms this: "There is no doubt in my mind that Frank would have hated the kind of rhetoric of Fried, which he never participated in" (e-mail to author March 24, 2003).

60. This designation was important to Sandler, who used it as the title of his 2003 memoir, *A Sweeper-Up After Artists*. Sandler also cites O'Hara as an advocate: "Early in my career, he tried to help me along — that is, not just talked about it but really tried, without saying anything to me. In 1966, shortly before his death, he asked if I would co-curate a retrospective of the painting of Bradley Walker Tomlin at the Museum of Modern Art. I was delighted and touched by his offer" (207).

61. Here is how Sandler describes the problem of speaking for the Abstract Expressionists themselves: "There is a widely held notion that when the events of the 1940s are fully researched, certain 'truths' will be established. Indeed, many persons who kindly contributed information to this study have expressed the hope that it would 'set the record straight.' Most will be disappointed, for what they really desired was not so much a record of events as the assertion that certain events were more significant than others. Yet different artists' assessments of 'significant' events were so varied and even contradictory that it soon became clear that there was not one 'truth' but many, each determined by the vantage point from which an artist viewed developments" (2–3).
62. Later, using the language of "confession," Sandler continues the rhetoric of privacy in his account of gestural painting: "The gesture painters on the whole believed that when painting is deeply felt by the artist, its felt quality is communicable and can be experienced by the sensitive viewer as 'real' or 'moral' — and as aesthetically valid, for a fully felt shape or color was deemed formally correct. Therefore, the primary content of gesture painting was thought to be the 'confession' of the artist's particular creative experiences — the embodiment of his unique artistic temperament" (97). His description of Pollock's work, too, relies on this division of public and private: "Pollock's gesturing reflected his inner compulsions and was in this sense autographic. But his 'living' on the canvas appeared so delirious as to transcend the diaristic, to transform the autographic into the ideographic. The painting became a kind of private ritual made visible" (110).
63. O'Hara's 1965 article on Motherwell is a case in point: "[P]op and op have tended to stimulate a way of looking, particularly at abstract expressionists and hard-edge painters, which reveals new qualities in their works. . . . you see more in Motherwell rather than less if you have just been studying a Rosenquist or a Dine" (SS 177).
64. Though it was not until 1967 (the year after O'Hara's death) that the real fault lines were drawn between what became known as the minimalist or literalist position of Tony Smith, Judd, and Morris, and the "optical modernism" of Greenberg and Fried, already by the mid-1960s Smith, Judd, Morris, and Flavin had all had several solo exhibits. After being included in the influential 1964 *Black, White, and Gray* show at the Wadsworth Atheneum in Hartford, Connecticut, Smith had two solo shows in 1966, the first also at the Wadsworth and the second in Philadelphia at the Institute of Contemporary Art. In New York, Judd's first exhibition was in 1957 at the Panoras Gallery, and he did not exhibit again until 1963 at Green Gallery. Morris's first solo show was at the Green Gallery in fall 1963; his second — with plywood sculptures — was in December 1964. After exhibiting calligraphic abstractions based on literature in 1961, Flavin began to show his minimal work in

March 1964 at Kaymar Gallery. LeWitt's first solo exhibition was at the John Daniels Gallery in 1965. Andre began exhibiting in group shows in 1964. Hesse showed drawings in group exhibitions in 1961; her first solo show was in 1963 at the Allan Stone Gallery. In addition to *Black, White, and Gray*, other group exhibitions significant to the formation of minimalism included *8 Younger Artists* at the Hudson River Museum in Yonkers in October 1964, curated by E. C. Goossen. More important, perhaps, is *Shape and Structure: 1965*, held at the Tibor de Nagy Gallery in January 1965. The best account of the period is James Meyer's *Minimalism: Art and Polemics in the Sixties*, to which this chronology is indebted.

65. Similarly, in his 1967 essay "Recentness of Sculpture," Clement Greenberg had claimed that "[m]inimal art remains too much of a feat of ideation, and not enough anything else. Its idea remains an idea, something deduced instead of felt and discovered. The geometrical and modular simplicity may announce and signify the artistically furthest out, but the fact that the signals are understood for what they want to mean betrays them artistically" (4: 254).
66. As Robert Smithson noted in *Artforum* in his 1967 letter to the editor, "Fried, the orthodox modernist, the keeper of the gospel of Clement Greenberg has been 'struck by Tony Smith,' the agent of endlessness" (*Robert Smithson: The Collected Writings* 66).
67. In her (ultimately far more precise and focused) account of Smith's sculpture, Rosalind Krauss elides this early recognition by Frank O'Hara of Smith's figurative qualities: "Throughout the 1950s and 1960s his major pieces appeared, to others, to be nonrepresentational, which seems to have been caused by a heightening of the principle of discontinuity" (*Passages in Modern Sculpture* 165).
68. In contrast, O'Hara's 1966 MoMA catalog essay for Ruben Nakian and his 1964 *Art News* feature on George Spaventa promote artists who look back more directly to the generation of the Abstract Expressionists.
69. In her 1972 book on the artist, Lucy Lippard notes that Smith has at once "been associated with the 'Primary Structure,' or 'Minimal Art'" and has been, "since the 1940's, a respected friend and colleague of Newman, Still, Rothko and Pollock, considered an equal (but happily for his personal relationships, not a rival) by the leaders of the Abstract Expressionist generation" (8).
70. D'Harnoncourt mentions in his introduction, "*La sélection des oeuvres présentées dans cette exposition a été assurée avec le concours de M. Frank O'Hara, Conservateur-adjoint au Département des expositions intinérantes de peinture et de sculpture du Musée d'Art moderne sous la direction de M Waldo Rasmussen*" (n.p.).
71. The full list of artists is as follows: Leonard Baskin, Lee Bontecou, Louise Bourgeois, John Chamberlain, Joseph Cornell, Herbert Ferber, John B. Flan-

nagan, Dimitri Hadzi, Raoul Hague, Frédéric Kiesler, Gaston Lachaise, Ibram Lassaw, Seymour Lipton, Robert Mallary, Escobar Marisol, Elie Nadelman, Reuben Nakian, Louise Nevelson, Barnett Newman, Isamu Noguchi, Claes Thure Oldenburg (whose phone is pictured in the catalog), George Rickey, José de Rivera, James Rosati, David Smith, George Spaventa, Richard Stankiewicz, Mark di Suvero, Wilfred Zogbaum, and William Zorach. The exhibition was supplemented by what was referred to as "Ateliers Américains en France." These included Alexander Calder, Mary Callery, Claire Falkenstein, David V. Hayes, Caroline Lee, and Ralph Stackpole.

72. Donald Judd, "In the Galleries," *Arts Magazine* (January 1963); reprinted in Judd, *Complete Writings* (65). Two years earlier, Judd described the voids in Bontecou's work as "threateningly concrete holes to be among" (27).
73. The terms of O'Hara's response remain largely speculative: aside from recommending in "Art Chronicle II" that the new Lincoln Center commission works from Chamberlain (among eight other sculptors), O'Hara mentions Chamberlain in the art writing only briefly and without detail. O'Hara's only mention of Bontecou that I've encountered is simply the name among lists of artists to be included in *ModernSculpture USA*.
74. By April 1966, MoMA curator Kynaston McShine (whom O'Hara had brought to MoMA) was opening *Primary Structures*, one of the major minimalist exhibitions at the Jewish Museum. As James Meyer notes, the categories at play in McShine's show were looser than those that came to be associated historically with minimalism (*Minimalism* 22–24).
75. In "Notes on Sculpture," Morris argues for sculpture that uses "simpler forms that create strong gestalt sensations" and whose "parts are bound together in such a way that they offer a maximum resistance to perceptual separation." Morris goes on to associate the term *detail* negatively with "all factors in a work that pull it toward intimacy by allowing specific elements to separate from the whole, thus setting up relationships within the work. . . . Every internal relationship, whether set up by a structural division, a rich surface, or what have you, reduces the public external quality of the object and tends to eliminate the viewer to the degree that these details pull him into an intimate relationship with the work and out of the space in which the object exists" (226, 232–33). This two-part essay was initially published in the February and October 1966 issues of *Artforum*.
76. O'Hara, *Helen Frankenthaler: Paintings* (n.p.).
77. In her chapter on O'Hara and Warhol, Reva Wolf cites a passage of O'Hara's "Art Chronicle III" that seems to be alluding negatively to Warhol: "Some preconceptions in imagery stand still at their freshest (soup cans, newspaper pages, road signs), like a high school performance of *The Petrified Forest*" (SS 151). The context is a contrast with Robert Motherwell's imagery. "But the Elegies mean something," O'Hara continues, "and you can't beat that"

(ibid.). Wolf concludes, unconvincingly, to my mind, that because O'Hara liked other pop artists his dislike of Warhol *must* be personal: "This acerbic judgment was not only a defense of abstract expressionism. O'Hara did have positive things to say about other pop artists. His dislike of Warhol, then, cannot be attributed solely to Warhol's seemingly anti-expressionist methods, but operated on a personal level" (18).

78. In O'Hara's words, "There is no hint of mysticism, no 'significance,' no commentary, in the work" (SS 142).

79. O'Hara's long description is worth considering: "Where most of the other artists grouped by opinion into the 'new realists' or 'pop art' movement tend to make their art *out of* vulgar (in the sense of everyday) objects, images and emblems, Oldenburg makes the very objects and symbols themselves, with the help of papier-mâché, cloth, wood, glue, paint and whatever other mysterious materials are inside and on them, *into* art. His was one of the most amusing, cheering and thought-provoking exhibitions this year. Beautifully modeled and painted bacon-and-eggs or slices of pie on real (old) kitchen plates, on low pedestals, led one towards a monumental pair of work pants on a hanger and another over a chair, each heavier-looking than bronze, and just beyond them a seven-foot pistachio ice cream cone (painted cloth) lay on the floor, flanked by a monstrous wedge of chocolate and vanilla layer cake of the same materials and scale and a hamburger (with pickle round on top) which, if used as an ottoman, could sit at least twenty fairly large persons. The juxtapositions of scale in the show, the use of 'real' plates, kitchen utensils, chairs and commercial display cases of chrome and glass (pie racks, etc.) in conjunction with the created 'food,' each executed with an acute esthetic attention to shape, texture and variety of color, were bewildering in the very best sense, causing one to halt (an unusual occurrence in New York except at intersections), and appreciate" (SS 141–42).

80. Rosalind Krauss claims that "[t]he two major formal devices Oldenburg used to transform the ordinary object are the strategies of giganticism and/or softness. They are obstructions in the viewer's space because they have become colossal variants on their natural scale, and because they promote a sense of interaction in which the viewer is a participant, their mass being construed in terms that suggest his own body — pliant and soft, like flesh. The viewer is then forced into two simultaneous admissions: 'They are *my* things — the objects I *use* everyday'; and 'I resemble them'" (*Passages* 229).

81. During the time of their collaboration, Brainard was living with the poet Tony Towle, a former student of O'Hara's at the New School and later a friend.

82. Brainard acknowledged O'Hara's support: "I remember the night Frank O'Hara bought a construction of mine. Before I had a gallery or anything.

Partly because he liked it. Partly (I think) because he liked me. And partly (I think) because I was broke. Frank was generous" (H 168).

83. In an April 18, 1963, letter to Larry Rivers, O'Hara mentions that he is "making some cartoons with Joe Brainard, a 21-year-old assemblagist genius you will like a lot, as he looks remarkably like Joe Riv though not so handsome and far more shy. (Kenneth is doing some too, and Tony Towle and Bill Berkson.) It is a cartoon revival, because Joe Brainard is so astonishingly right in the drawing etc." (G 430–31).
84. Perhaps that is the intention of the addition of the "l" in the Red Rydler title —pushing "rider" toward "riddler."
85. There is a long tradition of New York School writers (both queer and straight) being fascinated with cowboys, from Ted Berrigan's novel *Clear the Range* to Bill Luoma's *Western Love*. Daniel Kane considers the cowboy in early 1960s New York as a figure used to encode the idea of roughing it in the not yet fully "settled" East Village (see *All Poets Welcome* 17–23).
86. One of many examples is Lee Krasner's angry response to the fact that, in his book on Pollock, O'Hara thanked Larry Rivers and Grace Hartigan for helping him understand Pollock's work. See LeSueur, *Digressions on Some Poems by Frank O'Hara* (202).
87. The word "usually" is here appended in pencil.
88. O'Hara also touches on galleries: "As much as possible for many reasons it is necessary to visit the major galleries at least once a month, especially those which are cooperative lenders, both from the point of view of 'keeping up' with what's going on in general and with individual artists' development, but [also] to maintain good relations with the dealers and artists" (MoMA April 8, 1965).

BIBLIOGRAPHY

When an entire book has been translated into English, the date of publication in the original language follows in parentheses.

Agamben, Gorgio. *The Coming Community*. Trans. Michael Hardt. Minneapolis: University of Minnesota Press, 1993 (1990).

Ahearn, Barry, ed. *Pound/Zukofsky: Selected Letters of Ezra Pound and Louis Zukofsky*. New York: New Directions, 1987.

Allen, Donald. Archive. Mandeville Special Collections Library, University of California, San Diego.

———, ed. *The New American Poetry, 1945–1960*. New York: Grove, 1960.

Allen, Donald, and Warren Tallman, eds. *The Poetics of the New American Poetry*. New York: Grove, 1973.

Als, Hilton. "Frank Appraisal." *Artforum* 38, no. 2 (October 1999): 27–28.

Altieri, Charles. *Painterly Abstraction in Modernist American Poetry*. University Park, PA: Penn State University Press, 1989.

———. "Frank O'Hara." *Enlarging the Temple: New Directions in American Poetry during the 1960s*. Lewisburg, PA: Bucknell University Press, 1979.

Andrews, Bruce, and Charles Bernstein, eds. *The L=A=N=G=U=A=G=E Book*. Carbondale, IL: Southern Illinois University Press, 1984.

Apollinaire, Guillaume. *Alcools*. Trans. Anne Hyde Greet. Berkeley: University of California Press, 1965.

Ashbery, John. "The Heritage of Dada and Surrealism." In *Reported Sightings*, ed. David Bergman. Cambridge: Harvard University Press, 1989.

———. "Introduction." In *The Collected Poems of Frank O'Hara*, ed. Allen.

———. *Other Traditions*. Cambridge: Harvard University Press, 2000.

———. "A Reminiscence." In *Homage to Frank O'Hara*, eds. Berkson and LeSueur.

———. *The Tennis Court Oath*. Middletown, CT: Wesleyan University Press, 1962.

———. *Turandot and Other Poems*. New York: Tibor de Nagy Gallery, 1953.

Ashton, Dore. "57th Street: Robert Rauschenberg." *Art Digest* (September 1953): 21, 25.

Auden, W. H. *The English Auden: Poems, Essays and Dramatic Writings 1927–1939*. Ed. Edward Mendelson. London: Faber, 1977.

———. *Prose and Travel Books in Prose and Verse*, vol. 1. Princeton, NJ: Princeton University Press, 1996.

Auden, W. H., and Lewis MacNeice. *Letters from Iceland*. London: Faber, 1985.

Auricchio, Laura. "Lifting the Veil: Robert Rauschenberg's *Thirty-four Drawings for Dante's Inferno* and the Commercial Homoerotic Imagery of 1950s America." In *The Gay 90s*, eds. Foster, Siegel, and Berry.

Austin, J. L. *How to Do Things with Words*. Cambridge: Harvard University Press, 1962.

Baraka, Amiri [Leroi Jones]. *The Dead Lecturer*. New York: Grove, 1964.

———. *The LeRoi Jones/Amiri Baraka Reader*, ed. William J. Harris and Amiri Baraka. New York: Thunder's Mouth, 1995.

———. *Preface to a Twenty Volume Suicide Note*. New York: Totem/Corinth, 1961.

Baraka, Amiri, and Fundi (Billy Abernathy). *In Our Terribleness*. New York: Bobbs-Merrill, 1970.

Barr, Alfred. *Defining Modern Art: Selected Writings of Alfred. H. Barr, Jr.* Eds. Irving Sandler and Amy Newman. New York: Abrams, 1986.

Barthes, Roland. *Barthes by Barthes*. Trans. Richard Howard. New York: Noonday, 1977 (1975).

———. *S/Z*. Trans. Richard Miller. New York: Noonday, 1974.

Bataille, Georges. "The College of Sociology." In *The College of Sociology 1937–1939*, ed. Denis Hollier. Minneapolis: University of Minnesota Press, 1988.

Battcock, Gregory. *Minimal Art: A Critical Anthology*. New York: Dutton, 1968.

Beach, Joseph Warren. *The Making of the Auden Canon*. Minneapolis: University of Minnesota Press, 1957.

Bendiner, Kenneth. "Robert Rauschenberg's *Canyon*." *Arts Magazine* 56, no. 10 (June 1982): 57–59.

Benjamin, Walter. *The Origin of German Tragic Drama*. Trans. John Osborne. London: New Left Books, 1977 (1928).

———. "The Task of the Translator." Trans. Harry Zohn. In *Walter Benjamin: Selected Writings, Vol. 1, 1913–1926*. Cambridge: Harvard University Press, 1999 (1923).

Bergman, David, ed. *Reported Sightings*. Cambridge: Harvard University Press, 1989.

Berkson, Bill. "Afterword." In Frank O'Hara, *What's with Modern Art: Selected Short Reviews and Other Art Writings*, ed. Bill Berkson. Austin: Mike and Dale's Press, 1999.

———. "Companion to Biotherm." In *Biotherm [For Bill Berkson]*. San Francisco: Arion, 1990.

———. "Frank O'Hara and His Poems." In *Homage to Frank O'Hara*, eds. Berkson and LeSueur.

Berkson, Bill, and Joe LeSueur, eds. *Homage to Frank O'Hara*. Bolinas, CA: Big Sky, 1988.

Bernstein, Charles. "Artifice of Absorption." *A Poetics*. Cambridge: Harvard University Press, 1992.

Bernstein, Michael. *The Tale of the Tribe: Ezra Pound and the Modern Verse Epic*. Princeton, NJ: Princeton University Press, 1980.

Berrigan, Ted. "The Business of Writing Poetry." In *On the Level Everyday: Selected Talks on Poetry and the Art of Living*, ed. Lewis.

———. "The Chicago Report." In *Nice to See You: Homage to Ted Berrigan*, ed. Waldman.

———. *Clear the Range*. New York: Coach House/Adventures in Poetry, 1977.

———. Review of *Lunch Poems*. *Kulchur* 5, no. 17 (1965): 91.

———. *The Sonnets*. New York: Grove Press, 1964.

Blasing, Mutlu Konuk. *Politics and Form in Postmodern Poetry*. Cambridge, UK: Cambridge University Press, 1995.

Bois, Yve-Alain, and Rosalind Krauss. *Formless: A User's Guide*. New York: Zone, 1997.

Boone, Bruce. "Gay Language as Political Praxis: the Poetry of Frank O'Hara." *Social Text* 1 (1979): 59–93.

Boym, Svetlana. *Death in Quotation Marks: Cultural Myths of the Modern Poet*. Cambridge: Harvard University Press, 1991.

Brainard, Joe. "Frank O'Hara." In *Homage to Frank O'Hara*, eds. Berkson and LeSueur.

Breslin, James. "Frank O'Hara." *From Modern to Contemporary: American Poetry, 1945–1965*. Chicago: University of Chicago Press, 1984.

Breton, André. *Manifestoes of Surrealism*. Trans. Richard Seaver and Helen R. Lane. Ann Arbor: University of Michigan Press, 1969 (*First Manifesto* 1924; *Second Manifesto* 1930; *Third Manifesto* 1934).

Breunig, Leroy, ed. *Apollinaire on Art: Essays and Reviews 1902–1918*. Trans. Susan Suleiman. New York: Da Capo, 1972.

Buchloch, Benjamin. "Allegorical Procedures: Appropriation and Montage in Contemporary Art." *Artforum* 21 (September 1982): 43–56.

———. *Neo-Avantgarde and Culture Industry: Essays on European and American Art from 1955–1975*. Cambridge: MIT Press, 2000.

Bürger, Peter. *Theory of the Avant-Garde*. Trans. Michael Shaw. Minneapolis: University of Minnesota Press, 1984 (1974).

Bush, Ronald. "'Quiet, Not Scornful'? The Composition of *The Pisan Cantos*." In *A Poem Containing History: Textual Studies in The Cantos*, ed. Lawrence S. Rainey. Ann Arbor: University of Michigan Press, 1997.

Butler, Judith. *Antigone's Claim: Kinship Between Life and Death*. New York: Columbia University Press, 2000.

———. *Gender Trouble*. New York: Routledge, 1990.

Butterick, George, ed. *Charles Olson and Robert Creeley: The Complete Correspondence*. Vol. 7. Santa Rosa, CA: Black Sparrow Press, 1987.

Caillois, Roger. "Brotherhoods, Orders, Secret Societies, Churches." In *The College of Sociology 1937–1939*, ed. Denis Hollier. Minneapolis: University of Minnesota Press, 1988.

Carpenter, Humphrey. *A Serious Character: The Life of Ezra Pound*. New York: Delta, 1990.

Charters, Ann, ed. *The Portable Beat Reader*. New York: Viking, 1992.

Clark, T. J. *Farewell to an Idea: Episodes from a History of Modernism*. New Haven, CT: Yale University Press, 1999.

———. *The Painting of Modern Life: Paris in the Art of Manet and His Followers*. New York: Knopf, 1984. Reprint, Princeton, NJ: Princeton University Press, 1986.

———. "Phenomenality and Materiality in Cézanne." In *Material Events: Paul de Man and the Afterlife of Theory*, eds. T. Cohen, B. Cohen, Miller, and Warminski.

Clay, Steven, and Rodney Phillips. *A Secret Location on the Lower East Side: Adventures in Writing, 1960–1980*. New York: Granary/New York Public Library, 1998.

Clements, A. L., ed. *John Donne's Poetry*. New York: Norton, 1966.

Cockroft, Eva. "Abstract Expressionism, Weapon of the Cold War." In *Pollock and After*, ed. Frascina.

Cohen, Tom, Barbara Cohen, J. Hillis Miller, and Andrzej Warminski, eds. *Material Events: Paul de Man and the Afterlife of Theory*. Minneapolis: University of Minnesota Press, 2001.

Cole, Mary. "57th Street in Review: Bob Rauschenberg." *Art Digest* 25 (June 1951): 18.

Coles, Alex, ed. *Site-Specificity: The Ethnographic Turn*. London: Black Dog, 2000.

Cottom, Daniel. "'Getting It': Ashbery and the Avant-Garde of Everyday Language." *SubStance* 73 (1994): 3–23.

Creeley, Robert. *Contexts of Poetry: Interviews 1961–1971*. San Francisco: Four Seasons, 1973.

Crimp, Douglas. "On the Museum's Ruins." In *The Anti-Aesthetic*, ed. Foster.

Crow, Thomas. "Modernism and Mass Culture in the Visual Arts." In *Pollock and After*, ed. Frascina.

Culler, Jonathan. "Apostrophe." *The Pursuit of Signs*. Ithaca, NY: Cornell University Press, 1981.

———. *Structuralist Poetics*. Ithaca, NY: Cornell University Press, 1975.

Damon, Maria. *The Dark End of the Street: Margins in American Vanguard Poetry*. Minneapolis: University of Minnesota Press, 1993.

Davidson, Michael. "Ekphrasis and the Postmodern Painter Poem." *Journal of Aesthetics and Art Criticism* 42 (Fall 1983): 69–79.

———. *The San Francisco Renaissance: Poetics and Community at Mid-Century*. New York: Cambridge University Press, 1989.

Davie, Donald. "The Black Mountain Poets: Charles Olson and Edward Dorn." In *The Survival of Poetry: A Contemporary Survey*, ed. Martin Dodsworth. London: Faber, 1970.

Debrot, Jacques. "Present, The Scene of My Selves, The Occasion of These Ruses: Frank O'Hara's Collaborations with Grace Hartigan, Larry Rivers and Jasper Johns." *Arshile* 11 (1999): 64–81.

Deleuze, Gilles. *Difference and Repetition*. Trans. Paul Patton. New York: Columbia University Press, 1994 (1968).

De Man, Paul. *Allegories of Reading*. New Haven, CT: Yale University Press, 1979.

———. *Blindness and Insight*. Minneapolis: University of Minnesota Press, 1971.

———. *The Resistance to Theory*. Minneapolis: University of Minnesota Press, 1986.

Dennis, Donna. "Excerpts from Journals." In *Nice to See You: Homage to Ted Berrigan*, ed. Waldman.

Derrida, Jacques. *Of Grammatology*. Trans. Gayatri Chakravorty Spivak. Baltimore: Johns Hopkins University Press, 1976 (1967).

D'Harnoncourt, Rene. *ModernSculpture USA*. New York: Museum of Modern Art, 1965.

Diggory, Terence, and Stephen Paul Miller. *The Scene of My Selves: New Work on New York School Poets*. Orono, ME: National Poetry Foundation, 2001.

Di Prima, Diane. *Recollections of My Life as a Woman*. New York: Penguin, 2001.

Dollimore, Jonathan. *Sexual Dissidents: Augustine to Wilde, Freud to Foucault*. New York: Oxford University Press, 1991.

Donne, John. *John Donne's Poetry*. Ed. A. L. Clemens. New York: Norton, 1966.

Duncan, Robert. "Letter to Allen Ginsberg." In *Homage to Frank O'Hara*, eds. Berkson and LeSueur.

Eliot, T. S. *Notes towards the Definition of Culture*. London: Faber, 1948.

———. *On Poetry and Poets*. New York: Noonday, 1974.

———. *The Use of Poetry and the Use of Criticism*. London: Faber, 1933.

Elledge, Jim, ed. *Frank O'Hara: To Be True to a City*. Ann Arbor: University of Michigan Press, 1990.

———. "'Never Argue with the Movies': Love and the Cinema in the Poetry of Frank O'Hara." In *Frank O'Hara: To Be True to a City*.

Ellingham, Lewis, and Kevin Killian. *Poet Be Like God: Jack Spicer and the San Francisco Renaissance*. Hanover, NH: Wesleyan University Press, 1998.

Epstein, Andrew. "'I Want to be at Least as Alive as the Vulgar': Frank O'Hara's Poetry and the Cinema." In *The Scene of My Selves: New Work on New York School Poets*, eds. Diggory and Miller.

Fainsod, Merle. *Smolensk under Soviet Rule*. New York: Vintage, 1958.

Feinstein, Roni. *Robert Rauschenberg: The Silkscreen Paintings, 1962–64*. New York: Whitney Museum, 1990.

Feldman, Alan. *Frank O'Hara*. Boston: Twayne, 1979.

Feldman, Morton. "Lost Times and Future Hopes." In *Homage to Frank O'Hara*, eds. Berkson and LeSueur.

Ferguson, Russell, ed. *Hand Painted Pop: American Art in Transition, 1955–62*. Los Angeles: Museum of Contemporary Art, 1992.

———. *In Memory of My Feelings: Frank O'Hara and American Art*. Berkeley: LAMOCA/University of California Press, 1999.

Fineman, Joel. "The Structure of Allegorical Desire." *October* 12 (1980): 47–66.
Fitzsimmons, James. "Art." *Arts and Architecture* 70 (October 1953): 33–34.
Foster, Hal, ed. *The Anti-Aesthetic*. Seattle: Bay Press, 1983.
———. "Death in American." *October* 75 (Winter 1996): 37–59.
———. *Recodings: Art, Spectacle, Cultural Politics*. Seattle: Bay Press, 1985.
———. *The Return of the Real*. Cambridge: MIT Press, 1996.
Foster, Thomas, Carol Siegel, and Ellen E. Berry, eds. *The Gay 90s: Disciplinary and Interdisciplinary Formation in Queer Studies*. New York: New York University Press, 1997.
Foucault, Michel. "Nietzsche, Genealogy, History." Trans. Donald F. Bouchard and Sherry Simon. In *The Foucault Reader*, ed. Paul Rabinow. New York: Pantheon, 1984.
Frascina, Francis, ed. *Pollock and After: The Critical Debate*. New York: Harper and Row, 1985.
Fried, Michael. *Art and Objecthood*. Chicago: Chicago University Press, 1998.
———. "How Modernism Works: A Response to T. J. Clark." In *Pollock and After*, ed. Frascina.
Friedlander, Benjamin. "Strange Fruit: O'Hara, Race and the Color of Time." In *The Scene of My Selves: New Work on New York School Poets*, eds. Diggory and Miller.
Gaugh, Harry F. *Willem de Kooning*. New York: Abbeville, 1983.
Ginsberg, Allen. *Improvised Poetics*. Ed. Mark Robison. San Francisco: Anonym, 1972.
———. "Letter to Robert Duncan." In *Homage to Frank O'Hara*, eds. Berkson and LeSueur.
———. "Notes for *Howl* and Other Poems." In *The New American Poetry, 1945–1960*, ed. Allen.
———. "Prose Contribution to Cuban Revolution." In *The Poetics of the New American Poetry*, ed. Allen and Tallman.
———. "'When the Mode of the Music Changes the Walls of the City Shake.'" In *The Poetics of the New American Poetry*, ed. Allen and Tallman.
Golding, Alan. *From Outlaw to Classic: Canons in American Poetry*. Madison: University of Wisconsin Press, 1995.
Gooch, Brad. *City Poet: The Life and Times of Frank O'Hara*. New York: Knopf, 1993.
Goodman, Paul. "Advance-Guard Writing, 1900–1950." *Kenyon Review* 13, no. 3 (Summer 1951): 357–80.
Gray, Camilla. *The Russian Experiment in Art, 1863–1922*. London: Thames and Hudson, 1962.
Greenberg, Clement. *The Collected Essays and Criticism, Volume 1: Perceptions and Judgments, 1939–1944; Volume 2: Arrogant Purpose, 1945–1949; Volume 4, Modernism with a Vengeance, 1957–1969*. Ed. John O'Brian. Chicago: University of Chicago Press, 1986.

Greenwald, Ted. "Frank O'Hara: A Personal Memoir." In *Homage to Frank O'Hara*, eds. Berkson and LeSueur.

Guest, Barbara. *Dürer at the Window: Reflections on Art*. New York: Roof, 2003.

Guilbaut, Serge. *How New York Stole the Idea of Modern Art*. Trans. Arthur Goldhammer. Chicago: University of Chicago Press, 1983.

Guillory, John. *Cultural Capital: The Problem of Literary Canon Formation*. Chicago: University of Chicago Press, 1993.

Hapgood, Susan. *Neo-Dada: Redefining Art, 1958–62*. New York: American Federation of Arts, 1994.

Harris, William J. *The Poetry and Poetics of Amiri Baraka: The Jazz Aesthetic*. Columbia, MO: University of Missouri Press, 1985.

Hegel, Georg Wilhelm Friedrich. *The Philosophy of History*. Trans. J. Sibree. New York: Dover, 1956.

Hejinian, Lyn. *The Language of Inquiry*. Berkeley: University of California Press, 2000.

———. *My Life*. Los Angeles: Sun and Moon, 1991.

Hess, Thomas. *Abstract Painting: Background and American Phase*. New York: Viking, 1951.

———. *Willem de Kooning*. New York: Braziller, 1959.

Heyman, David. *Ezra Pound: The Last Rover*. New York: Viking, 1977.

Honig, Edwin. *Dark Conceit: The Making of Allegory*. Hanover: Brown/New England University Press, 1959.

Hopps, Walter. *Robert Rauschenberg*. Washington, DC: Smithsonian, 1977.

Hopps, Walter, and Susan Davidson, eds. *Robert Rauschenberg: A Retrospective*. New York: Guggenheim, 1997.

Jakobson, Roman. *Language in Literature*. Eds. Krystyna Pomorska and Stephen Rudy. Cambridge: Harvard University Press, 1987.

Jameson, Fredric. *Fables of Aggression: Wyndham Lewis, the Modernist as Fascist*. Berkeley: University of California Press, 1979.

Joseph, Branden W. *Random Order: Robert Rauschenberg and the Neo-Avant-Garde*. Cambridge: MIT Press, 2003.

Judd, Donald. *Complete Writings 1959–1975*. Halifax: Nova Scotia College of Art and Design Press, 1975.

Kalaidjian, Walter. *Languages of Liberation: The Social Text in Contemporary American Poetry*. New York: Columbia University Press, 1989.

Kane, Daniel. *All Poets Welcome: The Lower East Side Poetry Scene in the 1960s*. Berkeley: University of California Press, 2003.

Kaprow, Allan. *Essays on the Blurring of Art and Life*. Berkeley: University of California Press, 1993.

Katz, Jonathan. "The Art of Code: Jasper Johns and Robert Rauschenberg." In *Significant Others: Creativity and Intimate Partnership*, eds. Whitney Chadwick and Isabelle de Courtivron. London: Thames and Hudson, 1993.

Keats, John. "Letter to George and Tom Keats." December 21/27, 1817. In *Romantic Poetry and Prose*, eds. Harold Bloom and Lionel Trilling. New York: Oxford, 1973.

Kenner, Hugh. *The Poetry of Ezra Pound*. London: Faber, 1951.

———. *The Pound Era*. Berkeley: University of California Press, 1971.

Kinnell, Galway. "Review of Frank O'Hara's *Meditations in an Emergency*." *Poetry* (June 1958): 178–79.

Knabb, Ken, ed. and trans. *Situationist International Anthology*. Berkeley, CA: Bureau of Public Secrets, 1981.

Koch, Kenneth. "All the Imagination Can Hold (The Collected Poems of Frank O'Hara)." *New Republic* 8 (January 1972). Reprinted in *Homage to Frank O'Hara*, eds. Berkson and LeSueur.

———. *I Never Told Anybody: Teaching Poetry in a Nursing Home*. New York: Random House, 1977.

———. *Making Your Own Days: The Pleasures of Reading and Writing Poetry*. New York: Scribners, 1998.

———. *Rose, Where Did You Get That Red? Teaching Great Poetry to Children*. New York: Random House, 1973.

———. *When the Sun Tries to Go On*. Los Angeles: Black Sparrow, 1969.

———. *Wishes, Lies and Dreams: Teaching Children to Write Poetry*. New York: Random House, 1970.

Koolhaas, Rem. *Delirious New York*. New York: Monacelli, 1994.

Kors, Alan Charles. *D'Holbach's Coterie: An Enlightenment in Paris*. Princeton: Princeton University Press, 1976.

Kotz, Mary Lynn. *Robert Rauschenberg: Art and Life*. New York: Abrams, 1991.

Kozloff, Max. "American Painting during the Cold War." In *Pollock and After*, ed. Francis Frascina.

Krauss, Rosalind. *The Optical Unconscious*. Cambridge: MIT Press, 1993.

———. *The Originality of the Avant-Garde and Other Modernist Myths*. Cambridge: MIT Press, 1985.

———. *Passages in Modern Sculpture*. Cambridge: MIT Press, 1981.

———. "Perpetual Inventory." In *Robert Rauschenberg: A Retrospective*, eds. Hopps and Davidson.

———. "Rauschenberg and the Materialized Image." *Artforum* 13 (December 1974): 36–43.

Kripke, Saul. *Naming and Necessity*. Cambridge: Harvard University Press, 1972.

Kropotkin, Peter. *Mutual Aid: A Factor in Evolution*. Boston: Porter Sargent, 1955.

Laclau, Ernesto, ed. *The Making of Political Identities*. London: Verso, 1994.

Lefort, Claude. *Democracy and Political Theory*. Trans. David MacEy. Minneapolis: University of Minnesota Press, 1988 (1986).

Lehman, David. *The Last Avant-Garde: The Making of the New York School of Poets*. New York: Doubleday, 1998.

Leja, Michael. *Reframing Abstract Expressionism*. New Haven, CT: Yale University Press, 1993.

LeSueur, Joe. *Digressions on Some Poems by Frank O'Hara*. New York: FSG, 2003.

Lévi-Strauss, Claude. *The Elementary Structures of Kinship*. Trans. James Harle Bell and John Richard von Sturmer. Boston: Beacon, 1969 (1949).

———. *The Savage Mind*. Trans. George Weidenfeld. Chicago: University of Chicago Press, 1973 (1962).

———. *Tristes Tropiques*. Trans. John and Doreen Weightman. New York: Atheneum, 1973 (1955).

Lewis, Joel, ed. *On the Level Everyday: Selected Talks on Poetry and the Art of Living*. New York: Talisman, 1997.

Lippard, Lucy. *Tony Smith*. New York: Abrams, 1972.

Lucie-Smith, Edward. "An Interview with Frank O'Hara." In *Standing Still and Walking in New York*, ed. Donald Allen. San Francisco: Gray Fox Press, 1983.

Luoma, Bill. *Western Love*. New York: Situations, 1996.

Lyons, John. *Semantics*. Cambridge: Cambridge University Press, 1977.

Mac Low, Jackson. "Museletter." In *The L=A=N=G=U=A=G=E Book*, eds. Andrews and Bernstein.

———. "The Poetics of Change and the Politics of Simultaneous Spontaneity, or the Sacred Heart of Jesus (Revised & Abridged)." In *Talking Poetics from Naropa Institute: Annals of the Jack Kerouac School of Disembodied Poetics*, vol. 1. Eds. Waldman and Webb.

———. *Stanzas for Iris Lezak*. Millertown, NY: Something Else, 1971.

Magee, Michael. "Tribes of New York: Frank O'Hara, Amiri Baraka, and the Poetics of the Five Spot." *Contemporary Literature* 42, no. 4 (2001): 694–726.

Marotti, Aurthur. *John Donne, Coterie Poet*. Madison: University of Wisconsin Press, 1986.

Mattison, Robert. *Grace Hartigan: A Painter's World*. New York: Hudson Hills, 1990.

Mayakovsky, Vladimir. *The Bedbug and Selected Poetry*. Ed. Patricia Blake. Trans. Max Hayward and George Reavey. Bloomington: Indiana University Press, 1975.

———. *How to Make Verse*. Trans. Valentina Coe. Willimantic, CT: Curbstone, 1985 (1926).

———. *Selected Verse*. Ed. Patricia Blake. Trans. Victor Chistyakov. Moscow: Raduga, 1985.

Mayer, Bernadette. *The Desires of Mothers to Please Others in Letters*. West Stockbridge, MA: Hard Press, 1994.

———. "Experiments." In *The L=A=N=G=U=A=G=E Book*, eds. Andrews and Bernstein.

———. *Memory*. Plainfield, VT: North Atlantic Books, 1975.

———. *Moving*. New York: Angel Hair, 1971.

———. *Studying Hunger*. New York and Bolinas, CA: Adventures in Poetry and Big Sky, 1975.

McCaffery, Steve and bp Nichol. *Rational Geomancy: The Kids of the Book Machine.* Vancouver: Talonbooks, 1992.
McGann, Jerome. *The Romantic Ideology.* Chicago: University of Chicago Press, 1983.
———. *Towards a Literature of Knowledge.* Chicago: University of Chicago Press, 1988.
Melville, Stephen. "Notes on the Reemergence of Allegory, the Forgetting of Modernism, the Necessity of Rhetoric, and the Conditions of Publicity in Art and Criticism." *October* 19 (1981): 55–92.
Mendelson, Edward. *Early Auden.* New York: Viking, 1981.
———. *Later Auden.* New York: Farrar, Strauss and Giroux, 1999.
Meyer, James. *Minimalism: Art and Polemics in the Sixties.* New Haven, CT: Yale University Press, 2001.
———. "Nomads: Figures of Travel in Contemporary Art." In *Site-Specificity: The Ethnographic Turn*, ed. Coles.
Miller, J. Hillis. "Paul de Man as Allergen." In *Material Events: Paul de Man and the Afterlife of Theory*, eds. T. Cohen, B. Cohen, Miller, and Warminski.
Molesworth, Helen. "Before Bed." *October* 63 (Winter 1993): 69–82.
Morris, Robert. "Notes on Sculpture." In *Minimal Art: A Critical Anthology*, ed. Battcock.
Morrison, Paul. *The Poetics of Fascism: Ezra Pound, T. S. Eliot, Paul de Man.* New York: Oxford, 1996.
Moses, Robert. *Working for the People: Promise and Performance in Public Service.* New York: Harper, 1956.
Mouffe, Chantal. "Democratic Citizenship and the Political Community." In *Dimensions of Radical Democracy*, ed. Chantal Mouffe. London: Verso, 1992.
Myers, John Bernard, ed. *The Poets of the New York School.* Philadelphia: University of Pennsylvania Press, 1969.
———. *Tracking the Marvelous.* New York: Random House, 1981.
Naifeh, Stephen, and Gregory White Smith. *Jackson Pollock: An American Saga.* New York: Harper, 1991.
Nielsen, Aldon Lynn. *Black Chant: Languages of African-American Postmodernism.* New York: Cambridge, 1997.
Nietzsche, Friedrich. *The Birth of Tragedy.* Trans. Walter Kaufmann. New York: Vintage, 1967 (1872).
Notley, Alice. *Margaret and Dusty.* St. Paul, MN: Coffee House Press, 1985.
O'Hara, Frank. Archive. Thomas J. Dodd Research Library, University of Connecticut, Storrs.
———. *Art Chronicles: 1954–1966.* New York: Braziller, 1975.
———. *A City Winter and Other Poems.* New York: Tibor de Nagy Gallery, 1952.
———. *The Collected Poems of Frank O'Hara*, ed. Donald Allen. New York: Knopf, 1972.
———. *Early Writing*, ed. Donald Allen. Bolinas, CA: Grey Fox, 1977.

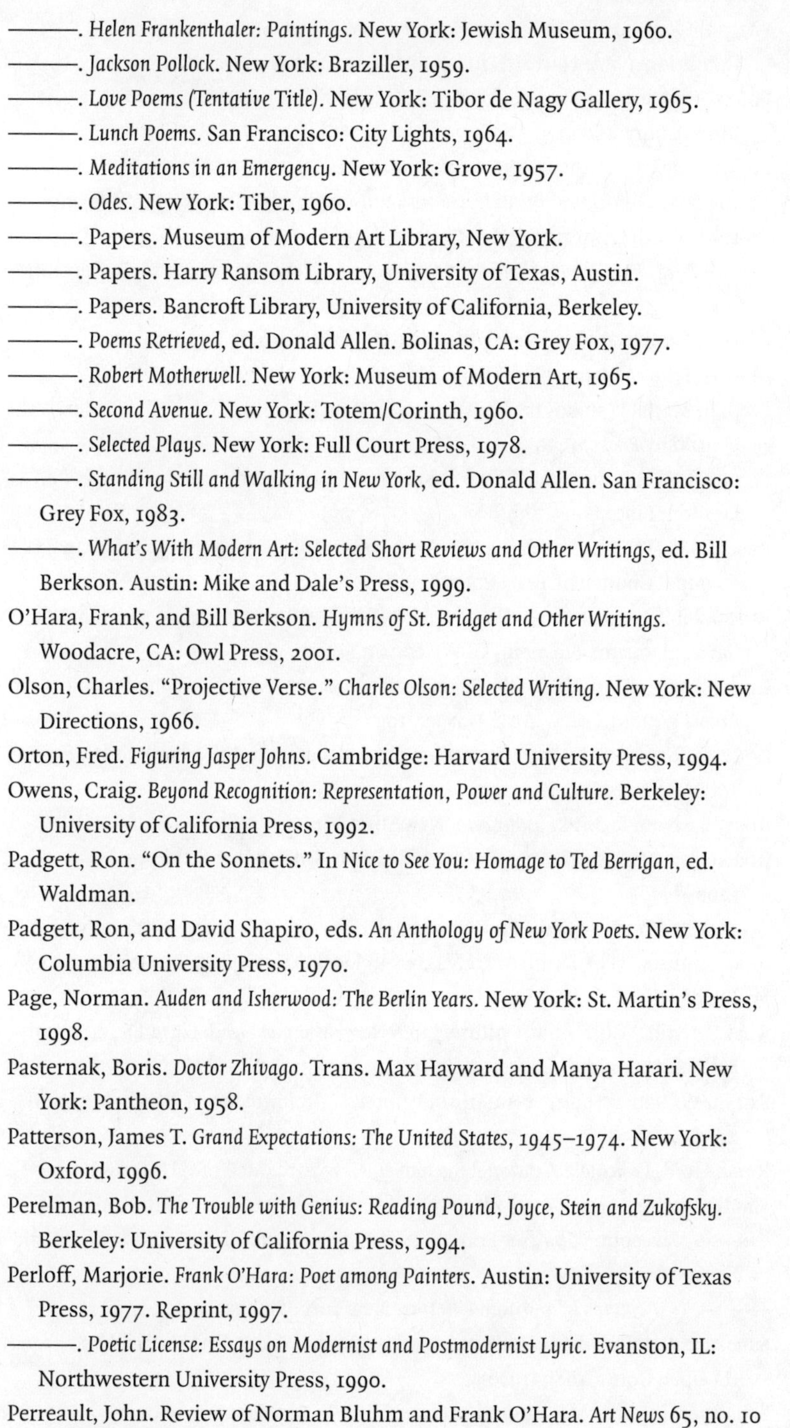

———. *Helen Frankenthaler: Paintings*. New York: Jewish Museum, 1960.

———. *Jackson Pollock*. New York: Braziller, 1959.

———. *Love Poems (Tentative Title)*. New York: Tibor de Nagy Gallery, 1965.

———. *Lunch Poems*. San Francisco: City Lights, 1964.

———. *Meditations in an Emergency*. New York: Grove, 1957.

———. *Odes*. New York: Tiber, 1960.

———. Papers. Museum of Modern Art Library, New York.

———. Papers. Harry Ransom Library, University of Texas, Austin.

———. Papers. Bancroft Library, University of California, Berkeley.

———. *Poems Retrieved*, ed. Donald Allen. Bolinas, CA: Grey Fox, 1977.

———. *Robert Motherwell*. New York: Museum of Modern Art, 1965.

———. *Second Avenue*. New York: Totem/Corinth, 1960.

———. *Selected Plays*. New York: Full Court Press, 1978.

———. *Standing Still and Walking in New York*, ed. Donald Allen. San Francisco: Grey Fox, 1983.

———. *What's With Modern Art: Selected Short Reviews and Other Writings*, ed. Bill Berkson. Austin: Mike and Dale's Press, 1999.

O'Hara, Frank, and Bill Berkson. *Hymns of St. Bridget and Other Writings*. Woodacre, CA: Owl Press, 2001.

Olson, Charles. "Projective Verse." *Charles Olson: Selected Writing*. New York: New Directions, 1966.

Orton, Fred. *Figuring Jasper Johns*. Cambridge: Harvard University Press, 1994.

Owens, Craig. *Beyond Recognition: Representation, Power and Culture*. Berkeley: University of California Press, 1992.

Padgett, Ron. "On the Sonnets." In *Nice to See You: Homage to Ted Berrigan*, ed. Waldman.

Padgett, Ron, and David Shapiro, eds. *An Anthology of New York Poets*. New York: Columbia University Press, 1970.

Page, Norman. *Auden and Isherwood: The Berlin Years*. New York: St. Martin's Press, 1998.

Pasternak, Boris. *Doctor Zhivago*. Trans. Max Hayward and Manya Harari. New York: Pantheon, 1958.

Patterson, James T. *Grand Expectations: The United States, 1945–1974*. New York: Oxford, 1996.

Perelman, Bob. *The Trouble with Genius: Reading Pound, Joyce, Stein and Zukofsky*. Berkeley: University of California Press, 1994.

Perloff, Marjorie. *Frank O'Hara: Poet among Painters*. Austin: University of Texas Press, 1977. Reprint, 1997.

———. *Poetic License: Essays on Modernist and Postmodernist Lyric*. Evanston, IL: Northwestern University Press, 1990.

Perreault, John. Review of Norman Bluhm and Frank O'Hara. *Art News* 65, no. 10 (February 1967): 11.

Poggioli, Renato. *The Theory of the Avant-Garde*. Trans. Gerald Fitzgerald. Cambridge, MA: Harvard University Press, 1968 (1962).

Polizzotti, Mark. *Revolution of the Mind: The Life of André Breton*. London: Bloomsbury, 1995.

Pollock, Jackson. "Answers to a Questionnaire." *Arts and Architecture* 61 (February 1944): 14. Reprinted in *Art in Theory 1900–1990*, eds. Charles Harrison and Paul Wood. Cambridge, MA: Blackwell, 1996.

Pound, Ezra. *The Cantos of Ezra Pound*. New York: New Directions, 1970. Reprint, 1991.

———. *Guide to Kulchur*. New York: New Directions, 1938. Reprint, 1970.

———. *Literary Essays of Ezra Pound*. New York: New Directions, 1968.

Prather, Marla. "Catalogue." In *Willem de Kooning: Paintings*. National Gallery/Yale University Press, 1994.

Prynne, J. H. *A Discourse on Willem de Kooning's "Rosy-Fingered Dawn at Louse Point."* London: Pluto Press, 1996.

Rasula, Jed. *The American Poetry Wax Museum: Reality Effects 1940–1990*. Urbana, IL: National Council of Teachers of English, 1996.

Rifkin, Libbie. *Career Moves: Olson, Creeley, Zukofsky, Berrigan, and the American Avant-Garde*. Madison: University of Wisconsin Press, 2000.

Rivers, Larry. *What did I do? the Unauthorized Autobiography of Larry Rivers, with Arnold Weinstein*. New York: Harper, 1992.

Rodefer, Stephen. "Strange To Be Gone in a Minute." In *Nice to See You: Homage to Ted Berrigan*, ed. Waldman.

Rose, Barbara. *Robert Rauschenberg*. New York: Vintage, 1987.

Rosenberg, Harold. *The Anxious Object*. Chicago: University of Chicago Press, 1966.

———. *The Tradition of the New*. Chicago: University of Chicago Press, 1960.

Ross, Andrew. "The Death of Lady Day." In *Frank O'Hara: To Be True to a City*, ed. Elledge.

Ross, Kristin. "Commune Culture." In *A New History of French Literature*, ed. Denis Hollier. Harvard: Cambridge University Press, 1989.

Rubin, William. "Younger American Painters." *Art International* 4 (January 1960): 24–31.

Ruge, Gerd. *Pasternak: A Pictorial Biography*. New York: McGraw-Hill, 1959.

Sandler, Irving. *A Sweeper-Up After Artists*. New York: Thames and Hudson, 2003.

———. "Sweeping Up After Frank." In *Homage to Frank O'Hara*, eds. Berkson and LeSueur.

———. *The Triumph of American Painting*. New York: Praeger, 1970.

Saussure, Ferdinand de. *Course in General Linguistics*. Trans. Roy Harris. La Salle, IL: Open Court, 1986 (1916).

Schaffner, Ingrid. "Storage and Art over Time: A Conversation with a Conservator: Ingrid Schaffner talks to Elizabeth Lunning." In *Deep Storage:*

Collecting, Storing and Archiving Art, eds. Ingrid Schaffner and Matthias Winzen. New York: Prestel, 1998.

Schiff, Richard. "Water and Lipstick: De Kooning in Transition." In *Willem de Kooning: Paintings*. Washington, DC/New Haven, CT: National Gallery/Yale University Press, 1994.

Schimmel, Paul. "The Faked Gesture: Pop Art and the New York School." In *Hand Painted Pop: American Art in Transition, 1955–62*, ed. Ferguson.

Schjeldahl, Peter. "Frank O'Hara: 'He Made Things & People Sacred.'" In *Homage to Frank O'Hara*, eds. Berkson and LeSueur.

Schumacher, Michael. *Dharma Lion: A Biography of Allen Ginsberg*. New York: St. Martin's Press, 1992.

Schuyler, James. *Selected Art Writings*, ed. Simon Pettet. Santa Rosa, CA: Black Sparrow, 1998.

Searle, John. "Proper Names." *Mind* 67 (1958): 166–73.

Seelye, Catherine, ed. *Charles Olson and Ezra Pound: An Encounter at St. Elizabeths*. New York: Grossman, 1975.

Shapiro, David. *John Ashbery: An Introduction to the Poetry*. New York: Columbia University Press, 1979.

———. "On a Poet." In *Nice to See You: Homage to Ted Berrigan*, ed. Waldman.

Shattuck, Roger. *The Banquet Years: The Origins of the Avant-Garde in France, 1885 to World War 1*. New York: Vintage, 1955.

Shaw, Lytle. "Book Review." Alan Golding's *From Outlaw to Classic* and Jed Rasula's *The American Poetry Wax Museum*. *Criticism* 41, no. 3 (1999): 403–9.

———. "Faulting Description: Clark Coolidge, Bernadette Mayer and the Site of Scientific Authority." In *Never Get Famous: Essays on New York Poetry beyond "The New York School,"* ed. Daniel Kane. Normal, IL: Dalkey Archive, forthcoming.

———. "The Labor of Repetition: Silliman's 'Quips' and the Politics of Intertextuality." *Quarry West* 34 (1998): 118–33.

———. "Poet as Action Figure: The New York School Out of History." *Arshile* 11 (1999): 112–21.

———. "Smithson, writer." In *Robert Smithson: Spiral Jetty*, eds. Lynne Looke and Karen Kelly. New York/Berkeley: DIA Art Foundation/University of California Press, 2005.

Shklovsky, Viktor. *Mayakovsky and His Circle*. Trans. Lily Feiler. New York: Dodd, 1972 (1940).

———. *The Third Factory*. Trans. Richard Sheldon. Normal, IL: Dalkey Archive, 2002 (1926).

Shoptaw, John. *John Ashbery: On the Outside Looking Out*. Cambridge: Harvard University Press, 1994.

Silliman, Ron. *Tjanting*. Berkeley: Figures, 1981.

Smith, Hazel. *Hyperscapes in the Poetry of Frank O'Hara: Difference / Homosexuality / Topography*. Liverpool: Liverpool University Press, 2000.

Smith, Rod, ed. *Aerial 8: Barrett Watten*. Washington, DC: Edge, 1995.

Smithson, Robert. *The Collected Writings of Robert Smithson*. Ed. Jack Flam. Berkeley: University of California Press, 1996.

Sollors, Werner. *Amiri Baraka/LeRoi Jones: The Quest for a "Populist Modernism."* New York: Columbia University Press, 1978.

Sontag, Susan. "Notes on 'Camp.'" *Against Interpretation*. New York: Anchor, 1990.

Sorrentino, Gilbert. "Review." *Bookweek* 1 (May 1966): 19.

Spicer, Jack. *The Collected Books of Jack Spicer*, ed. Robin Blaser. Santa Rosa, CA: Black Sparrow, 1989.

Spring, Justin. *Fairfield Porter: A Life in Art*. New Haven: Yale University Press, 2000.

Steinberg, Leo. "Footnote." *Arts Magazine* 32 (May 1958): 9.

———. "Month in Review: Contemporary Group at Stable Gallery." *Arts Magazine* 30 (January 1956): 46–47.

———. *Other Criteria: Confrontations with Twentieth-Century Art*. New York: Oxford University Press, 1972.

Stich, Sidra. *Made in USA: An Americanization in Modern Art, the '50s and '60s*. Berkeley: University of California Press, 1987.

Stock, Noel. *The Life of Ezra Pound*. New York: Pantheon, 1970.

Storr, Robert. *Tony Smith: Architect, Painter, Sculptor*. New York: Museum of Modern Art, 1998.

Stuckey, Charles. "Reading Rauschenberg." *Art in America* 65, no. 2 (March–April, 1977): 74–84.

Sweet, David LeHardy. *Savage Sight/Constructed Noise: Poetic Adaptations of Painterly Techniques in the French and American Avant-Gardes*. Chapel Hill: North Carolina Studies in the Romance Languages and Literatures, 2003.

Tashjian, Dickran. *A Boatload of Madmen: Surrealism and the American Avant-Garde, 1920–1950*. New York: Thames and Hudson, 1995.

Thomas, Lorenzo. *Extraordinary Measures: Afrocentric Modernism and Twentieth-Century American Poetry*. Tuscaloosa, AL: University of Alabama Press, 2000.

Towle, Tony. *Memoir 1960–1963*. Cambridge, MA: Faux Press, 2001.

Trotsky, Leon. "Futurism." *Literature and Revolution*. Trans. Rose Strunsky. New York: International Publishers, 1925.

Tucker, Marcia. Foreward to *Blasted Allegories: An Anthology of Writings by* Contemporary Artists, ed. Brian Wallis. New York: New Museum of Contemporary Art and MIT Press, 1987.

Tytell, John. *Ezra Pound: The Solitary Volcano*. New York: Doubleday, 1987.

Veeser, H. Aram, ed. *The New Historicism*. New York: Routledge, 1989.

Wagner, Anne. "Warhol Paints History, or Race in America." *Representations* 55 (Summer 1996): 98–119.

Waldman, Anne. "Interview." In *Talking Poetry: Conversations in the Workshop with Contemporary Poets*, ed. Lee Bartlett. Albuquerque: University of New Mexico Press, 1987.

———. "My Life A List." In *Talking Poetics from Naropa Institute*, vol. 2., eds. Waldman and Webb.

———, ed. *Nice to See You: Homage to Ted Berrigan*. Minneapolis: Coffee House Press, 1991.

Waldman, Anne, and Marilyn Webb. *Talking Poetics from Naropa Institute.* 2 vols. Boulder, CO: Shambhala, 1978–1979.

Ward, Geoff. *Statutes of Liberty: The New York School of Poets*. New York: Saint Martin's Press, 1993.

Warner, Michael. "Zones of Privacy." In *What's Left of Theory?*, eds. Judith Butler, John Guillory, and Kendall Thomas. New York: Routledge, 2000.

Warsh, Lewis. "Introduction / Lewis Warsh." In *The Angel Hair Anthology*, eds. Anne Waldman and Lewis Warsh. New York: Granary, 2001.

Watkin, William. *In the Process of Poetry: The New York School and the Avant-Garde.* Lewisburg, PA: Bucknell University Press, 2001.

Watten, Barrett. "After Ted." In *Aerial* 8, ed. Rod Smith.

———. "The Conduit of Communication in Everyday Life." In *Aerial* 8, ed. Rod Smith.

———. *Total Syntax*. Carbondale: Southern Illinois University Press, 1985.

Watten, Barrett and Andrew Ross. "Reinventing Community: A Symposium on/with Language Poets." In *Aerial* 8, ed. Rod Smith.

Whitman, Walt. *Leaves of Grass*. Eds. Sculley Bradley and Harold W. Blodgett. New York: Norton, 1973.

Wolf, Reva. *Andy Warhol, Poetry, and Gossip in the 1960s*. Chicago: University of Chicago Press, 1997.

INDEX

CONTEMPORARY NORTH AMERICAN POETRY SERIES

Jorie Graham: Essays on the Poetry
Edited by Thomas Gardner
University of Wisconsin Press, 2005

Gary Snyder and the Pacific Rim: Creating Countercultural Community
By Timothy Gray

Paracritical Hinge: Essays, Talks, Notes, Interviews
By Nathaniel Mackey
University of Wisconsin Press, 2004

Frank O'Hara: The Poetics of Coterie
By Lytle Shaw